Professor Fisher,
    I thought you might
like this book. It is
an excellent read.
        yours,
        Bill Ward

Acting Like Men

Acting Like Men

Gender, Drama, and Nostalgia in Ancient Greece

Karen Bassi

Ann Arbor

THE UNIVERSITY OF MICHIGAN PRESS

2001   2000   1999   1998   4   3   2   1

A CIP catalog record for this book is available from the British Library.

Library of Congress Cataloging-in-Publication Data

Bassi, Karen.
    Acting like men : gender, drama, and nostalgia in ancient Greece /
Karen Bassi.
        p.   cm.
    Includes bibliographical references and index.
    ISBN 0-472-10625-2 (cloth : alk. paper)
    1. Greek drama—History and criticism.   2. Literature and society—
Greece.   3. Gender identity in literature.   4. Drama—Psychological
aspects.   5. Masculinity in literature.   6. Nostalgia in literature.
7. Gender identity—Greece.   8. Masculinity—Greece.   9. Men in
literature.   10. Nostalgia—Greece.   11. Men—Greece.   I. Title.
PA3136.B37   1998
882'.0109353—dc21   98-36063
                                                                          CIP
ISBN13 978-0-472-10625-7 (cloth)
ISBN13 978-0-472-02695-1 (electronic)

For Peter and Nick

Acknowledgments

I wish to acknowledge the sustained encouragement and much appreciated criticism of my colleagues in Pre- and Early Modern Studies at the University of California, Santa Cruz, among whom Catherine Soussloff, Margo Hendricks, Deanna Shemek, Linda Lomperis, Sharon Kinoshita, Carla Freccero, and Harry Berger, Jr., deserve special thanks. Other friends and colleagues provided thoughtful appraisals and comments through correspondence and conversations. Thanks are owed to Nancy Rabinowitz, Carol Dougherty, Leslie Kurke, Mark Griffith, Charles Segal, Seth Schein, Amy Richlin, Sandra Joshel, Mark Edwards, Gary Meltzer, Sharon James, Lauren Taaffe, Victoria Wohl, and Lisbeth Haas. I also wish to acknowledge the support of my colleagues in classics at Santa Cruz: Mary-Kay Gamel, Gary Miles, John Lynch, Charles Hedrick, and Dan Selden. Audiences at Stanford University, San Francisco State University, the University of California, Berkeley, and a meeting of the Bay Area Pre- and Early Modern Studies Group provided necessary feedback at an early stage of the work. Holly Coty and Max Goldman deserve special commendation for proofreading the manuscript in draft. Dan Wenger helped me to make the computer do what I wanted it to do. I am also very grateful for the excellent staff support provided by Lisa Leslie and Marianna Alves at Cowell College. This project was supported by faculty research funds granted by the University of California, Santa Cruz, and by a University of California President's Fellowship in the Humanities granted in 1992–93. Part of chapter 2 has been previously published in *Arethusa* as "Orality, Masculinity, and the Greek Epic," *Arethusa* 30 (1997): 315–40. Part of chapter 3 has been previously published in *Helios* as "Male Nudity and Disguise in the Discourse of Greek Histrionics, *Helios* 22 (1995): 3–22. I am grateful for permission to reprint amended versions of these articles.

I owe a special debt of gratitude to Dolores Pratt, whose intelligence and wit sustained me in critical moments, and whose text editing saved me from numerous infelicities of expression. The responsibility for all remaining errors and omissions rests with me. Finally, I am most deeply indebted to Peter Harris for his humor, loyalty, and love.

The abbreviations used in citing ancient authors and works are generally those found in the *Oxford Classical Dictionary,* 3d ed. (cited as *OCD*), or in H.G. Liddell and R. Scott, eds., *A Greek–English Lexicon,* 9th ed., revised by H. Stuart Jones (cited as LSJ).

Contents

Introduction: The Search for Origins

Greek drama demands a story of origins. The most seductive of these, and the one that has persistently attracted scholarly adherents in the history of European drama, begins with an act of transcendence. In this anthropological narrative, dramatic mimesis has its primeval ancestor in early cult or ritual practices in Greece in which some form of mimetic enactment is preparatory to the taking on of a new identity.[1] Less seductive, but also focused on what might be called a consummate moment of transformation, is the story of drama's formal origins in which earlier modes of cultural production, in particular choral lyric and the Panhellenic epics, evolve into a new kind of civic performance—one that exemplifies the political and artistic values of the Athenian democracy.[2] Each of these stories demands

---

1. See Seaford 1981, 259, for a discussion of the origin of drama in rites that "function to deprive the initiand of his previous identity so that he may assume a new one." More recently, see Seaford 1994, esp. chaps. 7 and 8. Else 1965, chap. 1, gives a good overview of the scholarly tradition that finds tragedy's origins in ritual and cult practice. See also Burkert 1966. Foley (1985, 52–64) discusses the theories of Gerard and Guépin. Nietzsche's *Birth of Tragedy* must also be mentioned in this context, on which see Silk 1981. The formal or literary antecedents to Greek drama are discussed by Hall (1989, 63); see also Herington 1985. On the "bourgeois esthetics" that has been dominant in the study of dramatic texts, see Longo 1990, 15.

2. Easterling and Kenney (1989, 87–88) epitomize this teleological narrative of Greek drama: "we have inherited from late antiquity and Byzantium a selection from the work of three tragic poets which represents, all too inadequately, the splendid flowering of this native Athenian art in the great period of imperial democracy." Cf. Else 1965, 24: "Tragedy was a peculiarly and uniquely Athenian invention, from Thespis to Theodectes." But that Attic drama is the product of a pure or unambiguous Greek imagination, what Burkert (1966, 94) refers to as the "autochthonous origin of tragedy in Attica," begs more questions than it answers. Complex cultural artifacts—especially those that develop during times of cultural dissemination and expansion (like that of Greek colonization ca. 750–550)—are not likely to be sui generis.

our attention precisely because the historical, political, and social processes by which ritual mimesis evolved into dramatic mimesis or by which preexisting genres evolved into a new genre continue to elude us; moreover, the relationship between the institution of the Athenian theater and the emergence of Athenian democracy is not easily explained.[3] The search for the origins of drama—as for any form of cultural production—necessarily involves a kind of myth making, one in which there is an a priori assumption that the myth is "isomorphic with [a] purported reality."[4] In the originary stories of Attic drama, this purported reality is embedded in hypothetical, fragmentary, late, or internal evidence (i.e., internal to the dramatic texts themselves) for actual religious or performance practices that predate the plays; as a result, the truth-value of these accounts is compromised by their own built-in burden of historical or empirical evidence. This compromise does not mean, of course, that attempts to understand the processes by which Athenian drama came into existence should be abandoned; it means only that the search for drama's origins reduces the scope of that attempt and limits the usefulness of its conclusions.

Another kind of origin story takes Aristotle's *Poetics* as its principal text and regards Aristotle as what Foucault calls the "author of a tradition" whose works—like those of Homer, Freud, and Marx—generate an inevitable necessity for a return to the origin.[5] The search for what in this case might be called the formal origins of drama—or, more precisely, for its aesthetic first principles—has a different trajectory than the search for its ritual or generic origins but serves a similar function and raises similar questions. To establish the *Poetics* as a prescriptive template for what constitutes the best sort of tragedy, the critic must paradoxically confer authority on a text that is itself "disjointed, full of interruptions, of digressions, and of failures in connec-

---

3. Griffith 1995 provides an analysis of the positivism that characterizes the scholarship on Greek drama.

4. The quote is from Burkert 1979, 4; he is describing attempts to locate the meaning of myth in some empirical reality existing either in nature or history. Cf. his p. 27: "The concept of 'origin' is mythical thinking, applying the tale of birth or creation to the constant flux of reality."

5. Foucault 1979, 156. Foucault mentions Homer, Freud, and Marx; I would include Plato and Aristotle in this list of primary suspects. See chap. 1.

tion."[6] It is not that these textual difficulties make the *Poetics* useless as a guide to the ancient (or modern) understanding of Attic tragedy. But the persistent return to and authorization of the *Poetics* is indicative of the modern critic's desire to comprehend Greek drama from the privileged point of view of an elite Athenian, like Aristotle.[7]

It is easy to take this desire for granted and perhaps even to think of it as a necessary motivating principle in the history of classical scholarship. It deserves our attention, however, as a persistent feature in the history of theater criticism in general. Like the search for drama's historical origins, the return to Aristotle's aesthetic principles is part of a larger project of valorizing and reanimating (as it were) a normative and universalized masculine subject—as ritual initiate, tragic sufferer, soldier-citizen, and literary critic or philosopher— who plays his role in the unique cultural and political destiny of ancient Athens. The search for drama's origins, then, is founded on a nostalgic desire both to create and "to be at one with" the ideal subject of the ancient past.[8] Represented in Foucault's notion of "continuous history," that search also initiates and helps define a linear progression of past events that, in the end, brings that subject into being.

Continuous history is the indispensable correlative of the founding function of the subject; the guarantee that everything that has eluded him may be restored to him; the certainty that time will disperse nothing without restoring it in a reconstituted unity; the promise that one day the subject—in the form of historical consciousness—will once again be able to appropriate,

---

6. Lucas 1968, x.

7. A similar desire characterizes the history of textual criticism, as summarized by Greetham (1992, 320): "Such an attitude [that the Romantics did not 'know enough'] is clearly going to promote a textual practice in the editing of vernacular texts which parallels the earlier textual treatment of classical texts: a desire for uniformity and polish over roughness and idiosyncrasy, and a consequent elevation of the textual critic to the position of virtual co-author in the attainment of a refined text purged of both historical accretions and of improprieties in the composer." Greetham notes that this approach is now out of favor with textual critics, and he illustrates this point (322) with reference to Wolf's *Prolegomena ad Homerum*, published in 1795.

8. The phrase is quoted from Wilshire 1982, 27–28.

to bring back under his sway, all those things that are kept at a distance by difference, and find in them what might be called his abode. (Foucault 1972, 12)

Foucault's characteristically provocative description invokes a metaphorical nostalgia in which discovering and mastering the past is coincident with discovering and returning to one's "abode." With their implicit appeals to "intrinsic, autochthonous, and universally recognizable characteristics,"[9] the various aforementioned approaches to the origins of Greek drama testify to a similar appeal to what might be called a reunion with the normative masculine subject of antiquity, a subject perpetually at risk of losing his privileged position at the center of the stage of history. One purpose of this book is to show how this nostalgia is a constituent feature of the critical histories of European drama in general and of Greek drama in particular.

I begin with the obvious point that Athenian drama has played a significant role in the history of European theater and cultural identity, the role of a progenitor whose own obscure origins remain lost to view and longed for. Subsumed within this observation is a less obvious one, namely, that the search for drama's origins signifies a desire to attempt "to master time" by filling in the lost sequences of events that culminate in Attic drama and, in so doing, to prove such mastery possible.[10] This formulation provides a concise expression of the nostalgic enterprise previously described, both because mastery is ideally and historically the prerogative of masculine subjects (and the aim of traditional scholarship) and because the will to master time is compromised by its necessary claims to historical specificity; like all narratives about the origins of cultural phenomena, it "must end up in a vicious

---

9. The phrase is from Foucault 1972, 21–22. Cf. Lévi-Strauss 1963a on the concept of evolutionism. The "universal" applicability of Greek drama is expressed in Freud's analysis ([1900] 1965, 296) of Sophocles' *Oedipus the King* as a play about "the fate of all of us." I discuss Freud's text in chap. 1. This universalism is also evident in Lévi-Strauss' discussion (1963b) of the Oedipus play as a model for the structuralist method. These famous "returns" to Sophocles' *Oedipus* also reference that play's importance in the *Poetics* despite the fact that they do not explicitly mention Aristotle. For a relevant discussion of universalism as a problem for feminist theater criticism, see Dolan 1988, chap. 2.
10. On the notion of mastering time, see Foucault 1972.

regress."[11] Is this predicament inescapable, or is there another way to approach the development and significance of the theater in ancient Greece? If we abandon the search for drama's origins, where do we begin?

To answer this question, I propose a broadly defined field of inquiry that does not owe allegiance to a sequence of actual historical events. In general, this field is constituted by representations of activities and experiences that can be predicated of formal theatrical performance—spectatorship and disguise, for example—but that are found in narrative and visual sources that are additional to, prior to, or even subsequent to the dramatic performances of the fifth century. Adopting a term coined by Bruce Wilshire, I refer to these activities and experiences as "theater-like."[12] Although the notion of performance is essential to this concept, I avoid using the term *performance*, because of the tendency in performance studies and in gender studies to rely on a slippage between the notion of performance in the theater and the notion of life as a performance. This slippage is not without some justification, of course, and in this book, I will take up the significance of the conflation of dramatic characters and actual social subjects.[13] But, I want to maintain a focus on the theatricality of the activities and experiences represented in the sources I will be discussing, or, to put it another way, on the fact that not every human activity and speech act is a literal or metaphorical performance. My aim throughout this book is to better understand the cultural context in which Greek theatrical performance developed as a civic institution.

The epic poems will be a recurring point of reference in the chapters that follow. The epics qualify as pretheatrical or extratheatrical texts because—like formal dramatic productions—they were originally presented as oral or live performances and because their narratives are built around first-person speeches.[14] Plato, who calls Homer the "first

---

11. The phrase is from Burkert 1979, 27.

12. Wilshire 1982, 138–39.

13. For a discussion of the history and application of the term *performance*, see Roach 1996, 3–4.

14. See Martin 1989, 46: "it has been estimated that nearly half of the *Iliad* is composed of direct speech, and slightly more of the *Odyssey*." For the statistics, see Griffin 1986. The performance of the Homeric rhapsode is best exemplified in Plato's *Ion*. Cf. Else 1965, 64–70. Aristotle says of Homer that

teacher and leader of the tragic poets" (*Republic* 595c and 607a), criticizes both epic and tragedy because of this shared quality. Aristotle
calls Homer a "dramatizer" (δραματοποιήσας, *Poetics* 1448b37–38). But
if Greek drama is indebted to Homer, it is not only by virtue of the later
philosophical tradition, or because so many of the tragic plots are based
on the epic narratives, or because of the prevalence of first-person
speeches in those narratives.[15] It is also because, by virtue of their
cultural primacy, the epics establish models for representing human
speech and the display of the human body in a public context. These
models operate across genres and over time and ultimately have currency in the spectatorial and communicative systems of the theater in
Athens. I hope to demonstrate the ways in which these representations
function in Greek and Athenian self-representation—for example,

---

"he alone combined dramatic form with excellence of imitation" (μιμήσεις
δραματικὰς ἐποίησεν, *Poetics* 1448b34–35; the translation is from Butcher
[1894] 1951). Cf. *Poetics* 1459b12–17, 1449b14–20, 1451a22–30.

15. Cf. Aristotle *Poetics* 1453a17–22. Else (1957a) argues for the relationship
between the rhapsodic contests and the "earliest stage" of the tragic contests.
Seaford (1994, 275–80) takes exception to Else's arguments, particularly his
contention that "[a]ffiliations [of tragedy] with cult-myths and cult rituals,
especially those of Dionysos, are secondary both in extent and performance."
But Else does not deny such affiliations, as Seaford contends; he simply
relegates them to a secondary status. Moreover, while it is true, as Seaford
shows, that a number of extant plays end with the "foundation of cult," none
of those he mentions are related to Dionysus (which seems to be the point
Else is trying to make). Likewise, I find problematic Seaford's attack on
Herington 1985 for crediting the dramatic quality of rhapsodic performance as
antecedent to formal dramatic mimesis. It may be that choral lyric is dramatic
"in principle," as Seaford argues. But to criticize Herington for providing "no
evidence" to support the contention that the rhapsode may have mimed
certain scenes is to ignore the fact that such miming is also possible "in
principle." Seaford maintains that "[t]ragic impersonation has four features
that rhapsodic impersonation lacks: it is *visual* (notably through the mask),
exclusive (the actor cannot while on stage step in and out of the part), *active* (he
enacts what the rhapsode narrates), and part of a group performance. These
features are in fact more likely to be found in choral lyric than in rhapsodic
recitation" (277–78). These distinctions are plausible but not incontestable.
Rhapsodic recitation is also visual, and insofar as the individual voice of the
male rhapsode impersonates the first-person voices of epic personae, his
performance is closer to that of an actor than is the performance of a lyric
chorus. But the merits of these various arguments are not crucial for mine.

how the notion of spectatorship in the Homeric epics can contribute to a formulation of spectatorship in the theater, including its relation to citizenship in what Simon Goldhill has referred to as Athenian civic ideology.[16]

While the epics are a fundamental source for the theater-like activities and experiences I have mentioned, these representations can be identified in a wide variety of other texts and artifacts spanning several centuries and including historical narratives, philosophical treatises, visual media, and finally the dramatic texts themselves (as so-called metatheatrical texts). As I suggested earlier, an account of these representations culminates not in a story of drama's origins and formal development—a story that often trades on the lack of available data—but in a broader analysis. There is no doubt that such an eclectic approach risks the charge of effacing historical specificity, of disregarding generic differences, and of relying on an indiscriminate notion of what constitutes evidence. Appeals to evidence, however, depend on the factors by which the evidence is defined.[17] This dependence does not mean that we have no access to the past or that what we can know about it is so contingent as to be meaningless, but it does imply that historical meaning is not restricted to an objective accounting or quantitative sequencing of events or dependent on the legitimacy or accuracy of historical sources as guides to a social or political reality.[18] One interpretation of the past may be demonstrably more plausible than another, but, still, past events are imbedded in the representational strategies that *create* the past as an object of inquiry.[19]

Given this way of understanding the ancient past and of under-

---

16. Goldhill 1990.

17. See Daston 1994 and the exchanges that follow her essay.

18. These have been the traditional principles of historical inquiry, especially for what has been called "high political history." That term is used by Keith Thomas in his 1994 review of Wilson 1994.

19. Speaking about historical narrative, White (1980, 23) states "Unless at least two versions of the same set of events can be imagined, there is no reason for the historian to take upon himself the authority of giving the true account of what really happened." This same principle is applicable to fictional narratives in which, while there may be no need (stated or implied) to verify facts, an author often proceeds from the assertion that he is telling the "better" or more convincing version of a story. Cf. Peradotto 1989. On the question of the document in historical inquiry, see Foucault 1972, 3–21.

standing the Greek theater as part of that past, the search for historical origins begins to lose its allure. At the same time, whether Solon
actually met Thespis (said to be the first dramatic actor) or whether
the Athenian tyrant Pisistratus ever dressed up a woman as Athena,
for example, become less important than the question of how these
and similar possibilities—stated or implied in the ancient sources—
contribute to a broadly defined understanding of theatrical performance in Greece. Moreover, the unreliability of Plutarch as a source is
of less concern than the fact that the stories he tells contribute to what
might be called a cultural database. Searching that database may or
may not yield what actually happened in the past, but it will produce
a plausible narrative of the social, political, and ideological factors that
contribute to the ancient and modern understandings of Athenian
drama.[20] When positing such a narrative, one must obviously consider the context in which a text or artifact is produced and the exigen-
cies that contribute to its preservation. But hypotheses relating to the
historical circumstances of a given text or artifact or to its preservation
over time function within a representational complex in which past
events are, in Hayden White's words, "never given directly to perception."[21] The events that culminate in the establishment of the Athenian theater can never be given directly to perception and can never
reveal their transcendent origins. The impossibility of discovering
those origins is productive of the thesis of this book, namely that the
history of the theater in Greece, including the critical discourses it
generates, is also a history of the construction and preservation of the
masculine subject of Greek antiquity. Together these histories tell us
what it means for ancient Greeks to act like men.

Chapter 1, "Nostalgia and Drama," presents an overview of the methodology that guides the subsequent arguments. I begin by considering the lexicon of ancient Greek drama—namely, the activities of acting, watching, and impersonating—and propose that watching or
spectatorship is the principal element in any analysis of the meaning
of Greek and European drama. This proposal leads to a discussion of
spectatorship in the context of Plato's and Aristotle's analyses of dra-

---

20. Cf. Foucault's notion (1972, part 2) of "discursive formations."
21. White 1992, 92.

matic impersonation, in the psychoanalytical narrative of sexual object choice and identity formation (i.e., in Freud's reading of the *Oedipus Tyrannus*), and in contemporary drama criticism and performance
studies. I argue that spectatorship as a practice is problematized in
each of these critical discourses insofar as it is defined by the presence
of bodily impersonations. Such impersonations pose an inherent
threat to the notion of a core of masculine identity by presenting the
possibility that this core may only be an *effect* of bodily acts, and not
their cause. Based on the assumption that bodily impersonations dis-
rupt the immutable disposition of an idealized masculinity, the preservation of that ideal is a persistent feature in the history of drama and
of the Greek theater.[22]

Chapter 2, "Scripted Speech," treats the gender-specific rules that
distinguish mediated from nonmediated forms of communication in
archaic and classical Greek thought. I introduce the term *scripted
speech* to designate a form of mediated, or secondhand, communication, one that occupies a middle position within the oral-literate binary that dominates discussions of communicative practices in the
West. Scripted speech is first exemplified in the message-sending
scenes in the *Iliad*, where it is antithetical to direct first-person speech
among elite males. This antithesis is operative in the representation of
martial practices as well, so that direct, or man-to-man, speech is
analogous to direct, or man-to-man combat in the epic. In the wartime
culture of the *Iliad*, the epic hero is ideally "experienced in deeds and
in words." (Iliad 9.443) This heroic subject persists as a nostalgic ideal
in democratic and militaristic Athens, witnessed, for example, in the
first-person speeches in Thucydides' *History* and, in Plato's dialogues.
Modes of speech in general are shown to be gendered categories, and
scripted speech in particular is shown to be the negative corollary to
fully articulated direct speech between males. This distinction forms
the basis for talking about the political and social significance of dramatic speech in the fifth-century theater.

In contrast to the focus on modes of communication and their
importance for the construction of masculine subjectivity in chapter 2,

---

22. Cf. Zeitlin (1990a, 85): "by virtue of the conflicts generated by her
social position and ambiguously defined between inside and outside, interior
self and exterior identity, the woman is already more of a 'character' than the
man, who is far more limited as an actor to his public social and political role."

chapter 3, "The Theatrical Body," considers the conspicuous display of the masculine body in the visual and literary traditions of archaic and classical Greece. The argument begins with an analysis of corporeal and vestmental codes operating along a continuum of bodily display that consists of the nude body, the clothed body, and the disguised body as gendered categories. With particular attention paid to the body of Odysseus, it offers a formulation of the disguised body as the theatrical body in the post–Trojan War and domestic context of the *Odyssey*. I argue that the culture- and gender-specific issues relating to this element of disguise in the *Odyssey* prefigure those relating to disguise as a necessary element in Attic drama. In both mimetic regimes, the disguised body represents a threat to the ontological integrity of the normative male, a threat counteracted by public displays of unambiguous manhood.

Chapter 4, "The Theater of Tyranny," represents a transition from the exposition of theater-like practices and events to a consideration of the theater as an institution in fifth-century Athens. The primary tests are those that narrate the early political history of Athens, in particular the Pisistratid tyranny. In these narratives, the tyrant credited with instituting the dramatic contests in Athens is himself the subject of theater-like display in the city, so, in effect, he gains mastery over the Athenians by turning them into passive spectators. Passivity is defined as the failure to meet the requirements of a masculine identity; it is also equated with feminine and non-Greek behavior. At the same time, the representation of failed resistance to the tyrant in these narratives is witness to the fading of that idealized identity in Athenian self-representation. The result is an essentially ambiguous notion of spectatorship in the formative narratives of the Athenian polis and, by extension, in the history of the theater as polis-specific.

Chapter 5, "The Theater of Dionysus," considers the connection between the god Dionysus and the Greek dramatic festivals, as a means of understanding the role of Greek masculine identity in the context of theatrical experience. The chapter begins with a discussion of the god's entry into Greek culture in ethnographic and historical accounts. These accounts often focus on some potential threat that Dionysus poses to Athenian masculinity and provide clues to the god's role in the theater as a secular and civic institution. The meaning of this threat is the subject of a comparative study of Euripides' *Bacchae* and Aristophanes' *Frogs*, the two extant plays from Greek antiquity in which Dionysus is a main character. I argue that both in his tragic manifestation (in the *Bacchae*) and in his comic manifestation (in the *Frogs*), Dionysus plays a part similar to that of the tyrant Pisistratus in the historical record. Just as tyranny is represented as theater in the Pisistratid narratives, so theater is represented as tyranny—embodied in the persona of Dionysus—in the *Bacchae* and the *Frogs*. The power of Dionysus in these plays is manifested in the passivity of a spectator, with implicit reference to the theatrical spectator. I end with the conclusion that, as the topic of these late plays, theatrical experience does not unambiguously valorize the social and political virtues of the Athenian polis, as is so often argued. Rather, that experience epitomizes the way in which Greek democracy and Greek masculinity are mutually reinforcing mimetic regimes.

1

Nostalgia and Drama

In the introduction, I discussed the critic's desire to inhabit the position of the masculine subject of antiquity and the persistence of that desire in the critical history of Greek and European drama. Here I want to elaborate on that claim by discussing this form of nostalgia in the context of four historically dominant—if very different—approaches to dramatic production: Plato's critique of dramatic mimesis in the *Republic*, Aristotle's formal analysis of tragedy in the *Poetics*, Freud's narrative of sexual object choice and identity formation in his reading of Sophocles' *Oedipus Tyrannus*, and the account of theatrical experience in contemporary drama criticism and performance studies. It is obvious that I will not be presenting a comprehensive survey of approaches to theatrical experience but a highly selective one with some particular aims in mind. Plato and Aristotle must necessarily be included in any account of the social and cultural meaning of drama in ancient Greece. My discussions of the *Republic* and *Poetics* are aimed at demonstrating how, in the context of their analyses of dramatic performance, a defining feature of each is the desire to create and preserve an internal and essential core of masculine identity. Then I want to make a more far-reaching claim, namely, that this desire is a defining feature of Western drama as a conceptual category. While this proposition must remain provisional, I illustrate its plausibility in the context of Freud's analysis of the *Oedipus* and in the context of contemporary drama and performance studies, where the desire for an essential masculine identity is manifested, for example, in the concept of identification. The overall aim of this chapter is to show how the preservation of an idealized and normative masculinity is a motivating principle in ancient Greek analyses of dramatic production and persists as a nostalgic effect in the history of drama since the ancient Greeks.

Before entering into this larger discussion, however, I want to establish a general outline for what I mean when I talk about drama and the activities and representations it comprehends. The lexicon of formal

theatrical performance in ancient Greece is comprised of terms meaning to do or act (δράω), to watch (θεάομαι), and to imitate or impersonate (μιμέομαι). From these terms, we derive the principal concepts that
describe the European theater: the drama (δρᾶμα); the spectator and
the theater (θεατής, θέατρον); and imitation or impersonation (μίμησις)
as the vehicle of the dramatic performance.[1] A common approach to
the development of Greek drama is to analyze the semantic ranges and
privileges of occurrence of these terms as they constitute an emerging
aesthetic vocabulary. I mention this lexicon not to talk about specific or
shifting usage, however, but to establish an inventory of activities that,
while they come to function within the context of formal theatrical
production in fifth-century Athens, also have semantic and ideological
value outside that context. It is true that once we uncouple these activities from their dramatic or theatrical moorings, we face a seemingly
limitless variety and number of references to human beings acting,
watching, and impersonating—especially acting and watching—in
the Greek narrative and visual traditions. At the same time, restrictions
obviously apply to the sorts of human actions and visual experiences
that are available or suitable for representation in any cultural context.
In the Greek context, this restrictive criterion is perhaps most obvious
with respect to impersonations, as Plato's critique of dramatic mimesis
in the *Republic* illustrates.[2]

But whether we are talking about seemingly indiscriminate activities like acting and watching or about more readily circumscribed
ones like impersonating, each operates in a representational system
that enforces cultural norms and hierarchies. The first general proposition I wish to make, then, is that it is possible to identify in Greek
culture at large the representation of activities that are analogous to
the formal dramatic practices of acting, watching, and impersonating
(whether or not they are specified by forms of δράω, θεάομαι, or

---

1. I am obviously referring not to English cognates but to theatrical concepts; and these are not the only terms in the Greek dramatic lexicon. For a
useful recent discussion of the terms *mimesis* and *drama,* see Nagy 1990, 42–
43, 388. See also Sörbom 1966. I adopt "impersonation" rather than "imitation" as a translation for the term *mimesis* wherever it seems appropriate to
specify the dramatic sense of imitating human actions and behaviors.
2. At *Republic* 396a2–6, Socrates warns the guardians against imitating
madmen, worthless men, and women. I discuss this passage in chap. 5.

μιμέομαι); that doing so allows us to configure the cultural prescriptions at play with respect to these activities outside the theater; and that, as a consequence, we can better understand the meaning of theatrical experience itself. In this respect, it seems noteworthy to me that the general lexicon of Greek drama is not unique to the medium. This lack of specificity suggests a semantic link between the generic activities this lexicon names outside the theater and the specific practices it names within it.[3]

But according to what criteria do representations of these generic activities contribute to an understanding of theatrical production? Is it not in fact dangerously anachronistic to propose such a possibility? I will respond to this last question first, by noting that the charge of anachronism is only valid if the terms in question have no meaning apart from their chronologically deferred referents. While the generic activities to which I refer look forward to the conventions and lexicon of the fifth-century Athenian theater, their status as pretheatrical or extratheatrical concepts and activities is not part of an originary tale. I will not argue that the activity of watching in the context of Greek visual culture (e.g., what it means to look at monumental sculpture) or the activity of impersonation in the epic narratives (e.g., Odysseus' disguise in the *Odyssey*) anticipate these activities in the Theater of Dionysus.[4] Even disregarding the problems of chronology, there can be no strictly historical account of whether fully dramatized spectacle was prepared for by looking at sculptural representation, by examining the narrative elements of figures painted on a vase, or by studying the rhapsode's use of gesture, voice, costumes, or props.[5] Because

---

3. In contrast, the terms *tragedy* (τραγῳδία) and *comedy* (κωμῳδία) are unique to these media, but their history and meaning remain obscure despite repeated attempts at decipherment—beginning with Aristotle *Poetics* 1448a36–b1.

4. Golder (1996, 11) argues for a "sculptural style of tragic acting" and maintains that the "visual forms and meanings of the chorus . . . derive from the visual arts as well." I agree with Golder that the dramatic spectacle takes its place among other forms of visual culture in Athens at the time, but I am skeptical about the model of derivation he proposes. Moreover, the closed system of actors and chorus he investigates is only part of the picture.

5. See my introduction on the relevant arguments of Else, Herington, and Seaford. The introduction of masks, costumes, and props to visually enact a narrative might seem a first plausible step in the transition from

these questions posit origins or antecedents as answers, they ignore the more complex question of how these various practices contribute to a culture of public spectacle that transforms the citizen into a dramatic spectator or, more accurately, into a citizen-spectator in the Theater of Dionysus. The significance of this transformation can only be understood by considering acting, looking, and impersonating as long-standing and culturally discrete activities whose social and political effects come into play when the audience in the fifth-century theater witnesses the presentation of actors moving and speaking in accordance with a plot and a script.

I stated earlier that the sorts of activities available for representation in any given cultural and historical context are necessarily subject to restrictions and that these restrictions are key to the ideological content of those activities. We can apply this principle to the first question previously raised and begin to establish the criteria—or restrictions—that pertain to the generic activities of acting, watching, and impersonating as they become particularized in dramatic activities. It seems reasonable to combine acting and impersonating into a single category for analysis, one in which impersonating is the marked, or defining, activity (e.g., it is the activity that Plato finds so problematic).[6] In dramatic terms, to act is to impersonate, and to impersonate comprises both bodily acts and speech acts. These acts are the subject of the following two chapters, focused, respectively, on the representation of relayed, mediated, or what I call "scripted" speech (chap. 2) and on the overt public display of the disguised or theatrical body (chap. 3). In this chapter I want to focus attention on the criteria that pertain to the activity of watching and on the centrality of the spectator, as a theoretical construct.

Privileging the spectator over the actor or impersonator in this way

---

rhapsodic to dramatic performance. But again such an originary tale seems to me to raise more questions than it answers. Aristotle does not speculate about the origins of the mask in the *Poetics*. See Jones 1962, 42–43. Pickard-Cambridge (1968, 190–91) notes that "the primitive use of masks in the worship of a number of deities in Greece is well attested" and was therefore not particular to the worship of Dionysus (i.e., to that of the god of tragedy). On the ritual use of masks in the presumed ritual antecedents of tragedy, see Girard 1977, 166–68.

6. I use the word *marked* rather loosely here. See Nagy 1990, 5–8.

may at first seem reductive or arbitrary.[7] But if we consider that the institution of the theater is, first of all, a social or civic phenomenon and that the dramatic spectator is, above all else, a social agent, this emphasis on the spectator seems justified.[8] We should recall too that it is from the point of view of the spectator that imitation or impersonation is dangerous in Plato's critique of drama; the problem is that the spectator may become an impersonator. In principle, impersonation requires the visualized apprehension of a preexisting human model whose bodily acts and speech acts are the subject of the impersonation. Thus visualization is prior to impersonation whether or not the model is an actual social or historical person or a character out of myth or legend. What defines a spectator, moreover, is not some technical skill or specialized activity, such as the skill required of an actor,[9] but the sociopolitical environment in which the spectator is made to watch; a principal criterion of spectatorship is that it take place in a public or civic arena. In this context, it should be noted too that Plato's critique of imitation or impersonation is not directed at the actor as a professional, since his impersonations are (it is implied) only the temporary and proximate causes of the moral, ethical, and political dangers Plato proposes in the *Republic*. Rather, it is directed at a citizen whose own possible impersonations are the immediate and long-lasting causes of those dangers in the city. The point of recognizing

---

7. The actor is the privileged subject in those accounts of drama's origins that posit the taking on of a new identity. Likewise, performance studies commonly privilege the actor or performer. The opposite seems to be true for film studies, namely, that the emphasis there is on the subject position, or gaze, of the spectator. Perhaps this emphasis occurs because the film actor, unlike the actor in the theater, is only virtually present in the viewing situation.

8. See the introduction to Parker and Sedgwick 1995 for the relevant notion of the "compulsory witness" whose real or imagined presence enables performance both in the mundane world and in the theater proper: "like a play," they write, "marriage exists in and for the eyes of others." I argue, however, that as "witnesses," wedding guests and theatrical spectators occupy discrete and historically distinct sociopolitical positions.

9. That the actor qua actor requires some technical skill is true whether he is part of a professional class or simply a citizen who plays dramatic parts; in some cases, he is known to have been the poet himself. On the technical training of actors, see Pickard-Cambridge 1968, chap. 3. See also Lucas 1968 on *Poetics* 1448a1.

the primacy of the spectator is thus both theoretical (with an intended reference to the Greek θεωρία) and political. Spectatorship, by which I mean the representation of attentive or disciplined watching, is a shared feature of Athenian drama and of Athenian citizenship.

But when I talk about spectators and spectatorship, I am not talking about spectators as actual social subjects but about their representation in visual and narrative media.[10] This crucial distinction is all too often ignored in critical discussions of ancient Greek drama and is the source of that easy slippage between ourselves as critics and our ancient subjects. The failure to make this distinction also results in the too easy conflation of the ancient Athenians (as actual social subjects) and mythological characters, a conflation best exemplified in analyses of dramatic texts as though they were unmediated commentaries on contemporary Athenian life. The history of scholarship on Greek drama, even very recent history, demonstrates how difficult it is not to talk about what actual Athenians felt or thought in relation to the plays they witnessed or about mythological personae as if they were actual people (i.e., Athenians). To be sure, these texts were part of contemporary Athenian life: the Athenians seemed to prefer mythological plots and attended the theater to see them enacted (cf. Aristotle *Poetics* 1453a17–23). But this perceived preference is in part the result of statistical circumstance, that is, of the fact that almost all the extant plays and fragments of plays are based on mythological stories. The assumption that "the Athenians" preferred these stories ignores the diverse social factors that contribute to cultural production, while it naturalizes a narrative of unanimity and personal taste. Representations of social relations, whether these are founded on statistics or on the statements of dramatic characters, neither "reflect" nor "mirror" actual social relations in any simple or straightforward manner.

But if we do away with the actual Athenian spectator, how can we talk about the meaning of theatrical experience in ancient Greece? The answer is provided in part by Jack Winkler, when he says that the

---

10. In analyses of performance and identity, whether or not reference is made to visual or literary media (as in Freud's use of the *Oedipus Rex*), the aim is to understand the formation of actual social subjects as gendered subjects, for example, or as analysands.

"notional or proper audience [of Attic drama] is one of men."[11] Taking
the liberty of applying his idea with less historical and generic specificity, I propose a more general class of notional spectators, who play
their roles in the texts of Homer, Herodotus, Euripides, Aristotle,
Plato, and Freud (to name a few). It might be objected that the idea of
notional spectators in fact presupposes knowledge of their actual or
historical counterparts, that is, of spectators in the Theater of Dionysus during the fifth century. But similar to the charge of anachronism
mentioned earlier, this objection only begs the question of our ignorance of those actual spectators and resists the fact that our knowledge of ancient Greek culture is a product of representation. It also
accedes to a chronological imperative that would deny the existence
of spectators as a conceptual category until the time of their appearance as "actual" dramatic spectators in the Attic theater. As I have
already suggested, this objection also works to deny that the act of
interpretation itself is a manifestation of the desire for a seamless
interdependence between the representation of social relations (e.g.,
as moral or ethical exampla) and actual social relations, or, once again,
of the critic's desire to be as one with his ancient predecessor.

I mentioned at the beginning of this chapter that I intended to
discuss the trope of nostalgia in the critical history of drama and that
my primary texts would include Plato's and Aristotle's critiques of
dramatic impersonation, Freud's narrative of sexual object choice and
identity formation, and contemporary accounts of theatrical experience in drama and performance studies. I want to enter into that
discussion now, beginning with a look at Plato's model citizens in the
Republic (the guardians or φύλακες) as examples of the notional spectators I have just described. The decision to begin with Plato is perhaps
predictable and requires some explanation for precisely this reason. If
I had wanted to talk about the conceptualization of spectators and
spectatorship in terms of a chronological development, I would necessarily begin with Homer. I want to avoid a narrative of origins and
development, however, in favor of one that begins in medias res. The
primacy of Plato's fourth-century critique in such a narrative can be

---

11. Winkler 1990a, 39 n. 58. Cf. Dolan 1988, 2: "Performance usually addresses the male spectator as an active subject, and encourages him to identify with the male hero in the narrative."

explained in two ways. First, Plato's historical vantage point and philosophical purpose have established him as the arbiter of dramatic production in the context of political and social life. As Foucault would say, he is the author of a tradition.[12] Second, Plato's critique of dramatic impersonation in the *Republic* is itself inherently nostalgic. The tradition that Plato can be said to have authored is already retrospective, since he looks back to fifth-century Athens to implicitly condemn the city that condemned Socrates. Perhaps the best evidence of Plato's nostalgic enterprise is the fact that it is embedded in dramatic dialogue, a form that simultaneously expresses a desire to reanimate the dead Socrates and the necessarily failed satisfaction of that desire.[13]

Plato bases his critique on the possibility that social and political structures can be destabilized by bodily or visually manifested impersonations. This critique operates within the more general Platonic condemnation of the physical body and assumes an incommensurability between the reality and truth to which the eternal soul has access and the approximations and falsehoods that lead the mortal and ephemeral body astray (see Spelman 1982). In book 3 of the *Republic*, Socrates argues that fully enacted first-person impersonation—that is, "to impersonate both in voice and in looks" (393c5–6)—is dangerous in the ideal state, in which no citizen may be "double or multiple, since each one does one thing" (397e1–2).[14] In this political context, the baser sort of citizen is one who is wholly indiscriminate and will "attempt to imitate everything in earnest before many people" (397a3–4). The danger inherent in such indiscriminate imitations is that, if they are practiced from an early age, they can become habitual and naturalized in "body and voice and thought" (395d1–3). The repudiation of such multiplicity is then illustrated by the numerous examples Socrates offers of classes of people who should not be imitated by good men (ἄνδρας ἀγαθούς, 395d6), beginning with the example of women (395d5–396b7, 397a1–b2). In book 10, Socrates argues that the unreasonable or irrational part of the soul is the agent of these indiscriminate impersonations and that the theater is the site of its most conspicuous effects (604e1–6), because the dramatic poet, as the imitative poet par

---

12. I discuss this reference in my introduction.

13. I discuss this aspect of the Platonic dialogue in chap. 2.

14. Cf. Schechner's reference (1988, 175) to Artaud's positive definition of the actor as "doubled." I discuss Schechner's reference later in this chapter.

excellence (605a2), pleases a multitude of spectators by treating them to imitations and impersonations of every sort. External bodily dispositions and behaviors are clearly the focus of Socrates' critique of imitation or impersonation, in particular of the sorts of human dispositions and behaviors that good men, in their roles as good citizens, must avoid impersonating. Thus Plato's discussion corroborates what I have suggested earlier, namely, that visualization must precede impersonation. His critique is posited from the point of view of an ideal spectator (the good man or guardian), for whom the city is like a stage on which a variety of possible negative models or roles (women, slaves, madmen, cowards, working men, storytellers, etc.; 395d5–396a6) are presented. This analogy between the city and the theater is explicitly suggested in the *Republic*, when Adeimantus' question about whether or not tragic and comic impersonations ought to be allowed in the city (394d5–6) quickly becomes a question of the sorts of human behaviors the city provides for its best citizens to impersonate and not to impersonate.[15] In short, impersonation and its effects are first localized in the theater and then generalized in the city at large.

But whether we are talking about Plato's critique of the theater per se or of the city as a theater-like space, that critique functions as part of a disciplinary regimen. This regimen extends to the *Republic* as a whole, of course, and is best exemplified in the principle of justice according to which "everyone ought to perform the one function in the city for which his nature is best suited" [ὅτι ἕνα ἕκαστον ἓν δέοι ἐπιτηδεύειν τῶν περὶ τὴν πόλιν, εἰς δ' αὐτοῦ ἡ φύσις ἐπιτηδειοτάτη πεφυκυῖα εἴη] (433a3–5). The guardians must be the "master craftsmen of freedom for the city" [δημιουργοὺς ἐλευθερίας τῆς πόλεως] (395c1) and must avoid imitating those acts that are not conducive to this role. They may engage in impersonation, but only if they imitate

---

15. Socrates also mentions animal behaviors and natural phenomena as extreme examples of what the guardians should avoid imitating (*Republic* 396b5–8). But these seemingly extreme examples are not distinguished from the examples of human subjects (women, madmen, workmen, etc.) who are also to be avoided. In other words, all are to be equally avoided as models. In fact, they are just the sorts of things that the worse sort of man imitates (*Republic* 397a1–b2).

from childhood virtues and behaviors that are assumed to be "fitting" [προσήκοντα].

ἐὰν δὲ μιμῶνται, μιμεῖσθαι τὰ τούτοις προσήκοντα εὐθὺς ἐκ παίδων, ἀνδρείους, σώφρονας, ὁσίους, ἐλευθέρους καὶ τὰ τοιαῦτα πάντα, τὰ δὲ ἀνελεύθερα μήτε ποιεῖν μήτε δεινοὺς εἶναι μιμήσασθαι, μηδὲ ἄλλο μηδὲν τῶν αἰσχρῶν, ἵνα μὴ ἐκ τῆς μιμήσεως τοῦ εἶναι ἀπολαύσωσιν.

[If they do imitate, they should imitate from childhood what is fitting for them—men who are brave, temperate, pious, free, and all things of that sort; but things not for the free they should neither do nor be clever at imitating, nor should they imitate anything that shameful men do, so that they may not enjoy [or benefit from] what they imitate.] 395c2–d1

The guardians are defined here by their (innate?) ability to recognize and impersonate those people whom they ought to be like. This definition may not be strictly tautological, but it does suggest that to become a guardian, a man must already possess the ability to see himself as such. Another way of viewing this situation is to recognize that whereas imitation in its negative register ("do not imitate x") relies on a distinction between imitator and imitated, imitation in its positive register ("do imitate y") relies on the lack of such a distinction. These registers necessarily work together, but the ultimate positive aim of Plato's disciplinary regimen is the preservation and replication of a normative masculine subject as citizen and spectator. Now we can begin to see the full effect of Plato's analogy between impersonation as a theatrical and a political activity. Implicitly defined as a place where indiscriminate impersonations are allowed and encouraged among the worst sorts of citizens (i.e., as a place without discipline), the theater is the negative corollary to the ideal city, where impersonation is allowable only insofar as the best citizens perpetually impersonate (or replicate) themselves.

As I have already mentioned, civic discipline is enforced in Plato's regimen by reference to the visual and aural apprehension of external forms and gestures, that is, of bodily acts and speech acts. These external manifestations are the immediate source of the analogy between theatrical impersonations (those on the stage) and political ones (those in the city at large). But these external forms are only transitory; bodily acts and speech acts come and go both on the stage and in the city. And Plato's interest in these transitory conditions of impersonation is itself only transitory. What matters is how these conditions affect the internal and essential dispositions of the citizen's mind or soul. The passage just quoted tacitly assumes such an inner essence or core of identity, one that preexists and is separable from the changing scene of imitable bodily acts and speech acts. This inner core, comprising behavior that is "fitting," or natural, for the guardians, is described according to the standard lexicon of Athenian masculinity: the guardians are to be brave, temperate, pious, and free (ἀνδρείους, σώφρονας, ὁσίους, ἐλευθέρους).

Greek cultural identity in general is predicated on behaviors that normalize and naturalize the elite Greek male as a model human in terms of age, sexual maturity, bodily form, and what might be called reproductive power or agency;[16] he also possesses elite or aristocratic virtues, especially martial virtues.[17] Males can certainly be barbarians, slaves, or noncombatants; masculinity is not guaranteed by biology or by being an elite by birth or a soldier by occupation. Indeed, it can even be predicated of a biological woman. But the possibility that not

---

16. On this topic, see Spelman 1988; Hall 1989; Hartog 1988; Vidal-Naquet 1986; Loraux 1990; duBois 1982; Long 1986, 131–32; Lloyd 1983, 26–43; Arthur-Katz 1989, 172; Rousselle 1988, 26. Hall (95) notes the " 'law' of Greek ethnography that the more barbarian a community [is,] the more powerful its women [are]." De Ste. Croix (1981, 300) notes: "As early as 380 B.C. Isocrates (IV.50) had declared that being a Greek was not a matter of race (genos) but rather of mental attitude (dianoia), and that the name 'Hellenes' was given to those who shared a particular culture (paideusis: the process of education and its effects) rather than a physical relationship (a koine physis)." Said (1979, 40) describes the western construction of "Orientals" as "irrational, depraved, childlike, different." De Lauretis (1984, 121) notes the "mythical mechanism [that] produces the human being as man and everything else as, not even 'woman,' but non-man, an absolute abstraction" and adds that "this has been so since the beginning of time, since the origin of plot at the origin of culture."

17. Courage, or ἀνδρεία, is essential to the guardians' education and to the preservation of the city (Republic 429a–430c). Mason (1984, 105) points out that the transition from boyhood to manhood in classical Greek society is simultaneously a transition to the "citizen body and hence into the armed body at puberty."

all males are masculine, or that bodily acts and speech acts are transitory and illusory, only proves the need to postulate an essential core of immutable masculinity. Plato's censorship of bodily or visualized impersonations thus illustrates how the critique of dramatic impersonation is a manifestation of disciplinary practices that are ultimately aimed at establishing an inner core of unchanging masculinity. Dramatic impersonation, aligned with the irrational part of the soul, threatens to destabilize that core, not least of all by exciting the possibility that it too (that core) may only be an *effect* of bodily acts. This possibility motivates Plato's nostalgic antitheatrical enterprise.

This nostalgic enterprise is also descriptive of Aristotle's *Poetics*, even though the *Poetics* is commonly believed to be a corrective to Plato's condemnation of dramatic impersonation in the city.[18] Of course, Aristotle is concerned neither with the effects of impersonation per se nor with the political effects of tragedy but with analyzing the constituent formal features of the dramatic plot. In fact, he makes very few direct references to the effect of the dramatic performance on a spectator. But that he has so little to say about the audience's reaction to tragedy may indicate that he assumes a great deal in his readers. More accurately, it indicates that he assumes a homogeneous readership that holds common views about what it means to watch a tragedy. This homogeneity is overtly figured in the *Poetics*, in Aristotle's reference to the necessary fellow feeling with tragic characters who, says Aristotle, are "like us" [περὶ τὸν ὅμοιον] (*Poetics* 1453a6). It seems fair to say that Aristotle assumes an ideal reader who is equated with an ideal spectator. Although not as overtly disciplinary as Plato's critique of drama, Aristotle's discussion addresses this reader/spectator in a similar rhetorical register; the *Poetics* sets out to establish what is proper, fitting, appropriate, and natural with respect to imitation in general and tragic imitation in particular (e.g., κατὰ φύσιν, 1447a12; αὗται φυσικαί, 1448b5; σύμφυτον τοῖς ἀνθρώποις,

---

18. Cf. the provocative 1992 article by Nehamas, who argues against the proposition that Aristotle offers such a corrective. At times Nehamas seems to make this issue a question of biography, however, that is, of whether or not Aristotle actually intended a direct answer to Plato (see his p. 306). From my point of view, the relationship between Plato and Aristotle on the question of drama is a question not of biography but of the cultural meaning(s) of spectatorship.

1448b5–6). Thus, while Aristotle's ideal tragic spectators are not as clearly personified as Plato's guardians, they are naturalized in accordance with the proper effect of tragic mimesis. They even make a rather conspicuous appearance, so to speak, when Aristotle implicitly compares them to those spectators whose "weakness" is the source of inferior tragic plots (τὴν τῶν θεάτρων ἀσθένειαν, 1453a34–36). In general terms then, the *Poetics* is not a corrective to the *Republic*. Rather, it expands on the premises of the *Republic* by contextualizing drama within a normative and hierarchical order of representation and a disciplinary order of spectatorship.[19]

What Aristotle does have to say about the overt effect of tragedy on an audience constitutes one of the most controversial passages in the *Poetics*, namely, his all too brief claim that the *catharsis* of pity and fear is the benign and therapeutic purpose of tragedy.

ἔστιν οὖν τραγῳδία μίμησις πράξεως σπουδαίας καὶ τελείας μέγεθος ἐχούσης, ἡδυσμένῳ λόγῳ χωρὶς ἑκάστῳ τῶν εἰδῶν ἐν τοῖς μορίοις, δρώντων καὶ οὐ δι᾽ ἀπαγγελίας, δι᾽ ἐλέου καὶ φόβου περαίνουσα τὴν τῶν τοιούτων παθημάτων κάθαρσιν.

[Tragedy is an imitation of action that is serious, complete, and of great import, using speech that has been embellished by each of the kinds [of adornment] separately in the different parts [of the play], [speech spoken] by those performing the action and not through narrative, [an imitation of an action that] by means of pity and fear accomplishes the catharsis of such emotions.] (1449b24–28)[20]

---

19. Nehamas (1992, 297) argues that inasmuch as the emotions in the *Rhetoric* and elsewhere involve "rational elements . . . Aristotle presents a picture of our mental life which is in fact continuous with Plato's."

20. Nehamas (1992, 306–8) takes παθήματα as coordinate with πρᾶξις (meaning "incident") and proposes that "the *catharsis* of the sort of action of which the tragic plot consists is reached only through a series of incidents that are themselves pitiful and fearful—characteristics which it is quite reasonable to attribute to the events that constitute the tragic plot." He translates the final phrase of Aristotle's definition of tragedy as "and carrying such incidents to their appropriate resolution through a course of events that provoke pity and fear." This reading is suggestive, but the translation seems to me to involve a redundancy. Segal (1996, 55) argues for the traditional translation, that is, "through pity and fear accomplishing the purification of such emotions."

It is not my intention to enter into the debate over the strict meaning of the term *catharsis* in the *Poetics*, and for that reason I have intentionally not translated it in the preceding passage.[21] Rather, I would like to attempt a preliminary accounting of its subsequent dominance in the critical history of theatrical experience. Within that history, catharsis has been variously defined as a cognitive or an emotional effect, as a purification or a purgation. It is also an effect that is paradoxically independent of the visual experience of the theater. This paradox is ultimately attributable to Aristotle himself, who claims that pity and fear—the emotions so enigmatically associated with catharsis—do not rely on seeing events enacted on stage, that is, on *opsis*.

Ἔστιν μὲν οὖν τὸ φοβερὸν καὶ ἐλεεινὸν ἐκ τῆς ὄψεως γίγνεσθαι, ἔστιν δὲ καὶ ἐξ αὐτῆς τῆς συστάσεως τῶν πραγμάτων, ὅπερ ἐστὶ πρότερον καὶ ποιητοῦ ἀμείνονος. δεῖ γὰρ καὶ ἄνευ τοῦ ὁρᾶν οὕτω συνεστάναι τὸν μῦθον ὥστε τὸν ἀκούοντα τὰ πράγματα γινόμενα καὶ φρίττειν καὶ ἐλεεῖν ἐκ τῶν συμβαινόντων· ἅπερ ἂν πάθοι τις ἀκούων τὸν Οἰδίπου μῦθον.

[There is a sort of fear and pity that comes from the spectacle and another that comes from the arrangement of the events itself; this latter is the superior sort and the work of the better poet. For even without seeing how the plot is arranged [on stage], it is possible for one who hears the sequence of events to both shudder with fear and feel pity from what happens in the plot. These are the very things that someone who hears the Oedipus story [or plot] would experience.] (1453b1–7)

---

21. See Golden 1992, 5–39, for a summary of the scholarly debate, although I find Golden's own conclusions somewhat reductive. For him, *catharsis* refers to "intellectual clarification" and not to any emotional effect (whether a purification or purgation of the emotions). As a metaphor, however, the term traverses several semantic ranges. Nussbaum (1986, 388–91) discusses *catharsis* and related words and concludes that "We can, then, say without hesitation that all along the meaning 'clearing up' and 'clarification' will be appropriate and central ones for *katharsis*, even in medical and ritual contexts." She also argues for the cognitive value of such clarification: "the being who has achieved *katharsis* [is associated] with the true or truly knowing." See also Nehamas 1992 and Segal 1996 on this issue.

26 Acting Like Men

I will return to catharsis (and to Oedipus) in a moment. First, I want
to consider why Aristotle's definition of tragedy as an "imitation of an
action" is disengaged from what is arguably tragedy's most distinctive
formal feature, namely, the visual enactment.[22] In the following discussion I consider three related questions: How can the proper effect of
tragedy (catharsis) be achieved in the absence of one of tragedy's
principal elements (opsis)? What is the purpose of the assimilation of
what might be called the dramatic auditor and the dramatic spectator?
And finally, what place does the dramatic spectator occupy in Aristotle's theory of tragedy?

According to Aristotle, drama proceeds by a combination of bodily
acts and first-person speech acts, with no narrative interludes (cf.
Plato Republic 392d5 ff.). These acts are expressive, in turn, of internal
or psychological dispositions, that is, of ethos, or "character," and of
dianoia, or "intellect."[23]

ἐπεὶ δὲ πράξεώς ἐστι μίμησις, πράττεται δὲ ὑπό τινῶν
πραττόντων, οὕς ἀνάγκη ποιούς τινας εἶναι κατά τε τὸ ἦθος
καὶ τὴν διάνοιαν (διὰ γὰρ τούτων καὶ τὰς πράξεις εἶναί
φαμεν ποιάς τινας, [πέφυκεν αἴτια δύο τῶν πράξεων εἶναι,

---

22. It might be objected that what Aristotle disapproves of is not the visual
enactment of the dramatic plot per se but the kind of spectacle made possible by
lavish "expenditure" [χορηγία] (Poetics 1453b8). Certainly, Aristotle's opposition to spectacle suggests a common opinion that the visual apparatus of the
stage needed to be kept in check. Cf. Poetics 1450b16–21. But this opposition is
only one aspect of the more general disavowal of visual enactment that I am
arguing for. So, for example, Aristotle maintains that "the power of tragedy
exists even without the performance at public cost and the actors" [ἴσως γὰρ τῆς
τραγῳδίας δύναμις καὶ ἄνευ ἀγῶνος καὶ ὑποκριτῶν ἔστιν] (Poetics 1450b19–
20). Cf. Lucas 1968, on 1450b18: "A. is emphatic (cf. 53b4, 62a12) that the 'effect'
of tragedy does not depend on its being performed."
23. Ethos and dianoia admit various translations and are not always clearly
distinguished in the Poetics. See Blundell 1992. What interests me, however, is
how they are generally understood to be internal dispositions revealed
through the dramatic impersonation. Butcher [1894] 1951, 335) comments:
"The πρᾶξις of the drama has primary reference to that kind of action which,
while springing from the inward power of will, manifests itself in external
doing." A similar phenomenon, although in a different mimetic context, is
argued for with respect to Winckelmann's notion of the "mythic oneness of
body and idea, of nature and the ideal"; see Potts 1994, esp. 145–65.

ἦθος καὶ διάνοια] καὶ κατὰ ταύτας καὶ τυγχάνουσι καὶ ἀποτυγχάνουσι πάντες), ἔστιν δὲ τῆς μὲν πράξεως ὁ μῦθος ἡ μίμησις [24]

[Since [tragedy] is an imitation of action, and since action is accomplished by people who act and who are necessarily of a certain sort according to *ethos* and *dianoia* (for it is on account of these that we say actions are of a certain sort [and these, that is, *ethos* and *dianoia*), are the two natural causes from which actions arise], everything succeeds or fails on account of these for the plot is an imitation of action.] (Aristotle *Poetics* 1449b36–50a6)

In Aristotle's analysis of the constituent parts of the drama, he suggests that *ethos* is revealed primarily in bodily acts, while *dianoia* is revealed primarily in speech acts (1449b38–1450a7).[25] *Ethos*, he says, is a distinguishing feature of men in action (πράττοντας, 1448a1), and he offers as an analogy the types of *ethe* that can be distinguished in paintings of various human types (1448a5–6). The inference is clearly that visual appearance or externally perceived activity is expressive of *ethos* and, conversely, that *ethos* is what "gives rise to action."[26] From the point of view of Aristotle's analysis of dramatic impersonation, then, there exists an interdependence between the apprehension of internal feelings and thoughts and the apprehension of external acts and speech. We might say that this interdependence is a first principle of Aristotle's understanding of dramatic mimesis. But why does Aristotle weaken the argument for this interdependence by stating that the visual apparatus of tragedy *(opsis)* is unnecessary for achieving the tragic effect? In other words, why does he neutralize tragedy as a spectacle of bodily action by insisting on its efficacy as a verbal expression of internal and invisible mental states and feelings?

---

24. Lucas (1968, ad loc.) brackets πέφυκεν δὲ αἴτια δύο τῶν πράξεων εἶναι, ἦθος καὶ διάνοια as a "marginal explanation of the previous clause." See Blundell 1992, 162.

25. Cf. *Poetics* 1450b4–12; 1456a37. See Lucas 1968, on 1449b38. Blundell (1992) offers a revealing analysis of the relationship of *ethos, dianoia,* and *praxis* in Aristotle's *Ethics* and *Poetics,* according to which the *Poetics* responds to "the challenge of representing [*dianoia* and *ethos*] through language and stage action." See also p. 175 n. 82.

26. Blundell 1992, 157.

These questions bring me back to catharsis. It seems clear that
when Aristotle talks about catharsis in his definition of tragedy at
Poetics 1449b24–28, he is not talking about an effect on the characters
in the play. This interpretation is borne out at 1453b1–7, in which the
"someone" [τις] to whom Aristotle refers is the hearer of the [Oedi-
pus] plot, who, as Segal remarks, stands in for the spectator.[27] The
feelings of pity and fear to which that hearer is subject are the same
feelings that bring about the proper effect of the tragic performance,
that is, catharsis. Thus, catharsis is what ideally happens to the auditor *and* the spectator of the Oedipus plot. It is true, of course, that the
definition of tragedy does not overtly refer to the spectacular apparatus of the stage performance. The men in action whom Aristotle mentions there (δρώντων) need not be the actors per se; they may be only
the characters in the story. But this possibility begs the question of the
role of *opsis* as a necessary feature of tragedy. When Aristotle begins to
enumerate the six parts or elements of tragedy, he in fact begins with
its visual element.[28]

ἐπεὶ δὲ πράττοντες ποιοῦνται τὴν μίμησιν, πρῶτον μὲν ἐξ
ἀνάγκης ἂν εἴη τι μόριον τραγῳδίας ὁ τῆς ὄψεως κόσμος, εἶτα
μελοποιία καὶ λέξις·

[Since persons in action [or acting] are what make the [tragic]
imitation, it is necessary first of all that the arrangement of the
visual spectacle be a part of tragedy, and next comes song and
diction.] (1449b31–33)

Thus, even though Aristotle maintains that *opsis*, or visual spectacle—
especially the spectacle of bodily acts expressed in δρώντων and
πράττοντες— is a vital part of the tragic genre, he is willing (perhaps
even anxious) to eliminate that part when talking about the proper
tragic effect (i.e., feelings of pity and fear). To my mind, this willingness presents one of the most interesting and difficult conundrums in
the *Poetics*, even though it is more or less ignored in the critical litera-

---

27. Segal 1996, 154.
28. Aristotle lists μῦθος, or "plot," as the first of the six elements at
1450a9–10, where ὄψις is listed fifth. But this ordering only attests again to
the uncertain status of visual spectacle in Aristotle's scheme.

ture, in favor of the persistent search for an accurate meaning of cathar-sis. This situation is symptomatic of a desire to locate and preserve internal and essential dispositions in the face of dramatic practices.

We have already seen that Aristotle's notion of tragic action relies on the principle that internal dispositions and external or bodily ac-tions are interdependent. This interdependence relies in turn on an uneasy slippage between dramatis personae and actual social sub-jects or, more accurately, between tragic action and action in "real life." The basis of this slippage is the proposition that all action, including tragic action, is an unmediated expression of *ethos* and *dianoia*. But the appeal to this "real life" principle only begs the ques-tion of its credibility as a principle of mimetic performance. As a formal or technical practice, dramatic impersonation contradicts the proposition that external actions are revelatory of internal disposi-tions, that is, of those dispositions that prove a person is of a "certain kind" (1449b36–50a1). And the visual apparatus of the stage—the masks, the costumes, the choreography, and the theatrical space itself—attests most fully to the incommensurability of dramatic action and action in "real life." The force of the slippage, then, is to deny the threat of tragic action, namely (as I mentioned earlier), the threat that internal dispositions may only be the effect of visually apprehended bodily acts. This possibility is especially relevant for the story of Oedipus, which serves as Aristotle's model mythos, or plot. Bodily acts are the most significant features of the Oedipus narrative (incest and murder) and the most vivid feature of the stage production of the *Oedipus Tyrannus* (the presentation of the self-blinded Oedipus). Aris-totle (1452a22–33) praises the Oedipus plot most of all for its fully developed coincidence of peripeteia (reversal of the situation) and anagnorisis (recognition); since his analysis is essentially formal, he has little to say about the particulars of Oedipus' acts and their conse-quences or about the question of Oedipus' agency within the fictional universe of the plot. We can assume that those acts are the expression of Oedipus' *ethos* and *dianoia*, but Aristotle offers no detailed analysis of this expression.[29]

---

29. Aristotle does mention Oedipus as an example of the sort of man who suffers not on account of some evil or wickedness (κακίαν καὶ μοχθηρίαν) but on account of *hamartia* (*Poetics* 1453a7–10). The meaning of *hamartia* and its relationship to *ethos* and *dianoia* is beyond the scope of the present discussion.

Instead, he illustrates his claim that tragic plots (and actions) need not be seen to have their tragic effect, by the example of the Oedipus plot (1453b1–7). From the point of view of the dramatic spectator (rather than the dramatic character), the disavowal of *opsis* in Aristotle's theory suggests a desire to keep Oedipus' bodily acts out of sight. I include among these acts even those that would not have been literally presented on stage, that is, the incest and the murder. For the body of Oedipus as a dramatis persona on the stage necessarily communicates to a spectator the corporeality of those acts, even though they are not actually performed or visualized. In principle, Aristotle's tragic auditor—the one who only hears the Oedipus plot (ἀκούων τὸν τοῦ Οἰδίπου μῦθον)—can visualize Oedipus' bodily acts. But this visualization is internal and private rather than external and public. That Oedipus' infamous acts are always unseen—or rather, that they are only to be seen in the mind's eye—epitomizes Aristotle's anxiety over the body as a visually presented phenomenon and helps explain why *Oedipus* is his model tragedy. In general terms, when Aristotle maintains that seeing a play is not necessary for achieving the desired effect of tragedy, he simultaneously dissociates that effect from the bodily acts of the dramatis personae and from the bodily presence of the dramatic spectator. This denial of the corporeal basis of tragic impersonation accomplishes two ends. First, as I have already suggested, it works to deny the possibility, inherent in that impersonation, that internal dispositions may only be the effect of bodily acts. Second, it suggests that the visual corporeality of the tragic genre— epitomized in the Oedipus plot—is somehow dangerous for the spectator. If there is a critique of bodily acts and impersonations in the *Poetics*, here is its founding principle.

But what is the meaning of this critique? Like Plato's political regimen, Aristotle's therapeutic regimen works to subsume dramatized performance as a spectacle of bodily heterogeneity under a dominant discourse of invisible and essential dispositions and feelings. Plato would preserve the notion of an inner and essential soul idealized and localized in the masculine spectator (the guardian). For all its differences from Plato's critique, Aristotle's *Poetics* is engaged in a similar act of preservation. The repudiation of the effect of bodily impersonations—overt and political in Plato, curiously paradoxical in Aristotle—functions in the service of creating and maintaining the integrity and stability of the masculine subject, a subject who is, above all else, not Oedipus. The answer to the conundrum raised by Aristotle's disavowal and disapproval of dramatic *opsis* lies in a critique of bodily impersonations as unnatural acts in two senses: first, because dramatic impersonation in general uncouples the ontological and "natural" interdependence of internal dispositions and external acts; and second, because Oedipus' acts in particular are emblematic of this uncoupling, since he committed them, we might say, in defiance of his *ethos* and *dianoia* (he acted without knowing that he was doing exactly what he wanted to avoid doing). This Oedipal predicament—the crisis of an unstable and uncontrollable self-identity—summarizes the predicament posed by dramatic impersonation.

In Sophocles' *Oedipus Tyrannus*, Jocasta observes that Oedipus' acts are commonly committed in men's dreams: "Do not be afraid of marrying your mother; many men share their mother's bed in dreams" (979–82). This observation, offered as a means of disavowing the reality of that act and forestalling its terrible consequences, illustrates Aristotle's critique of dramatic *opsis* as I have described it; it internalizes those acts and would keep them in control and out of sight. But more to the point, this explanation helps to contextualize Jocasta's statement as a source for Freud's analysis of Sophocles' play in *The Interpretation of Dreams*, a text that represents perhaps the most conspicuous example of a critique of dramatic production in the service of preserving a dominant masculinity. After quoting Jocasta's reference to the dream, Freud ([1900] 1965, 297) comments, "Today, just as then, many men dream of having sexual relations with their mothers, and speak of the fact with indignation and astonishment." Thus Freud reinscribes the conflation of ancient Greek dramatis personae and contemporary social subjects that persists in the history of drama in the West. The effect of Freud's reference to the dream, like Jocasta's, is to assuage the indignation that the incestuous desire brings with it (and the repulsion that Freud speaks of later) by appealing to its common occurrence. Like Jocasta, Freud naturalizes Oedipus' "unnatural" acts in the context of dreaming and as a means of assuaging fear (or anxiety), and thus like Aristotle, he enlists the *Oedipus* as part of a therapeutic regimen. In the *Poetics*, that therapy consists of the catharsis of pity and fear as tragedy's proper effect. In Freud's text the Oedipal drama is dream material in which "a repressed wish [the little boy's sexual desire for his mother and hatred of his father] has found a means of evading censorship—and the distortion that censorship involves." Freud continues:

> The invariable concomitant is that painful feelings are experienced in the dream [and not in waking life]. In just the same way anxiety-dreams only occur if the censorship has been wholly or partly overpowered; and, on the other hand, the overpowering of the censorship is facilitated if anxiety has already been produced as an immediate sensation arising from somatic sources. We can thus plainly see the purpose for which the censorship exercises its office and brings about the distortion of dreams: it does so *in order to prevent the generation of anxiety or other forms of distressing affect.* (297–301)

In this formulation, Sophocles' drama is abstracted from its historical and civic context, and its plot is made universally available for men's private dreams. Freud does not describe the particular painful feelings that are experienced in the dream, but like pity and fear in Aristotle's text, they arise in response to what is arguably a mimetic phenomenon (the dream), and, as mentioned earlier, they provide a therapeutic benefit similar to Aristotle's catharsis.[30] In Freud's theater of the mind, the boy-spectator of psychoanalysis becomes a dreamer whose dreaming saves him from experiencing painful feelings in his waking existence and also enables him to take on his proper sociosexual role. We might say that the analysand's childhood is internally dramatized in conformity with the psychoanalytical script of sexual identity and object choice: following a therapeutic regimen, he becomes a mature heterosexual male.[31] It is noteworthy that Aristotle's dicta that "imitation is natural in humans from childhood" and that a man "learns his earliest lessons through imitation" (*Poetics* 1448b4–8) seem to anticipate this Freudian model of internalized spectatorship: the lessons of childhood in Aristotle's account of mimesis are suggestive of the disciplining of the "little boy" in Freud's Oedipal drama.[32]

---

30. Cf. Lucas 1968, appendix II.
31. On the difficulty of fitting feminine development into Freud's Oedipal scheme, see Meltzer 1990, 152–53.
32. Aristotle is talking about mankind (ἄνθρωποι) and not necessarily about masculine subjects, although the latter essentially constitute the former.

But the question before us is how does the little boy of psychoanalysis come to inhabit the figure of the disembodied Oedipus, that is, the Oedipus of dreams. The centrality of incest (or its avoidance) in the psychoanalytical account of sexual object choice and in anthropological and structuralist accounts of social formations is certainly germane to this question.[33] I am interested less in incest as a psychological or social phenomenon, however, than in the relationship between bodily acts and internal dispositions in Freud's analysis of the Oedipal plot and, more specifically, in the relationship between spectatorship and masculinity in that analysis.

At the end of the *Oedipus Tyrannus*, Oedipus blinds himself to avoid seeing his father, mother/wife, and children/siblings in Hades (1268–74, 1371–77). In general terms, his blindness signifies both the end, or resolution, of the external or bodily acts that drive the plot (the murder and incest) and the internal understanding of the truth of who Oedipus is and what he has done. For Freud, as Françoise Meltzer explains, Oedipus' self-inflicted punishment is a "substitute for the 'proper' one: castration."[34] Thus, the disavowal of spectatorship or, more accurately, Oedipus' willed blindness is essential in the ancient tradition to his self-recognition and to his role as the archetypal subject of psychoanalysis. When Freud describes the way in which that subject may be expected to react to the realization of his incestuous and murderous desires, he invokes this disavowal.

Like Oedipus, we live in ignorance of these wishes [to sleep with our mothers and murder our fathers], repugnant to morality, which have been forced upon us by Nature, and after their revelation we may all of us well seek *to close our eyes to the scenes of our childhood.* (Freud [1900] 1965, 297, emphasis added)

Freud's appeal to nature, like Aristotle's, disregards the ideological bases of social or political practices and expresses once again the nostalgic desire to be as one with the masculine subject of Greek

---

33. On incest, see Freud 1952; Levi-Strauss 1963b; Rubin 1975. Cf. deLauretis 1984 on Oedipal desire and narrative production.

34. Meltzer 1990, 154–55. Freud's substitution theory also illustrates how the refusal to see can be coextensive with a refusal to see the ruined or castrated male.

antiquity ("Like Oedipus, we . . .")—a desire that is naturalized in the context of Oedipus' ignorance of his own desires or wishes. In effect, Freud plays the role of an Oedipus figure who—unlike his ancient ancestor—knows what he wants and what he wants to see.[35] When Freud refigures Oedipus' self-blinding as an urge "to close our eyes to the scenes of our childhood," he summons the will to discipline the spectator, to turn him away from bodily acts and desires and toward the therapeutic construction of an inner and knowing self. This injunction to "close our eyes" to the Oedipal scene is acted on by the chorus in Sophocles' play, whose members are themselves loath to look at the blinded Oedipus.

ἀλλ᾽ οὐδ᾽ ἐσιδεῖν δύναμαί σ᾽ ἐθέλων
πόλλ᾽ ἀνερέσθαι, πολλὰ πυθέσθαι,
πολλὰ δ᾽ ἀθρῆσαι·
τοίαν φρίκην παρέχεις μοι.

[But I am not able to look at you, even though I wish
to ask you many things, and to learn many things,
and to consider many things [as I look on you];
such is the shiver of fear you cause in me.]

(Oedipus Tyrannus 1303–6)

In effect, the chorus members' revulsion and their own refusal to look replicate Oedipus' blindness. And that revulsion and refusal in turn present a negative corollary to the viewing position of the spectators in the theater, who, insofar as they are spectators, must look at Oedipus.[36] The implicit conflict between refusing to look and the compulsion to look, together with Oedipus' blindness, is emblematic of the ambivalence that characterizes spectatorship as a category of

---

35. See Page duBois' discussion of Freud's relationship to antiquity, in du-Bois 1988, chap. 2, esp. pp. 21–22. She offers a succinct reading of Freud's use of the Oedipus plot in *The Interpretation of Dreams*: "He attributes universality to the very thing that is alleged to grant universality to his own views" (21).

36. On Aristotle's statement at *Poetics* 1448b10–12, that mimesis affords pleasure in what ought to give pain, see chap. 5. Obviously actual spectators could refuse to look at Oedipus on stage; my point depends on the principle that, by definition, spectators are in the theater to watch.

analysis in the critical history of drama. In the works I have been discussing, attention is deflected from the body as a corporeal object of empirical observation and onto a stable and internal essence of [masculine] selfhood. In Freud's case that selfhood emerges out of a dream, and as Kaja Silverman notes, Freud thus "refuses to specify a physical location for psychical reality" in *The Interpretation of Dreams*.[37] But this reading of Freud is not entirely accurate. For in Freud's analysis of the *Oedipus Tyrannus* (as well as in his subsequent analysis of *Hamlet*), the dramatic stage is the physical location that paradoxically awakens a desire to see through the body to an internal essence that corresponds to a normative heteromasculinity.[38]

This desire to see through the body is also explanatory of the concept of identification that is common to psychoanalysis and to contemporary critical analyses of dramatic performance. I know of no historical basis for their shared use of the term, nor am I relying on the fact that one exists; identification does similar conceptual work in both theoretical domains, however. Generally descriptive of the pre-Oedipal or Oedipal desire to be or become the other, *Identifizierung* in the psychoanalytical literature is initiated and achieved through that desire.[39] Terms and phrases that frequently circulate around it are *fusion, connectedness, match, mesh,* and *to be at one with;* a similar lexicon is employed to explain the notion of theatrical identification, in which we hear of *fusions, meltings,* and *breachings* of individuation.[40] In Freud's

---

37. Silverman 1996, 9. Silverman's book elucidates the psychoanalytical ambivalence toward the corporeal body, especially with respect to the concept of identification. On the unconscious as "unseeable" and on the use of concrete metaphors as a way in which "the unconscious manifests itself for psychoanalysis," see Meltzer 1990, 147–52.

38. Cf. de Lauretis 1987b, 44: "If Oedipus has become a paradigm of human life and error, narrative temporality and dramatic structure, one may be entitled to wonder whether that is purely due to the artistry of Sophocles or the widespread influence of Freud's theory of human psychic development in our culture; or whether it might not also be due to the fact that, like the best of stories and better than most, the story of Oedipus weaves the inscription of violence (and family violence, at that) into the representation of gender." See also duBois 1988, chap. 2.

39. See Laplanche and Pontalis 1973, 205–8; Fuss 1995 introduction and chap. 1; Silverman 1996, esp. 22–37.

40. See Wilshire 1982, 27–28.

The Ego and the Id, as Silverman explains, identification is a process by which "the other is interiorized as the self."[41] It is moreover a mimetic process in which "an idealized [masculine] image" is the means by which the other can be "interiorized" as the same.[42] A full appreciation of Silverman's analysis of this concept is outside the scope of this discussion. But even a brief glance at her arguments helps demonstrate the emphasis on internal and unseeable ("interiorized") phenomena in the psychoanalytical narrative of identification. External, visible, and somatic phenomena are vaguely ancillary to the child-spectator's primary goal of achieving an idealized and internalized masculine selfhood.

In performance studies, the concept of identification is similarly based on a hierarchical distinction between internal and external (bodily) phenomena. With obvious roots in psychoanalysis, but also indebted to anthropological approaches to drama that were prevalent in the 1960s, it has remained a dominant feature in conceptualizing the essential dramatic act, that is, the act of acting itself.[43] Thus, for example, in his much quoted 1975 book *The Actor's Freedom: Toward a Theory of Drama*, Michael Goldman suggests that "the covert theme of all drama is identification, the establishment of a self that in some way transcends the confusions of the self" (122–24). Like Aristotle and Freud, Goldman offers up a therapeutic regimen that would guarantee an essential and inner selfhood, even godhood. He overtly denies the idea that dramatic impersonation poses a threat to this essential identity, and he displaces this idea with the counterassertion that dramatic impersonation in fact eliminates identity "confusion." This elimination, he says, is "the actor's achievement." Identification is thus naturalized and valorized as a unifying "mechanism" by which the actor, the spectator, and the character occupy undifferentiated

---

41. Silverman 1996, 23; see also Fuss 1995, 4–5.

42. Silverman 1996, 24–25. In contrast to the idealized masculine image is that of the castrated female: "The castration crisis can perhaps best be understood as the moment at which the young female subject first apprehends herself no longer within the pleasurable frame of the original maternal imago, but within the radically deidealizing screen or cultural image repertoire, which makes of her body the very image of 'lack' " (Silverman 1996, 33). Cf. Butler 1990a, 66–72; de Lauretis 1984, 136–41. Girard (1977, 169–92) argues for Freudian identification as a process of "mimetic desire." See also Mulvey 1975.

43. See Schechner 1985, 1988. Cf. Geertz 1980.

positions. The homogeneity of these positions is a means of presuming sameness in the face of multiplicity and difference. In Foucault's words (1972, 12) it is a means by which the subject is founded in the process of bringing "back under his sway, all those things that are kept at a distance by difference."

When Goldman turns or returns to Greek tragedy, as all critics must, this founding process overtly apprehends him and his implied or ideal reader. Like Aristotle and Freud, he envisions himself and his readers as elite male citizens in fifth-century Athens.

> We are far from the hero. A good portion of the entire city's population sits around us. We all look down the vast cupped slope into the stone bull's-eye, the dancing ring with an altar at the center. (Goldman 1975, 126)

This picture of oneness with the citizens of Athens is the essential expression of the unifying power of identification, a power that establishes "a self that in some way transcends the confusions of the self." Here that transcendence is transhistorical—even eternal. It has its roots (once again) in the ritual origins of drama and the spiritual rebirth of the hero. And it invents the drama critic as an Athenian, to guarantee his own stable, eternal, and authoritative "self."

Goldman's analysis of theatrical experience may seem idiosyncratic, but it is not unique in scholarly literature. The desire for oneness with the ancient Greeks is a notable feature in the work of some of the most renowned classical scholars of ancient drama. For example, J.P. Vernant concludes his influential 1981 article by collapsing the dramatic dates of plays ("a past that is still alive") and their historical dates (the fifth century) to argue for tragedy's therapeutic effect in the fifth-century city, an effect occasioned by the civic "anxiety" or "tension" inherent in the tragic production. Like Goldman's ideas, but now translated back into the social reality of fifth-century Athens, Vernant's arguments rely in principle on an assimilation of Athenian citizens and mythological heroes. He finds in the tragic hero a reliable, if hyperbolic, model for the contemporary Athenian spectator.

> Even as the setting and the mask confer upon the tragic protagonist the magnified dimensions of one of the exceptional beings

that are the object of a cult in the city, the language used brings
him closer to the ordinary man. And even as he lives his legendary adventure this closeness makes him, as it were, the contemporary of the public so that the tension that we have noted
between past and present, between the world of myth and that
of the city, is to be found again within each protagonist. At one
moment the same tragic character appears projected into a far
distant mythical past, the hero of another age, imbued with a
daunting religious power and embodying all the excesses of the
ancient king of legend. The next, he seems to speak, think, live
in the very same age as the city, like a "bourgeois-citizen" of
Athens amid his fellows. (Vernant 1981, 19)

Vernant's prose takes us out of the mundane world of historical
specificity and into a marvelous landscape that melds together past
and present, hero and citizen. In doing so, he presents a genealogy
of spectator positions in which the citizens of fifth-century Athens
become like the heroes of a distant mythical past. At the same time,
the bourgeois citizens of a European present (Vernant's readers)
are themselves implicitly likened to those mythical Athenian hero-
citizens. In his genealogy, moreover, a "tragic consciousness" is hero-
ically experienced by "tragic man" (Vernant 1981, 7). Thus, even
though Vernant does not talk about identification per se, he does
illustrate how such a concept, broadly conceived, universalizes and
dehistoricizes Greek drama and idealizes the masculine subject of
Greek antiquity.

An excerpt from Richard Schechner's *Performance Theory* illustrates
a similar role for the concept of identification in contemporary American performance studies. Schechner offers a global perspective on the
actor in his or her role as a dramatis persona.

Looking at performing worldwide, two processes are identifiable.
A performer is either "subtracted," achieving transparency, elimi-
nating "from the creative process the resistance and obstacles
caused by one's own organism" (Grotowski 1968a: 178); or s/he is
"added to," becoming more or other than s/he is when not performing. S/he is "doubled," to use Artaud's word. The first tech-

nique, that of the shaman, is ecstasy; the second, that of the Balinese dancer, is trance. (Schechner 1988, 175)[44]

Schechner's language of transcendence is similar to Goldman's and, if less obviously so, to Vernant's. Each critic appeals to a kind of religious experience that results in a more meaningful identity, one freed from mundane confusions or obstacles. Schechner identifies certain Western actors who exemplify the two types of performance styles he mentions (i.e., trance and ecstasy), but like Goldman, he too evokes what amounts to a universally held principle of transcendence, even though he locates this transcendence in the exotic bodily states (ecstasy and trance) of non-Europeans.[45] In Schechner's view, acting is a state of mind to which the actor's body is somehow subject, although obviously this subjection is very different from that implied by Aristotle's insistence on the relationship of external action to internal thoughts and dispositions: ecstasy and trance are a long way from *ethos* and *dianoia*. In the time of performance, according to Schechner, the actor is somehow "subtracted from" or "added to," is made either transparent or is doubled. These states would seem to refer to material or bodily phenomena. But these are only metaphorical propositions, and if we ask what is "subtracted from" or "added to," we have to assume some already existing inner state or identity. Thus Schechner illustrates how the acting or impersonating body is made the locus of internal and already existing dispositions and how the theoretical contemplation of that body calls forth the validation of those dispositions in the spectator/critic.

Schechner's pronoun *s/he* is clearly meant to refer to actresses and actors as gender-specific categories and to avoid privileging one over

---

44. de Lauretis (1987b, 44) finds a "daring parallel between shamanistic practices and psychoanalysis" in Lévi-Strauss's "The Effectiveness of Symbols." Fuss (1995, 4) describes Freud's scientific conception of identification as oppositional to "[P]revious models that seek to conceptualize the influence of other on self—demonic or ecstatic possession, contagious passion, animal magnetism, mesmerism, hypnosis," arguing that "all represent otherness in mystical rather than rational terms, subsuming science into religion."

45. In equating the state of the actor with a state of ecstasy and trance, Schechner (1988), like Goldman (1975), implicitly alludes to the ritual origins of western drama—origins that he himself discounts.

the other. Yet the compound paradoxically signifies a lack of differentiation, an androgynous actor/ess. Thus, while Schechner's Aristophanic s/he resists acquiescing to the male as the default subject, it also denies the possibility for a multiplicity of subjects and reinscribes the notion that behind every act of dramatic impersonation, there resides an essential and unitary selfhood.[46] Of course, the compound also implicitly alludes to the fact that the performing body of the actor, distinguished from an everyday or mundane body, signifies hyperbolic embodiment. In Greek and other performance contexts, this hyperbolic embodiment is most conspicuous in the "doubling" that takes place when a male actor plays a female character. I am not suggesting that Schechner had the Greek actor (as female character) in mind when he used the compound pronoun in his definition of performing "worldwide." But the choice does illustrate how bodily acts are ultimately subsumed under an essential being that can be added to or subtracted from (as in the case of the Greek actor who puts on and takes off the costume of his female character) but that is itself immutable. As a consequence, the actor paradoxically becomes the subject of somatophobia in theatrical criticism and the catalyst for preserving and conveying a transcendent and inner subjectivity.

I have argued that the critical discourses of Greek and European drama are founded on a persistent desire to deflect attention from the external body as a site of empirical observation and mutability and onto an essential and eternal masculine selfhood.[47] In this reading, the story of theatrical experience is not independent of the story of a masculine transcendence and the search for Greek drama's origins is thus coincident with or, perhaps more accurately, motivated by the search for and preservation of the essential masculine subject of antiquity. In *Gender Trouble,* Judith Butler examines how gender identity functions within the kind of infinite regress that posits an ontologically "real" original. As a corrective to this originary myth, she argues that gender identity is the effect of a "stylized repetition of acts" that "create the illusion of an interior and organizing gender core."

---

46. In Plato's *Symposium* (189c2 ff.), Aristophanes tells the story of humans who were originally androgynous creatures. I discuss this story in chap. 3.

47. Cf. Wilshire (1982, 34–35) on what he calls the "body-self" in theatrical experience.

If the "cause" of desire, gesture, and act can be localized within the "self" of the actor, then the political regulations and disciplinary practices which produce that ostensibly coherent gender are effectively displaced from view. The displacement of a political and discursive origin of gender identity onto a psychological "core" precludes an analysis of the political constitution of the gendered subject and its fabricated notions about the ineffable interiority of its sex or of its true identity. (Butler 1990a, 136)

Butler's thesis is clearly focused on the social reality of gender-specific performances; she does not look at dramatic impersonation per se as part of that social reality. Nonetheless, her analysis illustrates the fact that the theater is precisely the place where the political regulations and disciplinary practices that produce an ostensibly coherent gender are effectively placed in view. In the critical discourses we have looked at, that "coherent" gender describes an illusion of normative masculinity whose status risks exposure, so to speak, when it becomes the subject of theatrical or theater-like practices. In this sense, dramatic performance is not so readily explained by Aristotle's statement that mimesis is innate in humans and that by means of it they learn their earliest lessons (*Poetics* 1448b4–19). Considered within the culture- and gender-specific prohibitions that establish masculine subjects as normative and essential, dramatic impersonation both affirms the law that, in Butler's words, "produces and regulates discrete gender identity and heterosexuality" (1990a, 64) and exposes its unstable foundation. For this reason, the related concepts of spectatorship and impersonation become focused on unseen psychological or mental processes whose effect is the validation of an internal core of masculine identity separate from the world of empirical, especially visual, perception— abstracted, that is, from the body as the vehicle of indiscriminate or unnatural acts. The critical history of Greek drama is thus part of a larger social and political drama in which Greek masculinity is historically reproduced in "a stylized repetition of acts" (Butler 1990a, 140). The formulation and representation of these acts are the subjects of the following chapters.

2

Scripted Speech

In the previous chapter, I argued that spectatorship and bodily impersonation are the principal features of drama as a practice and as a
conceptual category. But with the obvious exception of mime, dramatic impersonation comprises both bodily acts and speech acts. Despite the fact that Aristotle can do away with *opsis* and can simultaneously reduce the verbal articulation of a play to the reading or
recitation of its main events (*Poetics* 1453b1–7), formal dramatic performance advances by means of the first-person speeches of the actors.[1]
Indeed, the dramatic actor is referred to in the Greek lexicon as a
ὑποκριτής, whose primary meaning is generally given as "one who
gives an answer."[2] The historical route by which this term comes to
designate an actor and how its meaning is appropriate for an actor's
performance are uncertain. Nevertheless, it suggests that the dramatic actor is understood first of all in his role as a speaker, or, more
precisely, in his role as an impersonator whose impersonations con-
sist of speech acts (contra Aristotle, who emphasizes the tragic action). No matter what the history of the term, its use confirms the fact
that dramatic impersonation in ancient Greece must be understood

---

1. Aristotle certainly talks about language in the *Poetics:* λέξις is one of the
six parts of tragedy. But his interest is essentially philological (i.e., in chaps.
19–22). His definition of tragedy at *Poetics* 1449b24–28 explains the importance of λόγος and of the first-person speech of the actors. But as far as I can
tell, he does not talk about tragic speeches as imitations, although he implies
that dramatic speech is the vehicle of *dianoia*. See my discussion in chap. 1. Cf.
Martin 1989, 45–47, on the first-person speeches in epic.
   2. On ὑποκριτής as an actor on the stage, see Aristophanes *Wasps* 1279;
Plato *Republic* 373b; Aristotle *Poetics* 1449a15–19. Pickard-Cambridge (1968,
131–32) suggests that ὑποκριτής, meaning "one who answers," is a reference to the importance of the actor's voice in performance. Seaford (1994,
270 n. 153; contra Else 1957) insists that "interpreter" is the original meaning
of ὑποκριτής, in support of his contention that drama originally developed
out of mystery rituals whose "esoteric performance" required interpretation.

within the context of communicative practices. Based on the assumption that dramatic speech occupies a middle position between written speech (the script) and oral speech (in performance), this chapter begins with a look at the oral-literate binary in the Western tradition and goes on to define theatrical, or "scripted," speech as a gender-specific mode of communication within that binary. I will also argue that the nostalgia that governs the critical history of drama in the West is specified in the desire for an idealized speaking subject.

It is commonly understood that Western cultures define themselves in terms of a value-laden distinction between the spoken and the written word. Oral speech as direct or nonmediated communication and writing as indirect or mediated communication constitute the common terms of this oral-literate binary. What I am calling "scripted speech" occupies a position between these polarities.[3] The term *scripted speech* may seem oxymoronic at first glance but is meant to provoke a reconsideration of the terms of the opposition between oral speech and speech as a written text. It is also meant to allude to the dramatic script as a particular kind of speech act, an act that can be profitably positioned in the broader context of communicative practices and the ideological assumptions associated with those practices. In the introduction, I suggested that by virtue of their cultural primacy, the Homeric epics establish models for representing human speech and the display of the human body in Greek culture at large. Defined as communication in which there is a recognized or acknowledged dissociation between an original speaker and his words, scripted speech is first illustrated in the message-sending scenes in the epics, in which an intermediary delivers the words of one character to another.

I suggest no straightforward historical connection between the message-sending scenes in epic and the performance of a dramatic script but rather a connection based on some shared characteristics. In both cases, a human or divine entity speaks for another; in the case of

---

3. See Roach 1996, 11–12, on the different but related notion of *orature*, a term attributed to the Kenyan novelist and director Ngugi wa Thiong'o: "orature goes beyond a schematized opposition of literacy and orality as transcendent categories; rather, it acknowledges that these modes of communication have produced one another interactively over time and that their historic operations may be usefully examined under the rubric of performance."

verbatim first-person reports, the reporter or messenger speaks the words of the sender of the message (i.e., not his own words) and can be likened to an actor speaking as a dramatis persona.[4] Indeed, Socrates' assertion in Plato's *Ion* that the epic rhapsode and the dramatic actor both occupy a middle position is based on the notion that each speaks for or as another and that the position of each as an intermediary puts a limit on the truth-value of his utterances.[5] That messengers in the epic often come in disguise[6] suggests an early connection as well between the disguised body—like that of an actor—and the epistemological uncertainty occasioned by mediated, or reported, speeches. These resemblances between the rhapsode, the epic messenger, and the dramatic actor frame the argument of this chapter, namely, that scripted or mediated speech can constitute a category for analyzing dramatic speech.

The argument is also framed by some basic assumptions that will come into sharper focus later but that will be useful to prepare for here. The first of these is that Greek epic poetry—the *Iliad*, in particular— validates an idealized mode of direct first-person speech between elite males, in opposition to mediated speech (including oral and written messages) as suspect and feminine. At the same time, this gender-specific opposition between nonmediated and mediated speech is analogous in the epics to an opposition between the warrior who fights man-to-man and the fighter who fights from a distance; the archer is the paradigmatic example of the latter.[7] These contested modes of communication and of combat are essential and related variables in the construction of the heroic male, who, like Achilles, is to be "experi-

---

4. This definition of scripted speech holds whether or not we insist on the literal existence of the dramatic script in the fifth century. Cf. Svenbro 1990, 371–72. Svenbro's notion of dramatic performance as a vocal rewriting of the text is interesting if a bit confusing, since what is vocalized is not a rewriting but a reiteration of the written text in oral speech. See also Segal 1986.

5. *Ion* 535e9–536a1. This passage is discussed in more detail later in this chapter.

6. E.g., the dream as Nestor (*Iliad* 2) and Iris as Polites (*Iliad* 2.786 ff.).

7. Cf. Hanson 1989, 15: "[The] deliberate dependence on face-to-face killing at close range explains another universal object of disdain in Greek literature: those who fight from afar, the lightly equipped skirmisher or peltast, the javelin thrower, the slinger, and above all the archer (Eur. *HF* 157–63; Aesch. *Pers.* 226–80, 725, 813, 1601–3)." See also Loraux 1986, 34.

enced in deeds and in words."[8] In sum, the *Iliad* provides a basic profile of the Greek masculine subject defined by the ways in which he speaks and fights. As a related but more tentative conclusion, the recognition of these contested modes of speaking and fighting helps to clarify the essential distinction between the *Iliad* as a poem about (the Trojan) war and the *Odyssey* as a poem about war's aftermath. In the former, man-to-man combat and man-to-man speech are mutually reinforcing practices required of the heroic subject.[9] In the latter, Odysseus' return through and to the domestic space of the female is made possible by the mutually reinforcing practices of duplicitous or scripted (i.e., mediated) speech and bodily disguise (see chap. 3).

I begin with a brief sketch of how these assumptions function within the larger narrative of Western or European domination with particular reference to the role played by Greek epic within that narrative.[10] In very general terms, anthropological and philosophical explorations of human cultures in the West rely on a distinction between oral and literate societies, one that serves to substantiate the domination of writers over nonwriters. Recent work on the first encounters with the New World, for example, has shown how the Europeans validated and consolidated their superiority over the Amerindians not only by reference to this distinction in the abstract but also by the proliferation of written documents and proclamations that legitimated their "official" acts of "discovery" and subjuga-

---

8. Phoenix says that Achilles was sent on the expedition to Troy while still a child and not yet knowledgeable about warfare and debate (*Iliad* 9.440–41). Cf. Martin 1989, 26: "We can note that the heroic imperative as crystallized in Phoinix's words to Achilles demands that a hero learn to 'be a doer of deeds' and a speaker—not of words, but of muthoi, 'authoritative speech-acts': μύθων τε ῥητῆρ' ἔμεναι πρηκτῆρά τε ἔργων (9.443)." Martin (38) also notes that *epea* (as opposed to *muthoi*) in the *Iliad* denote "personal appeal, not authoritative performance," and that the latter are often spoken by women.

9. Cf. Goldhill 1990, 108: "The notions of single combat, a hierarchy of warriors, and the search for the perpetuation of a *name* are essential structurings of the heroic ethos of the Homeric poems." Achilles' withdrawal from and subsequent return to the battle in the *Iliad* only reinforces the dominance of this ethos.

10. Cf. Haraway 1991, esp. the first essay, "Animal Sociology and a Natural Economy of the Body Politic: A Political Physiology of Dominance," in which the author argues that competitive aggression, or the struggle for dominance, is the "chief form that organizes other forms of social integration" (18).

tion.[11] Here the realia of written treatises is proof of the cultural superiority that literacy affords. But this narrative of dominant writers and fighters does not mean that the cultural status of direct oral communication—of what Derrida calls "logocentrism"—has been erased in these explanations.[12] The persistence of this ideal finds expression in the notion of the nonliterate noble savage, for example, and in cultural *muthoi* about earlier and more authentic times before the intrusion of writing. In these *muthoi*, oral culture is an ever receding object of desire superseded in time by the development of literacy, and contemporary nonliterate societies become a nostalgic footnote; for them the development of literacy is only a matter of time.[13] Noteworthy in these narratives is how an idealization of oral culture or oral communication persists where literacy dominates.[14] Television may be the most obvious example of this phenomenon in the twentieth century, insofar as it maintains the appearance of living, speaking characters who "exist" in the private spaces of our everyday lives. We are prevented from speaking with (if not to) those characters, of course, but their transmitted images nevertheless respond to a desire to see and hear human beings speaking in our presence. As a historical phenomenon, this desire may well be a necessary and even predictable feature of the proliferation of literate (including electronic) technologies.[15]

---

11. Cf. Greenblatt 1991, 9. See also Hartog 1988, 287–89, on Jean de Léry's "lecture on writing" in *Histoire d'un voyage fait en la terre de Brèsil*. See also de Certeau 1988, 212–43 (cited by Hartog).

12. Derrida 1976, 11–12. See also Havelock 1986, 34–43.

13. On cultural authority and ethnographic writing, see Clifford 1988, 21–54. Manganaro (1992, 2), in a discussion of participant observation as an imperative in ethnographic writing, states: "Recent cultural theory has emphasized that this insistence upon an unmediated presentation (versus mediated representation) has motivations and effects other than hermeneutic naïveté, nostalgia, or optimism (though such logocentric impulses do play a part) . . . . the 'will to truth' is actually a 'will to power.' " I maintain that nostalgia is an expression of a will to power.

14. Cf., e.g., Ong 1982, 15: "Literacy can be used to reconstruct for ourselves the *pristine human consciousness* which was not literate at all—at least to reconstruct this consciousness pretty well, though not perfectly (we can never forget enough of our familiar present to reconstitute in our minds any past in its full integrity)" (emphasis added).

15. Ong (1982) defines "the telephone, radio, television, and other electronic devices" as examples of "secondary orality" and notes that "[p]rimary

This sketch is obviously incomplete and is offered only as a brief introduction to a more detailed discussion of the so-called orality question in classical studies. The historical and ideological features of the oral-literate binary are to a large degree indebted to the history of scholarship on Greek epic. Eric Havelock put it succinctly when he said, "The 'orality question' . . . from its inception in modern times, has been entangled with the 'Greek question' "[16] The "Greek question," formulated in Milman Parry's studies of the "acoustic mechanics of oral verse-making," is characterized by debates over the paradoxical nature of the epic as oral literature, that is, by the extent to which the advent of writing may have affected the formal properties of what is believed to have been orally composed poetry.[17] Statistical analyses of orality and literacy in ancient Greek society and historical accounts of when and how the *Iliad* and *Odyssey* were committed to writing are essential features of the "Greek question." But the metrical, grammatical, and syntactical arguments that have created the paradox of oral literature and the statistical, historical, and philosophical arguments that follow from them have recently and persuasively been called into question.[18] Now it seems that the distinction between orality and literacy is less absolute than had previously been supposed; it has been convincingly argued, for example, that formulaic poetry (like the Greek epics) is not necessarily the product of preliterate cultures. Absolute orality, in other words, is an attractive, if tenuous, proposition—a proposition that is made more attractive in the case of the Greek epics precisely because they have been committed to writing. Here again we are witness to the search for origins (the oral epic), moti-

---

orality" defines "a culture totally untouched by any knowledge of writing or print." These distinctions obscure the ideological similarities between primary and secondary oralities.

16. Havelock 1986, 37. Other standard works in English are Ong 1982 and Havelock 1982 and 1963. See also Harris 1989. For summaries of the topic, see the first chapters of Foley 1988, and see, more recently, Thomas 1992. Ong (1982, 10–15) discusses the phrase *oral literature*—a "monstrous concept." Cf. the critique of Havelock by Halverson (1992).

17. See Havelock 1986, 52. Havelock's book includes a good overview of Parry's work, including the relevant bibliography. See also the first chapter of Foley 1988.

18. See Thomas 1992, chap. 3.

vated in this case by a desire for what Derrida calls "the absolute
proximity of voice and being."[19]

Focused on the composition of the epic poems, the orality question
has diverted attention from the question of how orality and literacy
function within the epic narratives, that is, how they are part of epic
representation.[20] The notion of oral composition as a formal poetic
practice should not be confused with the notion of oral speech as a
mode of human intercourse, but these notions are not mutually exclusive; the medium (the poem as the idealized product of oral composition) is part of the message (the significance of idealized oral speech
between heroes). At the same time, of course, heroic speech acts are
mediated or transmitted through the poetic speech act, that is,
through the voice and body of the hypothetical poet in the act of
performance. The notion of the "absolute proximity of voice and being" as a principle of heroic or epic identity is thus always already an
object of desire. I want to make it clear that I am concerned not with
what Havelock calls an "oral consciousness" but with how the various
modes of communication that operate in the epic narratives function
in the construction of Greek cultural identity, especially the construction of masculine identity.[21]

In the texts of Hesiod and Homer, that identity is part of an account
of past events recorded in human memory and orally transmitted by
the poet, with divine assistance. In the originary scene of this account,
the poet receives at the whim of the Muses and passes on to his auditors an account of events worth remembering (*Theogony* 26–35; *Iliad* 1.1,
2.484–93; *Odyssey* 1.1). This is clearly not a representation of everyday
verbal intercourse (συνουσία) but a portrait of poetic instruction in the
service of establishing and maintaining a record of the dominant culture, in other words, in the service of creating a tradition. In defining a
tradition as "repeated instructions," Havelock argues that such repetition "is linked to a feeling of pleasure, a factor of primary importance in
understanding the spell of oral poetry."[22] But Havelock does not say
whose pleasure is in question, and so he conceals the way in which the

---

19. Derrida 1976, 11–12.
20. But see Martin's excellent 1989 study.
21. See Havelock 1986, chap. 10.
22. Havelock 1986, 68–70. Cf. Butler 1990a on gender as a "stylized repetition of acts."

enforcement of power relations is a factor in the "spell of oral poetry."[23] As the medium of this spell, oral transmission is a transcendent mode of communication—not only for the divinely favored poet, but also among the gods and mortal heroes about and for whom the poet speaks or sings. With its appeal to divine sanction and to the preservation of the exploits of gods and more-than-mortal Greek heroes, the originary scene of poetic production naturalizes oral transmission as a constitutive feature of legitimated domination.[24] Its premise is obviously agonistic in terms of poetic production (the divinely favored poet is the best) and perhaps less obviously so in terms of a cultural ethos that valorizes masculinity and martial valor.

As I have suggested, poetic production not only naturalizes an idealized version of oral transmission but also necessarily breaks the promise (or the "spell") of direct man-to-man speech as the validating practice of heroic identity. This contest between the idealization of oral transmission and the promise of heroic speech is prepared for in the originary scenes of Greek epic and didactic poetry. These scenes traditionally begin with an interchange between the female Muse and the male poet, in which her voice is subsumed under or resides within his. We can therefore say that the oral tradition, as the vehicle of communicating and preserving what matters in archaic Greek culture, originates in an act of gender-specific domination.[25] This act includes the poet's profession of his debt to the Muses, but the instruction for which he is thankful ultimately functions as a self-legitimizing gesture; it guarantees in advance the truth or persuasiveness of the story the

---

23. Cf. Foucault 1972, 21: "Take the notion of tradition: it is intended to give a special temporal status to a group of phenomena that are both successive and identical (or at least similar); it makes it possible to rethink the dispersion of history in the form of the same; it allows a reduction of the difference proper to every beginning, in order to pursue without discontinuity the endless search for the origin; tradition enables us to isolate the new against a background of permanence, and to transfer its merit to originality, to genius, to the decisions proper to individuals."

24. Whether or not the works of Homer and Hesiod are the product of a developing literate culture does not affect this idealization of oral transmission in their narratives, except insofar as that idealization may be an agonistic response to such a development. Cf. Havelock 1986, 79–82.

25. See de Lauretis 1987a on the female's "plot-space" in the mythological tradition.

poet is about to tell. In the *Theogony,* that story culminates in the
forcible victory of Zeus over the Olympian and chthonic realms; while
the *Iliad* does not end with the victory of the Greeks over the Trojans,
the larger "oral" tradition assumes that outcome.[26] In both poems,
then, oral or direct transmission is the medium that validates and
perpetuates the dominant social and political structures among gods
and men: Zeus' victory means the violent overthrow of female divinities and the monstrous Titans; the Greeks' victory means the defeat of
the non-Greek Trojans.[27] The persistent and nostalgic desire for oral
culture in the patriarchal and militaristic West cannot be dissociated
from this tradition of oral transmission in the service of dominant
political and cultural structures.

But at the same time, this poetics of domination is fraught with
doubt and uncertainty; it originates in a crisis of confidence. This
crisis is perhaps best illustrated in the well-known proem to the *Theogony,* where Hesiod receives his visit from the Muses.

αἵ νύ ποθ' Ἡσίοδον καλὴν ἐδίδαξαν ἀοιδήν,
ἄρνας ποιμαίνονθ' Ἑλικῶνος ὑπὸ ζαθέοιο.
τόνδε δέ με πρώτιστα θεαὶ πρὸς μῦθον ἔειπον,
Μοῦσαι Ὀλυμπιάδες, κοῦραι Διὸς αἰγιόχοιο·
Ποιμένες ἄγραυλοι, κάκ' ἐλέγχεα, γαστέρες οἶον,
ἴδμεν ψεύδεα πολλὰ λέγειν ἐτύμοισιν ὁμοῖα,
ἴδμεν δ', εὖτ' ἐθέλωμεν, ἀληθέα γηρύσασθαι.

[These women [the Muses] taught Hesiod a beautiful song
While he was shepherding his lambs under Holy Helicon,
And the goddesses first told me this in speech,
The Muses of Olympus, daughters of Zeus, who holds the aegis:
"Rustic shepherds, evil objects of reproach, mere bellies,
we know how to say many false things that seem like the truth,
and we know how to utter true things when we wish."]
                                                        (*Theogony* 22–28)

The Muses are employed here in a diversionary tactic implying that
they may have lied to others (e.g., Homer) but that they surely will not

---

26. Likewise, the *Odyssey* culminates with the victory of Odysseus over
the suitors.
27. In general, the monstrous chthonic realm is the realm of female power
beginning with Gaia.

lie to Hesiod.[28] In this competitive community of poets, the Muses'
first-person address fosters an intimacy between themselves and Hesiod, into whom they will breathe "a divine voice" [ἐνέπνευσαν δέ μοι
ἀυδὴν θέσπιν] (31–32). Invective is a common feature of addresses
from gods to men in Greek poetry, as is the self-deprecation of the
narrator (e.g., at *Iliad* 2.484–93). Here the Muses' less than complimen-
tary address ("Rustic shepherds, evil objects of reproach, mere bellies") functions rhetorically to give credence to their speaking presence, by saying what the narrator might be expected to refrain from
saying about himself.[29] The slippage between the first and third person, the switch from *Hesiod* in line 22 to *me* in line 24, represents another gesture toward presence and credibility. The construction may be
explained in part by the convention of an author naming himself as a
seal, or *sphragis,* on his work;[30] in this programmatic utterance, the
proper name might also constitute what Barthes calls a "reality effect."[31] But the point I want to make is that the somewhat awkward
switch to the first person (i.e., to *me*)—together with the direct quotation of what the Muses said—substantiates and vouches for their voice
and being and for the close proximity of the poet or narrating *ego* as
their addressee.[32]

---

28. For a discussion of the Muses in Hesiod, see Bassi 1997, 317–21 and
the sources cited there, esp. Pucci 1977, 8–45.

29. Cf. West 1966, 160, on *Theogony* 22–23.

30. The question still remains whether or not Hesiod wrote down his
poems. West (1966, 47–48) believes he did. But see the judicious discussion of
Thomas (1992, 101–2). If "a recurrent use of this early writing is to mark or
protect ownership" (Thomas 1992, 58), that Hesiod names himself may be an
indication that he was a writer—an indication in addition to the stylistic
reasons usually advanced when making this claim.

31. Cf. Barthes 1982b, 11–17. Grammatical signposts, possibly accompanied by gesture or voice change in oral performance, are necessary to mark
the introduction of a different speaking subject. First-person speeches in epic
and didactic poetry are commonly (if not always) marked off by some form of
a verb meaning "to speak" or "to answer," followed by an indefinite pronoun
meaning "the following thing(s)" (τόδε or τάδε). That punctuation is only
attested late in written documents may account for the persistence of such
signposts as a performance technique. See Immerwahr 1990 and Thomas
1992, 92–93.

32. For this scene as a part of Hesiod's biography, see West 1966, 158–61.
Cf. *Theogony* 81–103. I should make it clear that I consider the rustic Hesiodic
persona just that—that is, a persona that functions within a dominant cultural discourse.

But it is equally apparent that the passage represents a pretense to direct, or face-to-face, exchange as the originary or enabling moment of the "oral tradition."[33] No matter what interpretive point of view we assume, it is not the Muses who reveal their potential deceptiveness to Hesiod; Hesiod (or the speaking *ego*) reveals that deceptiveness while making it seem that the Muses are talking or, more precisely, that they did talk to him in the past. Insofar as direct quotation always signifies an absent speaker, their quoted speech is an example of those false things that can seem like true things; that is, its form exemplifies its content. Their speech thus occupies two (or maybe three) competing positions. On the one hand, it valorizes direct speech (as quotation). On the other hand, it epitomizes the epistemological dilemma of any reported speech (its deceptive potential). And despite the narrator's rhetorical moves, the Muses' quoted utterance ultimately puts his own credibility at risk: if the Muses can lie, they can make a liar out of him. As the first (πρώτιστα) and only words attributed to the Muses in the first person, their speech at this critical moment in the Greek "oral" tradition is complex and equivocal. It works to endorse direct first-person speech as the vehicle of cultural preservation. But, as mentioned earlier, the direct quotation of the Muses' cautionary tale is also only a pretense to direct speech. As such it constitutes both an implicit denial of the reliability of reported, or indirect (third-person), speech and an overdetermined validation of direct oral communication.[34] The result is an expression of the desire for bodily presence and direct speech that cannot be satisfied. It is also an expression of what might be called the predicament of divinity, that is, of the incommensurability between mortal and immortal existence. In this case, that incommensurability is expressed in terms of communication. Direct oral speech as a guarantor of masculine authority is implicitly contrasted with poetic production as the product of the Muses' mediation.

33. See Cohen 1991, chap. 3, discussing the anthropology of "face-to-face" societies in Mediterranean communities. I use the term face-to-face in a much more restricted sense, namely, to describe what is represented as an ideologically dominant mode of communication.

34. The lengthy encomium to the goddesses that follows the proem (*Theogony* 36–103) hardly rectifies this situation; the narrator seems to protest too much.

The proem to the Catalogue of Ships in the *Iliad* presents us with a similarly ambiguous scene.

ἔσπετε νῦν μοι, μοῦσαι᾽ Ὀλύμπια δώματ᾽ ἔχουσαι,
ὑμεῖς γὰρ θεαί ἐστε, πάρεστέ τε, ἴστέ τε πάντα,
ἡμεῖς δὲ κλέος οἶον ἀκούομεν οὐδέ τι ἴδμεν,
οἵ τινες ἡγεμόνες Δαναῶν καὶ κοίρανοι ἦσαν;
πληθὺν δ᾽ οὐκ ἂν ἐγὼ μυθήσομαι οὐδ᾽ ὀνομήνω,
οὐδ᾽ εἴ μοι δέκα μὲν γλῶσσαι, δέκα δὲ στόματ᾽ εἶεν,
φωνὴ δ᾽ ἄρρηκτος, χάλκεον δέ μοι ἦτορ ἐνείη,
εἰ μὴ Ὀλυμπιάδες μοῦσαι, Διὸς αἰγιόχοιο
θυγατέρες, μνησαίαθ᾽ ὅσοι ὑπὸ Ἴλιον ἦλθον;
ἀρχοὺς αὖ νηῶν ἐρέω νῆάς τε προπάσας.

[Tell me now, you Muses who have your homes on Olympus.
For you, who are goddesses, are there, and you know all things,
and we only hear the report of it and know nothing.
Who then were the chief men and lords of the Danaans?
I could neither tell of nor name the multitude,
not if I had ten tongues and ten mouths, not if there were
an unbreakable voice and a heart of bronze within me,
not unless the Muses of Olympia, daughters
of Zeus of the aegis, remembered all those who came beneath
    Ilion.
I will tell the lords of the ships and the ships' numbers.]

                                        (*Iliad* 2.484–93)

In this scene, the Muses' power of memory, one of the principal features of oral culture as it is commonly understood, has three related causes: their divinity, their physical presence, and their knowledge of all things. The relationship of these three is presumably sequential: the Muses' immortality insures their eternal presence, which in turn confers on them the knowledge of everything that comes to pass.[35] Although they do not speak to the poet directly here, the

---

35. Cf. the speech of the Sirens at *Odyssey* 12.189–91: "We know everything that the Argives and Trojans did and suffered in wide Troy through the gods' will. Over all the generous earth we know everything that happens."

Muses' eternal and infinite presence is the central feature of this triad, both in the sequence and in importance.[36] In contrast to them, the mortal poet knows nothing (οὐδέ τι ἴδμεν, 486), because of his physical—that is, spatial and temporal—limitations. His is a position of irredeemable absence from the past events he describes, exemplified first of all in the fundamental ontological difference between himself and the Muses.[37] His lament that even "ten tongues and ten mouths" and "an unbreakable voice and a heart of bronze" are inadequate to speak to the task at hand is a hyperbolic testament to the importance of an enduring physical presence in the discourse of oral memory and transmission.[38] Here the limits of human knowledge are figured by the metaphor of an impossibly monstrous body whose too many mouths and indestructible voice and heart only underline the fact of mortal insufficiency.[39]

In both these originary scenes, the authorizing voice of the Muses operates in the context of a desire for truth and completeness via divine presence and direct oral transmission, where desire specifies a potential lack of fulfillment. Perhaps implicit in each scene is a protestation, however inadequate, of the privilege of an idealized orality in the presence of writing, an agonistic response to the developing literate culture of the first half of the eighth century B.C.E.[40] But the question is not whether Hesiod and Homer composed with

---

36. Cf. *Odyssey* 8.492–93, where Odysseus praises Demodocus' song for an accuracy that suggests that he had been at Troy himself or heard about it from someone who was there. See Bakker 1993.

37. Cf. Derrida 1976, 141–65.

38. Cf. Kirk 1985, ad loc. "Aristarchus (Arn/A) judged the hyperbole to be typically Homeric and compared *Odyssey* 12.78, where Scylla's cliff is unclimbable 'even if a man had twenty hands and feet.' " Yet each hyperbolic utterance must be considered in context. For Kirk, the poet's physical inability refers only to the number of the troops (ὅσοι, 492), not to the names of the leaders (οἵ τινες, 487), which the Muses tell him and which he recounts. This distinction is plausible, but I am more convinced by the ambiguity of the passage.

39. The metaphorical effect of "an unbreakable voice and a heart of bronze" (φωνὴ δ' ἄρρηκτος, χάλκεον δέ μοι ἦτορ) is to give enduring tensile strength to what is only fleetingly embodied in mortal flesh. The word ἄρρηκτος is commonly used of strong walls and chains; cf. *Odyssey* 10.3–4 where that adjective and χάλκεον occur together to describe the wall around Aiolos' island: τεῖχος/χάλκεον ἄρρηκτον.

40. See Thomas 1992, 53.

the aid of writing or even whether writing constituted some kind of threat in a predominantly oral (i.e., nonliterate) society. These originary scenes raise theoretical as well as historical questions. What rhetorical purpose does this ambiguity about the Muses serve? Why is direct oral speech represented as the vehicle of divine omniscience and presence but then compromised in the confession of human insufficiency and absence? In short, why does the appeal to divine sanction via the divine voice seem to "transgress its own system of values?"[41]

As the framing scenes of early Greek poetry, these proems evoke a logocentric ideal rooted in nostalgia and disenchantment. Expressed in the context of an ambiguous confidence in feminine speech (that of the Muses) and an overdetermined confidence in direct speech (exemplified in the Homeric narrator's ten tongues and ten mouths"), this disenchantment is rooted in the desire for an unambiguous and eternally authorizing presence and voice. Outside these originary scenes, this desire continues to be a persistent feature of the epic narratives at large, where it finds expression in the competition between two distinct modes of oral communication. The first is exemplified by characters speaking face-to-face (or ἀντιβίοις ἐπέεσσι), the second by orally delivered messages in which the speech of character A is repeated by character B and delivered to character C. The second sort of communication constitutes the category of scripted speech.

In the context of the oral-literate binary discussed earlier, and as a prelude to discussing message sending as a form of scripted speech in the epics, I want to consider the single reference to a written message in the epic, namely, that in the Bellerophon episode in *Iliad* 6. This episode is pertinent both because it represents a unique counterexample to direct oral speech and because its very uniqueness testifies to the gender-specific criteria that define communicative practices in the *Iliad*. In book 6, the Trojan hero Glaucus and the Greek hero Diomedes meet as enemies on the battlefield, where Glaucus tells the story of his ancestor Bellerophon.

---

41. The quotation is from Spivak's introduction to Derrida 1976, xlix. The poet's insistence on his own insufficiency at *Iliad* 2.484–93 is obviously also an insistence on the Muses' omniscience; it functions as a gesture of praise for the divinities. But this literal reading does not obviate the way in which the truth claims of the passage are undermined.

τῷ δὲ γυνὴ Προίτου ἐπεμήνατο, δῖ᾽ Ἄντεια,
κρυπταδίη φιλότητι μιγήμεναι· ἀλλὰ τὸν οὔ τι
πεῖθ᾽ ἀγαθὰ φρονέοντα, δαΐφρονα Βελλεροφόντην.
ἡ δὲ ψευσαμένη Προῖτον βασιλῆα προσηύδα·
τεθναίης, ὦ Προῖτ᾽, ἢ κάκτανε Βελλεροφόντην,
ὅς μ᾽ ἔθελεν φιλότητι μιγήμεναι οὐκ ἐθελούσῃ.
ὣς φάτο, τὸν δὲ ἄνακτα χόλος λάβεν οἷον ἄκουσε·
κτεῖναι μὲν ῥ᾽ ἀλέεινε, σεβάσσατο γὰρ τό γε θυμῷ,
πέμπε δέ μιν Λυκίηνδε, πόρεν δ᾽ ὅ γε σήματα λυγρά,
γράψας ἐν πίνακι πτυκτῷ θυμοφθόρα πολλά,
δεῖξαι δ᾽ ἠνώγειν ᾧ πενθερῷ, ὄφρ᾽ ἀπόλοιτο.

Beautiful Anteia, the wife of Proetus, was mad
to lie in love with Bellerophon, and yet she could not
persuade the noble man, whose thought was virtuous.
So she lied to Proetus, the king, and said:
"Would you be killed, Proetus? Then murder Bellerophon,
who tried to lie with me in love, although I was unwilling."
So she spoke, and anger seized the king because of what he had
    heard.
But he shrank from killing Bellerophon, because he feared to do
    so in his heart,
and instead sent him away to Lycia and gave him murderous
    symbols,
having written many deadly things in a folding tablet,
and told him to show it to his wife's father, so that he would die.
                               (Iliad 6.160–70)[42]

Precisely what these "murderous symbols" [σήματα λυγρά] (6.168)
are is unclear. The verb used to indicate how they were put on the
tablet, γράφω (6.169), later acquires the meaning "to write" in the
sense of writing alphabetic characters, but in the epic it more accurately means simply to scratch or draw signs.[43] In any event, inscribed

---

42. Cf. *Iliad* 7.175 ff., where the Achaeans make signs on lots (κλῆρον
ἐσημήναντο). These symbols or signs, however, do not constitute a message
in the way that Proetus' do.

43. See Kirk 1990, ad loc. The symbols may refer to a syllabic script—
perhaps a descendent of the Mycenaean Linear B script—or to a private form
of communication between son-in-law and father-in-law, especially since we

symbols are the vehicles of private knowledge and deception and are treated with suspicion; more precisely, the narrative associates them with a feminine deceptiveness that puts masculine prerogatives at risk.[44] This risk is illustrated not only by the obvious threat to Bellero-

---

can infer that if Bellerophon had access to the symbols, he did not understand them. Leaf (1960, ad loc.) believes that the fact that Proetus sent the message ἐν πίνακι πτυκτῷ indicates that it was "closed and sealed, and allows us to infer that Bellerophon would have understood the σήματα had they been left open." But πτυκτός simply means "folded," not necessarily "sealed." I think it more likely that Bellerophon is depicted not only as the innocent victim of a woman's desire (which she would keep secret [κρυπταδίη φιλότητι]), but also as innocent of written symbols whose secret message he could not understand. Cf. Harvey 1966, 48 with n. 17: "Perhaps he [Homer] even saw writing itself as sinister. He certainly insists on the evilness of Proetus' letter (θυμοφθόρα πολλά 169; σῆμα κακόν, 178)." See also Heubeck 1979, 128–46.

44. The perception that women and writing are a dangerous combination is expressed in a comic fragment tentatively attributed to Menander (702 Kock): γυναιχ᾽ ὁ διδάσκων γράμματ᾽ [οὐ] καλῶς [ποιεῖ] ἀσπίδι δὲ φοβερᾷ φάρμακον. The meaning of the fragment is somewhat obscure; Edmonds (1961) offers the following translation: "Whoever teaches a woman letters does not do well but provides a fearful snake with additional poison." Although it may be a late interpolation, Herodotus' story of Gorgo (*Histories* 7.239) can also be mentioned in this context. On learning of Xerxes' intention to invade Greece, Demaratus sends a message to the Spartans telling them of the Persian plan. When the message arrives, Gorgo, the wife of Leonidas, is the only one able to discover the message hidden under the wax layer on the tablet. Although Herodotus does not say that Gorgo could read the message, the story suggests that women are particularly adept at finding hidden messages. The discovery is beneficial to the Spartans, although the written text is again part of a narrative of deceit and possible danger: Herodotus hints that Demaratus may have treacherous designs against the Persians. Other late examples include two stories from Plutarch (*Moralia* 252a–c and 254d–e). In the first, the tyrant Aristotimos tries to force the women of Elis to write letters to their husbands to trick them into leaving off fighting. In the second, Polykrite of Miletos saves her friends by sending a note to her brothers inscribed on a piece of lead and hidden inside a cake. Both of these stories are mentioned by Cole (1981, 233). See also Svenbro 1990, 382–83, for a discussion of the *ABC Show*, or *Grammatike theoria*, by the Athenian poet Kallias (Athenaeus 7.276a, 10.448b, 453c–454a (= Kallias frag. 31 Edmonds), in which a chorus of twenty-four women represent the Ionian alphabet. Cf. Pöhlmann 1971. DuBois (1988, 136–37) discusses the metaphorical connection between women and the writing tablet, or *deltos*. Segal (1984, 56) notes that the *Trachiniae*, the *Hippolytus*, and Euripides' *Stheneboea* "associate writing,

phon but also by Proetus' compromised masculinity in the narrative. His wife's desire for another man, together with her ability to convince the king of the truth of what is a lie, undermines Proetus' position as husband and king in general. But his decision to send the secret, or hidden, message signifies a more complex condemnation.⁴⁵ Folded within a tablet and calling for Bellerophon's death, the message resonates with Anteia's secret desire for sex with Bellerophon (κρυπταδίη φιλότητι). And even though it is sent by the husband, the message is closely aligned in the text with the desires and tactics of the wife. Indeed, that Proetus sends a written message is an explicit sign of his less than heroic stature; ideally, Greek men and kings do not use written messages to accomplish their goals.

The censurable status of the written message in Greek culture is illustrated by the fact that letter writing is used almost exclusively by the Persian kings in Herodotus' *Histories*. According to Hartog, "the [royal] letter was a means of transmitting intelligence or instructions, a secret means of communication, and, all in all, a way of exercising power."⁴⁶ Hartog does not note—though it seems equally important—that these kings must exercise their power over a vast empire, in implicit distinction to the smaller compass of the Greek *poleis*, where face-to-face speech is again the idealized mode of communication. The practice of sending written messages thus distinguishes Greeks from Persian barbarians in the related discourses of tyranny, empire, and fighting prowess. At *Histories* 5.49, Aristagoras, the Greek tyrant of Miletus, describes how the Persians differ from the Spartans as fighters. The Persians, he says, are "an unwarlike people" who "use bows and arrows and a short spear." He adds:

---

trickery, concealed love, female desire as all related distortions of the truth." On women who write in tragedy in general, see Cole 1981, 224–25. Other possible evidence for the negative association of women with writing includes Sophocles frag. 811, "I write the oaths . . . of a woman in water" [ὅρκους . . . γυναικὸς εἰς ὕδωρ γράφω]; Philonides Comicus frag. 7 (Kock); *Trachiniae* 155–60, 683; Euripides' *Iphigenia among the Taurians* 735; Demosthenes 18.55. See also Lloyd 1983, 76–78, and the passages cited there.

45. Cf. Euripides' *Iphigenia in Aulis*, in which the secret letter that Agamemnon writes to Clytemnestra, telling her not to bring Iphigenia to Aulis, could have prevented the Trojan War and therefore the means of epic *kleos*. On this play, see Zeitlin 1994.

46. Hartog 1988, 278.

"they wear trousers in the field, and cover their heads with turbans. So easy are they to vanquish." Letter writing, the use of bow and arrows, a particular style of dress, susceptibility to defeat, and tyranny are here the defining characteristics of non-Greeks.

When Glaucus maintains that Proetus shrank from killing Bellerophon outright, because he feared to do so in his heart (*Iliad* 6.167), it may be indicative of Proetus' reverent and commendable treatment of a guest who had become an enemy.[47] But it is more persuasively indicative of his failure to act like a warrior and a king, that is, like Achilles, who—instead of sending "murderous symbols"—would kill his enemy outright. This negative comparison is verified some lines later, when Andromache tells how Achilles killed Eëtion but "did not strip him of his armor, because, out of respect, he feared to do so in his heart" (6.417; cf. 6.167).[48] Even though she is describing Achilles' behavior on the battlefield, the shared phrase σεβάσσατο γὰρ τό γε θυμῷ suggests a comparison with Proetus' behavior on behalf of his wife; in both cases an aristocratic warrior should not hesitate to kill his enemy.[49] Proetus and his secret message thus represent the negative corollaries to man-to-man combat and face-to-face speech among elite Greek males; in this case the written message is a cowardly substitute for single combat.

It is worth noting too that the story of Bellerophon is told on the Trojan battlefield, where Glaucus and Diomedes "avoid each other's

---

47. At *Iliad* 13.355–57, Poseidon "shrank from defending the Argives outright but secretly, up and down the ranks, was forever urging them on in a man's likeness" [τῶ ῥα καὶ ἀμφαδίην μὲν ἀλεξέμεναι ἀλέεινε,/λάθρη δ᾽ αἰὲν ἔγειρε κατὰ στρατόν, ἀνδρὶ ἐοικώς]. Hesitation to act outright—here against Zeus—expressed by ἀλέεινε plus the infinitive, is again accompanied by secret dealings, manifested in a god who impersonates a human being. Unlike Proetus, Bellerophon excels in the face-to-face encounter. As an exemplary hero, "he defeats two types of monstrous females (Khimera and Amazons) and resists a third, Anteia" (Martin 1989, 128). The would-be victim of a woman's trick, Bellerophon proves himself against her kind figured as monstrous.

48. See Leaf 1960, on *Iliad* 6.418, for a discussion of Achilles' decision to burn Eetion's body along with his armor.

49. The Trojan War is, of course, a domestic dispute writ large; it is waged over the abduction of a guest-friend's wife. Other pertinent examples of warriors who kill those who have violated their wives include Odysseus, who kills Penelope's suitors (although they had not attempted to rape her), and Theseus, who has his own son killed for allegedly raping Phaedra.

spears" (6.226) by speaking to one another. Whereas Proetus avoided Bellerophon's spear in effect by sending a message and instructing his father-in-law to exact his revenge, Glaucus and Diomedes engage in direct face-to-face talk, which serves as an effective or positive substitute for direct man-to-man fighting; their encounter on the battlefield leads to face-to-face speech, which takes the place of hand-to-hand combat. As a final gesture, Glaucus and Diomedes exchange armor so that they will be recognized as "guest-friends from the time of their fathers" [ξεῖνοι πατρώϊοι] (6.231).[50] Insofar as armor is the signifier par excellence of personal identity, an identity reified in the body or bodily appearance,[51] the verbal and material exchanges between Glaucus and Diomedes illustrate the privileged presence and authority of the (male) speaking subject. It is as if this full-bodied exchange on the battlefield is an answer or antidote to the story of Bellerophon embedded within it and to the sinister written message he is made to deliver.[52]

Graphic communication (Proetus' "symbols") is characterized in this episode by the geographical distance between the original writer or sender of the message and his addressee (Proetus and his father-in-

---

50. It does not matter whether the τεύχεα (*Iliad* 6.235) they exchange is full body armor or shields only.

51. The transference of Achilles' armor from Achilles to Patroclus to Hector exemplifies the role of armor in marking identity through bodily appearance. See *Iliad* 16.40–43. The commonly narrated genealogy of armor as it is passed down from the hero's ancestors to the hero is also relevant.

52. The unequal exchange of armor between Glaucus and Diomedes may even serve to illustrate the story of Bellerophon. Leaf (1960) comments on 6.200–202: "There was evidently some legend of the madness of Bellerophon. . . . At least his role as messenger of his own intended destruction casts him as somewhat 'witless.' " Thus Glaucus' "witless" exchange of gold armor for bronze (*Iliad* 6.232–36) may serve to establish his credentials as Bellerophon's descendant. For an extended list of possible explanations of this exchange, see Kirk 1985, ad loc.; Calder 1984. Calder interprets it as an expression of Glaucus' superiority, insofar as Diomedes is put in his debt; the narrator's "editorial comment," namely, that Zeus took away Glaucus' wits or φρένας, is credited by Calder to his imperfect understanding of a Mycenaean exchange pattern. It might be pointed out that while the uneven exchange is described in terms of the symbolic value of the metals, bronze certainly offers more effective protection than gold and is the stuff of which epic armor is made (cf. *Odyssey* 21.431 ff.). But this fact only makes it more difficult to account for the narrator's "editorial comment."

law), by its deadly potential (although Bellerophon ultimately escapes death), and by the ability to hide what it says both by virtue of the fact that it can be concealed and because it requires decipherment. It is also associated with women and with putting male aristocratic and martial virtues in jeopardy. As I have suggested, these associations operate in the context of competing modes of speaking and fighting, in which face-to-face speech is the counterpart to man-to-man combat. But this conclusion is not limited to a singular example. It is borne out in the broader context of the epic's martial code, in which a prominent distinction is made between two sorts of combatants, the archer and the frontline fighter.[53] At *Iliad* 11.369 ff., Diomedes addresses Paris after he has sustained a surface wound from Paris' bow.

τοξότα, λωβητήρ, κέρᾳ ἀγλαέ, παρθενοπῖπα,
εἰ μὲν δὴ ἀντίβιον σὺν τεύχεσι πειρηθείης,
οὐκ ἄν τοι χραίσμῃσι βιὸς καὶ ταρφέες ἰοί·
νῦν δέ μ' ἐπιγράψας ταρσὸν ποδὸς εὔχεαι αὔτως.
οὐκ ἀλέγω, ὡς εἴ με γυνὴ βάλοι ἢ πάϊς ἄφρων·
κωφὸν γὰρ βέλος ἀνδρὸς ἀνάλκιδος οὐτιδανοῖο.

[You archer, wretch, man of brilliant hair, ogler of girls,
If you were to make trial of me with arms in combat,
neither your bow nor your dense arrows would do you good.
Now you boast because you have scratched the flat part of my foot.
But I care as little as if a woman or a witless child were to strike me;
for yours is the dull arrow of an unwarlike and worthless man.]

(11.385–90)[54]

---

53. Cf. Herodotus *Histories* 5.49, mentioned earlier. Cf. also *Histories* 8.128, in which Artabazus is aided in his attempt to lay siege to Potidaea by the Scionean collaborator Timoxenus. The two communicate with one another by sending attached written messages to arrows. Here archery is the vehicle of the written message in the service of treachery. Svenbro (1990) discusses this passage in connection with the question of ancient literacy. In general, the bow is the recognized weapon of non-Greeks, that is, of Scythians, Ethiopians, and Persians. Cf. Hartog 1988, 43–45. Deanna Shemek tells me of a relevant analogue in Italian Renaissance culture in which the use of firearms is negatively compared to chivalric combat with swords and lances.
54. Other examples of the comparatively low status of the archer include *Iliad* 13.713 ff., where the Locrians are described, and Sophocles' *Ajax*, where

As an adjective in Homer, ἀντίβιος (βία) only occurs in the phrase
ἀντιβίοις ἐπέεσσι [with fighting words]—for example, to describe the
quarrel between Achilles and Agamemnon at *Iliad* 1.304. Its use here
in the phrase ἀντίβιον σὺν τεύχεσι [with arms in combat] and, in
opposition to the archer's mode of fighting, helps to substantiate a
positive analogy between the frontline fighter and direct man-to-man
communication, on the one hand, and a corresponding negative analogy between the archer and mediated speech, on the other. As another indicator of this analogy, the use of ἐπιγράφω to describe the
wound made by Paris' bow can be compared to the use of γράφω to
describe the "murderous symbols" inscribed by Bellerophon in the
passage discussed earlier (6.160–70) and of ἐπιγράφω to describe the
inscribed marks that distinguish a particular hero when lots are
drawn.[55] Once again, the shared lexicon is suggestive of the way in

---

Teucer (ὁ τοξότης) is attacked by Menelaos (*Ajax* 1120 ff.) and by Agamemnon,
who accuses him of being a lowborn barbarian (*Ajax* 1226 ff.). See also *Iliad*
8.268–72, where Teucer is said to run behind Ajax' shield, like a child into its
mother's arms. The antiarcher prejudice is clearly not consistent in archaic
culture, however: Apollo and Heracles are archers. But see Loraux 1990 on
Heracles' "hyperfemininity." The story of Odysseus' bow at *Odyssey* 21.1–41
gives greater scope to the prejudice. Odysseus gives Iphitos a "sharp sword
and strong spear" [ξίφος ὀξὺ καὶ ἄλκιμον ἔγχος, 21.34] in exchange for the bow,
which he then never took to war but always kept in the house (ἐνὶ μεγάροισι,
21.41) and used in his own country, presumably for hunting. Together with the
somewhat pathetic fate of Iphitus, the narrative contrasts Odysseus, as a man
of the sword and spear, with the man of the bow. The subsequent contest of the
bow planned by Athena and Penelope in *Odyssey* 21 and Odysseus' use of the
bow to kill the suitors at the beginning of *Odyssey* 22 associate archery with
female tactics, pseudocombat (i.e., contests), and domestic rivalries rather
than foreign warfare. The battle with the suitors begins with the bow but is
finally won with the sword, in grisly hand-to-hand combat.
    55. At *Iliad* 7.187, the lot on which Ajax had engraved his distinctive mark
(ἐπιγράψας) leaps out of the helmet. Cf. *Iliad* 4.139, where Pandaros wounds
Menelaus (ἀκρότατον δ' ἄρ' ὀϊστὸς ἐπέγραψε χρόα φωτός). It must be
stressed that in none of the instances in which γράφω or its compounds mean
to inscribe on a tablet or lot do they necessarily mean "to write" alphabetic
characters. On ἐπιγράφω, LSJ I reads, "In Homer the word has not the sense
of *writing*." Nonetheless, in these instances it does signify a form of communication that is distinct from direct, or face-to-face, communication. On *graphein*
in the epics, see Saussy 1996, esp. 301–4.

which archery is aligned with graphic or mediated communication: both signify physical distance—between combatants, on the one hand, and speakers and their addressees, on the other. That the archer's bow often lacks deadly force—that it only scratches the surface of his enemy's body—also illustrates how this alignment is based on a hierarchy of communicative and martial practices.[56] In short, the characteristics that distinguish the idealized Greek warrior from the unwarlike and effeminate archer (and the Persian warrior) are expressive not only of codes of martial behavior but also of distinct modes of communicating.

That graphic, or mediated, forms of communication are antithetical to direct, or face-to-face, forms and that these antithetical forms are gender-specific can also be argued for in a very different cultural context, namely, in the context of domestic life, in which weaving is primarily (if not exclusively) figured as women's work. My intent here is not to belabor a point that has been well argued by others but to emphasize the way in which weaving as women's work constitutes a kind of communicative practice and to argue for the implications of that practice.[57] Greek women are described as weavers and sewers as

---

56. The word ἐπιγράφω is also used to describe instances when spears (i.e., not arrows) graze but fail to kill (i.e., at *Iliad* 13.551–53, 17.599–600). At 11.390 Paris' arrow is called κωφός, an adjective that means "dull," but also "noiseless" or "mute," e.g., at *Iliad* 14.16. Thus, the silence of the arrow suggests a metaphorical equivalence with the absence of face-to-face or direct speech.

57. Keuls (1985, 233) discusses those "woven garments [that] feature heavily in myths of female rebellion,"—for example, Clytemnestra's net and the poisoned garments used by Eriphyle, Medea, and Deianeira—and the fact that Pandora learns weaving from Athena (Hesiod *Works and Days* 64). On weaving as women's work in general, see the sources in Lefkowitz and Fant 1982 and Jenkins 1985. Geddes (1987, 310) notes: "clothes had always been produced by women in the household and so were not demanded or supplied in the market-place. Women working at home always made a large part of the cloth that was worn in Greece—and therefore a large part of the clothes, since Greek clothes for the most part were not sewn or fitted, but simply draped." Gould (1980, 48) points out that time-consuming tasks like weaving are meant to keep women "out of mischief." But men also engage in time-consuming tasks, which may or may not be meant to keep them "out of mischief." The point seems to be that as a time-consuming task, weaving is performed by certain classes of people, including women (elite or not), slaves,

early as the archaic period (*Iliad* 6.490–93; *Odyssey* 1.357–69, 21.351–
53). The view that weaving belongs to the domain of women persists
even when it is observed that men can also engage in this activity. So,
for example, in his account of Egyptian practices (equivalent to won-
ders, or θαύματα), Herodotus notes that Egyptian men do the weaving but that those doing so act more like women than men (*Histories*
2.35.2).[58] When Oedipus likens his sons to Egyptians who stay at
home and weave like girls (παρθένοι), it is to be understood that this
constitutes a reversal of the expected or natural order: his sons play
the roles accorded to women, while his daughters act like men (Sophocles *Oedipus at Colonus* 337–45). From the archaic to the classical period, then, weaving is a feminine practice.

That practice constitutes a means of communication or, more to the
point, it constitutes the visual means by which women convey what
they cannot or should not speak in the public (i.e., male) domain.[59] It
is obvious that this proposition does not apprehend all the ways in
which textiles function in the ancient Greek context, either as representations (in narrative or visual form) or in social reality. It is also the
case, as David Cohen remarks, that the absence of women from the
public sphere and hence from speaking in public may be a dominant
"cultural ideal" but is not a verifiable feature of social reality: as Cohen

---

and other marginalized or subservient groups, not by elite males. In the
Roman context, Cicero (*De oratore* 277) equates working wool with effeminacy; cf. Juvenal 2.54–56.

58. Weaving can also be used metaphorically to describe barbarian evils, as
when Andromache calls the Spartans "weavers of wicked schemes" (Euripides *Andromache* 447). On the *Andromache*, see Hall 1989, 214. In Euripides'
Orestes (1434–36), the purple cloth Helen is weaving for Clystemnestra's tomb
comes from the Phrygian spoils.

59. See Bergren 1983, 71–75, on the analogy between women's weaving
and language. As she notes, women's weaving is often an iconic representation that partakes of falsehood. DuBois (1988, 161) argues that weaving belongs to "the preliteracy of women's work." While weaving is obviously not
the same thing as alphabetic writing, it often fulfills a similar function;
namely, it conveys messages that need to be deciphered. The proposition that
women were more likely to be illiterate than men in the archaic and classical
periods does not preclude conceptual associations between women and
graphic (but nonalphabetic) forms of communication. On literacy in antiquity,
see Harris 1989, 94–96, 103–8; Cole 1981.

shows, numerous sources depict women going about their business outside the house.[60] Thus, when I say that weaving represents a particular form of graphic communication engaged in by women and distinct from the oral and public form of communication engaged in by men, I do so with the understanding that these distinctions are promulgated within the context of a dominant cultural ethos that validates the primacy of masculine subjects. Within this ethos, the notion that women do not engage in "face-to-face" communication does not describe social reality but rather validates the cultural pre-scription that women be kept out of the public domain. We have seen that face-to-face combat and face-to-face speech describe normative and mutually reinforcing behaviors among Greek men in archaic cul-ture; the former describes what men do, the latter how they speak. Similarly, weaving and silence describe normative and mutually re-inforcing behaviors among women; the former describes what they do, the latter how they (do not) speak.

The most prominent descriptions of women weaving in the epic narratives—Penelope weaving Laertes' funeral shroud in the *Odyssey* and Helen weaving her tapestry in the *Iliad*—illustrate the complex nature of these gender-specific behaviors. In the process of weaving and unweaving the shroud in Odysseus' absence, Penelope success-fully forestalls her marriage to another man and maintains the hege-monic structure of the royal house (*Odyssey* 2.91–105, 19.137–56). In other words, her weaving and unweaving keep her at home and prevent her from committing what would amount to adultery.[61] The shroud's silent message is the message of Penelope's fidelity and the promise that she will wait for Odysseus, as the narrative eventually confirms. Penelope speaks to the suitors directly, but the silent and hidden message of the shroud proves to be the true message of a

---

60. The quotation is from Cohen 1991, 152. Cohen's analysis (148–70) offers an important corrective to arguments that confuse idealized representa-tions of women's behavior with actual social practice. See also Gould 1980, 46 ff.; Zeitlin 1982a.

61. Cohen (1991, 155) argues that the restriction on a woman's public presence is related to the fear of her committing adultery: "Adultery served as a focus of obsessive sexual fears in the ancient and modern Mediterranean precisely because women regularly engaged in activities which brought them into some sort of contact with other men."

proper wife.[62] Here weaving is a graphic message that communicates a woman's social position, a position ideally guaranteed by her silence in the presence of men other than her lawful husband. And in this sense her conversations with the disguised Odysseus convey and confirm her fidelity, rather than compromising it as might be the case were she talking to a "real" stranger. The process and product of Penelope's weaving, with their interchange of deferral and repetition, can be said to provide an antidote for Socrates' condemnation of writing in the *Phaedrus:* "If ever, out of a desire to learn, you ask [written words] about any of the things they say, they point to just one thing, the same each time" (*Phaedrus* 275d5 ff.).[63] Freed from a critique of writing as an impediment to the acquisition of knowledge (and power) guaranteed by face-to-face verbal exchanges among men, the graphic sameness of Penelope's weaving is the source of maintaining dominant social structures and, most importantly, the wife's place within those structures.

Despite its brevity, the description of the tapestry Helen weaves in the *Iliad* provides another prominent illustration of women's weaving as a form of graphic communication.

τὴν δ' εὗρ' ἐν μεγάρῳ; ἣ δὲ μέγαν ἱστὸν ὕφαινε,
δίπλακα πορφυρέην, πολέας δ' ἐνέπασσεν ἀέθλους
Τρώων θ' ἱπποδάμων καὶ Ἀχαιῶν χαλκοχιτώνων,
οὓς ἕθεν εἵνεκ' ἔπασχον ὑπ' Ἄρηος παλαμάων·

[She [Iris] found her [Helen] in her chamber, she was weaving a
    great web,
purple and double folded, and she worked into it many contests
of horse-taming Trojans and bronze-armored Greeks,
which they had endured for her sake by the hands of Ares.]
                                                        (*Iliad* 3.125–28)

---

62. At *Odyssey* 18.259 ff., Penelope addresses the suitors and hints that she will soon marry one of them. But much of her speech consists of a first-person recitation of the speech Odysseus had made to her before he left for Troy, including his admonition to marry once Telemachus has grown up (17.259–70). By playing the part of Odysseus in this scene, that is, by speaking his words, the narrative tempers the fact of her own presence and speech before the suitors.

63. I discuss the *Phaedrus* in more detail later in this chapter.

The contrast here, of course, is between the woven pictures worked by Helen's hands and the flesh-and-blood bodies of the "horse-taming Trojans and bronze-armored Greeks," that is, between women as weavers and men as warriors. In this respect it is difficult to agree with Kirk that the unique phrase "by the hands of Ares" [ὑπ' Ἄρηος παλαμάων] is "not completely successful," since παλάμη is frequently used in archaic texts to refer to the hand of a craftsperson and in this case successfully sets up a contrast between what the hands of Ares accomplish and what those of Helen are weaving.[64] At the same time, the reference helps to emphasize the distinction between the war being fought at the hands of Ares (here also referring by extension to the hands of the Greek and Trojan warriors) and the representation of the war woven by Helen's hands. The overall effect of the passage is to establish the incommensurability of these activities, or, more precisely, the spatial, material, and temporal differences that separate the woman as she weaves in her chamber from the men as they fight on the battlefield. As a graphic or nonverbal representation of the Trojan War, Helen's tapestry simultaneously limits the scope of the epic narrative and impedes or defers its linear progression of events; it constitutes what might be called a visual epitome of the *Iliad*.[65]

The implied differences between Helen's tapestry and the epic narrative that contains it are differences in modes of communicating essential cultural data. The questions raised by these differences are, Who can tell the story of the Trojan War, and how shall it be told? Or it may be more accurate to ask, How is the verbal art of the epic narrator distinct from Helen's textile art? And this question begs another: Why does the epic narrator invite us to contemplate this distinction at all? These questions begin to come into focus when Iris admonishes Helen to leave her loom so that she might see the deeds of the "horse-taming Trojans and bronze-armored Achaeans" who she is weaving into her tapestry. At this point in the narrative, the scene Iris describes to Helen is a static one in which the battle at

---

64. Kirk 1985, ad loc. Cf. *Iliad* 15.411, *Theogony* 580, and Pindar *Pythian* 2.40, where the παλάμαι of Zeus fashion a deceptive image of Hera for Ixion.

65. As has often been remarked, Helen is here the creator of the war in a figurative or artistic sense. Cf. Bergren 1983, 79: "She [Helen] is both the passive object of the war and the creator of its emblem." See also Kennedy 1986; Austin 1994, 37–41.

large has ceased in anticipation of the one-on-one combat between
Menelaos and Paris.

δεῦρ᾽ ἴθι, νύμφα φίλη, ἵνα θέσκελα ἔργα ἴδηαι
Τρώων θ᾽ ἱπποδάμων καὶ Ἀχαιῶν χαλκοχιτώνων·
οἵ πρὶν ἐπ᾽ ἀλλήλοισι φέρον πολύδακρυν Ἄρηα
ἐν πεδίῳ, ὀλοοῖο λιλαιόμενοι πολέμοιο,
οἳ δὴ νῦν ἕαται σιγῇ, πόλεμος δὲ πέπαυται,
ἀσπίσι κεκλιμένοι, παρὰ δ᾽ ἔγχεα μακρὰ πέπηγεν.

[Come with me, dear girl, to see the marvelous deeds
of the Trojans, breakers of horses, and the bronze-armored,
    Achaeans,
who before were waging sorrowful war against each other
in the plain, desirous of the deadly battle;
now they are all seated in silence, and the battle has ended;
they lean on their shields, next to where their long spears are
    fixed.]

                                                    (3.130–35)

This interlude, emphasized by a lexicon of silence and fixity (ἕαται
σιγῇ, πέπαυται, κεκλιμένοι, πέπηγεν) reflects the graphic sameness of
Helen's woven tapestry, in contrast to the ever changing configuration
of the epic battles it depicts. Another way of putting it is to say that Iris'
description of the battlefield is simultaneously a description of Helen's
tapestry. But this conflation of the actual battlefield with its graphic de-
piction does not equate the two. Instead, it validates the former over
the latter. Like a fixed and ever repeating piece of writing, as it is described by Socrates in the *Phaedrus* (275d5 ff.), and in contrast to the epic
narrative as a representational practice, Helen's tapestry signifies the
end of heroic action; she weaves the battle scene when the battle itself
has ceased.[66] As a piece of woman's work done within the women's

---

66. That Aphrodite interrupts the one-on-one combat between Paris and
Menelaos and transports Paris to Helen's bedroom exemplifies Helen's paradoxical role as the cause of the war who, at the same time, can arrest heroic
action. Cf. *Iliad* 22.440–41, where Andromache is described as weaving a web
when news reaches her of Hector's death. Just as Helen's weaving coincides
with a lull in the battle (due to the impending one-on-one combat between

quarters (ἐν μεγάρῳ), Helen's silent and static weaving exemplifies the silencing and deferral of the narrative of direct man-to-man exchanges in words and deeds on the battlefield.[67]

Comparison of the description of Helen's tapestry and the Shield of Achilles in *Iliad* 18 illustrates this conclusion. Together these artifacts constitute the most conspicuous examples of graphic or ecphrastic representation in the epics. On first glance, the two objects are easily distinguishable in terms of the length of their descriptions: 129 lines for the shield as compared to 4 for the tapestry. It is to be expected, of course, that shields and weaponry are elaborately featured in the epics as the implements of martial combat. But this does not necessarily explain the differences in kind between the shield and Helen's tapestry. It has often been remarked that the elaborate scenes engraved on the shield are moving and changing—that they are living, in effect.[68] In this sense, they occupy a different mimetic register than the tapestry scenes, one in which the narrator animates (as it were) lifeless and static pictures, by giving a story to the movements and actions that the pictures can only suggest. In contrast, Helen's woven scene, so briefly sketched and lacking the many details of the "battles of Greeks and Trojans" that it depicts, also obviously lacks what the shield scenes offer: the verbal animation of the dynamic details of those battles.[69] As an artifact that circulates among the epic's greatest heroes and is used on the battlefield in the war's most crucial encounter, the shield attests to the public and active nature of epic militarism and heroism and contrastively defines Helen's weaving as an inferior and lifeless object.

---

her lovers), Andromache's weaving coincides with the temporary end of the battle (due to the death of her husband). Cf. Scheid and Svenbro 1996, 115–16, on Helen's weaving.

67. This understanding of women's weaving as a silent and graphic mode of communication analogous to writing is not compromised by the fact that the Greeks seem to have read out loud until the end of the sixth century B.C.E. Writing—like women's weaving—is a nonvocal or nonaural form of communication until the reader (who acts as an intermediary) gives it "voice." See Scheid and Svenbro 1996, 127 with n. 54.

68. Cf. Hephaestus' lifelike attendants, described at *Iliad* 18.417 ff. See Kris and Kurz 1979, 68–71.

69. Cf. the shield scenes in Aeschylus' *Seven against Thebes*, in which written messages help to explain or interpret the pictorial representations. These scenes are discussed by Zeitlin (1982b) and Svenbro (1990, 376–77).

So even though we might say that Helen is the antithesis of Penelope, that one is defined by her marital faithlessness while the other is defined by her faithfulness, their weaving positions both women within a dominant social structure in which they are far removed from the masculine world of face-to-face encounters, whether in speech or in battle.

I have been arguing that weaving as women's work functions as a graphic form of communication in the epic, one that is distinguished from direct oral speech as the normative form of communication among males. How, then, do we account for the fact that weaving (ὑφαίνω) and sewing (ῥάπτω) are common Greek metaphors for poetic production, beginning in the archaic period (Hesiod frag. 357; Pindar frag. 179; Bacchylides 5.9)?[70] Does this metaphor accord with or counter the gender-specific analysis I have been proposing? We have already seen that the originary scenes of the epic and didactic poems, that is, those in which the Muses appear, are equivocal with respect to poetic production and transmission, and I have noted that this equivocation is an expression of a desire for an idealized presence of body and voice. In a recent book, John Scheid and Jesper Svenbro point out that characters in the epic, Odysseus and Menelaus in particular, can be said to weave stories and counsels (μύθους καὶ μήδεα πᾶσιν ὕφαινον, Iliad 3.212), in other words, that weaving can be used metaphorically in the epics to describe speech between males.[71] In this case "weaving" is not an overt signifier of "women's work," although we might suspect that speech described as such is of a particular sort. Scheid and Svenbro argue that it is distinguishable first of all from the song of the bard or epic narrator, who does not use the metaphor to describe the production of the poem itself.

---

70. The word ῥάπτω is used of straightforward sewing at Euripides Bacchae 243 (Dionysus is sewn into the thigh of Zeus; cf. Homeric Hymn 1.2) and at Aristophanes Ecclesiazousae 24–25 (the women's beards are sewn on). Both occasions involve deceptive ruses; in the former Zeus would play the woman, in the latter the women would play men. On the Ecclesiazousae, cf. Taaffe 1991, 99: "Errammenous underlines the deceptive costume theme and the involvement of women in a plot which requires costumes, for women sew and, like Penelope, could stitch or weave a deception easily." Both ὑφαίνω and ῥάπτω are also used of contriving and plotting, usually in a negative sense (e.g., Iliad 6.187, 18.367; Odyssey 3.118, 4.678, 9.422, 16.379, 16.423; Hesiod Shield of Heracles 28).

71. Scheid and Svenbro 1996, 114–15.

Whereas verbal "weaving" is in keeping with the context of the quasi-public gathering, characterized by the confrontation of opposing interests, it does not necessarily suit the bard's singing in the midst of a group with which he identifies—and must identify, in order not to jeopardize the automatic nature of his performance. To put it another way, whereas verbal "weaving" defines the receiver of the spoken words as an other, a stranger or a hostile party, the bard's song presupposes an identification between the sender and receiver that makes the metaphor unsuitable. (Scheid and Svenbro 1996, 115)

According to this analysis, what distinguishes "verbal weaving" from the "automatic" poetic production of the epic narrator is the fact that the latter "identifies" with his audience. Conversely, the verbal weaving of Odysseus and Menelaus in *Iliad* 3 (quoted earlier) is a sign that the heroes are "avoiding any spontaneous discourse" (Scheid and Svenbro 1996, 113), that is, that their speeches do not presuppose an identification with their audience (the assembled Trojans). In chapter 1, I noted that in a performance context, identification operates in a process of validating an idealized and internalized masculine selfhood. Here it can be observed that, as an interpretive concept, identification functions in a similar fashion. I am not quite sure from what or whose point of view it operates, that is, whether the bard's performance naturally testifies to an identification with his audience or whether Scheid and Svenbro simply will it to do so; nor is it clear why the "automatic nature" of the bard's singing would be jeopardized without this identification. Their conclusion does illustrate the persistence of an idealized notion of oral performance in which there is a direct and unmediated communication between the poet and his audience, the same sort of ambiguous persistence we have noted in the previously discussed originary scenes in which the Muses are invoked.

According to Scheid and Svenbro, the epic narrator refrains from using the metaphor of weaving or stitching to describe his songs because he "does not consider himself to be the author of his own words": the Muses "fill him with song." But at the same time they note that rhapsodes weave or "resew" their songs because they are not Homer, that is, they are not the original author of the Homeric poems (112).[72] But if verbal stitching or weaving signifies the existence of a prior and originary verbal act and if the Homeric narrator does not consider himself to be the author of his own words, we would expect that he would describe himself as a weaver or sewer of songs. The notion that stitching or weaving is an appropriate metaphor for a secondary order of poetic production also works against Scheid and Svenbro's argument that the choral poet (i.e., Pindar or Bacchylides) used weaving as a metaphor for his art because he had to "assert himself as author of his poem" (119): verbal weaving does not easily signify both that the poet is the original author of his poem and that the Homeric rhapsodes are dependent on a previously existing poetry. If I have read Scheid and Svenbro's arguments correctly, they convey a complex confusion over direct and indirect communication as competing modes of telling an originary tale, that is, the tale of an original poet or an original poem.

Scheid and Svenbro's argument does confirm a distinction in the Greek poetic tradition between an original poet, or Ur-poet (ὁ ποιητής), and the rhapsode or secondary order of poet, who weaves or stitches poems together. As part of a tale of origins, the textile metaphor works within this hierarchical framework to distinguish the original maker of the poem from those who subsequently copy or imitate his work. Although it represents a later commentary on these issues, Plato's *Ion* provides the most vivid portrait of this secondary order of poetic production and one that best illustrates the cultural assumptions that contribute to this hierarchy.[73] In describing what he knows best, the rhapsode Ion says that the kind of speech he knows is not the kind that suits a slave or a woman who is spinning wool (γυναικὶ . . . ταλασιουργῷ) but the kind that suits "a general exhorting his soldiers" (*Ion* 540–41). Ion's equation of the rhapsode (i.e., himself) with the

---

72. See Else 1957b, 26–34, on the etymology of *rhapsoidos* as meaning "stitch-singer." Else believes that *rhapsoidos* was a "derisive or deprecatory epithet," because "sewing is not a heroic pursuit." He explains: "It connotes if anything banausic labor, a sedentary life, a spirit given to petty concerns. In legend, tailors are apt to be spiteful, malicious fellows, suspicious of their wives and all the world." He also maintains that "there is no doubt about the contempt in which the rhapsodes were held by cultivated men in the fifth and fourth centuries," and he proposes Plato's *Ion* as the "archetype."

73. The *Ion* is not discussed by Scheid and Svenbro.

general (as opposed to slaves and women) is seriously challenged by Socrates, however, as is everything Ion professes to know. In particular, Ion's insistence that he knows what a general needs to know proves that he has more in common with his counterexample, that is, with "a woman who is spinning wool," than he does with a general in command of his troops. According to Socrates, the rhapsode, like the actor, is a mediator or middleman who occupies a position between the original poet and his audience: ὁ δὲ μέσος σὺ ὁ ῥαψῳδὸς καὶ ὑποκριτής (535e9–536a1).[74] The simile of the magnet and the iron rings in the dialogue is a further illustration of this point. As a teller of tales, the rhapsode, or "stitcher of words," in Plato's text neither fights nor speaks like a "real" general. He is a go-between who has more in common with slaves, women, and actors. And in this sense he shares a common attribute with writing as the object of Socrates' critique in the *Phaedrus* (275d5 ff.); both mediate rather than communicate directly, and, consequently, neither fosters true knowledge.

The Platonic critique of the rhapsode is based on associations between weaving or sewing as woman's work and verbal weaving or sewing as a metaphor for indirect, insufficient, or deceptive speech.[75] This basis is in keeping with the earlier discussions of Helen's weaving and Proetus' inscribed "symbols" as examples of graphic communication in the epic itself, all of which may help explain why the Homeric narrator does not use the metaphor to describe his own poetic enterprise. The Platonic critique also offers another instance of the link between martial and communicative practices in the construction of Greek masculinity; a general ordering his troops is the antithesis of the

74. At *Republic* 395a8, Socrates says that men "cannot be reciters and actors at the same time" [Οὐδὲ μὴν ῥαψῳδοί γε καὶ ὑποκριταὶ ἅμα], but this proscription does not obviate their similarity as middlemen. Intermediacy is also responsible for the diminished truth-value of objects that are only approximations or imitations of the Forms in *Republic* 10, a discussion that culminates in the expulsion of the tragic poet from the city.

75. Cf. the review of Scheid and Svenbro 1996 by Simon Goldhill, *Bryn Mawr Classical Review* 96.8.3: "The authors surprisingly give little time to the sense of the trickery with which weaving becomes associated. . . . From Calypso, Circe and Penelope in the *Odyssey*, through the robes in which Agamemnon and Heracles die, to the weaving of plots in male spheres of activity, 'the web' develops a negative sense of deception and subtlety that constantly threatens to undermine its normative and positive value."

rhapsode stitching his poems. But it also does something more interesting for our purposes, by situating the conflict between direct and mediated forms of speech in the context of theatrical performance, in which the actor, like the rhapsode, is the model practitioner of the latter. Whether or not verbal weaving or sewing is a stable metaphor throughout the periods that encompass the epic poems and the Platonic dialogues, the *Ion* testifies to a gender-specific discourse of communicative practices in which mediated speech is the recognized mode of the dramatic actor.

I mentioned early in this chapter that the message-sending scenes in the *Iliad* best exemplify the functioning of mediated or scripted speech in the context of the epic poems themselves. In the most sustained and important example, Agamemnon sends Ajax, Odysseus, and Phoenix to convey his promises to Achilles and to entreat him to return to the fighting. As the means by which Agamemnon would persuade Achilles to return to the battlefield so that the Greeks can win victory, the message qua message is already implicated in the poem's narrative of martial failure or success. The form of the message is the key to how it operates in that narrative. The promised gifts (*Iliad* 9.122–57) are repeated mutatis mutandis by Odysseus (9.264–99), so that Odysseus is the mouthpiece of Agamemnon. As a narrative device, this repetition emphasizes the fact that Agamemnon's promises are made secondhand; it can also help us to recognize that because they are secondhand, they ultimately fail to persuade Achilles.[76] This failure occurs even though it is Nestor who recommends that men be appointed to carry the message (9.165–66) and even though the messengers are "men who are most dear" to Achilles (φίλτατοι ἄνδρες, 9.204). Thus the failure of the embassy, even though it conforms to protocol, emphasizes the way in which second-

---

76. Heralds, of course, make secondhand speeches by definition. But with heralds as a formal class (ἄγγελοι), the problem too is that—contra Létoublon 1987—they may not get the message right or tell it truthfully. Messengers who are not officially heralds but who have a more personal relationship to the parties in question are also very often implicated in some potential to deceive. Cf. Lichas' lying message in Sophocles' *Trachiniae*; Oedipus' charges against Creon as the messenger from Apollo's oracle in Sophocles' *Oedipus Tyrannus*; the message brought by the lone survivor of Laius' party that numerous men had attacked the king in the same play; and the false message of Orestes' death in the *Choephoroi*. See Longo 1978, 72–86.

hand, or mediated, speech is oppositional to face-to-face, or man-to-man, speech as the validated and persuasive mode of communication among the epic warriors.[77] Two statements by Achilles illustrate this opposition. In the first, he makes the following reply to Odysseus:

διογενὲς Λαερτιάδη, πολυμήχαν᾽ Ὀδυσσεῦ,
χρὴ μὲν δὴ τὸν μῦθον ἀπηλεγέως ἀποειπεῖν,
ᾗ περ δὴ φρονέω τε καὶ ὡς τετελεσμένον ἔσται,
ὡς μή μοι τρύζητε παρήμενοι ἄλλοθεν ἄλλος.
ἐχθρὸς γάρ μοι κεῖνος ὁμῶς Ἀΐδαο πύλῃσιν
ὅς χ᾽ ἕτερον μὲν κεύθῃ ἐνὶ φρεσίν, ἄλλο δὲ εἴπῃ.
αὐτὰρ ἐγὼν ἐρέω ὥς μοι δοκεῖ εἶναι ἄριστα·
οὔτ᾽ ἔμεγ᾽ Ἀτρεΐδην Ἀγαμέμνονα πεισέμεν οἴω
οὔτ᾽ ἄλλους Δαναούς, ἐπεὶ οὐκ ἄρα τις χάρις ἦεν
μάρνασθαι δηΐοισιν ἐπ᾽ ἀνδράσι νωλεμὲς αἰεί.

[Godly son of Laertes, resourceful Odysseus,
it is necessary that I answer straightforwardly
in the manner I have in mind [φρονέω], and tell what will be
    accomplished
so that you may not sit and mutter at me one after another.
For as I hate the gates of Hades, so I hate that man
who hides one thing in his mind [φρεσίν] and says another.
But I will speak as seems best to me;
and I think Agamemnon, the son of Atreus, will persuade neither
    me
nor the rest of the Danaans, since there was no gratitude given
for always fighting without pause against hostile men.]
                                        (9.308–17)

Coming just after Odysseus has enumerated the gifts promised by Agamemnon, the statement may be (as Leaf suggests) "an excuse for

---

77. Cf. *Iliad* 1.324–25, where Agamemnon says that if the heralds are unable to bring back Briseis, he will go himself with many others to get her (ἐγὼ δέ κεν αὐτὸς ἕλωμαι / ἐλθὼν σὺν πλεόνεσσι). The statement implies both that there is a need to use force (σὺν πλεόνεσσι) and that the success of intermediaries—that is, the heralds—is in doubt.

the freedom with which Achilles means to speak."[78] But the reproach
also pertains to Agamemnon, whose promises Achilles has just heard
from Odysseus, with the implied accusation that Agamemnon is the
sort who "hides one thing in his mind and says another." The distinction Achilles makes between what a man hides in his mind (ʾενὶ φρεσίν)
and what he says out loud is implicitly a distinction between truthful,
or complete, speech (insofar as thought and speech are ideally commensurate) and false, or incomplete, speech. Thus when Achilles professes
to say what is on his mind (φρονέω) and what will be accomplished (ὡς
τετελεσμένον ἔσται), namely, that Agamemnon will not persuade him,
the point is that Achilles hides nothing and that what Achilles says is
persuasive.[79] Achilles' reference a few lines later to the time when
Agamemnon "remained by the ships" while others fought for the
spoils of war (9.332) once again confirms the correspondence between
martial and communicative systems in the *Iliad*; whereas Achilles is in
principle "always fighting against hostile men" and speaks what is on
his mind, Agamemnon hides from the fighting and sends others to
speak for him.[80]

The second relevant passage occurs in Achilles' final rejection of
Agamemnon's gifts.

τῷ πάντ' ἀγορευέμεν, ὡς ἐπιτέλλω,
ἀμφαδόν, ὄφρα καὶ ἄλλοι ἐπισκύζωνται ᾿Αχαιοί,
εἴ τινά που Δαναῶν ἔτι ἔλπεται ἐξαπατήσειν,
αἰὲν ἀναιδείην ἐπιειμένος· οὐδ' ἂν ἔμοιγε
τετλαίη κύνεός περ ἐὼν εἰς ὦπα ἰδέσθαι·

---

78. Leaf 1960, ad loc.

79. Leaf (1960, ad loc.) takes Δαναούς at 316 as the subject (not the object)
of πεισέμεν, along with ᾿Αγαμέμνονα, and he takes ἐμέ as the object in both
clauses. He admits, however, that the "phrase is ambiguous." In either case,
persuasiveness (or the failure to persuade) is Agamemnon's problem more
than it is a problem for "the rest of the Danaans."

80. At *Iliad* 6.79, Helenus refers to Hector and Aeneas as "the best in battle
and in thought" (ἄριστοι . . . ἐστε μάχεσθαί τε φρονέειν τε). This implicit
equation of fighting and thinking helps to illustrate the point I am making for
Iliad 9.308–17 and 332, namely, that Achilles' vow to say what is on his mind
(φρονέω) is implicitly equated with his fighting prowess, while Agamemnon's failure to fight makes him susceptible to the accusation that he hides
what is on his mind.

οὐδέ τί οἱ βουλὰς συμφράσσομαι, οὐδὲ μὲν ἔργον·
ἐκ γὰρ δή μ' ἀπάτησε καὶ ἤλιτην· οὐδ' ἂν ἔτ' αὖτις
ἐξαπάφοιτ' ἐπέεσσιν.

[Go back and tell him all that I command you,
openly, so other Achaeans may turn against him in anger
if he wishes still to trick some other Danaan,
wrapped as he always is in shamelessness: yet he would not
dare to look me in the face, he is so like a dog.
I will neither join with him in any counsel nor in any action.
For he cheated me and offended me. May he not trick me
with words again.]

(9.369–76)

The repeated lexicon of trickery (ἀπάτησε, ἐξαπάφοιτο) and the emphasis on the deceptiveness of Agamemnon's words (ἐπέεσσιν) register the connection between potentially false speech and the absence of the person whose speech is in question, a connection made vivid by the accusation that, though "wrapped as he always is in shamelessness," Agamemnon "would not dare to look [Achilles] in the face."[81] Since the embassy to Achilles is arguably the most extended and marked example of a relayed message in the *Iliad*, it establishes such messages as inferior forms of communication, the sort that undermine the persuasiveness and truthfulness assured by the presence of the speaking subject speaking for himself. It is worth noting too that when Achilles does accept Agamemnon's gifts in book 19, Agamemnon has offered them in person and refers to himself with the emphatic *I* as a marker of his bodily presence in the proceedings (ἐγὼν ὅδε, 19.140).

It must be admitted, of course, that Achilles does not go directly to Agamemnon with a reply, but Agamemnon has established the precedent of relayed messages. As part of this message-sending system,

---

81. An analogy can be made with the relationship between autopsy and truth-value in historical narratives, that is, in Herodotus. See Woodman 1988, 15–28. For the phrase εἰς ὦπα ἰδέσθαι see also *Iliad* 15.147 and *Odyssey* 23.107. Cf. *Odyssey* 11.425 where Agamemnon, now in Hades, calls the deceitful Clytemnestra κυνῶπις.

the truth-value of Achilles' reply is also compromised. In comparison
with the almost word-for-word report of Agamemnon's promises to
Achilles, Odysseus brings back to Agamemnon only the briefest
sketch of all that Achilles had said.[82] There are two obvious explanations for this discrepancy. First, it makes sense that the gifts promised
by Agamemnon had to be enumerated to Achilles without deviation;
second, we can imagine a certain circumspection on Odysseus' part,
since, for example, he would not benefit from reporting Achilles'
rejection of Agamemnon's daughter word for word (9.388–92). But
why not report back the circumstances of Achilles' double destiny
(διχθαδίας κῆρας, 9.411), knowledge of which would presumably be
important for further negotiations with Achilles? The question of
Odysseus' abbreviated report to Agamemnon is a matter not of the
character's unknown motives, however, but of what the report includes and what it leaves out. An opportunity to judge the report on
just this point is provided by Achilles, when he offers two versions of
what he intends to do: first he says he will leave Troy (9.355 ff.), and
then he says he will not fight until Hector reaches his own ships
(9.650 ff.; cf. 9.619).[83] Odysseus reports the former, but he fails to
report the latter, even though Achilles had specifically told him to do
so (ἀλλ'ὑμεῖς ἔρχεσθε καὶ ἀγγελίην ἀπόφασθε, 9.649; cf. 9.369–70).[84]
This omission signals the potential insufficiency or inaccuracy of reported, or mediated, speech, especially given the overall importance
of what Achilles says in the poem and the repetitive nature of the epic
narrative in general.

Another important message-sending scene occurs at the beginning
of book 2 of the Iliad, when, in an effort to satisfy Thetis' request to
give honor to Achilles, Zeus sends a dream (οὖλον Ὄνειρον, 2.6) to
Agamemnon, with the message that he is to prepare for battle, since

---

82. Achilles' reply comprises approximately 128 lines (Iliad 9.308–425,
644–55); Odysseus' report of the reply comprises only 7 lines (Iliad 9.680–87).

83. Cf. Leaf 1960, on line 650: "Achilles has apparently by this time abandoned his idea of returning home, though Odysseus in 682 reports only the
original threat. This difficulty was a popular ἀπορία in the Alexandrian
schools, and is not solved by expunging the present passage; see 601, 619."
Cf. further de Jong 1987, 184–85.

84. See Martin 1989, 218, on the emphasis achieved by the enjambment of
ἀμφαδόν at Iliad 9.369–70; cf. Agamemnon's similar phrase at 2.10.

the time has now come for him to conquer Troy.[85] We know, of course, that the opposite is in store for Agamemnon and that the ensuing battle will bring disaster; the dream leaves him "pondering things in his heart that are not to be accomplished" [τὰ φρονέοντ' ἀνὰ θυμὸν ἃ ῥ' οὐ τελέεσθαι ἔμελλον], (2.36). Later Nestor will maintain that, had the dream's message been reported to the princes by any man other than Agamemnon, it would have been taken to be a lie (ψεῦδος, *Iliad* 2.81). The irony lies both in the fact that the message itself is not true and in the fact that Agamemnon will lie to his men outright about the content of the dream's message.

The dream is sent in the likeness of Nestor (Νηληΐῳ υἷι ἐοικώς, 2.20), and Agamemnon's faith in its veracity is implicitly related to this guise, since Nestor is so often praised as the giver of sound advice.[86] But along with Proetus' written message, this dream represents the only other example in the *Iliad* of a message based on an overt lie.[87] Its status as a message is marked by the number of times it is repeated or passed on in the narrative, first from Zeus to the dream, then from the dream to Agamemnon, then from Agamemnon to the Greek princes, and finally—in revised form—from Agamemnon to the Greek fighting men.[88] Leaf finds these repetitions to be "really too much," but precisely the weight of the repetitions focuses attention on the message qua message.[89] In effect, they emphasize the falseness

---

85. There are no explicit messages relayed either to Achilles by the heralds sent to bring Briseis to Agamemnon (cf. *Iliad* 1.32 ff.) or to Chryses by the men sent to return Chryseis to him (*Iliad* 1.441 ff.). Nor is Thetis' request to Zeus explicitly a message from Achilles (cf. *Iliad* 1.493 ff.). But see Létoublon 1987, 138–42, on the chiastic relationship between the communicative scheme of book 1 (Achilles to Thetis to Zeus) and that of book 24 (Zeus to Thetis to Achilles).

86. Cf. Kirk 1985, ad loc.: "One would suppose that Agamemnon might dream either of Nestor advising him *or* of a truly divine messenger doing so; Nestor himself in the role of the latter might seem to break the Dream's verisimilitude." Cf. *Iliad* 10.496.

87. Cf. Létoublon 1987, 143 n. 16.

88. See Kirk 1985, ad loc., on the authenticity of these repetitions. The words of introduction (*Iliad* 2.23–26) and salutation (2.33–34) that the dream adds to Zeus' message are not, strictly speaking, deviations from the text of the message.

89. Leaf 1960, on Iliad 2.60. This repetition is hyperbolic; it is in excess of the epic's formal conventions. But cf. Kirk 1985 ad loc. Leaf approves of

of the message by insisting too much on its truthfulness—insofar as
Agamemnon believes it to be true. The scene also contrastively illustrates the validation of an ontological and epistemological integrity of
body and voice in the discourse of direct, or man-to-man, speech: the
true Nestor, present and' speaking as himself, would tell the truth, but
the false Nestor, as an apparition and a messenger, tells a lie.

Agamemnon reports the exact message from Zeus to the princes of
the army but a different message to the fighting men, a lie of his own.

ὦ φίλοι ἥρωες Δαναοί, θεράποντες Ἄρηος,
Ζεύς με μέγα Κρονίδης ἄτῃ ἐνέδησε βαρείῃ,
σχέτλιος, ὃς πρὶν μέν μοι ὑπέσχετο καὶ κατένευσεν
Ἴλιον ἐκπέρσαντ' εὐτείχεον ἀπονέεσθαι,
νῦν δὲ κακὴν ἀπάτην βουλεύσατο, καί με κελεύει
δυσκλέα Ἄργος ἱκέσθαι, ἐπεὶ πολὺν ὤλεσα λαόν.

[Danaan heroes, friends, servants of Ares, Great Zeus, the
son of Kronos, has ensnared me in a heavy delusion.
He is cruel. For he promised me before, and he nodded his head,
that I would sack strong-walled Troy and then return home.
But now he has planned an evil deceit, and he orders me
to return to Argos in disgrace, when I have lost many people.]
                                                    (2.110–15)

Again the language of delusion (ἄτη) and trickery (ἀπάτη), combined
with the irony that Agamemnon's lie is close to the truth behind Zeus'
false message, is a reminder that Zeus has planned an evil deceit,
although not the one Agamemnon invents. Agamemnon's lie is similar to Zeus' but with opposite intent. The god sends a message of
victory only to defeat the Greeks and give honor to Achilles (2.3–4);
Agamemnon sends a message of early homecoming (which is also a
message of defeat) only to rouse the soldiers to stay and fight. In

---

Zenodotus' two-verse condensation of the passage. Létoublon (1987, 132)
seems to agree with Leaf and argues that it is "as if the fidelity of the messenger in the archaic epic was never in doubt." But Létoublon makes no clear
distinction between the content of the message and the accuracy of the message as delivered. Cf. Longo 1978, 74–78; de Jong 1987, 281 n. 71; Thalmann
1988, 7.

effect, the tactic of the god is adopted by the general.[90] The difference between Zeus' message and Agamemnon's is that the former eventually has its desired effect, that is, "to destroy many beside the ships of the Achaeans" (2.4). In contrast, Agamemnon's lie comes close to having an effect opposite what he intends. The Homeric narrator affirms that the men would have returned home if Hera had not intervened (2.155–56). The possibility for a "premature and fruitless return home" may be ascribed to mythical revision, as Kirk maintains.[91] But what that revision means is the complete sabotaging of the poem's martial ethos, an ethos based on Greek victory in face-to-face combat: Agamemnon's message is predicated on withdrawal without a fight. In this sense, Agamemnon resembles Proetus, whose message sending compromises his status as a warrior and a king. Even though the professed intent of Agamemnon's false message is to instill a fighting spirit in the men, it is left to others (Odysseus, in particular) to marshal the troops in person and to see to it that they do stay and fight.[92]

I have argued that Agamemnon's failure to convince Achilles to reenter the war in book 9 is due in part to his failure to face Achilles directly (εἰς ὦπα ἰδέσθαι) and that the *Iliad* encodes its valorization of direct, face-to-face communication not only by representing messages as potentially untruthful but also by exposing their potential failure to persuade their recipients. The different mode of transmitting those messages is also a clue to the distinction between indirect and direct oral speech in the poem. Messages are reported either in the first or third person. On the one hand, the indirect, or third-person, reporting of a message is a grammatical marker of indirect, or mediated,

---

90. Thalmann (1988, 8–10) notes that, "unlike Zeus, [Agamemnon] wishes his hearers to do the opposite of what he seems to be urging" and that the lies of Zeus and Agamemnon indicate a "crisis of kingship itself and its ideology." But Agamemnon's position has been at risk since the quarrel with Achilles at the beginning of the *Iliad*. Moreover, Hesiod's account of Zeus' ascendancy to kingship (i.e., the story of the stone Gaia gives to Cronos as a substitute for the infant Zeus, at *Theogony* 453 ff.) and of his actions while king (i.e., the creation of Pandora, at *Theogony* 561 ff.) suggests that deception is a prerogative of legitimate kingship and operates within its ideology, not outside it.

91. Kirk 1985, ad loc.

92. See Thalmann 1988, 11–14. Cf *Iliad* 9.17–28, where Agamemnon repeats the message to return home—this time in earnest.

speech. On the other hand, direct quotation, or first-person reporting, is a grammatical marker of direct speech in the form of a
pretense, as in the case of Hesiod's direct quotation of the Muses,
discussed earlier.[93] Thus the fact that Agamemnon's promises are
delivered by Odysseus in the third person is another indicator of
Agamemnon's failure to face Achilles directly and perhaps of some
uncertainty about his intent to deliver on those promises. A better
case for this hypothesis can be made for the two messages delivered
by Agamemnon in book 2, however, where their interdependence
and proximity invite comparison.

The dream message that Agamemnon believes to be true and that he
reports to the Greek princes in book 2 is delivered in the first person and
includes the phrase "I am a messenger from Zeus." To his fighting men,
however, Agamemnon presents his own false message as the message
brought to him by the dream, and he does so using the third person.
Homer's audience, of course, knows that both messages are false. Thus
Agamemnon's use of different grammatical persons reflects the difference in the truth-value that *he* assigns to each of them: he relates the
message he believes to be true in the first person but uses the third
person when relaying the message that he knows to be a lie (2.110 ff.).[94]
But the meaning of this relationship between grammatical person and
truth-value is not explained by Agamemnon's beliefs or intentions.
Rather, the difference between the use of the third or the first person in
reporting a message reveals a complex hierarchical relationship be-

---

93. Svenbro (1993, chap. 2) argues that first-person writing on "egocen-
tric" inscriptions or objects, conceived of as being read aloud, "gives the
impression of being a direct speech-act" (p. 29). Cf. Benveniste 1971, 199, on
the third person as nonpersonal.

94. The problem is a bit more complicated if we consider the truth-value of
the content of a message as distinct from the accuracy of the message qua
message. We know that the content of Zeus' message is false, because we
know that he does not intend to give victory to the Greeks. But the message
Agamemnon reports to the Greek leaders is an accurate report of what Zeus
and the dream had said. In stressing what Agamemnon believes or knows to
be a true or false message, I elide these two and, in the process, obscure the
irony in the fact that his lie is closer to the truth of what Zeus intends. But the
point about the choice of grammatical persons still holds. In general, that
choice refers to the class-based relationship between the speaker and the
recipient of a message, on the one hand, and the truth-value of the message
assigned by the speaker, on the other.

tween the sender of the message and the messenger. On the one hand, first-person reporting, in which the messenger effectively speaks as the sender of the message, suggests some affinity between the sender and the messenger (either desired or actual). Third-person reporting, on the other hand, suggests the messenger's subservient position with regard to the sender. So, for example, when the dream reports Zeus' message to Agamemnon in the third person, the dream's status as the god's underling is emphasized.[95] Likewise, that Odysseus reports Agamemnon's message to Achilles in the third person verifies his position as Agamemnon's second in command. Conversely, that Agamemnon reports the dream's message to the Greek leaders in the first person reveals his desire for and belief in his privileged access to divine agency (cf. 2.35–40). Of course, the irony of the situation is clear, since Zeus is obviously not Agamemnon's ally at this point in the narrative.[96]

My point is that Agamemnon's use of direct, or first-person, speech to communicate what he believes to be a true message from Zeus to his fellow princes validates direct, or first-person, speech as the vehicle of truth between elite warriors. Conversely, his use of indirect, or third-person, speech to communicate what he knows to be a lie to the common soldiers aligns mediated, or indirect, speech with deception and falsehood. The difference between first- and third-person reporting in this instance also suggests that falsehoods are construed in the poem as most easily persuasive when perpetrated by a member of the elite warrior class against those over whom he has power; a similar case might be made for Zeus' lying message to Agamemnon in book 2. Even though Agamemnon intends that his message will fail to persuade the men, that is, that it will in fact make them want to stay and fight, that failure is ironically dependent on the possibility that they will believe the message to be true, that is, that they will believe he really wants them to return home. His lie also marks a point in the narrative where his own martial and political authority is at high risk; even if Agamemnon does not know it, Zeus is planning his defeat. Agamemnon's ignorance illustrates his perilous position by demonstrating his susceptibility to the dangerously

---

95. Cf. Iris' use of the third person to report Zeus' message at *Iliad* 8.397 ff.

96. See de Jong 1987, chap. 5, for a discussion of message sending, although class differences do not figure in her analysis. Létoublon (1987, 124) attributes changes in grammatical person to "the positions of the interlocutors," but without reference to their class or status. Cf. Svenbro 1993, 26–27.

persuasive potential of Zeus' false message of victory. His at-risk position is also signified by the content of the lie he tells the men (to
retreat before the Greeks have been victorious) and by the fact of his
lying to test them. This signification may help account for what has
been thought to be the anomalous episode of Agamemnon's testing of
the soldiers, or πεῖρα, in the epic. When we recall Plato's Ion, who
claims to know the kind of speech that suits "a general exhorting his
soldiers" (Ion 540–41), but whose claim only proves his marginal status, Agamemnon's lying speech to his soldiers seems to provide Ion
with a suitable model.

Another example of the gender- and class-specific problematic of
mediated, or indirect, speech in the Iliad is provided by the "unmea-
sured" and "disorderly" speech of Thersites in book 2. Thersites does
not deliver a message per se, but what he says is a reiteration of an
earlier and equally transgressive speech in the poem, namely, Achilles' insults against Agamemnon in book 1. Richard Martin notes the
repetitive or predictable nature of Thersites' speech.

> [A]t times [Thersites] appears simply to make use of arguments
> available in any aggrieved hero's traditional stock. For the tack of
> toting up one's opponents' goods, compare 2.226–27—"the huts
> are full of bronze, many select women are in the huts" with
> Antilokhos's sharp words to Achilles (23.549–50): "Much gold
> you have in your hut, much bronze and movable goods, women-
> slaves and single-hoofed horses." (Martin 1989, 109)

But Thersites' taunt to Agamemnon at Iliad 2.225 ff. is so closely
aligned with Achilles' speech in book 1—both in content and proximity—that the appeal to "the hero's traditional stock" is not entirely
explanatory. At the same time, Thersites' nonheroic status makes his
use of the speech of an "aggrieved hero" all the more noteworthy for
its inappropriateness. Like Achilles, Thersites rebukes Agamemnon
for greed and the abuse of power.[97] He even quotes Achilles directly;

---

97. Cf. Iliad 1.121 ff. and 1.149 ff. with 2.225 ff.; cf. the narrator's comment
that Thersites "quarrels with kings" at Iliad 2.214 (οὐ κατὰ κόσμον, ἐριζέμεναι
βασιλεῦσιν) and Nestor's admonition that Achilles not fight with a king at
1.277–78 (μήτε σὺ, Πηλεΐδη, ἔθελ᾽ ἐριζέμεναι βασιλῆϊ / ἀντιβίην).

Iliad 2.240 (ἑλὼν γὰρ ἔχει γέρας, αὐτὸς ἀπούρας) repeats *Iliad* 1.356 and 507, first spoken by Achilles to Thetis and then by Thetis to Zeus. Yet Thersites is the speaker in the *Iliad* whose speech is most overtly marked as nonconformist. He does not contend with the kings according to protocol (ἀμετροεπής, 2.212; ἔπεα ἄκοσμα 2.213; οὐ κατὰ κόσμον ἐριζέμεναι βασιλεῦσιν 2.214) and will say whatever seems likely to be considered "laughable" among the assembled troops (ἀλλ ὅ τι οἱ εἴσαιτο γελοίϊον Ἀργείοισιν ἔμμεναι, 2.215–16).⁹⁸ He is most hated (ἔχθιστος, 2.220) by Achilles and Odysseus, "who," notes Nagy, "happen to be the best of the Achaeans in the *Iliad* and *Odyssey* respectively, and thereby the two prominent figures of Panhellenic Epos."⁹⁹ As the ugliest (αἴσχιστος, 2.216) man who came to Troy, his physical presence is in accord with his unruly speech and proleptically establishes the criterion by which that speech (following his physical description) is to be judged. Not only is Thersites' physical nonconformity indicative of a lack of manly virtue, but it guarantees the condemnation of what he says and proves that he is in need of discipline.¹⁰⁰ So why is he given a speech that recalls Achilles' speech in so many details? Are we to conclude that Achilles' speech against Agamemnon in book 1 is thereby retrospectively condemned?¹⁰¹

Thersites' reference to the quarrel between Achilles and Agamemnon has puzzled critics who think it does not seem appropriate to the

---

98. The word ἀμετροεπής is found only here in Homer; γελοίϊον is also a hapax legomenon in Homer. On Thersites' style of speaking, see Martin 1989, 109–13.

99. Nagy 1979, 260.

100. The correspondences between Thersites' physical appearance and the words he speaks are clear. In general they are both οὐ κατὰ κόσμον and γελοίϊον. On the presentation of Thersites' body, see chap. 3. Cf. *Odyssey* 8.169 ff., where Odysseus equates beautiful looks with comely words. Spelman (1988) discusses the persistence of somatophobia in feminist theory and its complicity in racism. See also Parker 1987, esp. chap. 2; Rousselle 1988. Cf. Thalmann 1988, 15.

101. This interpretation is one way of understanding the correspondences between the two speeches and adds substance to the notion that both Achilles and Thersites are marginalized. See Martin 1989, 24; cf. 109 with n. 41. The question remains, By what criteria or against what standards is marginalization established in the epic?

present situation.[102] But this apparent inappropriateness only high-
lights what constitutes the essential point of comparison between the
speeches of Achilles, Agamemnon, and Thersites: the threat of returning home before the proper end of the war (i.e., before a Greek victory). First introduced by Achilles (1.169–71) and subsequently proposed by Agamemnon when he makes trial of the troops, this threat
constitutes the most notable feature of what might be called the
Thersites script (2.236). The critical import of this threat for the Iliadic
narrative has already been mentioned; when it is put into the mouth
of this worst of the Achaeans, its radical negation of the poetic and
martial enterprise of the epic becomes parodic and hyperbolic. His
appropriation of the threat helps to explain why Thersites' condemnation is authorized at a less contingent narrative level. Whereas the
elite warriors who threaten to return home are condemned by another
warrior within the narrative (Nestor condemns Achilles at 1.277 ff.
and Agamemnon at 2.336 ff.), Thersites is more absolutely condemned by the extradiegetic narrator. The admonition to return home
constitutes a significant and repeated message of heroic failure in the
Iliad, one that is conspicuously repeated by the character whose status
as a hero is most vehemently denied.[103] In this sense, this particular
message represents a prominent example of repeated, or scripted,
speech as a sign of compromised masculinity within the epic's code of
martial virtue.

   The Greek epic validates an idealized mode of communication,
what I have termed face-to-face or man-to-man verbal exchange, by
contrastively ascribing epistemological ambiguity to mediated, or

---

   102. Nagy (1979, 263) argues that Thersites misrepresents Achilles in his
speech when Thersites says that Achilles' anger is "nonexistent, since such a
superior hero would surely have killed Agamemnon if he had really been
angry (II 241–242)." But Thersites does not say that Achilles' anger is "nonexistent," only that it is not so great as to have caused him to kill Agamemnon:
we are meant to remember Athena's intervention in preventing Achilles from
drawing his sword at *Iliad* 1.193 ff. See Kirk 1985, on *Iliad* 2.240; Leaf 1960, on
Iliad 2.241; Nagy 1979, 313, §4 n. 5; Whitman 1958, 161. Thalmann (1988, 19–
21) argues that Thersites' speech is parodic and that he is Achilles' "comic
double" (19).
   103. Thersites' admonition to return home in the ships at *Iliad* 2.236
(οἴκαδέ πεϱ σὺν νηυσὶ νεώμεθα) is close to Achilles' at 1.170 (οἴκαδ' ἴμεν σὺν
νηυσὶ κοϱωνίσιν).

scripted, speech whether graphic or oral. This validation is recognized in pejorative references to the absence of an original speaker
(who, in Achilles' words, does not dare to look him in the face), in
ambiguity about the truth-value of relayed messages, and in the
shared class- and gender-specific protocols operating in the poems'
martial and communicative systems—even at the level of grammatical
person. As an ideological concept, direct oral speech is codified in the
epic as a vehicle of cultural preservation specified in the related discourses of Greek masculinism and militarism, a concept that persists
in Athenian democratic ideology. According to Nicole Loraux, the
Athenian democracy "distrusted writing, or what amounts to the
same thing, never used it, as an instrument of theoretical reflection."
Loraux notes that "only speech enjoyed the freedom of Athens in the
political sphere."[104] Literacy and public speech making were not mutually exclusive; the extent to which the orators of the fourth century
depended on carefully written speeches lies hidden under the pretense of what Ober identifies as an "Athenian political culture [that]
remained at its heart an oral culture."[105] Socrates' condemnation of
Lysias' written speech in the *Phaedrus* is emblematic of this pretense.
So are the traditional stories told about Pericles, who is said not to
have written down his speeches (Plutarch *Pericles* 8.6–7), and about
Socrates, who is said to have written nothing at all.[106] As conspicuous
figures in the representation of fifth-century Athens, Pericles and
Socrates occupy diverse and even seemingly contradictory social and
political positions.[107] Yet they share a reputation as warriors and
as men who refused to write, a refusal that attests to an implicit

---

104. Loraux 1986, 179. See also Matson, Rollinson, and Sousa 1990 on
Alcidamas' *On Those Who Write Written Speeches*.

105. Ober 1989, 158. See also Ober's discussion of the orator's pretense to
spontaneity (187–91).

106. See Loraux 1986, 178. There seems to be no evidence for written
speeches before the fourth century. See Cole 1981, 240 n. 35; Turner 1952, 18
(cited by Cole). This lack of evidence may itself be symptomatic of a persistent
validation of and pretense to direct oral speech.

107. Thucydides' Pericles is the privileged aristocrat who exemplifies a life
of public action and speech making. Plato's Socrates is the self-proclaimed
gadfly whose philosophical inquiry, carried out in more or less private conversations, leads to the proposal of a strictly hierarchical political system based
on education and training rather than on the perquisites of the great families.

validation of direct speech in the democratic and militaristic ideology of fifth-century Athens.

This validation is perhaps best represented in the first-person speeches that Thucydides and Plato put into the mouths of Pericles and Socrates, respectively. To appreciate its significance, we only have to recognize the use of a narrative technique (first-person speeches) whose effect is to disguise or compensate for the absence of these men as speaking subjects, an absence to which the written record of their speeches necessarily attests. It might be argued that since first-person speeches are part of the epic tradition, their inclusion in later historical or philosophical texts is simply traditional. But appeal to the formal properties of the epic cannot adequately explain the persistent use of first-person speeches across a broad spectrum of literary genres, historical periods, and political regimes. It could in fact be argued that the epic presentation of characters speaking in the first person is an unsuitable model for recording the speeches of historical contemporaries. More convincingly, the use of first-person speeches attests to a general nostalgia for bodily presence and direct oral speech as the markers of a normative masculine identity in what has become—by the time of Thucydides and Plato—an increasingly literate culture.

At the same time, the use of speeches in the first person amounts to an implicit denial of any discrepancy between what Pericles and Socrates "actually" said and the written account of what they said. As in the epic message-sending narratives, it functions to invest mediated speech with the persuasiveness of truth in the absence of an original speaker. Thucydides' much discussed explanation of the general method he adopts in writing down his speeches (*History* 1.22) is perhaps the most concise expression of this investment. In the absence of verbatim sources, Thucydides makes the truth and accuracy of any given speech commensurate with what seems most plausible to him.

Καὶ ὅσα μὲν λόγῳ εἶπον ἕκαστοι ἢ μέλλοντες πολεμήσειν ἢ ἐν αὐτῷ ἤδη ὄντες, χαλεπὸν τὴν ἀκρίβειαν αὐτὴν τῶν λεχθέντων διαμνημονεῦσαι ἦν ἐμοί τε ὧν αὐτὸς ἤκουσα καὶ τοῖς ἄλλοθέν ποθεν ἐμοὶ ἀπαγγέλλουσιν· ὡς δ' ἂν ἐδόκουν ἐμοὶ ἕκαστοι περὶ τῶν αἰεὶ παρόντων τὰ δέοντα μάλιστ' εἰπεῖν, ἐχομένῳ ὅτι ἐγγύτατα τῆς ξυμπάσης γνώμης τῶν ἀληθῶς λεχθέντων, οὕτως εἴρηται·

[With reference to the speeches in this history, some were delivered before the war began, others while it was going on; some I heard myself, others I got from various quarters; it was in all cases difficult to carry them word for word in one's memory, so my habit has been to make the speakers say what was in my opinion demanded of them by the various occasions, of course adhering as closely as possible to the general sense of what they really said.] (1.22.1)[108]

The scholarly debate over the meaning of this passage is long-standing and complex. I am less interested in explaining Thucydides' methodology, however, than in the question of first-person speech as a narrative technique in his history, or rather in the pretense to unmediated speaking, or direct, face-to-face speaking, that the speeches represent. We may well ask why Thucydides emphasizes the problem of historical veracity in terms of the speeches. The answer, I think, has to do with the lost ideal of the masculine speaking ego, the resulting persistence of written speeches as a performance of that ego, and the guarantee of truth and persuasiveness as its reward.[109] Thus the speeches in Thucydides—and perhaps the speeches in historical narrative in general—attest once again to that desire to preserve and inhabit the position of the masculine subject of antiquity, most conspicuously that of the greatest generals of the Peloponnesian War. These speeches are, in fact, constitutive of their greatness.

The history of theatrical performance in the West is in part a history of scripts, or, in the words of Aristophanes, "little books" (βιβλία, cf. *Frogs* 1114). These scripts are meant to be spoken out loud and in the first person, but like Thucydides' speeches, with which they are contemporary, they constitute a similar (if more vivid) pretense to direct

---

108. This translation is Crawley's. On this passage, see Woodman 1988, 11–15; Gomme 1959, ad loc.

109. Cf. Gomme 1959, on Thucydides *History* 1.21: "Owing to the prevalence of the spoken over the written word, at least to the end of the fifth century, listening was commoner than reading in all kinds of literature and λέγειν and ἀκούειν tended everywhere to be used, in this connexion, in place of γράφειν and ἀναγιγνώσκειν. We still say of a writer—poet, novelist, historian, or orator—'he says,' not 'he writes so-and-so.' "

oral speech. It is perhaps not surprising, therefore, that Plato's fully developed critique of writing in the fourth century shares important features with his critique of dramatic performance. Both are predicated on the possibility for a kind of disembodied speech and on the epistemological crisis this possibility entails. As I mentioned earlier, Socrates asserts in the *Phaedrus* that the problem with written speeches is their inability to be part of direct verbal exchange and, as a consequence, their inability to foster knowledge (*Phaedrus* 275d5 ff.). The graphic sameness of the written artifact—the necessary precondition of its repeatability—and the arrested knowledge that it fosters are further specified in the *Phaedrus* as the absence of the father.

ὅταν δὲ ἅπαξ γραφῇ, κυλινδεῖται μὲν πανταχοῦ πᾶς λόγος ὁμοίως παρὰ τοῖς ἐπαΐουσιν, ὡς δ' αὕτως παρ' οἷς οὐδὲν προσήκει, καὶ οὐκ ἐπίσταται λέγειν οἷς δεῖ γε καὶ μή. πλημμελούμενος δὲ καὶ οὐκ ἐν δίκῃ λοιδορηθεὶς τοῦ πατρὸς ἀεὶ δεῖται βοηθοῦ· αὐτὸς γὰρ οὔτ' ἀμύνασθαι οὔτε βοηθῆσαι δυνατὸς αὑτῷ.[110]

[When anything is written down, the entire speech is tumbled about everywhere among those who may or may not understand it, and it does not know to whom it should speak and to whom not; and it is maltreated and unjustly abused; it always needs the help of its father; it is unable to defend or help itself.] (275d10–e5)

The indictment of writing in the *Phaedrus* is circumscribed by Socrates' philosophical argument about eros but is not case specific. The general premise, that writing presents an impediment to truth and knowledge because it can continue to speak in the absence of the body and voice of an original speaker, is the culminating expression of an established cultural prejudice.[111] Here direct speech is specified as

---

110. Both ἀμύνω and βοηθέω operate in martial contexts, although not exclusively.

111. In the story of Theuth, Egypt is associated with intellectual skills, including writing, but these skills are suspect. On the specific dangers of writing and the irony of the Platonic dialogue as a product of writing, see Griswold 1986, 202–29. On Plato and Egypt, see Bernal 1987, 105–8. On Egypt and writing, cf. duBois 1988, 140–43: "Egypt, source of papyrus, is the land of

the speech of the most persistently valorized masculine subject, the father.[112] Conversely, the written representation of that speech, like a child, woman, or slave, is weak and—despite its repeatability—is unable to defend itself; repeatability is in fact the cause of its weakness.[113] The metaphors of bodily weakness and abuse in this passage demonstrate that as a text, writing is subservient and inferior to the strong and self-reliant physical body (and voice) of the father.[114]

This critique of writing, in which there is an absence of an authorizing and paternal body and voice, may help explain what seems to have been a rule for fifth-century drama, namely, that only the plays of living poets were allowed to be produced. The rule is proven by the exception the Athenians reportedly made of Aeschylus. According to the author of the *Life of Aeschylus*, the Athenians were "so fond of Aeschylus that they voted after his death that anyone wishing to produce his works could have a chorus" (*Vit. Aesch.* 12).[115] The exception

---

writing, of all inscription. . . . Writing and counting and repetition are the Egyptians' characteristically human skills." DuBois notes that in Aeschylus' *The Suppliants*, "[t]he Danaids and Egypt, their home, are associated with the ephemeral writing on papyrus and tablets, while the Greek city is bound by laws inscribed in stone or bronze." There is a contradiction, I think, in describing Egypt as the home both of "ephemeral writing" and of writing as "repetition" in a "land of records, of the preservation of the past." In Aeschylus' *Prometheus Bound* (459–61), Prometheus—a problematic figure in Greek culture—is the divine originator of writing. Cf. Derrida 1981, 84–94.

112. See Derrida 1981, 75–84, on the figure of the father in the *Phaedrus*.

113. Svenbro (1990, 378) notes that the voice of the actor "is the mere instrument of an unchanging text and not the voice of someone in possession of knowledge, episteme." Cf. Plato *Ion* 532d (cited by Svenbro). See also Aristotle *On Rhetoric* 1413b, where the philosopher discusses the oral delivery of the written text and the sort of text best suited for the actor. On actors' interpolations, see Bain 1975. Cf. Wilshire 1982, 21: "Hence the theatre event has at least two temporal dimensions. First, it must be repeatable from one performance to the next. Second, each performance must occur for a given stretch of time."

114. The maxim "War is the father of all" [Πόλεμος πάντων μὲν πατήρ ἐστι], attributed to Heraclitus (DK 22.B53), functions within this Greek discourse of paternity in which the father embodies martial virtues.

115. Evidence for reproductions of tragedy date from 386 B.C.E., of comedy from 339 B.C.E. See Pickard-Cambridge 1968, 86, 99–101. Cf. Aristophanes *Acharnians* 9–12 and *Frogs* 866 ff. The posthumous performance of Euripides' *Bacchae* also seems to represent an exception to the rule.

invites a number of explanations. The author of the *Life of Aeschylus* says somewhat blandly that the exception was enacted because the Athenians were very fond of the playwright, but political or aesthetic issues of the sort dramatized in the *Frogs* may have had more to do with it.[116] Whatever might explain the exception, however, the rule suggests a preference for the presence and voice of the poet in the process of producing dramatic texts and a corresponding prejudice against the written script as an inadequate or incomplete means of transmitting the play for production; Aristotle says that originally the poets themselves acted in their tragedies (*On Rhetoric* 1403b). Thus the narrative of theatrical performance in Athens resists the dangerous potential of the dramatic script, specified in the *Phaedrus* as the potential for written texts to "tumble about everywhere." Illustrated by the fact that the script provides speaking parts for as many as three actors playing several roles, that potential is constrained by the authorizing body and voice of the playwright as a putative father.

Havelock believes that "surviving orality . . . explains why Greek literature to Euripides is composed as a performance, and in the language of performance."[117] This explanation seems somewhat circular, although Havelock acknowledges that orality survives in literary genres only as a performance. At the same time, the explanation raises the question of what the survival of "orality" really means. Havelock posits that its perseverance, by which he essentially means the oral transmission of cultural information in verse, validates a conventional set of moral and ethical behaviors in Greek culture. There are two objections to this proposition. First, survival in this analysis is misleading, because what survives in the literary tradition is mediated through the written text and is perhaps best described as an echo of what Havelock refers to as primary orality. Drama, in particular, may have "preserved the means by which primary orality controlled the ethos of its society through a repeated elocution of stored information, guidance preserved in living memories,"[118] but only if we ignore the fundamental formal and performance differences between drama and epic as the vehicle of primary orality. Havelock's theory tends to

---

116. I discuss the *Frogs* in chap. 5.
117. Havelock 1986, 93.
118. Havelock 1986, 94.

conflate epic and other poetic forms so that he can talk about the "continuing pressure [on the dramatic poets] to compose didactically for oral memorization." He notes the "crucial role played by the [tragic] choruses in the conservation of current tradition, communicated through the orality of song, dance, and melody," and concludes that "[t]he typicalization previously noted as characteristic of the Homeric narratives lasts on in Greek drama."[119] But even if it can be maintained that the choruses of Greek drama are routinely engaged in the "conservation of current tradition," it does not necessarily follow that they were composed for the purpose of facilitating the oral memorization of the themes and ideas they present. Choral lyrics vary widely in their intricate metrical and syntactical patterns, are very often imagistic or obscure to the modern reader,[120] and may have had only a single performance. They are therefore not comparable, either in form or in terms of performance practices, with epic as the repetitive vehicle of cultural memory.[121]

Second, the distinction between verse and prose that Havelock's

---

119. Havelock 1986, 15.

120. The contest between Aeschylus and Euripides at *Frogs* 1245 ff. suggests that dramatic lyrics were subject to controversy in the fifth century. At one point, Euripides attacks Aeschylus for composing lyrics that are monotonous insofar as they rely too heavily on dactylic rhythms (*Frogs* 1261–77). According to this comic critique, what is wanted in tragic lyrics is variation, not memory-enhancing repetition. See Dover 1993, ad loc.

121. Havelock (1986, 94) says that "repetitions of dramatic performances in the countryside were regular in Plato's day; he says so himself (*Rep.* 475d)." Socrates says, however, only that there are people who "have hired out their ears to hear all the choruses and run around to the Dionysiac festivals, leaving out neither those in the cities nor those in the towns" [ὥσπερ δὲ ἀπομεμισθωκότες τὰ ὦτα ἐπακοῦσαι πάντων χορῶν περιθέουσι τοῖς Διονυσίοις οὔτε τῶν κατὰ πόλεις οὔτε τῶν κατὰ κώμας ἀπολειπόμενοι]. The Rural Dionysia may have included reproductions of plays that had appeared earlier at the City Dionysia, but it is not clear that Socrates is referring to these reproductions. Even if such reproductions were frequent—and there is no evidence that they were—it does not follow that the tragic choruses were meant to be widely memorized. More to the point, the possibility that some dramas were reproduced does not support Havelock's general claim that drama is a manifestation of "primary orality." Certainly, the actors and chorus members memorized their lines. But this sort of memorization is not equivalent to the sort of cultural memorization Havelock speaks of. See Pickard-Cambridge 1968, 99–101.

formulation presupposes tends to obscure the issue, especially his notion that Plato put prose (coextensive with the advent of literacy) in competition with verse (coextensive with the survival of orality) on account of the persistent didactic efficacy of the latter. Havelock argues that Plato objected to the epic and tragic poets' "didactic function" and to "the authority that went with it."[122] In his view, the authority accorded the poets is a function of their verse, that is, the "spell" of orality, which Plato condemns as a necessary prelude to establishing his own authority in prose.[123] It seems clear that Plato recognizes the didactic authority of epic and tragic poetry, but his objection to them is not based on their shared poetic form. Rather, it relies on a distinction between registers of mimetic representation or impersonation, that is, on a distinction between mediated and direct, or first-person, speech. This distinction is summarized by Socrates as follows:

Ὀρθότατα, ἔφην, ὑπέλαβες, καὶ οἶμαί σοι ἤδη δηλοῦν ὃ ἔμπροσθεν οὐχ οἷός τ' ἦ, ὅτι τῆς ποιήσεώς τε καὶ μυθολογίας ἡ μὲν διὰ μιμήσεως ὅλη ἐστίν, ὥσπερ σὺ λέγεις, τραγῳδία τε καὶ κωμῳδία, ἡ δὲ δι' ἀπαγγελίας αὐτοῦ τοῦ ποιητοῦ—εὕροις δ' ἂν αὐτὴν μάλιστά που ἐν διθυράμβοις—ἡ δ' αὖ δι' ἀμφοτέρων ἔν τε τῇ τῶν ἐπῶν ποιήσει, πολλαχοῦ δὲ καὶ ἄλλοθι, εἴ μοι μανθάνεις.

["You have it exactly," I said, "and I think I make clear to you now what was not clear before, namely, that poetry and fables are

---

122. Havelock 1986, 8.

123. Cf. Havelock 1963, 208–9. The implicit assumption that prose is less amenable than verse to memorization is questionable. Certainly, verse is the conservative vehicle of cultural preservation or memory, and part of Socrates' critique of epic poetry is that it fosters rote memorization and precludes discussion and criticism (e.g., in the *Ion*). But this argument is also the basis of his critique of writing (e.g., in the *Phaedrus*). Thus, when Havelock links writing and prose in opposition to orality and verse in Plato and bases this opposition in large measure on Plato's objection to the primacy of oral memory, he occludes the Platonic correspondence between epic or oral poetry and written prose treatises: both "say the same thing" (*Phaedrus* 275d5 ff.; cf. *Ion* 532b2–7), and both foster rote memorization, as does the written speech of Lysias in the *Phaedrus*.

either wholly through imitation, as you say, in the case of tragedy and comedy, or through the report of the poet himself—you would find this best expressed in the dithyramb—or through both these techniques, as in the making of epic poetry and in many other examples too, if you understand me."] (*Republic* 394b8–c5)

Socrates makes a clear distinction between epic and drama, based on the degree to which they are produced through imitation or imperson-ation (διὰ μιμήσεως).[124] He goes on to criticize not the effect of poetry (as verse) or its content per se but the manner in which that content is performed. Speech that is "wholly through imitation," that is, speech in which a character speaks in his or her own (first) person, is the most politically and socially dangerous, because what one imitates in this way can become integrated into one's "habits and nature" [ἔθη τε καὶ φύσιν] (395d1–3). Socrates criticizes tragedy especially because, unlike epic, in which the mimetic pretense is mediated by those narrated interludes that come between the first-person speeches, drama is all impersonation or mimesis (ἁπλῇ διηγήσεις ἢ διὰ μιμήσεως, 392d5–6; cf. 394b3–c5). The absence of those interludes in dramatic performance, together with the distribution of first-person speeches among several actors, fosters the fragmentation of the speaking subject, who imitates anything and everything—including animals, women, and slaves (397a1–b2, 398a1–b4). This sort of pretense to direct speech has a nega-tive ethical consequence predicated on the absence of the fully autho-rized speaking subject; Socrates asks whether the guardians ought to be allowed to practice such imitation at all (ἢ οὐδὲ μιμεῖσθαι, 394d4). Of course, the content of that imitation is crucial: the first-person imitation of good men is morally defensible, while that of bad men is not (395c3–d1). As we have seen, first-person imitation must be restricted to the speech of men who are "brave, temperate, pious, [and] free" [ἀνδρείους, σώφρονας, ὁσίους, ἐλευθέρους] (*Republic* 395c3–5),[125] and this restriction thus defines the ideal bardic or dramatic performance in Socrates' ideal state.

But in practice bardic and dramatic performances allow—even

---

124. Cf. Havelock 1963, 8–11.
125. See the discussion of this passage in chap. 1.

require—the first-person imitation of all sorts of people, including women and slaves, "before a large audience" (397a4). What might be called the performance imperative of epic and especially dramatic poetry is the source of their dangerous potential in Plato. By convention, the bard and the actor speak their first-person lines out loud and in public. In contrast, and despite their dramatic form, the Platonic dialogues formally resist this imperative simply by virtue of the obvious fact that they are neither plays nor epic poems. They may have been read aloud in public, but in principle they are not acted, recited, or performed in public as are epic and drama. This difference, coupled with the irony that Plato adopts the very mimetic strategy he attacks, has focused much critical attention on Plato's choice of the dialogue form.

Like characters in a play, Socrates and his interlocutors in Plato's dialogues speak outside a third-person narrative (διήγησις) and free from the authorizing voice of a poet (cf. 394c2, δι' ἀπαγγελίας αὐτοῦ τοῦ ποιητοῦ). According to Havelock, "the continuing partnership of orality and literacy, ear and eye, required Plato, writing in the crucial moment of transition from one to the other, to reassert the primacy of speaking and hearing in personal oral response, even as he wrote."[126] Havelock is not clear, however, about what constitutes this partnership and why it should require Plato to reassert the primacy of oral speech.[127] Since Plato's dialogues are themselves a form of scripted speech, his indictment of first-person imitation appears to be disingenuous. Havelock's attempt to defend Plato against this charge by arguing for Plato's final reassertion of the primacy of orality seems to make sense, especially when we consider Socrates' arguments against writing in the *Phaedrus*. But both the charge and the defense ignore the fact that the dialogues employ a mimetic register fundamentally different from epic and drama which, for Havelock, exemplify oral culture. In principle, Plato's dialogues are nonperformance (or antiperformance) works produced in the absence of the speaking intermediaries (the bard and the actor) who are essential for the production of these "oral" genres. Plato's use of prose may counter the spell of

---

126. Havelock 1986, 111.

127. Cf. my earlier discussion of Scheid and Svenbro 1996, especially their notion of the epic narrator's "identification" with this audience.

poetry, as Havelock contends. But it also makes his dialogues closer to actual oral speech than the first-person speeches in verse found in epic and drama. This potential equivalence, however, only emphasizes the fact that reading (and not speaking/performing/reciting) is the primary means by which the dialogues are produced. Whether or not reading in antiquity was done silently or out loud, the absence of a bard or actor to give voice to the words of Socrates and his interlocutors effectively silences the oral tradition as a formal performance practice.

Plato's critique of writing and first-person imitation is not disingenuous, but neither do his dialogues reassert the primacy of orality. For, if orality is the ideal mode of human communication and transmission in archaic and classical Greek culture, Plato's dialogues represent the irrevocable loss of that ideal. The absence of the mediating voice of the poet, bard, or actor is the overt marker of that loss, despite—or perhaps because of—the embedded layers of direct and reported first-person speeches in the dialogues.[128] Without the benefit of oral performance, those speeches only endorse Socrates' condemnation of first-person mimesis. Such mimesis is arrested, if not overtly denied, in the dialogues. And the moral dilemma posed by Socrates' admonition that first-person imitation be restricted to the imitation of men who are "brave, temperate, pious, [and] free" is also forestalled. This conclusion raises several related questions: whether or not it is possible to imitate or impersonate Socrates, whether Socrates ought to be imitated at all, and, if so, who should imitate him. Put in these terms, Socrates becomes the test case for the use or abuse of first-person imitation in the dialogues. If such imitation signifies the absence and silence of the ideal and normative masculine subject, the Platonic dialogues testify not to the survival of orality but to its death, just as they testify to the death of Socrates. The Platonic critique of speech as imitation thus documents a persistent pretense to direct oral speech that finally signifies the irrevocable absence of the masculine subject who is "preeminent in battle and in speaking." From the epic poet to the bard to the actor to the philosopher, that subject gradually comes into view as the subject of loss, desire, and impersonation—in terms

---

128. See Halperin 1992 for an analysis of first-person speech as a signifier of absence—and hence of desire—in the *Symposium*.

of both speech acts and bodily acts. In this chapter, I have focused on the former, that is, on the concept of scripted speech as it signifies the lost proximity of *voice* and an essential identity in the critical history of Greek drama. In the next chapter, I introduce the concept of the theatrical body—modeled on the disguised body of Odysseus—as the expression of the lost proximity of the *body* and an essential identity in that history.

3

The Theatrical Body

In chapter 1, I suggested that the concept of spectatorship is not born with the institution of the dramatic festivals in the sixth century but develops in the context of earlier Greek literary and visual traditions in which representations of the human body invite the attention of a spectator. In this chapter I want to consider the ways in which such representations invite the attention of an implied spectator, and to suggest how that invitation is pertinent to our understanding of spectatorship in the Athenian theater. More specifically, I will be looking at the representation of the disguised body as the model for what I am calling the theatrical body.

As the primary locus of meaning and attention in Greek visual culture, the human body functions within a continuum of bodily display in which the nude body, the clothed body, and finally the disguised body—as a hyperbolically clothed body—are distinct categories. Conceived of as occupying a historical moment along this continuum, the theater focuses particular attention on this last category, that is, on the disguised body of the actor, which is at once displayed and concealed by his costume and mask. Occupying the other end of the continuum is Greek monumental sculpture, whose dominant subject is the nude male body.[1] Indeed, this nude male is

---

1. Nudity was a convention in Greek sculpture from the seventh century B.C.E. For a general discussion of sculptural conventions, see Woodford 1982, 20–23. Ridgway (1977, esp. 53–54) offers a detailed discussion of the nude male kouros. Cf. Sutton 1992, 21: "Male nudity was a common convention in Greek art which attracts little attention except when first encountered, whereas female nudes are rare in Archaic and Classical Greek art except in the private medium of vase painting. . . . Pervasive male nudity is one of the more peculiar conventions of Greek art, one that is not easily explained." In this Sutton follows Ridgway, who notes (54) that although this representational convention may reflect nudity in athletic contests, it cannot be convincingly argued that the palaestra dictates male nudity in the plastic arts.

the model from which other forms of bodily display differ or deviate. In this respect, the proposed continuum comprehends categories of bodily display not only in terms of clothing and its absence but also in terms of gender specificity.

Larissa Bonfante offers a wide-ranging discussion of the overt and persistent display of male nudity, which she calls a "Greek innovation."[2] She points out that there are various registers of nudity, depending on the age, class, and gender of the subject and on the context (religious, magic, or athletic) in which it is encountered. What emerges is a "definition of [nudity] as heroic, divine, athletic, and youthful for men; and something to be avoided for women" (Bonfante 1989, 549).[3] Moreover, where male nudity is on public display, it amounts to the corporeal manifestation of those virtues that define Greek masculinity, virtues that females obviously do not possess.[4] The monumental male nude thus functions within the context of an elite martial ethos that persists from the archaic to the classical periods. So even though it is clearly a sign of weakness in the epics for a warrior to be stripped bare of his armor—it even makes him like a woman (cf. *Iliad* 22.122–25)—what is stressed in these instances is the transition from an armed to an unarmed state.[5] The assimilation of a lack of physical strength and the absence of armor (as a form of nudity) is also culture specific. In his assessment of the Persians,

---

Homosociality or homoeroticism may be put forward as an explanation for the athletic and artistic conventions (Sutton 1992, 21), but doing so only seems to beg the question. Bonfante (1989, 552 ff.) notes that female nudity is attested in initiation rituals, but insofar as nudity was a civic or public practice, the male nude predominates. Ferrari (1993) notes that kouroi sometimes have features, such as earrings and hairstyles, that may have been thought of as feminine. She comes to the provocative conclusion that these features refer "to the feminine skin that [the young male citizen of descent] has just cast off" (106).

2. Bonfante 1989, 549.

3. Cf. Plato *Republic* 452a7–b5. After proposing that women and men are to be similarly educated in his new society, Socrates observes that it would be considered particularly laughable (γελοιότατον) to see women and men naked together in the gymnasia.

4. See Bonfante 1989, 554. Cf. Potts 1994, esp. chap. 5, for an illuminating account of Winckelmann's role in formulating the art historical discourse around the male nude in the Greek sculptural tradition.

5. See MacCary 1982, 153–56.

Herodotus states, "What chiefly did them harm was that they wore no armor over their clothing and fought, as it were, naked (γυμνῆτες) against men fully armed" (*Histories* 9.63).[6] For Herodotus, armor and its lack distinguish Greeks from Persians and testify to the superior fighting power of the (armed) Greeks. The Persians are "naked" insofar as they have no armor; hence they are also inferior fighters. Outside this conflict between armed and unarmed, however, and apart from the stigma of the warrior who is stripped of his armor, male nudity in Greek visual culture specifies a " 'spectatorial' vision [that] glorifies the masculine."[7]

Conversely, the female body is most often clothed in the sculptural tradition, and as if to illustrate a rationale for this convention, the sight of a naked female in the literary tradition often signals imminent danger for the male spectator. Herodotus' famous story of Gyges offers a variation within a fully developed political narrative (Herodotus *Histories* 1.8–12; cf. Plato *Republic* 359c–360b). As an illicit but unwilling spectator, Gyges is not killed for looking at the naked wife of Candaules but, as a result of that act of looking, is made to choose between killing Candaules or being killed himself. In an explanatory note, Herodotus adds that even barbarian *men* are ashamed to be seen naked (cf. Thucydides *History* 1.5–6). This shame denotes the absence of a concept of idealized male nudity among barbarians, an absence that negatively distinguishes them from Greeks. In this story, moreover, the barbarian prohibition against male nudity has its counterpart in the prohibition (both Greek and barbarian) against female nudity, with the result that barbarian men are implicitly compared to women: both must not be seen naked.[8] This comparison becomes

---

6. Priam speaks of the beauty of a fallen youth at *Iliad* 22.71–73. But the passage does not specify the youth's nudity as Bonfante (1989, 547–48) implies it does.

7. Hwa Yol Jung 1991. On ocularcentrism and patriarchy, see, among others, Fox Keller and Grontkowski 1982; Owens 1983; Clover 1987.

8. Cf. Bonfante 1989, 544: "As it developed, Greek nudity came to mark a contrast between Greek and non-Greek, and also between men and women." What emerges from Bonfante's discussion is that nudity is oppositional in terms of gender: for men it signifies greater strength and manliness, while for women it signifies greater weakness and femininity. Cf. Plato *Republic* 452a–e on the prohibition against female nudity. See also McDonnell's discussion (1991) of mixed-gender symposia on Etruscan vases. In the philosophical

clearer in the representation of the behaviors of the barbarian men, who clearly do not meet the requirements of Greek masculinity in the Gyges narrative. Candaules is too much interested in his wife, and Gyges is forced by tyrannical rulers to commit two shameful acts, that is, to see the queen naked and to kill the sleeping king (Herodotus *Histories* 1.12).[9] The general warning is clear: to see a woman's naked body is both desirable and dangerous for a male spectator. The barbarian context may distance that warning from Herodotus' Greek readers, but at the same time, it gives them a glimpse of what they, like Gyges, may see to their peril.[10]

For the classical period, Bonfante suggests that the "civic significance" of male nudity in art is verification of a "readiness to stand up and fight even though one knew one was vulnerable." She continues, "It has to do with military valor which requires risking one's life, being fully exposed."[11] Geddes rightly surmises, "Greek warriors probably never went into battle wearing only their helmets and shields, even though they are sometimes portrayed nude in art."[12] We can also surmise, I think, that portraying fighters in the nude (or

---

tradition (e.g., in Aristotle), female bodies are "less sinewy and less articulated" than men's bodies (καὶ ἀνευρότερον δὲ καὶ ἀναρθρότερον τὸ θῆλυ μᾶλλον, Aristotle *Historia Animalium* 538b7–8); that is, the Greek male body has defining physical characteristics—the male buttocks are often the object of visual focus in Attic pottery—while clothing or drapery gives definition to the female body, which is ostensibly less well formed. When male figures are clothed on Attic vases, their clothing is often less elaborate and seems more likely to fall open than does the women's clothing. See, for example, figures 1.5A and B and 1.6 (vases from the mid-fifth century B.C.E.) reproduced in Sutton 1992, 17–20. See also Hollander 1978, chap. 1. Zweig (1992, 85–87), argues that the mute, nude female on the comic stage signifies the position of women as objects of the male gaze. It is uncertain, however, whether these nude mute roles were played by women. I argue, moreover, that in the Greek context, clothing is more convincingly a signifier of women's object status than is nudity. See Pickard-Cambridge 1968, 153 n. 1.

9. Cf. Plato *Republic* 452c. See McDonnell 1991; Bonfante 1989, 557. Gyges' reign is long but not especially noteworthy (see Herodotus *Histories* 1.14–15).

10. See duBois 1996, 132–33.

11. Bonfante 1989, 556. Although Bonfante asserts that nudity had been an expression of "vulnerability" before the classical period, her discussion does not bear this out—even if we consider nudity in initiation practices.

12. Geddes 1987, 308.

attired only in helmets and shields) is appropriate because it signifies an idealized masculinity; and here we might think of the Athenian pyrrhic, or armed, dance, which was performed "nude" at the Panathenaia.[13] Thus idealized male nudity is again not as much an acknowledgment of vulnerability in the face of an enemy as it is an overdetermined signifier of *in*vulnerability in the construction of Greek masculine identity. As a consequence, the plastic, or sculptural, presentation of the fully exposed male expresses an analogy similar to that which I have described between direct, man-to-man communication and man-to-man fighting, an analogy based on a visually manifested bodily presence. If armor and idealized male nudity are isomorphic cultural signifiers in Greek culture, we can conclude that the public display of the nude male body is framed within an ideology of martial virtue. Offering a succinct metaphor, Martha Nussbaum observes that "nudity, for the Greeks, was the dress of personhood."[14] The metaphor attests to the notion that the male body hides nothing, that there is no discrepancy between what is seen, that is, the full external view of the perfect human form, and what is not seen, that is, the internal perfection of human virtue. But if Greek "personhood" is specified in the male warrior and if nudity is the *metaphorical* dress of personhood, then armor is its literal analog; that is, armor is the *literal* dress of personhood.

Beginning with the epic arming scenes, armor generally has a nice ontological fit in Greek literature and history; it signifies the

---

13. See Bonfante 1989, 555; Lissarrague 1984, 37, fig. 54; Winkler 1990a, 55–57. On the evidence for "naked dances," or *gymnopaidia*, in Sparta, see Ferrari 1993, 103. On the *pyrrhica*, see Aristophanes *Clouds* 988–89; Plato *Laws* 815a; Lysias 22.1.

14. Nussbaum 1995, 32. Dover (1989, 70) observes: "Naked males greatly outnumber naked females in archaic and early classical vase-painting. In depicting the female figure the painter sometimes observes the differences of configuration between the male and the female pelvis. . . . On many occasions, however, the male and female bodies are distinguishable only by the presence or absence of the breasts and the external genitals." Female figures were assimilated to male figures in the iconographic conventions of archaic and early classical vase painting. Dover maintains that in the fifth century, however, men were "increasingly assimilated to women" (71). This means not necessarily that what were perceived to be female body types had become more aesthetically valued but that males with those body types had.

aggrandized militarism of the class of warrior-kings who wear it.
Passed down from father to son, a hero's armor is in fact a primary
marker of the correspondence between male attire and male identity.
So, for example, when Patroclus puts on Achilles' armor at *Iliad*
16.40–43, he can be mistaken for his friend. It can be argued, of
course, that armor here is precisely not a clear marker of identity, or
rather that it leads to mistaken identity. But in this very crucial
exchange, the two heroes share what might be called a dyadic identity, with the armor signifying their status as brothers in arms. Similarly, when Poseidon orders the Achaeans to exchange armor so that
the best fighters will have the best equipment (*Iliad* 14.371–77), the
point is that armor unambiguously identifies its wearer according to
his capabilities as a fighter. In a very different context, this point is
suggested by Xenophon, who, in his fourth-century account of the
March of the Ten Thousand, notes the need for a man going into
battle to be as beautifully outfitted as possible.

ἐκ τούτου Ξενοφῶν ἀνίσταται ἐσταλμένος ἐπὶ πόλεμον ὡς
ἐδύνατο κάλλιστα, νομίζων, εἴτε νίκην διδοῖεν οἱ θεοί, τὸν
κάλλιστον κόσμον τῷ νικᾶν πρέπειν, εἴτε τελευτᾶν δέοι, ὀρθῶς
ἔχειν τῶν καλλίστων ἑαυτὸν ἀξιώσαντα ἐν τούτοις τῆς τελευτῆς
τυγχάνειν.

[At this point, Xenophon got up, arrayed for war as beautifully
as possible. For he thought that if the gods should give him
victory, the finest adornment was fitting for victory; and if it
should be necessary for him to die, he thought it right that,
having accounted himself worthy of the most beautiful attire, he
meet his death in this attire.] (*Anabasis* 3.2.7)

Here battle dress signals to his opponent that the wearer deserves
either the beauty of victory or an honorable death in battle. In other
words, within the persistent Greek privileging of martial valor (from
the archaic period to the fourth century), splendid battle attire clearly
reflects the expectations of the male who wears it and the male who
sees it.[15] Military dress (like male nudity) is a principal signifier of

---

15. The rule is proven by the countertradition expressed by Archilochus
frag. 6 (Diehl), for example.

Greek masculinity and the model against which all male attire is judged.

This argument seems to be borne out by what is known about everyday male dress codes in Athens, that is, outside the context of military dress codes. In the classical period, ostentatious male clothing is specifically associated with the weakness or effeminacy of foreigners—as proved by their acceptance of tyranny, for example—while simple, coarse clothing (a Dorian look) speaks of the poverty that was supposed to promote masculine toughness, especially the toughness required for military service. Ostentatious clothing, with its attendant gender-, ethnic-, and class-specific connotations, distinguishes men lacking in martial valor from men whose bravery and toughness mark them as ideal males. To put the matter more succinctly, men who do not conform to the Greek masculine ideal dress like women or foreigners.[16] The elite male's preference for an unostentatious appearance, one that is equated with military toughness, can thus be understood as an antidote to the effeminacy and barbarism connected with ostentatious clothing.[17] In more general terms, when masculine prerogatives are in jeopardy, vestimentary codes play a role. According to those codes, military or military-like attire and nudity represent seemingly opposite but actually complementary positions on the continuum of bodily display.

The most flagrant transgression of these codes is expressed in the practice of cross-dressing, that is, when men wear women's clothing. As part of ritual practice, cross-dressing (both male and female) is generally explained as preparatory to assuming a new role in society. References to ritual cross-dressing—although scattered in the sources—point to the significance of gender-specific clothing, as opposed to some other cultural artifact, for distinguishing and establishing social norms.[18] In general terms, cross-dressing represents a

---

16. See the story of Callias, son of Cratias, who is nicknamed "the Mede" and is caricatured in Persian clothing on an ostracon. The Spartan general Pausanias is said to have "dressed in Median clothing" (Thucydides *History* 1.130) and played the Persian. Both stories are cited by Hall (1989, 59, 204). On Pausanias, see Blamire 1970. Cf. Herodotus' story of the Scythian Scyles (*Histories* 4.78–80), discussed in chap. 5.

17. See Geddes 1987.

18. On nudity as an initiation practice, see Bonfante 1989, 551–53; cf. Burkert 1985, 261–63.

transgression of those norms enacted in the display of the body and presented to a viewing public. Whatever the effect of cross-dressing on the initiate, ritual cross-dressing is by definition a public performance whose effect on the spectators offers a theoretical point of view from which to analyze its social functions. Looked at in terms of social or ritual reality, we may never know what that effect may have been. We have a better chance of understanding it in the context of those mythological narratives where cross-dressing is featured—for example, in the stories in which Achilles, Ajax, and Heracles are dressed as women. In these cases, wearing women's clothing signifies adult heroic identity at risk, while appeals to the nature of the opposite sex are less convincing.[19] Clothing is less a marker of nature (or its transgression) than a marker of social position and gender identity (or their transgression).

I have talked about some of the ways in which male nudity and men in armor represent analogous and idealized displays of the masculine body in Greek culture. I turn now to a consideration of women's clothing, to lay the foundation for understanding disguise—and the notion of the theatrical body—as a gender-specific phenomenon. In general, women's clothing is ontologically and epistemologically suspect throughout the Greek literary tradition. Pandora, the first woman, is both beautiful in external form *(eidos)* and elaborately dressed (Hesiod *Works and Days* 54 ff.). But her form and her clothes conceal, as it were, the lies and the deceitful nature that Hermes fashions within her (τεῦξε ἐν στήθεσσι, 77).[20] As Pandora's descendant, the Spartan Helen shares some of these attributes.[21] The suspicious nature of women's clothing is not restricted to early didactic and epic poetry, however. Passages from Aristophanic comedy demonstrate its persistence into the fifth century. It might be objected that

---

19. See Delcourt 1958, chap. 1, on sexual disguise or cross-dressing (i.e., that of Achilles, Ajax, Heracles) in the context of myth and ritual practices. Also, Vidal-Naquet 1983, 114–17. On Heracles, see also Loraux 1990 and Burkert 1985, 258–61. Dover (1989, 76) comments on a passage from Aeschines 1 *(Against Timarchus)* in which Demosthenes is ridiculed for wearing clothing that is indistinguishable from women's clothing: "Here 'unmanliness' and feminine clothes are unmistakably linked with passive homosexuality, and indirectly with feminine physique."
20. See Pucci 1977, esp. chap. 4.
21. On Helen's *eidolon*, see Bassi 1993.

comic transvestitism and hyperbole overdetermine any conclusions about women's clothing as a cultural signifier.[22] But comic hyperbole does not negate the significance of the belief or practice subjected to exaggeration or ridicule; if anything, it proves the audience's familiarity with the nonhyperbolic form of the belief or practice being scrutinized in the comic performance. Consequently, comic cross-dressing is one of the most vivid expressions of the significance of female clothing in Greek culture.

The *Lysistrata* illustrates the possibilities inherent in this conclusion. At the beginning of the play, Lysistrata tells Calonice that their clothing will take the fighting spirit out of their soldier husbands and that, as a result, the women of Greece will save their homeland.

Κα. τί δ᾽ ἂν γυναῖκες φρόνιμον ἐργασαίατο
ἢ λαμπρόν, αἳ καθήμεθ᾽ ἐξηνθισμέναι,
κροκωτοφοροῦσαι καὶ κεκαλλωπισμέναι
καὶ Κιμμερίκ᾽ ὀρθοστάδια καὶ περιβαρίδας;
Λυ. ταῦτ᾽ αὐτὰ γάρ τοι κἄσθ᾽ ἃ σώσειν προσδοκῶ,
τὰ κροκωτίδια καὶ τὰ μύρα χαἰ περιβαρίδες
χἠγχουσα καὶ τὰ διαφανῆ χιτώνια.
Κα. τίνα δὴ τρόπον ποθ᾽; *Λυ.* ὥστε τῶν νῦν μηδένα
ἀνδρῶν ἐπ᾽ ἀλλήλοισιν αἴρεσθαι δόρυ,—
Κα. κροκωτὸν ἄρα νὴ τὼ θεὼ ᾽γὼ βάψομαι.
Λυ. μηδ᾽ ἀσπίδα λαβεῖν,— *Κα.* Κιμμερικὸν[23] ἐνδύσομαι.
Λυ. μηδὲ ξιφίδιον. *Κα.* κτήσομαι περιβαρίδας.

[*Ca.* How can we women do something so conspicuously clever,
we who are accustomed to sit at home
and adorn ourselves with saffron gowns
and loose Cimmerian robes and slippers?
Lys. These are the very things that I think will save [Greece,]
putting on saffron gowns and myrrh and slippers
and diaphanous robes.

22. On cross-dressing in comedy and especially in the *Lysistrata*, see Foley 1982–83, 13 with n. 28 and Taaffe 1991.

23. Κιμμερικόν or Κιμβερικόν. In either case, the reference is obscure, but Cimmerian is clearly synonymous with foreign (cf. Herodotus *Histories* 4.11–13). See Stone 1977, 178.

Ca. How? *Lys.* So that no man will lift a lance against others . . .
Ca. I'll have my tunic dyed saffron, by the two Goddesses.
Lys. . . . nor take hold of a shield . . . *Ca.* I shall put on my
   Cimmerian gown.
Lys. . . . nor a little sword. *Ca.* I'll get a pair of slippers.]
                                             (*Lysistrata* 42–53)

Here women's clothing is explicitly presented as a means of making
friends of men who are enemies, by igniting their shared sexual desire
and thereby neutralizing their desire for war.[24] There is also a delicious
irony in the fact that insofar as these women are male actors in female
costume, men in this play indeed do not so naturally (i.e., according to
cultural norms) "wield the lance or take up the shield and sword."
Instead, they put on women's clothing and threaten to strip the fighting men of their fighting spirit by additional enhancements to their
feminine appearance. The quick juxtaposition of Lysistrata's assertions ("no man . . . will lift a lance . . .") with Calonice's answers
("I'll have my tunic dyed saffron . . .")—especially where the assertion and the answer constitute a single line of verse—illustrates
the way in which gender confusion is simultaneously vestimentary
confusion in the play.[25] Lysistrata's statements about what men will
not do is exemplified, as it were, by Calonice's assertions about what
she will wear.

   As a whole, the play toys with the bodies of the male actors. This
toying is perhaps best illustrated when Lysistrata tells the women that
they must abstain (or keep away) from the penis (ἀφεκτέα τοίνυν
ἐστὶν ἡμῖν τοῦ πέους, 124). Despite their earlier vows to secure peace
at any cost, the women refuse to give up the πέος: Calonice would
rather walk through fire (134). And Myrrhine, who had previously
said she would be willing to "cut herself in half" like a flatfish for the

------

24. Produced in 411 B.C.E., the *Lysistrata* seems to ridicule the possibility of
an Athenian victory. See Westlake 1980. On the play in general, see Konstan
1993.

25. For a discussion of clothing and gender ambiguity on vases, see
Frontisi and Lissarrague 1990, with Kurke 1992. See also Taaffe 1991 on incomplete gender disguise in comedy. More general studies of clothing and cross-
dressing include Hollander 1978 and Garber 1992. It is difficult to imagine
what the representation of neutral or culturally unmarked clothing might
look like; clothing always says something about the wearer.

sake of peace (115), wants nothing to do with Lysistrata's injunction (130). Myrrhine's refusal to comply is of special interest; for her, it seems that abstaining from the penis is worse than being cut in half. Being cut in half may have been part of a familiar joke in the fifth century or a familiar way of swearing loyalty. Most conspicuously, it forms the basis of Aristophanes' story of sexual object choice in Plato's *Symposium* (189c2 ff.).[26] According to the Aristophanes of Plato's dialogue, there were originally three kinds (γένη) of human beings: man, woman, and androgyne. Each was a round creature, with eight limbs, two faces, and two sets of genitals. But because of their terrible violence against the gods, Zeus cuts them in half, with the result that each half desired sexual intercourse with his or her other half.

My point is not that Plato had the scene from the *Lysistrata* in mind but that his Aristophanic story is suggestive of the way in which the threat of being cut in half has multiple meanings in the erotic and anatomically explicit context of the *Lysistrata*. On the level of the plot, Myrrhine's unwillingness to keep away from the penis is an expression of her sexual desire for men. But the reference to being cut in half— together with the actor's transvestitism—complicates this straightforward expression of heterosexual desire. The complication arises first of all because erotic desire is predominantly male desire in classical Greek culture. David Halperin observes that the gender system of classical Athens constructed male desire as "wide ranging, acquisitive, and object-directed," while it constructed female desire (in opposition to male desire) as "objectless, passive and entirely determined by the female body's need for regular phallic irrigation."[27] That female desire in Aristophanes' plays is "wide ranging, acquisitive, and object-directed" is a function of comic inversion but at the same time gestures to the bodily presence of the male actor beneath his female costume. Thus the characters' unwillingness to keep away from the penis in the

---

26. Henderson (1987, ad loc.) notes the shared use of the simile and that it "seems to refer to the practice of cutting sacrificial victims in two." On Aristophanes' speech, see Cohen 1991; Nussbaum 1986; Halperin 1986, 1990; Boswell 1980; Goldhill 1995.

27. Halperin 1990, 36. It should be noted that female desire can take the form of aggressive sexuality, e.g. in Semonides 7. But aggressive female sexuality is condemned.

Lysistrata makes reference to the actor's unwillingness (distinguished from that of his female character) to lose that part of his own anatomy. In the (homo)erotic economy of classical Athens, it is also, if less overtly, a reference to his unwillingness to deny the desire for his other (male) half: in each instance, the threat of being cut in half applies.[28]

In the play, the penis is both prominently displayed in the *phalloi* of the male characters and hidden, as it were, beneath the costumes of the female characters—costumes that wear thin throughout the play.[29] We might even say that the threat of losing or losing control over the penis as an anatomical member and as a prop is the primary focus of the plot. That threat is played out both visually and symbolically, by the actors' putting on and taking off women's garments and by the related enactment of what can only be called the male characters' hyperphallic impotence. Whether conceived of as a dramatic costume or as everyday articles of clothing (as when Myrrhine does her striptease for Cinesias, at *Lysistrata* 920 ff.), female clothing operates in an omni-erotic male fantasy in which the objects of male desire are at once women (as fictional characters desired by male characters), men (as fictional characters desired by female characters), and men dressed as women (as male actors implicitly desired by other male actors). There are, of course, no real women in this scheme, so women as object choices—and as desiring subjects—only exist in the play's mimetic frame. Within that frame and as a principal signifier in the play, women's clothing (as costume or

---

28. Since it seems likely that all roles were played by adult males on the Attic stage (as depicted on the Pronomos Vase, e.g.), the representation of male desire I am suggesting here is antithetical to normative male desire in classical Athens. Cf. Halperin 1990, 30: "Hence, an adult, male citizen of Athens can have legitimate sexual relations only with statutory minors (his inferiors not in age but in social and political status): the proper targets of his sexual desire include, specifically, women, boys, foreigners, and slaves." This fact does not argue against my suggestion, however, since the implicit desire between male actors would be most appropriate for comic ridicule, especially because it is disguised (so to speak) as female desire. Cf. Halperin 1990, 20–21, on Aristophanes' spherical creatures in the *Symposium*: "Although his genetic explanation of the diversity of sexual object-choice among human beings would seem to require that there be some adult males who are sexually attracted to other adult males, Aristophanes appears to be wholly unaware of such a possibility, and in any case he has left no room for it in his taxonomic scheme."

29. See Taaffe 1993.

disguise) is responsible for its successful outcome; in the end, martial aggression, with its homosocial and homoerotic underpinnings, is redirected into hetero-erotic desire, and the ideal soldier-citizen simultaneously loses his political and military dominance.[30] If this sort of subversion is to be expected in comedy, its vehicle is female clothing.

In a different but relevant context in the fourth century, Xenophon's Ischomachus chastises his wife for wearing makeup, clothing, and shoes that conceal her true form and stature—thereby giving an ironic twist to the Pandora paradigm and to the convention of dramatic transvestitism (*Oeconomicus* 10.2 ff.).[31] While not specifying a contradiction between his wife's inner character and what she wears, Ischomachus' advice makes reference to a common belief in the potentially deceptive nature of a woman's external appearance; his rhetoric relies on the lexicon of concealment (ἀποκρύπτω), deception, and trickery (ἐξαπατάω, ἀπάται).[32] But of even greater interest is the way in which he reproves his wife's cosmetic adornments by way of the counterexample of his own body.

Πότερως ἂν οὖν, ἔφην ἐγώ, τοῦ σώματος αὖ δοκοίην εἶναι ἀξιοφίλητος μᾶλλον κοινωνός, εἴ σοι τὸ σῶμα πειρώμην παρέχειν τὸ ἐμαυτοῦ ἐπιμελόμενος ὅπως ὑγιαινόν τε καὶ ἐρρωμένον ἔσται, καὶ διὰ ταῦτα τῷ ὄντι εὔχρως σοι ἔσομαι, ἢ εἴ σοι μίλτῳ ἀλειφόμενος καὶ τοὺς ὀφθαλμοὺς ὑπαλειφόμενος ἀνδρεικέλῳ ἐπιδεικνύοιμί τε ἐμαυτὸν καὶ συνείην ἐξαπατῶν σε καὶ παρέχων ὁρᾶν καὶ ἅπτεσθαι μίλτου ἀντὶ τοῦ ἐμαυτοῦ χρωτός;

[Therefore, I said, how should I seem more worthy of the affection that comes from our bodily union, by attempting to present my body to you taking care that it is in a healthy and strong

---

30. On homoeroticism as the basis of military success, see the speech of Phaedrus in the *Symposium* (178e3–179b3).

31. On this passage in Xenophon, see Pomeroy 1994, 304–6. It is interesting to note that when Western journalists wish to compliment a film actress in contemporary interviews, they frequently report that she is plainly dressed and not wearing makeup; such comments are rarely, if ever, made about male actors.

32. See also the story of the Spartan women who trick their kinsmen by trading clothes with their husbands (Herodotus *Histories* 4.145–46).

condition so that I shall be of good complexion in fact? Or should I show myself to you smeared with red paint and with flesh-tone under my eyes, should I have intercourse with you like that, deceiving you and causing you to see and to touch red paint instead of my own flesh?] (10.5)

The answer Ischomachus obviously expects indicates that he considers such enhancements unnecessary and at odds with the view he holds of what is appropriate for the masculine body. For his body to appear to be what he considers genuine or real (τῷ ὄντι), it must be unadorned. As part of this cosmological prohibition, Ischomachus compares his wife's deceitful adornments to imaginary household property and counterfeit silver (ἀργύριον κίβδηλον, 10.3).[33] The implied simile, that is, that a wife who enhances her appearance is like imaginary property and counterfeit money, assumes both that she is her husband's property and that her body functions metaphorically for the *oikos*. It also suggests that her body signifies the always present possibility that her husband is in possession of illusory and fraudulent goods, while, in contrast, his own genuine body guarantees his economic worth by virtue of possessing and disciplining her body.

Another sort of vestimentary discipline is found in Solon's social legislation, which is reported by Plutarch to have done away with women's disorderly and intemperate behavior in public by, among other things, prohibiting them from going outdoors wearing more than three garments.[34]

᾽Επέστησε δὲ καὶ ταῖς ἐξόδοις τῶν γυναικῶν καὶ τοῖς πένθησι καὶ ταῖς ἑορταῖς νόμον ἀπείργοντα τὸ ἄτακτον καὶ ἀκόλαστον· ἐξιέναι μὲν ἱματίων τριῶν μὴ πλέον ἔχουσαν κελεύσας, μηδὲ βρωτὸν ἢ ποτὸν πλείονος ἢ ὀβολοῦ φερομένην, μηδὲ κάνητα

---

33. Earlier in the dialogue, Socrates had attributed a "manly mind" to Ischomachus' wife for her willingness to look after the household possessions (τὴν ἀνδρικὴν διάνοιαν, *Oeconomicus* 10.1).

34. Else (1965, 74–76) connects Solon's funerary legislation with the *threnoi* of tragedy and suggests that tragic performances may have reinforced Solon's legislation by replacing the ostentatious funerary display of the elite with the opportunity for communal grief for the tragic hero. See also Segal 1994a.

πηχυαίου μείξονα, μηδὲ νύκτωρ πορεύεσθαι πλὴν ἁμάξῃ
κομιζομένην λύχνου προφαίνοντος.

[He also subjected the public appearances of women, their mourning, and their festivals to a law that did away with disorder and license. When they went out, they were not to wear more than three garments, they were not to carry more than an obol's worth of food or drink or a mat more than a cubit long, and they were not to travel about by night unless they rode in a wagon with a lamp to light the way.] (Plutarch *Life of Solon* 21.4)

The regulation seems to have been aimed at curtailing ostentation among the wealthy classes; its dress code specifies how women's clothes in particular are potentially dangerous or disruptive in the city, and in Plutarch's text this ostentation is implicitly an indicator of women's unruly behavior.[35] Here an excess of women's clothing reveals, rather than conceals, their true nature.

Thus, in contrast to the isomorphism that characterizes masculine vestimentary and ontological codes (including male nudity), female clothing and adornment signifies deceptiveness and an ambiguous relationship between one's inner being and outer appearance. As we have seen, this phenomenon functions on several levels of cultural analysis—martial, sexual, economic, and legal—and in a variety of genres and historical contexts. In examples from authors as diverse as Hesiod, Aristophanes, Herodotus, Xenophon, and Plutarch, clothing is encoded as feminine in Greek culture, and women's clothing in particular is encoded as dangerously, if not inherently, deceptive.[36] It

---

35. Both ἄτακτος and ἀκόλαστος are used to describe military troops in disarray. Cf. Herodotus *Histories* 6.93. At Herodotus 3.81, Megbyzus describes democracy as rule by the "unruly mob" (δῆμος ἀκόλαστος), suggesting that the adjective may also have been class specific.

36. See my discussion of weaving in chap. 2. See also Geddes 1987, 317. Clothing is also a marker of domesticity and hospitality (e.g., in the *Odyssey*; see Block 1985 for the relevant passages). Mention should also be made of the importance of clothing attended to by women in religious festivals—e.g., the *peplos* of Athena in the Panathenaea (see Parke 1977, 38–41). Herodotus (*Histories* 4.67) tells the story of the Scythian (i.e., barbarian) ἀνδρογύναι who, according to Hippocrates, put on women's clothes and thereby "played the woman" (*Airs, Waters, Places* 22). See also Herodotus' story (*Histories* 5.87) of

is worth noting too that the distinguishing characteristics of women are luxuriousness and weakness and that clothing is revelatory of these traits at least as early as the mid–sixth century (i.e., among the Ionians).[37] But more to the point, women's clothing is consistently associated with dissimulation and deception in the eyes of a male spectator. The convention of idealized male nudity in the visual tradition thus constitutes a denial of the dangerous potential of clothing as feminine adornment.

As a medium of deception, women's clothing is closely aligned with overt disguise on the continuum of bodily display referred to earlier, even when it is not the medium of such disguise (as it is in the case of dramatic cross-dressing). And conversely, the adoption of any overt disguise is aligned with feminine subjectivity. The most conspicuous examples of overt disguisings are found in the dramatic texts, where they constitute a recurring plot device. They include Menelaus disguised as the shipwrecked sailor in Euripides' *Helen*, Pentheus dressed as a maenad in the *Bacchae*, Dionysus disguised as a mortal in the same play, Dionysus disguised as his slave (and vice versa) in Aristophanes' *Frogs*, Euripides and his Relation disguised as women in the *Thesmophoriazousae*, and women disguised as men in the *Ecclesiazousae*. In the plots of these plays, disguise or costumed role playing signifies a radical change of status in which the integrity or constancy of the masculine subject—as the model subject—is at risk. In general, disguise signifies the vulnerability of that subject, often as a means of repositioning and redefining it against those mar-

---

the Athenians who compelled the women of Athens to switch from Dorian to Ionian dress and his story of Periander, who stripped the women of Corinth of their clothing and offered it up to his dead wife, Melissa (5.92). Ferris (1990, 28) argues that in Attic drama "women" *are* clothing: "Thus the drama limits and reduces its imagined women to items of clothing and attributes of adultery. The clothes are the women and the clothes that stand for them are instrumental to their well-practiced deceit. Men, however, expand, develop, grow and celebrate through their costume-sign, the phallus."

37. Geddes (1987, 317–20) discusses the Near Eastern antecedents to Greek clothing and the association of Ionian clothing in particular with "luxury and weakness." He offers Asios frag. 13 (Kinkel) and Xenophanes frag. 3 (J.M. Edmonds, *Elegy and Iambus*, vol. i.194) as evidence for this association as early as the seventh and sixth centuries B.C.E. See also duBois 1996, chap. 8, on Sappho and "Asianism."

ginalized others (women, slaves, and barbarians) who pose a potential threat to the sexual, political, and social order.[38]

In the famous contest between Aeschylus and Euripides in the *Frogs*, we are offered a glimpse of disguise as a feature of contemporary social and political life. Aeschylus charges Euripides with dressing his kings in rags (ῥάκια, *Frogs* 1063) with the result that the rich citizen "wraps himself in rags and complains, saying that he is poor," to shirk his civic duties (1066).[39] It is perhaps the case, as some commentators on the *Frogs* suggest, that the business about the rich man who wishes to avoid his liturgies reflects the tight wartime economy in fifth-century Athens.[40] Making use of comic hyperbole, Aristophanes thus attributes to the influence of Euripides' plays a practice that had cultural currency, whether or not rich Athenian citizens actually

---

38. A conflation of women, barbarians, and slaves whose dangerous and subversive natures are reified in their bodies is illustrated in Herodotus' description of the Scythian (i.e., barbarian) women who marry their slaves while their husbands are away on a mission of military conquest (*Histories* 4.1). On the husbands' return, the offspring of these unions wage war against them, and although the slave-born children are not successful, the story affirms a fear of women who are capable of producing offspring dangerous to the male ruling class. Cf. How and Wells 1968, on 4.3: "The idea of a slave-born class becoming dangerous is common in Greek tradition." Cf. Xenophon *Oeconomicus* 3.1–11 (where slaves, animals, and women are implicitly equated). The standard article on the feminine in Greek drama is Zeitlin 1990a. On the sexual and political dominance of elite males, see Halperin 1990, 30–33.

39. According to Geddes (1987, 331), the reference in the *Frogs* reflects social reality: "There was now [in the fifth-century] . . . every incentive for a rich man to conceal his wealth, to render it invisible and so retain the power of disposing it. In these circumstances he would be unlikely to wear it conspicuously." Geddes maintains that the adoption of the poor or Dorian look by the elite was an egalitarian gesture, that it operated in a social economy that condemned private expenditure, and that it stood for a willingness to honor public expenditure rather than an attempt to avoid it. Although Geddes does not make the connection, the joke is that Euripides' plays make men dress poorly in order not to undertake public expenditures. It may also indicate that those schooled in the Euripidean school of fashion went too far; a man could opt for a "poor but honest" look, but he should not dress like a beggar. For a relevant discussion of Aristophanes' parodic adaptation of Euripides' *Telephus* in the *Acharnians* and the *Thesmophoriazousae*, see Muecke 1982.

40. See Stanford 1968, ad loc.

disguised themselves as poor men.[41] That this practice was a persistent object of sociopolitical critique is illustrated in an observation made by Isocrates in the fourth century.

> When I was a boy, being rich was considered so secure and honorable that almost everyone pretended [προσεποιοῦντο] he owned more property than he actually did possess, because he wanted to enjoy the reputation [δόξα] it gave. Now, however, one has to defend oneself against being rich as if it were the worst of crimes . . . ; for it has become far more dangerous to give the impression of being well-to-do [τὸ δοκεῖν εὐπορεῖν] than to commit open crime; criminals are let off altogether or given trivial punishments, but the rich are completely ruined. (Isocrates 15.159–60)[42]

Isocrates' description of the way things used to be in the good old days is clearly self-interested. Nonetheless, together with the passage from the *Frogs* noted earlier, his description of dissimulation for political and economic advantage is compelling. Writing in 354–353 B.C.E., when he was in his eighties (Isocrates 15.9), Isocrates is looking back perhaps to the decade of 430–420 B.C.E. It seems plausible that as the Peloponnesian War went on, financial demands on the wealthier citizens increased, so that by the time of the production of the *Frogs* (405 B.C.E.) and continuing down to the time of Isocrates' old age, scenes of feigned poverty (like Euripides' rich man in rags) were common in civic life. But even if this hypothesis cannot be historically substantiated, these passages attest to a dramatic change in the representation

---

41. Dover (1993, 17) doubts that any "burning sincerity on Aristophanes' part inspired Aeschylus' claims that Euripides' portrayal of 'kings in rags' encouraged avoidance of liturgies," but he admits that such a topic could "arouse genuine anxiety." Cf. Taaffe 1991, 107, on the *Ecclesiazousae*: "His [Aristophanes'] serious statements to the citizens of Athens are that imposters can rule if allowed, that costumes change only appearances, and that political power can be won with the same persuasive tactics of illusion and artifice employed by actors."

42. This passage is cited by de Ste. Croix (1981, 297). Cf. Isocrates 7.31–35, where it is stated that, in the time of Solon and Cleisthenes, no one had to conceal (ἀπεκρύπτετο) his wealth. See also Ober 1989, 219–21.

of class affiliation in Athens after the 420s: rich men wanted to imitate poor men, rather than the other way round.

While disguise per se is not mentioned by Isocrates, avoiding the appearance of doing well in public (τὸ δοκεῖν εὐπορεῖν) can only be effected by appearing to be poor, that is, by adopting the sort of disguise to which Aristophanes refers in the *Frogs*. This change constitutes a reversal in the mimetic order in Athenian culture; it exemplifies in economic and class-specific terms the antithesis of what Plato and Aristotle called for in ethical terms, namely, the injunction to imitate good men rather than worthless men and women. As de Ste. Croix points out, economic status was not distinguished from ethical behavior in Greek civic ideology.

> The Greeks, from archaic times through the Classical and Hellenistic periods and on into the Roman age, habitually expressed political complexion and social status in a fascinating vocabulary which is an inextricable mixture of socio-economic and moral terminology, with two sets of terms applied more or less indiscriminately to the propertied and the non-propertied classes respectively. On the one hand we have not only words which mean property-owning, rich, fortunate, distinguished, well-born, influential, but also, as alternatives for virtually the same set of people, words having a basically moral connotation and meaning literally the good, the best, the upright, the fair-minded, and so forth. And on the other hand we find applied to the lower classes, the poor, who are also the Many, the mob, the populace, words with an inescapably moral quality, meaning essentially bad. (de Ste. Croix 1981, 425–26)

Based on dominant ethical criteria that translate into economic and political distinctions and advantages, the reversal described by Isocrates is tantamount to a sociopolitical transvestitism in which the need to appear poor is a sign of the moral and political decay of the city. This dangerous transvestitism is the same sort as that alluded to by Aeschylus in his charge against Euripides in the *Frogs*. That rich men go around town in rags pretending to be poor is only a piece of a larger argument in the play in which the older poet accuses the younger of weakening the ethical, moral, and martial spirit of Athens' citizens.[43] In the fifth and fourth centuries, then, there exists a social and political rhetoric in which bodily disguise—whether or not it is modeled on dramatic impersonation—is dangerous and subversive. And implicit in this rhetoric is a nostalgic desire for the good old days when good men could be recognized in the street for who they "really" were.

But the significance of disguise as a cultural practice, whether in the context of a dramatic production or in actual social relations, takes shape in the Greek epic. As noted in chapter 2, the *Iliad* and the *Odyssey* differ in general in that the former represents heroes at war while the latter represents the hero in the war's aftermath, as he returns to domestic life. This general difference between the two epics comprehends a difference as well between the representation of bodily display in each. In the *Iliad*, the heroic male body—fighting, eating, bleeding, and dying—is the constant object of visual attention from the point of view of other male warriors.[44] In the *Odyssey*, the body of Odysseus is the constant object of visual attention, but often in a compromising position, often from the point of view of a female spectator, and often in disguise. The literal interpretation of Odysseus' disguise in *Odyssey* 13, exemplified by a standard English commentary on the epic, argues that the disguise is necessary because were Odysseus to present himself at the palace in his own person, his chances for survival would be small.[45] But while Odysseus' disguise may be easily explained by appeals to the requirements of the plot or to characterization, these explanations are essentially tautological. Rather, Odysseus represents the locus classicus for Euripides' kings disguised as beggars, and in this respect his disguise and scripted speeches—to the extent that what he says is adapted to the disguised role he plays—are foundational to the concept of the theatrical body.

When Odysseus first lands in Ithaca, Athena fashions a landscape unfamiliar to him and makes him unrecognizable (ἄγνωστος) within that landscape.

---

43. For a fuller discussion of the *Frogs*, see chap. 5.

44. Cf. Mulvey 1989, 24, and for the concept of the "to-be-looked-at image."

45. See Stanford 1959 on 13.189. Odysseus also disguises himself as a beggar in Troy, at *Odyssey* 4.245, where only Helen recognizes him. Helen's ability to see through the disguise, coupled with the general association of women with deception, is noteworthy.

ὥς οἱ μὲν ῥ᾽ εὔχοντο Ποσειδάωνι ἄνακτι
δήμου Φαιήκων ἡγήτορες ἠδὲ μέδοντες,
ἑσταότες περὶ βωμόν. Ὁ δ᾽ ἔγρετο δῖος ᾽Οδυσσεύς,
εὕδων ἐν γαίῃ πατρωίῃ, οὐδέ μιν ἔγνω,
ἤδη δὴν ἀπεών· περὶ γὰρ θεὸς ἠέρα χεῦε
Παλλὰς ᾽Αθήναίη, κούρη Διός, ὄφρα μιν αὐτὸν
ἄγνωστον τεύξειεν ἕκαστά τε μυθήσαιτο,
μή μιν πρὶν ἄλοχος γνοίη ἀστοί τε φίλοι τε,
πρὶν πᾶσαν μνηστῆρας ὑπερβασίην ἀποτῖσαι.
τοὔνεκ᾽ ἄρ᾽ ἀλλοειδέα φαινέσκετο πάντα ἄνακτι,

[As they prayed to king Poseidon
The leaders and rulers of the Phaiacian people
Stood around the altar. But godlike Odysseus woke up
From sleeping in his fatherland, even though he did not know it,
Being absent for so long; for the goddess surrounded him in mist,
Pallas Athena, the daughter of Zeus, so that she could make him
Unrecognizable and could tell him everything in detail [under
      cover],
To prevent his wife and citizens and friends from recognizing him
Until he punished all the suitors for their violence.
For this reason then, everything appeared strange to the king.]
                                    (*Odyssey* 13.185–94; cf. 13.397–403)

The abrupt midline change of scene in this passage, from the Phaiacians sacrificing off the shore of Phaiacia to Odysseus awakening in
Ithaca (ἑσταότες περὶ βωμόν. Ὁ δ᾽ ἔγρετο δῖος ᾽ Οδυσσεύς, 13.187), is
like a quick cut in a film. In the briefest pause of the weak caesura, our
narrative gaze is refocused on the scene in Ithaca. The prominent
manipulation in this scene (both by Athena and by the narrator) results in what might be called a staged environment, in which Odysseus will play the part of someone he is not. Another way of putting it
is to say that the bold movement from Phaiacia to Ithaca, without any
narrative filler or interlude, signifies that the narrator is at work in
much the same way as the goddess is at work; both can change scenes
and appearances at will. And although Ithaca will be made clear to
Odysseus (13.344 ff.), he will remain unrecognizable to his wife and
to most of his fellow citizens and friends until the suitors are punished; his true identity remains consistently known only to the gods,

to the narrator, and to the poem's implied audience.[46] This disjunction between characters who do not recognize Odysseus and an audience that does anticipates the bifocal situation of the theater; within the fictional universe of the epic, Odysseus' fellow characters will play to his ragged beggar, which, as the audience knows, is only a temporary transformation.[47] And when Odysseus is in his beggar's rags, insofar as his visual transformation is from a higher to a lower status (from king to beggar), he prefigures those actors who will so often walk the tragic and comic stage in the personae of failed or degraded heroes.[48]

In this case, Athena disguises Odysseus as a wretched old man (γέρων, 13.432), a beggar or slave clothed in tattered rags.

ἀμφὶ δέ μιν ῥάκος ἄλλο κακὸν βάλεν ἠδὲ χιτῶνα,
ῥωγαλέα ῥυπόωντα, κακῷ μεμορυγμένα καπνῷ·
ἀμφὶ δέ μιν μέγα δέρμα ταχείης ἔσσ᾿ ἐλάφοιο,
ψιλόν· δῶκε δέ οἱ σκῆπτρον καὶ ἀεικέα πήρην,
πυκνὰ ῥωγαλέην· ἐν δὲ στρόφος ἦεν ἀορτήρ.

[Then she put another ugly rag on him, and a tunic
tattered, squalid, and blackened with the foul smoke, and around
it she put the great hide of a swift deer, with the hairs rubbed
off; and she gave him a staff, and an ugly wallet
that was full of holes, with a twisted strap attached.]

(13.434–38)

---

46. He will of course be revealed to Telemachus at *Odyssey* 16.172 ff., where his appearance is enhanced prior to his revelation.

47. As an anonymous reader of my manuscript for this book pointed out, "the playwright and actors are usually encouraging the audience to forget the actor's true identity, while the epic narrator deliberately keeps his audience aware of who Odysseus really is." This fact does not mean that epic disguise is unrelated to dramatic disguise, however, only that they operate in different mimetic registers.

48. Cf. Aristotle's definition of the best tragic plot as one in which the protagonist suffers a change from good to bad fortune (ἐξ εὐτυχίας εἰς δυστυχίαν, *Poetics* 1453a15). Such a plot subverts the epic paradigm of masculine heroism and seems to describe what in fact is often the case, namely, that tragedy's male protagonists are the failed or defeated heroes of epic (e.g., Agamemnon, Ajax, Jason, Menelaus).

At first glance this scene exemplifies the association of disguise with degradation and compromised masculinity in archaic Greek culture, here overtly played out in terms of age and class.[49] But the ambivalence that this transformation registers has often been glossed over by the common reading of the *Odyssey* as a story about spiritual death and rebirth.[50] The persistence of "rebirth" as an explanatory mechanism is illustrated by Sheila Murnaghan in her book on disguise in the *Odyssey*, in which she argues that "Odysseus' survival of [his] experiences represents the specifically Homeric version of what folklorists see as fundamental to every story of return and recognition: return from death, and rebirth." As an element within that myth, Odysseus' disguise mediates between concealment (commensurate with the hero's absence as death) and disclosure (commensurate with his return as rebirth). Murnaghan argues that Odysseus' disguise represents him as capable of "transcending normal human limits, as being like the gods for whom the experience of mortal limitation is a form of playacting."[51]

Murnaghan's reading is compelling, but at the same time this description of the disguised male body in the service of a religious transcendence assumes a negative equation of death with travel among foreign lands and peoples (which in general are to be abhorred, feared, and defeated) and an equation of rebirth (or the ability to transcend mortality) with the positive restoration of ethnic and cultural hegemony. Odysseus' wanderings among women and monsters illustrate the gender-specific assumptions operating in this myth of return and

---

49. This association is marked in reverse at *Odyssey* 17.549–50, where Penelope states that if the disguised Odysseus is telling the truth, she will give him fine clothes, and again at 19.250–60, where the beggar's description of Odysseus' clothing is the proof that he is telling the truth. In both passages, fine clothing is a sign of truth telling and of Odysseus' proper aristocratic status—not without irony in relation to Odysseus. Cf. Winkler 1990b, 148–52.

50. Frame (1978, 73 n. 68) offers linguistic evidence for *nostos* as meaning "return from death" and "return from darkness." But his emphasis on primitive sun worship (20 ff.) as a way of explaining the motif seems forced and is indicative of a zealous insistence on *nostos*, or heroic homecoming, as a religious phenomenon. In this insistence he follows Eliade (1963). On this topic, see also Holtsmark 1965–66; Powell 1977, 4–5.

51. Murnaghan 1987, 14 with n. 23. Cf. Block 1985.

recognition; his disguise as a foreigner and a slave specifies the subsequent revelation of his "true" self as a function of ethnicity and class. The Homeric narrative certainly privileges this revelation. But at the same time, the scholarly tradition fails to fully appreciate the assumptions inherent in equating godlike transcendence and selfhood with the revelation of an idealized Greek male.[52] Murnaghan's reference to mortal transcendence as a form of "playacting," also has obvious affinities with arguments about drama's ritual origins, rooted in the taking on of a new identity and therefore equivalent to achieving a kind of "rebirth."[53] Both explanations attest once again to the nostalgic desire for a transcendent masculine subject—not only in the epic narrative, but also in the scholarly tradition.

It is true that the disguised Odysseus emulates the gods who disguise themselves as mortals and that we should find in this emulation some clue to understanding the function of disguise in the epic.[54] But when divinities take on the shapes and voices of human beings, the effect is not to enhance their divinity (i.e., to inspire religious awe in mortal spectators) but to conceal it. They generally appear as mortals to facilitate human action, not to overtly demonstrate their power as divinities. In other words, like Odysseus' disguise as a beggar, divine disguisings in the epics effect a change from higher to lower status (ontological in the case of the gods, social and political in the case of Odysseus) that amounts to an implicit denial of visualized displays of

52. Cf. de Lauretis 1984.
53. In his foreword to Gaster 1961 (9), Gilbert Murray states: "It is hardly an exaggeration to say that when we look back to the beginnings of European literature we find everywhere drama, and always drama derived from a religious ritual designed to ensure the rebirth of the dead world." Cf. Seaford 1981, 259, on the relationship between drama and the ritual taking on of a new identity. More recently, see Seaford 1994, 299.
54. The gods' disguises in epic are discussed by Rose (1956, 66), who asks whether divine disguises were "assimilated to magical metamorphoses" or to "merely human attempts, surely not very elaborate at that date, at concealing one's real identity." Odysseus' disguise as a beggar, even though provided by Athena, indicates that the elaborate concealment of human identity was part of Homeric culture. It is useful for my argument that the second hypothesis seems to hold; disguise in the epics is not the restricted to shape changing that is a common folk motif (i.e., that of Proteus).

power.[55] On one level, that gods can disguise themselves as mortals is a sign of their power; on another level, their disguises are the visual enactment of a loss of power, that is, of mortality instead of immortality. If Odysseus' disguise is an expression of power residing in the protean capabilities of the gods, it is also an expression of power residing in the appearance of powerlessness.[56] In both the mortal and divine realms, then, disguise in the *Odyssey* is a paradoxical activity that often entails a visualized transformation from higher to lower status.

Compared to the presentation of the warrior culture in the *Iliad*, where external appearance is the true sign of a man's identity and status (Achilles and his armor exemplify the standard), the appearance of the *Odyssey*'s hero in rags marks the practice of disguise itself as antithetical to the heroic ethos.[57] In fact, the kind of disguise with which Odysseus is provided indicates how the epic encodes the fact of disguise as a sign of compromised manhood, expressed most concretely in the suspension and possible negation of face-to-face, or man-to-man, confrontation between elite males; this sort of confrontation is clearly jeopardized when a man speaks from behind a disguise.[58] Moreover, that Athena is the agent of Odysseus' disguise, together with the consistent association of women with clothing and with the mutability and deceptiveness of external appearance in general, marks disguise as a feminine tactic, even though the goddess herself is ambiguously gendered: it is noteworthy too that weaving is the metaphor for Athena's plan (ἀλλ᾿ ἄγε μῆτιν ὕφηνον, ὅπως ἀποτίσομαι αὐτούς, 13.386).[59] But if Odysseus' beggar's rags exemplify disguise in this

---

55. Cf. Athena's disguise as Deiphobus at *Iliad* 22.226 ff. The story of Zeus and Semele, recounted in the *Bacchae*, illustrates the danger incurred by a mortal who sees a god as a god.

56. For Murnaghan (1987, 8–9), Odysseus' disguise testifies to "an appreciation" of life's vicissitudes and to the true or unchanging heroic status which Odysseus will inevitably reclaim. See my chap. 5 on Dionysus' disguise as the Lydian stranger in the *Bacchae*.

57. Cf. Menelaus' lament over the loss of his splendid clothing, corresponding to his loss of warrior status, in Euripides' *Helen* (415–27).

58. Cf. *Iliad* 5.449, where Apollo makes an *eidolon* of Aeneas to remove him from the battlefield. On *eidola*, see Saïd 1987a, 309–30. See also Vernant 1991.

59. Odysseus' disguise is also meant to test Penelope, even though he is explicitly told of his wife's faithfulness (*Odyssey* 11.177–79, 13.379–81).

negative register, how do we interpret the scene in *Odyssey* 6 where Athena enhances his appearance? Are there good and bad kinds of disguise? Do they function within different or even opposing registers of bodily display? Or is the disguised male—when recognized as such—always under suspicion?

It may be objected that Odysseus' enhanced appearance in *Odyssey* 6 is not really a form of disguise and cannot be fairly compared with his beggar's rags. But while the rags constitute a more overt form of disguise, the scene of Athena's enhancement operates as part of a similar representational strategy and raises similar questions. In each instance, visual attention is directed at Odysseus' altered appearance. While Athena's attempt to make Odysseus more handsome in book 6 differs in purpose from her attempt to make him look like a beggar in book 13, both attempts nevertheless share the benefit of her machinations in attracting attention to the bodily display of the hero. Book 6, however, provides a more nuanced accounting of this attention, since the effect of Odysseus' bodily enhancement is immediately registered in Nausicaa. In other words, his enhancement is effected for the immediate benefit of a particular (female) spectator. This spectatorial arrangement in which a female is in the viewing position, is antithetical to and therefore illustrative of the dominant system in which men are both the viewers and the viewed.

Just prior to Athena's enhancement and just before he encounters Nausicaa and her maids, Odysseus attempts to hide his present state of nakedness with a leafy branch.

ἐκ πυκινῆς δ' ὕλης πτόρθον κλάσε χειρὶ παχείῃ
φύλλων, ὡς ῥύσαιτο περὶ χροῒ μήδεα φωτός.
βῆ δ' ἴμεν ὥς τε λέων ὀρεσίτροφος, ἀλκὶ πεποιθώς,
ὅς τ' εἶσ' ὑόμενος καὶ ἀήμενος, ἐν δέ οἱ ὄσσε
δαίεται· αὐτὰρ ὁ βουσὶ μετέρχεται ἢ ὀίεσσιν

Winkler (1990b, 139) states that "in the *Odyssey* that fear or suspicion of wives, so well attested in Mediterranean contexts, appears to be limited to this one character [Agamemnon]." But Odysseus' testing of Penelope is also evidence of this suspicion. The warning Agamemnon gives to Odysseus in the Nekyia works both ways; if only Agamemnon had returned home in disguise! In this sense, Odysseus' disguise ironically signifies the potential for men to be deceived by women. See Foley 1978; Doherty 1991, 161.

ἠὲ μετ᾽ ἀγροτέρας ἐλάφους· κέλεται δὲ ἑ γαστὴρ
μήλων πειρήσοντα καὶ ἐς πυκινὸν δόμον ἐλθεῖν·
ὣς Ὀδυσσεὺς κούρῃσιν ἐϋπλοκάμοισιν ἔμελλε
μίξεσθαι, γυμνός περ ἐών· χρειὼ γὰρ ἵκανε.

[From the thick foliage, with his massive hand, he broke off
a leafy branch to cover his body and hide his genitals
and went in the confidence of his strength, like some mountain-
    nurtured lion
who advances though he is rained on and wind blown
and his eyes gleam; he goes out after cattle or sheep,
or deer in the wilderness, and his belly urges him
to get inside the well-guarded house and to make an attempt on
    the sheep flocks.
So Odysseus was ready to mingle with the young girls with
well-ordered hair, naked though he was, for the need drove him.]
                                                        (6.128–36)

It is ironic that the branch (πτόρθος) only accentuates Odysseus' genitals in the process of hiding them. But at the same time, the gesture
suggests that the warrior ethos within which male nudity is valorized
requires that he be looked at by other males (cf. 6.221–22). Relevant
here is Odysseus' fear at *Odyssey* 10.339–41 that being naked before
Circe will make him weak and unmanned (ὄφρα με γυμνωθέντα
κακὸν καὶ ἀνήνορα θήῃς).[60] In other words, in the representation of
male nudity, to be naked in the presence of a woman is analogous to
being stripped by an enemy: males who inhabit these positions, that
is, the ἀνήνωρ and the defeated warrior, are more like women than
men. The implicit equation of women and enemies (i.e., non- or anti-
Greeks) as spectators is based on the potential threat each poses to the
male subject as the only subject who matters in this spectatorial system. Looking like a woman (as in the examples of Achilles, Ajax, and
Heracles), being looked at as a woman (as Hector imagines at *Iliad*
22.122–25), and being seen by a woman (Circe or Nausicaa) all illustrate this threat. Thus, when Odysseus covers his nakedness in the

---

60. Cf. Plutarch *Moralia* 139a on Circe's effect on Odysseus' companions.
This passage is discussed by Faraone 1992, 99.

presence of Nausicaa and her maids, his gesture testifies not so much to some moral code operating in the epic as to the risk that accompanies this transitional moment—a risk made manifest by the presence of a female spectator.[61]

The passage also registers the difference between the kind of natural but minimal covering with which the male provides himself (the branch, or πτόρθος) and the complete change in appearance made possible by the artifice of mortal and divine females, that is, by the clothing that Nausicaa gives Odysseus and by Athena's enhancements. In this respect, the lion simile (ὥς τε λέων ὀρεσίτροφος, *Odyssey* 6.130) operates as a kind of disguising mechanism in the text, since it represents an attempt to conceal Odysseus' weakened human state by likening him to a ferocious wild animal.[62] Similarly, the sexual reference registered in Odysseus' readiness to "mingle with the young girls" may be understood as a reference to masculine sexual prowess in this scene of masculine dependence, especially because it immediately precedes the reference to his nakedness (μίξεσθαι, γυμνός περ ἐών, 6.136). In short, Odysseus' exposed and vulnerable nakedness is (barely) covered up by his "leafy branch" and by his being compared with a powerful and aggressive lion. Overall, the scene provides a

---

61. Stanford (1959, ad loc.), notes the perceived inconsistency between this passage and *Odyssey* 3.464, where one of the daughters of Nestor bathes and anoints Telemachus. The situational difference to which Stanford alludes is crucial; in this moment of transition in *Odyssey* 6, Odysseus' nakedness signifies his need for hospitality or domestic protection, not the fulfillment of that need. At *Odyssey* 6.221–22, Odysseus professes to feel "awe [or reverence or fear] at being naked in the presence of the lovely-haired girls" [αἰδέομαι γὰρ/γυμνοῦσθαι κούρῃσιν ἐϋπλοκάμοισι μετελθών]. Stanford credits his awe, or αἰδώς, to his "filthy condition," but doing so does not adequately explain its obvious reference to his nakedness. The semantic range of αἰδέομαι is quite broad, but even if it is taken to mean something like "embarrassment," it does not compromise the reading I am suggesting. Odysseus' embarrassment at being naked before the girls is only another expression of the risk posed by the female spectator in the discourse of Greek masculinity. Cf. Freud's discussion ([1900] 1965, 279–80) of Odysseus' nakedness as illustrative of typical dreams.

62. Cf. *Iliad* 5.299, where the same simile is used of Aeneas just before he is struck by Diomedes, with fatal consequences had not Aphrodite intervened. The frequent representation of lions in Mycenaean sculpture and decorative arts, especially weaponry, may be relevant here.

vivid look at bodily display (including male nudity) and spectatorship
as gender-specific activities in the *Odyssey*, ones in which masculine
prerogatives are often at risk.

After Nausicaa gives the naked or near naked Odysseus clothing,
Athena makes his transformation complete.

ἀμφὶ δὲ εἵματα ἕσσαθ' ἅ οἱ πόρε παρθένος ἀδμής,
τὸν μὲν Ἀθηναίη θῆκεν, Διὸς ἐκγεγαυῖα,
μείζονά τ' εἰσιδέειν καὶ πάσσονα, κὰδ δὲ κάρητος
οὔλας ἧκε κόμας, ὑακινθίνῳ ἄνθει ὁμοίας.
ὡς δ' ὅτε τις χρυσὸν περιχεύεται ἀργύρῳ ἀνὴρ
ἴδρις, ὃν Ἥφαιστος δέδαεν καὶ Παλλὰς Ἀθήνη
τέχνην παντοίην, χαρίεντα δὲ ἔργα τελείει.
ὡς ἄρα τῷ κατέχευε χάριν κεφαλῇ τε καὶ ὤμοις.

[He put on the clothing that the unwedded girl had given him,
then Athena, daughter of Zeus, made him seem taller
and sturdier to look upon, and on his head she arranged
his thick hair like a hyacinth flower;
just as when a master craftsman works gold in with silver—
one whom Hephaestus and Athena had taught
in every art, and grace is on every work he finishes,
so Athena poured grace on his head and shoulders.]

(6.228–35; cf. 8.18–23)

This passage is striking first of all in the number of lexical items it
shares with the description of Athena's adornment of Pandora at
Theogony 573 ff. (cf. *Works and Days* 72 ff.). Taken together, the cosmetic attentions that Athena gives Homer's Odysseus and Hesiod's
Pandora recall each other in specific details, including an emphasis
on divine artifice (cf. *Odyssey* 6.230–37; *Theogony* 574–83).[63] So, for

---

63. These details include references to flowers, gold and silver adornment,
compelling appearance, and gracefulness, or *charis*. West (1966, on *Theogony*
583) states: "χάρις is the essential characteristic of the woman and her adornment." Cf. Hesiod *Works and Days* 65 and 73; Homer *Iliad* 14.183 and *Odyssey*
18.298. On the relative chronology of the Homeric and Hesiodic poems, see
West 1966, 46–47. Cf. the adornment of Penelope at *Odyssey* 18.185–200 and

example, when Nausicaa remarks that Odysseus "seems like [ἔοικε] the immortal gods" (*Odyssey* 6.243), we can recall Zeus' order to Hephaestus to make Pandora look like (εἴσκειν) the immortal goddesses (*Works and Days* 62).[64] But the effect of these shared references is not simply to confuse mortal and immortal physiognomy. Rather, they suggest that Athena's adornments make Odysseus like Pandora, whose falsehoods, deceptive lies, and deceitful nature are dangerous for men (*Works and Days* 77–78). There can be no doubt that Athena's enhancements at this point in the narrative are conducive to Odysseus' reception in Phaiacia, but this typical scene of *female* adornment also signifies his compromised status.

Such scenes of adornment are modeled on *Iliad* 14, where Hera beautifies herself to deceive the mind of Zeus (ὅππως ἐξαπάφοιτο Διὸς νόον αἰγιόχοιο, *Iliad* 14.160)[65]:

τῷ ῥ᾽ ἥ γε χρόα καλὸν ἀλειψαμένη ἰδὲ χαίτας
πεξαμένη χερσὶ πλοκάμους ἔπλεξε φαεινοὺς
καλοὺς ἀμβροσίους ἐκ κράατος ἀθανάτοιο.
ἀμφὶ δ᾽ ἄρ᾽ ἀμβρόσιον ἑανὸν ἔσαθ᾽, ὅν οἱ Ἀθήνη
ἔξυσ᾽ ἀσκήσασα, τίθει δ᾽ ἐνὶ δαίδαλα πολλά·
χρυσείης δ᾽ ἐνετῇσι κατὰ στῆθος περονᾶτο.
ζώσατο δὲ ζώνῃ ἑκατὸν θυσάνοις ἀραρυίῃ,
ἐν δ᾽ ἄρα ἕρματα ἧκεν ἐϋτρήτοισι λοβοῖσι
τρίγληνα μορόεντα· χάρις δ᾽ ἀπελάμπετο πολλή.

---

the adornment of Aphrodite at *Homeric Hymns* 5.59 ff. and 6.5–13. For a discussion of the "allurement type-scene," see Forsyth 1979. Although Forsyth admits that such scenes could generate a "range of variations," for him they are only descriptive of females: "Given the apparent occurrence of allurement scenes in non-Homeric poetry, the type must have been a part of the general Greek tradition, inherited by the singers as the normal way of composing a seduction scene, and applicable to a wide range of *female* characters" (117; emphasis added). The adornment of Odysseus in *Odyssey* 6 is in accordance with the elements Forsyth discusses. See also Edwards 1992, 312–13; Janko 1992, 173–79.

64. The words ἔοικα and ἐίσκω appear to be linguistically cognate. See Vernant 1991, 187 n. 7.

65. See Faraone 1990, 222 n. 5, on the correspondences between the adornment of Pandora in Hesiod and the tricking of Zeus in *Iliad* 14.

[When [Hera] had anointed her beautiful body and combed her
  hair,
with her hands, she plaited her shining locks,
beautiful and ambrosial, down from her immortal head.
Then she clothed herself in an ambrosial robe that Athena had
  worked
and smoothed, and on which she [Athena] placed many figures,
and [Hera] pinned it across her breast with golden brooches,
and attached a hundred tassels to her well-fitted girdle
and put earrings in her carefully pierced earlobes
with triple mulberry clusters; and grace radiated everywhere.]

(*Iliad* 14.175–83)

In addition to Athena's ambrosial robe, Hera wears the embroidered
ἱμάς, or magic girdle of Aphrodite (κεστὸν ἱμάντα / ποικίλον, 14.214–
15).[66] And together these adornments do not fail to beguile Zeus.[67]
The force of these adornments is complemented by Hera's tricky or
beguiling talk (δολοφρονέουσα, 14.300), the same sort of talk that
Helen charges against Aphrodite when she attempts to refuse the

---

66. The verb τεύχω, used to describe the lies that Hermes fashions in the
breast of Pandora (τεῦξε ἐν στήθεσσι, Hesiod *Works and Days* 77), is also used
of the adornments worked into Aphrodite's girdle at *Iliad* 14.215 and of
Athena's promise to make Odysseus unrecognizable at *Odyssey* 13.191 and
13.397. The verb is commonly used of works of art; it is also used of Apollo
fashioning the εἴδωλον of Aeneas at *Iliad* 5.449. While it appears in other
contexts as well, one important aspect of its semantic range includes the
notion of deceptively wrought appearances. On female adornments, especially the girdle or zone of Aphrodite, as aphrodisiacs, see Faraone 1990.
Faraone (1992) discusses the ability of the same erotic spells or objects to
facilitate erection or cause impotency. As he argues, variations of duration of
exposure and dosage are responsible for these seemingly contradictory out-
comes. I add that to the degree that the male's sexual state is due to the
external power of the aphrodisiac, both arousal and impotence are indicative
of his subjugation and passivity, especially when women are the agents of the
spell. This predicament also helps to explain why increased sexual arousal in
men due to an erotic spell is thought to weaken their self-control, as Faraone
(1992, 100–101) demonstrates. The common complaint in the Greek tradition
of women's promiscuity and subservience to their erotic desires is also
relevant.
67. The word ἑανός is also used of Helen's clothing at *Iliad* 3.385 and 3.419.

goddess' summons to the bed of Menelaus (δολοφρονέουσα, 3.405) and that Odysseus charges against Circe when he accuses her of asking him to have sex so that she can make him naked and unmanned (δολοφρονέουσα, *Odyssey* 10.339).[68] The deceptive adornments of the female, guileful speech, and the potential for putting masculine power at risk constitute what might be called the Pandora paradigm, according to which these attributes naturalize the female's affinity for visual and verbal deception from the point of view of male auditors and spectators.[69]

Thus the adornment of Odysseus, accomplished by Athena for the delectation of Nausicaa, enacts a pointed reversal.[70] Like those mortal men for whom the beautiful Pandora is a sheer deception (δόλον αἰπύν, *Theogony* 589), and like Zeus when he is tricked by Hera in all her divine finery, the Phaiacian princess is awed by Odysseus' splendid body only to be disappointed (if not tricked) when he fails to become her husband. This teasing possibility is manifested first of all in the clothes Nausicaa gives to Odysseus, clothes she had gone out to wash in anticipation of her wedding day (cf. *Odyssey* 6.277). Dressed in these clothes, Odysseus implicitly plays the role of the husband Nausicaa wishes for. In this respect his adornment is part of an elaborate disguise, even if, as I have admitted, it is less explicitly so than his beggar's rags. With the help of Athena, he occupies the subject position that the epic and didactic traditions consistently assign to females: he is the object of Nausicaa's desire, desire incited by the sight of his adorned body. And as in those scenes of female adornment, his adorned body is implicated in a deception that signals a potential threat to masculine prerogatives: marriage to Nausicaa would mean the sacrifice of Odysseus' return home and his failure to resume his kingship in Ithaca (6.228; cf. 6.244).[71] Odysseus' adornment thus represents a

---

68. The feminine participle of δολοφρονέω is also used at Archilochus 93 (Bergk), but the meaning of the fragment is unclear.

69. See Faraone 1992, 100–101, on the "usurpation of male power" as an effect of aphrodisiacs used by women against men, including the *kestos* of Aphrodite employed by Hera.

70. Cf. Foley 1978.

71. The relationship between bodily appearance and the possibility for deception is voiced in Alcinoos' address to Odysseus at *Odyssey* 11.363–66: "as we look at you [εἰσορόωντες], we do not take you for a cheat and thief; the black earth nourishes many such men who wander widely, making up lies, from

double-pronged threat: it testifies to his dependence on a woman for the assistance he needs to return home to Ithaca and, at the same time, to the possibility that he may not achieve that homecoming but may stay in Phaiacia and marry Nausicaa (cf. 6.175–77).

But what are we to make of Odysseus' predicament at *Odyssey* 23.153–62, where he is again given new clothing by a woman (Penelope) and where Athena repeats her cosmetic attentions? In contrast to the possible marriage with Nausicaa for which his adornment in book 6 prepares him, here Odysseus' body is beautified on the verge of his reestablishment as Penelope's husband and king in Ithaca. While any implication of trickery or false inducement is eventually negated (Odysseus will be reunited with his wife), his divinely adorned body is nevertheless again presented as posing a risk, namely, that Penelope will make love to someone who she is unaware is her legitimate husband. She does not immediately recognize Odysseus and thinks that he may be one of the immortals in mortal guise (cf. 23.63, τις ἀθανάτων, and 163). Nausicaa had compared Odysseus to a god in *Odyssey* 6 and here, as in that earlier scene, his adorned body represents a chance for an erotic encounter that could have disastrous consequences for the social and political order of Ithaca (cf. 23.215–16).

As in Phaiacia, Odysseus' body is adorned and erotically displayed in Ithaca for a woman's gaze at the moment of his entry into a domestic realm. And in both places that adornment precedes and predicts his dependence on a woman for his imminent homecoming and "true" recognition scene. Among the Phaiacians, Arete's friendly disposition can guarantee his homeward journey (6.303–15, 7.75–77, 11.335–41).[72] On Ithaca, Penelope devises a test to prove that Odysseus is the husband she has not seen for twenty years (23.173–230).[73] But whereas his adornment implicitly prepares him for a false or

---

which no one could learn anything." Of course, the suggestion that Odysseus is not a liar implies that he might be.

72. See Stanford 1959 on 6.303–15. The omission of these lines in many manuscripts, presumably because a king should be approached rather than a queen, is telling. For the reasons I argue here and based on the corresponding roles played by women in Odysseus' landing in Phaiacia and his return to Ithaca, the omission not only is unnecessary but eliminates a crucial element in the text. It should be remembered, too, that women facilitate or hinder Odysseus' *nostos* or homecoming all along the way.

73. See Winkler 1990b.

failed homecoming in book 6 (i.e., a home among the Phaiacians), in book 23 it prepares for his true homecoming, the homecoming that means the end of the battle and the end of the epic. Following one more abortive foray (24.496–544), Odysseus is destined for a life at home followed by a peaceful death.[74] His adorned body, displayed to Nausicaa, Arete, and finally to Penelope, thus demarcates the potential or actual end of the narrative of ever possible martial and sexual conquests for the male warrior. For the bulk of the poem is about the possibility of *nostos*, or homecoming, not its realization, and if we can define the Odyssean hero in part by his desire for *nostos* rather than by his realization of it, then home is the very place he should not be, especially insofar as it is the domestic domain of his wife. In this sense the Phaiacian interlude both holds out the possibility for a false homecoming and is a preview of what a true homecoming means: a time and place for telling and listening to stories and for engaging in games that, as Odysseus' remarks in *Odyssey* 8 suggest, are only substitutes for heroic action away from home.[75] In sum, Odysseus' adorned body is emblematic of the *Odyssey* as a poem about the transition from desired to achieved *nostos*, from the outlands of masculine heroism to the homeland of feminine domesticity, and from actual conquest and warfare to their approximation in songs and games.

By shifting the narrative of female adornment onto Odysseus' male body, these scenes also present imitations or performances of femininity that, by virtue of that shift, illustrate the gender-specific corporeal and vestimentary codes that operate in the epic. Without insisting on

---

74. Cf. the prophecy of Tiresias at *Odyssey* 11.121–37, repeated by Odysseus to Penelope at 23.266–84; cf. also Zeus' declaration of peace at 24.482–86.

75. Songs and games as substitutes for actual action, however, are different in kind. Noticing the weeping with which Odysseus responds to Demodocus' song of the Trojan War (*Odyssey* 8.83 ff.), Alcinoos immediately proposes games (ἀέθλοι) as an antidote to the grief occasioned by the songs about the war. While neither songs about war nor games exhibiting military skills compare to actual battle, the games at least demand physical activity as distinguished from passive listening. The famous simile that describes Odysseus "weeping like a woman lying over the body of her dear husband" [ὡς δὲ γυνὴ κλαίῃσι φίλον πόσιν ἀμφιπεσοῦσα] (8.523) after listening to Demodocus' song about the Trojan horse makes explicit the passive and womanlike subject position of the man who listens to songs. See Geddes 1987, 324–25, on games as practice for hoplite warfare.

the notion of formal performance, I want to suggest that Odysseus is made to play the woman when his male role is most threatened and that the disguise, in fact, signals the threat. Thus Odysseus' beggar's rags, on the one hand, and his female-like adornment, on the other, by virtue of their overt focus on identity and role playing manifested in disguise and bodily transformation, provide complementary, if seemingly antithetical, examples of threatened masculinity as a consequence of disguise.[76] In particular, the disguise of femininity signifies the unstable nature of masculine subjectivity and the possibility that gender identity is only an effect of vestimentary (or other external) phenomena.

But if Odysseus' beggar's disguise and feminine adornment are the defining attributes of the heroic body as a theatrical body in the *Odyssey*, the presentation of Thersites' nonheroic body in the *Iliad* can stand as a telling test case. While the display of the disguised and adorned body of Odysseus signifies the hero's transition to the domesticated space of women, Thersites provides an example of how the nonheroic body—as the deformed body—is feminized according to the martial codes of the *Iliad*. In chapter 2, I discussed Thersites' speech as a form of scripted speech because it is comprised of a series of repetitions and is therefore antithetical to direct man-to-man oral communication. In this chapter I will argue that his body—like Odysseus'—is a theatrical body by virtue of its prominent display value in the narrative and because of the gender confusion it represents.

The description of Thersites' body is emphatic in the *Iliad*, where detailed individuation based on the physical appearance of a character is unusual. Examples of such individuation are the descriptions of Helen's face (*Iliad* 3.158), of Paris (3.39), and of Dolon (κακός, 10.316). But these are quantitatively and qualitatively different from the description of Thersites. His closest relative may be the monkey-woman in Semonides' so-called *Satire on Women* (7.71–82): she is the "greatest of evils" [μέγιστον κακόν], has "a most ignoble face" [αἴσχιστα μὲν πρόσωπα], and is "laughable to all men" [πᾶσιν ἀνθρώποις γέλως].[77] Like this monkey-woman, Thersites is a sight to behold.

---

76. Cf. the notion of womanliness as masquerade in Riviere 1966 and as it is taken up in feminist film criticism by Doane (1991, chaps. 1 and 2).

77. See Thalmann 1988, 15.

φολκὸς ἔην, χωλὸς δ ἕτερον πόδα· τὼ δέ οἱ ὤμω
κυρτώ, ἐπὶ στῆθος συνοχωκότε· αὐτὰρ ὕπερθε
φοξὸς ἔην κεφαλήν, ψεδνὴ δ ἐπενήνοθε λάχνη.

[He was bandy-legged and lame in one foot; his shoulders were
hunched and caved into his chest. And above this
his head was pointed, and a thin wool was piled up.]

(*Iliad* 2.217–19)

The significance of these details is usually explained by reference to
a coincidence of physical beauty and heroic virtue in the epics:
Thersites' extraordinary ugliness proves the rule.[78] According to Kirk
(on *Iliad* 2.219), "The shambling, limping gait, the hunched back and
shoulders and the pointed, balding cranium combine to make Thersites a monstrosity by heroic standards."[79] But another way of describing human physiognomy in the epic poems is to say that because
male beauty defines its dominant model, such beauty needs no detailed elaboration, and that only what deviates from it requires description. This helps explain why Thersites' monstrous appearance is
also unusual in terms of its lexicon: φολκὸς (2.217) appears to be a
hapax legomenon, and the meaning of φοξὸς (2.219) is obscure.

But when Odysseus threatens to strip Thersites of his clothing and
expose his genitals, attention is directed away from this monstrous
exterior and onto what that exterior may conceivably conceal.

εἴ κ᾽ ἔτι σ᾽ ἀφραίνοντα κιχήσομαι ὥς νύ περ ὧδε,
μηκέτ᾽ ἔπειτ᾽ Ὀδυσῆϊ κάρη ὤμοισιν ἐπείη,

---

78. See Oribasius' *Libri incerti* (Daremberg) on physical appearance. This
work is cited by Rousselle (1988, 22).

79. Kirk 1985. Leaf (1960, on *Iliad* 2.214) calls Thersites "the only common
soldier mentioned by name in the *Iliad*." Kirk (on *Iliad* 2.212) thinks that a
common soldier "would not be permitted to open his mouth in assembly."
Thersites is the only character in the *Iliad* to lack both a patronymic and a
place of origin. Whether this aspect of his character designates him as a
"common soldier" is not clear in the text; it seems that he fights among the
frontline fighters in battle (*Iliad* 2.231). He is nevertheless an outcast among
the *Iliad*'s aristocratic males. See also Andersen 1982; Postlethwaite 1988; Rose
1988.

μηδ' ἔτι Τηλεμάχοιο πατὴρ κεκλημένος εἴην,
εἰ μὴ ἐγώ σε λαβὼν ἀπὸ μὲν φίλα εἵματα δύσω,
χλαῖνάν τ' ἠδὲ χιτῶνα, τά τ' αἰδῶ ἀμφικαλύπτει,
αὐτὸν δὲ κλαίοντα θοὰς ἐπὶ νῆας ἀφήσω
πεπλήγων ἀγορῆθεν ἀεικέσσι πληγῇσιν.

[If I find you playing the fool as you are now,
may Odysseus' head no longer sit on his shoulders,
and may I no longer be called Telemachus' father,
if I do not grab you and strip off your personal clothing,
your mantle and your tunic, which hide your genitals,
and send you back to the swift ships in tears
after I have driven you from the assembly place with insulting
     blows.]

                                                    (2.258–64)

Kirk notes that "the epic tradition generally avoided [reference to the]
genitals," although we have seen that Odysseus attempts to hide his
in front of Nausicaa (*Odyssey* 6.128–36). But just as Odysseus' attempt
is not sufficiently explained by reference to his feelings of shame, the
threat to remove Thersites' clothing here cannot simply be explained
by reference to shame connected with the exposure of "a deformed
person like Thersites."[80] In other words, at issue is not Thersites'
deformity but rather the stripping and exposure of his body.[81] The
verb ἀποδύω, used here of stripping Thersites' clothing, is commonly
used of stripping the armor from the heroic but defeated warrior.[82]
Thus, even though the verb functions to distinguish Thersites from a
heroic warrior, it also suggests a similarity between the act of stripping off his mantle and tunic and the degradation associated with the

---

80. Kirk 1985, ad loc. Even among the multifarious battle wounds, mention of the genitals occurs only one other time in the *Iliad* (13.567–69). The
goatherd Melanthius' μήδεα are ripped off and fed to the dogs in the *Odyssey*
(22.476). Cf. MacCary 1982, 152–53.
81. On the Thersites episode in general, see Thalmann 1988, although
Thalmann does not mention Odysseus' threat to strip Thersites.
82. Examples of ἀποδύω outside the epic include Herodotus *Histories* 5.92
and Aristophanes *Thesmophoriazousae* 636, *Ecclesiazousae* 668, and *Birds* 712.

warrior's loss of his armor. It also distinguishes the kind of nudity with which Thersites is threatened from the idealized male nudity I discussed earlier. What lies underneath Thersites' external covering is neither the wounded body of a noble warrior nor the body of an ideal male, but something else.

In the case of Thersites, we are dealing with a new category of analysis on the continuum of bodily display, that of exposure. In the mythological tradition, such exposure is most commonly revelatory of female genitalia. The paradigmatic example is Baubo, who exposes her genitals to cheer the grieving Demeter, a spectacle that delights the goddess but would presumably be frightful to men.[83] As in the case of the exposure of Candaules' wife in Herodotus' narrative of the Lydian kingship and in other Greek narratives featuring the exposure of female genitalia among barbarians (i.e., in Egypt, Lydia, and Persia), the threat of a woman exposing herself to men is subversive in terms of social disciplines (it is contrary to the Greek prescription that women be clothed) and political stability.[84] But because the genitals are considered to be the unambiguous indicators of sexual identity, the threat of their exposure also suggests some ambiguity about that particular aspect of identity. Again this ambiguity is best expressed in Attic comedy, where the possibility for such exposure is a frequent plot element.

In the *Ecclesiazousae,* for example, Praxagora warns one of the women disguised as a man not to expose herself to detection.

---

83. See Zeitlin 1982a, 144–45; Olender 1990, 99–113. Figures of what are thought to represent Baubo or Baubo types are found at Priene (on the coast of Asia Minor) and date from the fourth century B.C.E.

84. Herodotus tells the story of the festival in Bubastis in Egypt during which the women are said to mock other women and to lift up their own clothing (*Histories* 2.60). See also *Histories* 2.102, where the Egyptian king Sesostris erects pillars inscribed with "female genitalia, wishing to indicate that [the subject peoples] were weak." Cf. How and Wells 1968, ad loc.: "It was an Egyptian custom to set up columns in record of conquest, but the addition of sexual emblems (given more fully, Diod. i.55 *et al.*) is a Greek invention." There is also the story of the Spartan mother who, when she saw her sons retreating, shamed them by showing her genitals and saying: "Where have you fled to, you slavish cowards? Do you think you can slink back in here where you came from?" (Plutarch *Moralia* 241b). Cf. Plutarch *Moralia* 246a–b, where the same story is told about a group of Persian women. In these stories the exposure of female genitalia is a sign of male cowardice.

ἰδού γέ σε ξαίνουσαν, ἥν τοῦ σώματος
οὐδὲν παραφῆναι τοῖς καθημένοις ἔδει.
οὐκοῦν καλά γ' ἄν πάθοιμεν, εἰ πλήρης τύχοι
ὁ δῆμος ὤν κἄπειθ' ὑπερβαίνουσά τις
ἀναβαλλομένη δείξειε τὸν Φορμίσιον.

[Look at you combing wool! When you're not supposed to
expose even a glimpse of your body to those sitting around you.
We'd really do well if, when the whole town
happened to be crowded together, one of us would then leap up
and,
with her clothes all askew, show her Phormisius.]

(*Ecclesiazousae* 93–97)

Phormisius is a man known for his hairiness (cf. *Frogs* 966, where he is
one of the "lancer-whiskered-trumpeters" [σαλπιγγολογχυπηνάδαι]),
and, probably based on this passage, his name is glossed by Hesychius
as meaning τὰ γυναικεῖα αἰδοῖα, or "women's genitals."[85] That
women's genitals are metaphorically figured as a man with a hairy
beard or mustache is doubly significant, since the actors playing the
women dressed as men in the play are men.[86] More to the point, the

---

85. On this usage see Henderson 1991, 147–48. ξαίνω ("to comb wool") in
this passage implies that the woman is masturbating, although Henderson
does not include the verb in his study of obscenities in Aristophanic comedy.

86. Taaffe (1991, 99–100) explains the reference as follows: "The simple
logic behind this posits that women are not so different from men; they have
beards in a different place. Her [Praxagora's] comments emphasize the fragility of an actor's disguise." I agree that the actor's disguise is compromised but
think the metaphor is more complex. Cf. Arnobius *Adversus nationes* 5.25,
cited by Olender (1990, 88), who, in describing Baubo's exposure of her genitalia to Demeter, says that she made them "neat and smooth as a little boy
whose skin is not yet tough and hairy." But Olender does not comment on
this metaphoric transformation. The psychoanalytic explanation equates the
fear of the female genitalia with the fear of castration. Olender (88 n. 25) gives
the relevant bibliography. Cf. Freud [1922] 1940, 213: "What arouses horror in
oneself will produce the same effect upon the enemy against whom one is
seeking to defend oneself. We read in Rabelais of how the Devil took to flight
when the woman showed him her vulva." The function of the display of the
female genitalia is most commonly perceived as apotropaic, but this single
explanation is inadequate for the wide variety of contexts in which it occurs.

metaphor reveals the deep ambivalence about the sight of female genitalia, and their metaphoric transformation into male physiognomy can be construed as an attempt to diminish that ambivalence. But what is important here is how the threat of a woman exposing her genitalia is embedded in a series of comic disguisings in which the question of what will ultimately be exposed is ambiguous. We have seen that, generally speaking, bodily disguise is figured as a feminine or feminizing activity; it is therefore not surprising that Greek literature consistently figures the threat of exposing the body for what it "really" is as the exposure of a female body.

Another relevant scene occurs in the *Thesmophoriazousae*, where revealing Mnesilochus' penis shows him for the woman he is not (τὸ πέος, 643 ff.). Of course, the example of Mnesilochus overtly presents the threat of exposing male, rather than female, genitalia (since the audience knows who he is), but this possibility is subsumed under the fiction of Mnesilochus' role as a false female. In other words, the threat is carried out against a would-be woman. The ambiguity of sexual identity in the Greek comic tradition is often a function of this threat to expose the genitalia and is always part of a trick played with clothes.[87] On the comic stage this trick has multiple layers, of course, with the most obvious one revealed in the fact that the comic actors playing women are men in drag. But on all levels the threat is aimed at the sexual identity of males and is based on the implicit possibility that these men on stage may be exposed as not men.

It can be argued, of course, that the comic *phalloi* obviate any implied ambiguity, or rather that they are unambiguous markers of a male sexual identity that can hardly be covered or hidden by clothing.[88] Lauren Taaffe suggests that comic female personae may be intentionally compromised by some disarray in the actors' costumes that results in a peek at the *phallos*: "There is no way to determine the actual nature of the costumes for *Ecclesiazuusae*, but if the actors wore pads and the *phallos* protruded from these supposedly feminine bodies once in a while, the comic and metatheatrical effects would be hilarious." Her point is that the audience "may see actors, identified as comedians by

---

87. Cf. also *Lysistrata* 800–828 and the Agathon scene in the *Thesmophoriazousae*.

88. See Arthur-Katz 1989; Henderson 1991; Lissarrague 1990.

their stylized padded uniforms, consciously playing women."[89] But even if this is the case, a potential disjunction between gender roles and sexual identities is even more obviously in play. On another level, while Priapus, satyrs, and the ithyphallic comic actors evoke laughter, the hyperbolic exposure of the *phallos* as costume is the overt conceal-ment of the real thing, an overdetermined apotropaic gesture against emasculation. Thus it may be said that the comic *phalloi* are a means of disguising the frightful vulnerability—exemplified in Greek myths of castration—of the exposed male genitalia.[90] And it may be argued that the threat posed by such exposure is therefore displaced onto the threat of exposing the female genitalia.

In these comic examples, the threat of exposure is always the threat of men exposing themselves to other men, that is, of male actors exposing themselves to other male actors and to the male citizens in the audience.[91] It might be said, therefore, that the male gaze of comedy is a sort of cross-eyed version of the male gaze that validates male nudity. The play between actor, persona, and costume in terms of sexual or genital ambiguity is often what motivates the comic ac-tion, while the *phallos*—presumably the only "genital" object in view—exemplifies the performed nature of that ambiguity. Thus the comic *phallos* is antithetical to—and even subversive of—male nudity, since the former operates in the context of exposure and an attendant threat to identity, while the latter operates in the context of display and an attendant valorization of identity. In other words, valorized masculine nudity is exposure without the element of disguise. The comic spectacle made of Thersites in the *Iliad* (ἐπ' αὐτῷ ἡδὺ γέλασσαν, 2.270) must be viewed in light of these observations. Just as we can say that Odysseus is the locus classicus for Euripides' tragic king in rags, so we can say that Thersites is the locus classicus for the gro-tesque and sexually ambiguous body of comedy.[92]

---

89. Taaffe 1991, 98.
90. For example, castration as it is featured in the story of Kronos and Ouranos at *Theogony* 178–81. See Mason 1984, 63–67. Cf. my discussion of *Lysistrata* 115 earlier in this chapter.
91. See Winkler 1990a on the "notional or proper" audience of Attic drama as one of men.
92. Taaffe (1991, 93–107) discusses visual and linguistic references to the male actor underneath the comic female costume. Referring to vases that

In *Gender Trouble,* Judith Butler argues that "those who fail to do their gender right are regularly punished."[93] Thersites' punishment at the hands of Odysseus is perhaps the earliest example of this dictum in the European tradition. And if doing one's gender right in the epic means not only meeting certain physical and vestimentary requirements but also saying the right thing in the right way, Thersites fails on both counts.[94] It is not simply the case, then, that Odysseus' threat to expose Thersites' genitals suggests some nonspecific physical deformity; any implied deformity must be figured as a deviation from the elite male model. Odysseus' threat to expose Thersites thus prefigures the comic tradition by suggesting that Thersites is more like a woman than a warrior, and that he fails to do his gender right.[95]

As a cultural institution, Athenian drama reveals an inherited ambiguity about the monomorphous persona of the Greek citizen-soldier. This ambiguity finds its most conspicuous expression in the convention of men playing women on the Attic stage, that is, when a man (the

---

illustrate male actors playing women in comedy, she states: "No male actor in female dress is pictured without some reminder of his own sexual identity; the illusion of 'woman' is often disrupted." She concludes that such exposures contribute to a reaffirmation of the "male power base of Athenian society."

93. Butler 1990a, 273.

94. The feminization of Thersites may also be implied by Odysseus' threat to send him back to the ships weeping (κλαίοντα), since κλαίω is the verb commonly used of women in mourning (e.g., at *Iliad* 18.340, 22.515). In contrast, δακρύω is used of Achilles at *Iliad* 1.349 when he grieves over the loss of Briseis, while κλαίω is used of his mourning over Patroclus at 24.4. When Plato condemns this last passage at *Republic* 388a5–b5, he uses κλαίοντα and ὀδυρόμενον. The excessive nature of Achilles' grief—the point of Plato's condemnation—is marked in the *Iliad* as well. Plato specifically says that such grief (expressed in θρῆνοι, 387e9–388a3) belongs to women. At *Odyssey* 8.523, where Odysseus is said to weep like a woman, the verb is κλαίω. But cf. *Odyssey* 4.541 and 5.82, where κλαίω is used of Menelaus' and Odysseus' weeping. See also *Odyssey* 4.258, 705, 719.

95. The possibility that Thersites lacks the proper masculine genitalia also operates as part of the Greek cultural prejudice that assimilates women and Eastern barbarians. Cf. Hall 1989, 209: "In *Orestes* Helen has brought back with her from Troy exquisite riches and a troop of Phrygian eunuchs in whose mutilation the idea of eastern effeminacy is grimly reified: the connection in the Greek imagination of luxurious and transgressive women with feminized men is demonstrated by Hellanicus' allegation that it was Atossa herself who had introduced eunuchs to the Persian court (4 *FgrH* F 178a,b)."

universal subject) is made to look like a woman (the universal other). On the one hand, presenting men in women's clothing denies the possibility of women exposing themselves; it also conforms to the received views about the true nature of women (that they are not what they seem) and to the received views about the social position of women (that they are not to be seen in public). On the other hand, the impersonation of women's bodies, gestures, and speech is a means of maintaining and exhibiting women's oppression; when Greek males wear women's clothes in front of an audience, they at once display the duplicity they ascribe to women and wear, as it were, the trappings of their own power over women.[96] But that power is itself problematic within a dominant martial ethos where real or valorized power is power over men, not over women. In the previously discussed scenes from epic and the comic stage, the theatrical body is defined as a male body under the threat of exposure, where the threat itself reveals the unstable nature of an internal and unchanging essence of masculine identity.

In the spirit of speculation, I want to end this discussion with a statement made by the scholiast on Aeschines' *Against Ctesiphon* 66–68. In describing the so-called Proagon that took place a few days before the plays were performed in the Theater of Dionysus, the scholiast says that "the actors entered naked and without their masks" [εἰσίασι δὲ δίχα προσώπων οἱ ὑποκριταὶ γυμνοί]. Γυμνοί may simply be a gloss on δίχα προσώπων here and may mean, as Pickard-Cambridge thinks, that "[a]ctors who appeared in the Proagon did not wear masks or costumes."[97] But γυμνοί seems emphatic,[98] and if we consider pictorial evidence, we might tentatively accept that the actors were paraded before the city literally "naked and without their masks."[99] In a relevant narrative, Pausanias attrib-

---

96. Cf. Greenblatt 1991, 89, on "appropriative mimesis, imitation in the interest of acquisition." Greenblatt here refers to the Spanish imitation of Amerindian gestures.

97. Pickard-Cambridge 1968, 68.

98. On the meaning of γυμνός, see Bonfante 1989, 547 with n. 22. Bonfante states, "The word refers to total nudity." Its meaning in the scholiast's usage is still unclear, however. It is often used to mean "unarmed" (LSJ 2) and, with the genitive, "stripped bare of" (LSJ 4).

99. See Pickard-Cambridge's discussion of the naked figure labeled ΤΡΑΓΟΙΔΟΣ on a calyx krater from Apulia dated to about 400 B.C.E. (Pickard-Cambridge 1968, 217, fig. 105). The vase depicts a scene from a so-called phlyax

utes the custom of having trainers enter the arena naked to a historical incident.[100]

[[Callipateira] being a widow, disguised herself exactly like a
gymnastic trainer (ἐξεικάσασα αὑτὴν τὰ πάντα ἀνδϱὶ γυμναστῇ),
and brought her son to compete at Olympia. Peisirodus, for so
her son was called, was victorious, and Callipateira, as she was
jumping over the enclosure in which they keep the trainers shut
up, exposed herself (ἐγυμνώθη). And although it had been dis-
covered that she was a woman, they let her go unpunished out
of respect for her father, her brothers and her son, all of whom
had been victorious at Olympia. But a law was passed that for
the future trainers should be naked (γυμνούς) before entering
the arena.] (Pausanias, *Description of Greece* 5.6.7, Jones translation, with some modifications)

This *aition* about the parade of the nude trainers is analogous to the
anecdote about the parade of nude actors, with the additional explana-

---

comedy; the naked figure, according to Pickard-Cambridge, is presumably "a
tragic actor waiting for his turn to perform." Likewise, Beazley (1952, 194) thinks
that "[t]he tragic actor, his own performance over, or still to come, watches the
comedians." Trendall and Webster (1971, fig. IV, 13, p. 130) argue that "it is
probably right to associate the vase with the performance of an Attic comedy and
not a local farce." It is also worth noting that the nude actor is truly nude and is
not wearing the close-fitting tights that constitute stage nudity (see Trendall and
Webster 1971, 12). Of course, the question of costuming on vases believed to
show dramatic scenes is problematic, since a single scene can include figures
obviously in costume and mask together with those that are not. As far as I
know, little has been made of the fact that numerous tragic heroes (and some
heroines) are depicted nude in these scenes—where again nudity is not stage
nudity—although presumably these characters were not portrayed by nude
actors. These scenes demonstrate the persistence of idealized male nudity, but
what they tell us about costuming conventions is uncertain. Figure 32 in Pickard-
Cambridge 1968 shows an oenochoe fragment (470–460 B.C.E.) depicting a naked male carrying the mask of a female character. Might the naked mask carrier
in figure 32 be an actor on parade? According to Pickard-Cambridge (68), it is
uncertain whether a Proagon took place before the building of the Odeum in 444
B.C.E., that is, whether it was contemporaneous with the oenochoe fragment
under discussion. And we do not know whether the scholiast on Aeschines' text
is referring to a fifth- or fourth-century practice or both.

100. The Pausanias passage is discussed by Bonfante (1989, 558).

tion that the trainers' nudity is enforced with the specific aim of proving that they are really men. We should also recall that Greek athletes
competed nude in the fifth century and that "the formal procedure for
admission to the [Athenian] *deme* involved nudity."[101] In other words,
the public display of the nude male body is a persistent trope in Greek
cultural discourse and functions in the establishment of an unambiguous manhood.

Whatever other reasons might be suggested, the purported display
of the naked actors—like that of the naked trainers and athletes—
operates in the context of this valorized male nudity, with its denial of
ambiguity.[102] And if we can imagine those actors exposing themselves
in public, we can also imagine how their nudity functions as a visible
antidote to their later appearance as fully costumed dramatis personae.
This point can be made even if the actors' nudity mean that they appeared in the Proagon without their costumes and masks.[103] Thus, this
hypothetical parade reveals both the threatened masculinity of disguised or adorned males (insofar as the actors expose themselves to
diffuse that threat) and an overdetermined negation of the complicity
that the success of their disguises (as dramatis personae) demands of
the citizens. The significance of this complicity in the representation of
Athenian political history and identity is the subject of chapter 4.

---

101. Ferrari 1993, 104. Ferrari concludes that by means of such public
nudity, "the quality of *andreia* is offered for scrutiny to a community of men."

102. Cf. Aeschines *Against Ctesiphon* 154. In Herodotus *Histories* 6.67, we
find Demaratus, the ousted king of Sparta, in the theater, where he "took his
place among the onlookers" at the "Feast of the Naked Youths."

103. I am grateful to an anonymous reader of my manuscript for this book
for pointing this out to me.

4

The Theater of Tyranny

As a defining feature in the history of the developing Athenian polis, the Pisistratid narratives represent a transition from primarily mythological or legendary descriptions and explanations of past events to a more recognizably historical account of contemporary people and places. At the same time, the generic differences between myth (or poetry) and history that enable this notion of a transition ultimately fail to conceal the fact that historical narratives, like mythological ones, are "verbal fictions, the contents of which are as much *invented* as *found*."[1] We can credit Aristotle with establishing the naturalness of this distinction and for the subsequent and persistent attempt to maintain it in the history of European ideas.[2] For the difference between myth and narrative history has less to do with form and content per se and more to do with their reception in which history is subjected to questions of evidence while myth is subjected to questions of transcendent meaning. Indeed, myth and history are created as such by the sorts of questions they elicit. Adopting an approach between these two methods of inquiry—that is, between the search for social reality, on the one hand, and for transcendent meaning, on the other—we can bring the narrative of the Pisistratid tyranny into view as an expression of Athenian political and social ideology.[3] This ideological content is the common denominator that transcends the generic differences between narrative history and myth. The Pisistratid narratives in particular are subject to such an approach because, as suggested already, they occupy a middle position in Athenian self-fashioning between a distant mythological past and a more immediate historical past. And while this more immediate past is not strictly mytholo-

---

1. The quotation is from White 1978, 82.
2. Aristotle *Poetics* 1451a37–1451b32, 1461b10 ff.
3. See Ober 1989, 38–43, for an excellent discussion of the meaning of ideology in the context of Athenian social and political life.

gized, it is invented as a series of dramatized, or theater-like, events. The purpose of this chapter is to investigate this representational strategy and to show how the dramatic character of the Pisistratid tyranny—what I am calling the theater of tyranny in Athens— illustrates the proposition that gender ideology is a constituent feature of Athenian political ideology.

In Plutarch's *Life of Solon*, Pisistratus is implicitly compared to Thespis, the first tragic actor, whom Solon calls a "deceiver of the people" (29.4). In his 1957 article titled "The Origin of ΤΡΑΓΩΙΔΙΑ," Gerald Else argues that the account of tyranny in sixth-century Athens is an account of theater-like events in which the city is a stage, the tyrant is an actor, and the Athenian citizens are his captive audience.[4] Else's purpose, as the title of his article makes clear, is to give an account of the origin of tragedy in which Pisistratus' tactics take their place in the early development of the genre. I am interested, like Else, in the tyrant's theater-like activities, but I am not interested in proving their historicity as part of a story of tragedy's origins.[5] Rather, I want to show first of all how those activities are productive of a significant feature of the Pisistratid narratives, namely, a persistent ambivalence toward the tyrant's presence and power in Athens. Acquiescence to that power, represented in the Athenians' complicity or complacency, is both implied and resisted in the ancient sources; at stake in this narrative scheme is the validity of competing versions of Athenian political history and identity, both of which are founded on a normative version of Greek masculinity.[6] To anticipate my argument, Athens' citizens are positioned as passive spectators in the presence of the tyrant, spectators who risk failing to meet the gender- and culture- specific requirements that guarantee a normative history and identity; in the narrative of the tyranny, they are liable to act more like women

---

4. Else (1957b, 36 ff.) concludes that "the tragic actor [Thespis] . . . brought forth the political actor [Pisistratus]." Cf. Else 1965, 68–69.

5. In the introduction, I discuss the search for drama's origins.

6. McGlew (1993, 5) comes to a similar conclusion but with a different focus: "[J]ust as the city's initial complicity with its tyrant established the basis for resisting him, that resistance was the basis of an enduring complicity between the polis and tyranny." Wohl (1996) provides a suggestive discussion of the conflation of aristocratic and democratic ideals in the representation of Pericles as a "tyrant."

than men and more like barbarians than Greeks. The theater of tyranny in Athens, then, is a vehicle for locating and examining this phenomenon in the related histories of Athenian self-representation and theatrical performance as a polis-specific institution.[7]

The word *tyrannos* designates a single individual with absolute and extralegal powers.[8] He may have a bodyguard—he may even have the support of an army—but he is always uniquely distinguished in the Greek literary and historical sources as exercising power in his own person. In this sense, he is like the epic heroes who come before him and the tragic heroes who come after him.[9] In the vast compass of Herodotus' *Histories*, for example, he is the male who occupies a narrative space unto himself and whose power is attested to by virtue of that occupation. The ways in which that space is occupied varies from tyrant to tyrant, of course. Particular to the Athenian context is an overt focus on the effect of Pisistratus' bodily presence and activities in the city, or on what M. Christine Boyer refers to as "the basic relationship between theatricality and the fixed eyepoint of power."[10] While ostentatious display "can be traced in the activities of all the early tyrants," an emphasis on Pisistratus' theatrical body singles him out among them.[11]

The essential stories about Pisistratus come from four primary sources: the historical narratives of Herodotus and Thucydides, Aristotle's *Constitution of the Athenians*, and Plutarch's *Life of Solon*.[12] Herodotus is the earliest of these sources and in principle must be taken into account by the authors who follow him; he is also, of course, closer to

---

7. Wiseman (1994, 1–22) discusses the "possibilities of drama as a means of articulating [Rome's] civic identity."

8. On the semantic range of τύραννος, see Hall 1989, 154–56. Other discussions include How and Wells 1968, vol. 2, appendix 16, p. 339 n. 1; Sealey 1976, 38–39; McGlew 1993, 27–30.

9. Cf. Hartog 1988, 337.

10. Boyer 1996, 85.

11. The quote is from Sealey 1976, 45; cf. 57. See also Hölscher 1991, 362–68.

12. Herodotus *Histories* 1.59–64, 6.35–39, 6.103, 5.55–56, 5.62–65; Thucydides *History* 1.20, 6.53–59; Aristotle *Athenaion Politeia* 14–19; Plutarch *Life of Solon* 30–31. I refer to the author of the *Athenaion Politeia* as Aristotle for convenience. On the problem of authorship, see Rhodes 1981, 61–63. The question of the sources and of their relationship to one another is not easily sorted out. See Jacoby 1949, 152–68; Rhodes 1981, 189–99.

the time of the events he records.[13] I argue not that his account is in absolute terms more accurate or more readily verifiable than the others but that he can be held more accountable by his readers, both contemporary and modern. In this respect Herodotus' text can be considered the standard against which the other sources for the Pisistratid tyranny are to be read, and the ways in which those other sources agree with or diverge from him are crucial for understanding Pisistratus' place in the formation of Athenian civic identity. As part of this understanding, Herodotus' account of the Pisistratid tyranny as a series of theater-like performances should also be considered in view of the fact that the historian is writing during the time of the fully established theater in Athens.[14] I am not suggesting that Herodotus modeled his account on tragic or comic plot structures but that its dramatic elements can be perceived from the point of view of an Athenian audience familiar with the theater as a social and political institution. I should make it clear that when I talk about "dramatic elements" I mean generic practices, such as disguise; I am not talking about Aristotelian prescriptions or about the modern notion of history as tragedy.

Jacoby describes the primacy of the Pisistratid legacy in Herodotus' account of early Athenian history in the following way: "In Herodotus the tyranny is the first piece of Athenian history narrated in detail; he knows about Solon's legislation, but he does not set forth the epochal importance of it, nor does he realize Solon's position in the development of the Athenian State."[15] Herodotus' failure to give pride of place

---

13. See Jacoby 1949, 153.

14. On the dating of Herodotus' *Histories,* see Fornara 1971.

15. Jacoby 1949, 153 with n. 12. Jacoby argues that Herodotus' failure to acknowledge Solon's importance is because his "Athenian authorities (who may have known more about Solon, although it is not certain that they did) had a more lively interest in the political antagonisms that led to the reform of Kleisthenes, because these antagonisms were felt to be the step immediately preceding that phase of the struggle for democracy which most concerned them, i.e., that which began with the law of Ephialtes about the Areopagus and found its end at the time of Herodotus' sojourn in Athens, and, decisively for him, in the victory of Perikles over Thukydides Milesiou." It is somewhat difficult to accept, however, that Herodotus' Athenian sources would not have told him about Solon, especially if they knew more about him. The stories of Solon and Pisistratus—as later accounts (i.e., in Plutarch) attest—are certainly not mutually exclusive. In other words, an account of Solon would neither contradict nor weaken the "lively interest" of Herodotus'

to Solon is not easily explained, especially when we ask why a tyrant
receives more attention than the city's purported lawgiver: despite
Herodotus' failure to do so, other sources credit Solon with being the
progenitor of Athenian-style self-governance. Aristotle calls him the
first leader of the people (οὗτος δὲ πρῶτος ἐγένετο τοῦ δήμου προστάτης, *Athenaion Politeia* 2.2).[16] But whatever reasons might be given for
Herodotus' slight of Solon (if we can call it a slight), the result is a
tradition that puts the Pisistratids at the center of early Athenian history and the development of an Athenian political identity.[17]

In the archaeological and literary sources, the era of the tyranny can
be characterized by three related developments. First, the Athenian
polis is being defined spatially and visually in terms of its architecture
and public spaces; second, it is being defined culturally in terms of its
civic institutions and ceremonies; and third, it is being defined politically in terms of a transition from tyranny to democracy. Documenta-
tion of these developments is not without controversy, of course, and
the exact role the Pisistratids may have played in any of them is uncertain.[18] While acknowledging the impossibility of an accurate or factual
accounting of this period, I want to draw attention to those features
that contribute to the theatricality of the Athenian tyranny, beginning
with the city as a civic space in which Pisistratus played his part.[19]

---

sources as Jacoby describes it. Cf. Frost 1985, 67: "The only contemporary
source [for the sixth century] is Solon himself, to the extent that his poems
describe the social and political background from which Pisistratus emerged.
And we are most recently reminded by Bernard Knox that other than the
fragments of Solon's verse, not one scrap of Athenian writing from the rest of
the sixth century has survived." Cf. Knox 1978, 43. How and Wells (1968, on
Herodotus *Histories* 1.29), call Jacoby's interpretation "oversubtle": "The explanation of the omission [of mention of Solon's laws] is probably that H. has no
interest in constitutional history." But the Persian debate over the best sort of
government in book 3.80–82 suggests that Herodotus did have an "interest in
constitutional history."

16. On the meaning of τοῦ δήμου προστάτης, see Rhodes 1981, ad loc.

17. An anonymous reader of my manuscript for this book suggested that it
was not Herodotus' intent to give an outline of Athenian political history and
points out that Solon plays a significant role in the episodes with Croesus. No
matter what Herodotus' intent was, however, the Pisistratids occupy center
stage in his account of early Athens.

18. See, for example, Osborne 1994. Cf. Shapiro 1989, chap. 1.

19. For a general discussion of the European city as a theatrical space, see
Boyer 1996, chap. 3, "The City and the Theater."

Monumental building plans are commonly attributed to tyrants in the archaic Greek poleis.[20] So while the Pisistratid tyranny is not unique in this respect, the archaeological and literary evidence for such a plan under the Pisistratids—even though that evidence is far from straightforward—provides a backdrop against which to view the less tangible innovations with which the tyrants are credited in the early formation of the polis. The spatial development of the city during the sixth century is described by Hölscher.[21]

On the whole, this development (the separation of the living spaces of the social classes) introduced into the layout of the city of Athens a strong element of structure and monumentality. Most important was the decision to move the agora into the center of communal life. For centuries, the flat zone northwest of the acropolis had been the site of graves and chthonic sanctuaries, and more recently of increasing numbers of houses and potters' workshops; if it served, in addition, as a meeting place for the assembly, it did so only in the midst of this conglomerate of diverse spheres of life. But after 600 B.C. no more houses, graves or wells were built in a fairly large area between three important streets; the space was leveled, and a couple of wells refilled. Up to the middle of the sixth century, the open space was extended, particularly toward the east. This can only have been achieved through considerable expropriation of privately owned land, partly at the expense, and perhaps against the will, of influential families. Thus indeed, this was a measure that reflects not only forceful urban planning but also the precedence of central institutions over particular interests. (Hölscher 1991, 363–64)

As Hölscher describes it, the sixth century is a period of gradual transition from private dwellings in the area of the Athenian Agora to public administrative and religious buildings, a transition from private

---

20. As an example, Herodotus (*Histories* 1.14) concludes that the building known in his time as the Corinthian treasury at Delphi was built by Cypselus, tyrant of Corinth.
21. See also Shapiro 1989, 5–8.

to public space.²² Thus the early formation of the Athenian city-state can be described in terms of a demarcation of space for the purpose of public commerce and public display, or what Hölscher refers to as "monumentality." It is again true that a precise historical account of the relationship of the tyrants to the construction of particular public buildings is not possible;²³ it is also the case that some so-called monumental buildings may have been erected prior to the Pisistratids' coming to power.²⁴ Nonetheless, the archaeological evidence argues in favor of what will become a cultural trope in the fifth century, namely, that large public building plans in Athens are the work of tyrants. The most conspicuous example of this trope is the popular charge against Pericles that his sponsorship of such a program (among other things) meant that he aimed at tyranny: Plutarch quotes fifth-century comic poets who called Pericles and his supporters the "new Pisistratids" (*Pericles* 16.1.1–4).²⁵ Thus whether or not the Pisistratids were actually responsible for grand building schemes—and even if Plutarch's ac-

---

22. It has been argued that Building F on the west side of the Agora was built as a private "palace" for the Pisistratids (Camp 1986, 44–45). Cf. Frost 1985, 61 with n. 17; Kolb 1977; Hölscher 1991, 364. Still, this so-called palace was located in public space.

23. But Camp (1986, 40) attributes much of the reorganization of public space in the sixth century to the Pisistratids: "Several large projects were started under the Peisistratids: work was done on the Acropolis, the temple of Dionysos was built just below, and the colossal temple of Olympian Zeus— the largest on the Greek mainland—was laid out. During their reign the Agora took on a more monumental form. To judge from the filling of wells and the demolition of houses, the public area of the Agora expanded gradually to the east and south during the second and third quarters of the 6th century. In addition, new buildings and monuments were erected, several of which can be directly associated with the Peisistratids, and others which from the archaeological evidence seem to have been built during their tenure."

24. Cf., for example, Hölscher 1991, 367 with n. 49, on the earliest monumental temple to Athena: "for historical reasons it is impossible to connect this temple with Pisistratus."

25. The sources linking Pericles to tyranny are cited by Ostwald (1986, 185 n. 32). These include Aristophanes *Acharnians* 530–39; Thucydides *History* 2.65.8–10, 2.63.2; Plutarch *Pericles* 16.1–4, 7.4, 8.3. On opposition to Pericles' building plan, see Plutarch *Pericles* 12–14. Ostwald (187) notes the special significance of the building program in this regard: "of [Pericles'] populist measures the building program sustained the heaviest attack." See also Andrewes 1978; Wohl 1996.

count of Pericles "tyrannical" reputation in the fifth century cannot be verified—the Pisistratids came to have a reputation for making the city into a place for monumental public display. What is the source of this reputation, and what is its significance in the formulation of Athenian history and identity? The construction of public buildings and the monumentalizing of city space is a distinguishing activity of barbarian tyrants. Thus the barbarian or eastern tyrant is the model for any public figure who is described as a tyrant, and the building programs of Pisistratus or Pericles prove in a roundabout fashion their tyrannical ambitions.[26] Enormous wealth is often attributed to barbarian tyrants, so it may also seem obvious that the tyrant's wealth translates into large-scale public building programs. These barbarian associations are pertinent to the narrative of Athenian tyranny but not entirely adequate; rich tyrants could certainly spend their money satisfying their private desires, and—more to the point—great personal wealth is not a prominent feature in the Pisistratid narratives.[27] A related explanation is provided by Aristotle, who says that the building programs of tyrants, including the temple of Olympian Zeus undertaken by the Pisistratids, ensure "constant occupation and poverty among the subject people" (πάντα γὰρ ταῦτα δύναται ταὐτόν, ἀσχολίαν καὶ πενίαν τῶν ἀρχομένων, *Politics* 1313b124–25). But while this socioeconomic explanation is compelling, it also offers an inadequate and narrowly materialist account of the attribution of monumental urban and civic development to the tyrants.[28] Despite the many uncertainties about particular buildings or building plans in the archaeological and literary sources, the Athenian tyranny is "imagined" as a public spectacle to be viewed by Athens' citizens.[29]

Another development commonly associated with the tyrant and related to his role in the city's spatial definition is his role in the city's cultural definition, manifested in the introduction of particular civic

26. On the Greek characterization of barbarian tyrants, see Hall 1989, 154–59, 193–200. On Aristotle's description of the barbarian tyrant in the *Politics*, see my discussion later in this chapter.

27. However, Herodotus reports that on his third attempt at the tyranny, Pisistratus returned to Athens with a good accumulation of cash (συνόδοισι χρημάτων, *Histories* 1.63). On wealth and tyranny, see McGlew 1993, 26.

28. On tyranny and the Panathenaia, see Wohl 1996.

29. Cf. Anderson 1983 for the notion of "imagined" communities.

institutions, cults, and ceremonies. Pisistratus is reported to have brought the cult of Dionysus Eleuthereus into Athens, to have established the Greater Dionysia, to have reorganized the Panathenaea in 566 B.C.E., and to have introduced the tragic contests in Athens in 534 B.C.E.[30] Other tyrants (notably Cleisthenes of Sicyon) are said to have instituted or enhanced public festivals in their respective cities, and we might conclude that the Pisistratid legacy simply conforms to the standard narrative of tyranny. But the process of selection and invention that results in variations within these similar narratives make them polis specific. In the case of the Athenian tyranny, the dramatic institutions that Pisistratus purportedly founded or enhanced form part of the representation of his tyranny itself in terms of theatrical or theater-like practices. I am not insisting that Pisistratus is to be credited with any actual role in the establishment of the dramatic contests in Athens, only that his continuing reputation for doing so is significant.[31] In more general terms, what Robin Osborne calls the "orthodox" view of the city in the time of the tyrants—a view that accepts Pisistratus' role in the establishment of various cults, for example—is evidence of the modern scholarly desire to make Pisistratus into a culture hero that the ancient historical and archaeological sources cannot fully corroborate.[32]

The fullest appreciation of this desire can be found in the narrative tradition concerning the tyranny and, as I have mentioned, in Herodotus' *Histories* first of all. In Herodotus, the first account of the tyrant forms part of the story of Croesus, king of the Lydians, who wants to lead an expedition against the Persians. Croesus sends embassies to Delphi to ask if he should undertake this expedition and is told that

---

30. *Parian Marble, FGrH* 239 A43. See Frost 1985, 68–69; Pickard-Cambridge 1968, 57–58; Parke 1977, 34, 126, 129; How and Wells 1968, vol. 2, appendix 16.7; Nagy 1991, 391.

31. In a very suggestive 1990 article, Connor argues that the introduction of the cult of Dionysus Eleuthereus into Athens and the beginning of the City Dionysia may have happened after the overthrow of the tyranny (i.e., "a few years after 506 B.C.") and in "celebration of the success of the system [i.e., the reforms of Cleisthenes] that had replaced the Peisistratid regime" (12). See also West 1989.

32. Osborne 1994, 147–48. Cf. Shapiro 1989; and cf. Ober 1989, 65–67, on the "cult of personality" that surrounds Pisistratus in the sources.

he should make friends with the Spartans and the Athenians, who are the mightiest of the Greeks at this time. Croesus' inquiry about the Athenians is the point of Herodotus' digression on Pisistratus. Herodotus says that Athens was divided into two factions at this time and that Pisistratus, "aiming at the tyranny, put together a third faction" (*Histories* 1.59).[33] Now begins Herodotus' account of the manner in which Pisistratus' attempt was successful.

τρωματίσας ἑωυτόν τε καὶ ἡμιόνους ἤλασε ἐς τὴν ἀγορὴν τὸ ζεῦγος ὡς ἐκπεφευγὼς τοὺς ἐχθρούς, οἵ μιν ἐλαύνοντα ἐς ἀγρὸν ἠθέλησαν ἀπολέσαι δῆθεν, ἐδέετό τε τοῦ δήμου φυλακῆς τινος πρὸς αὐτοῦ κυρῆσαι, πρότερον εὐδοκιμήσας ἐν τῇ πρὸς Μεγαρέας γενομένῃ στρατηγίῃ, Νίσαιάν τε ἑλὼν καὶ ἄλλα ἀποδεξάμενος μεγάλα ἔργα. ὁ δὲ δῆμος ὁ τῶν ᾿Αθηναίων ἐξαπατηθεὶς ἔδωκέ οἱ τῶν ἀστῶν καταλέξας ἄνδρας τούτους οἵ δορυφόροι μὲν οὐκ ἐγένοντο Πεισιστράτου, κορυνηφόροι δέ. ξύλων γὰρ κορύνας ἔχοντες εἵποντό οἱ ὄπισθε. συνεπαναστάντες δὲ οὗτοι ἅμα Πεισιστράτῳ ἔσχον τὴν ἀκρόπολιν. ἔνθα δὴ ὁ Πεισίστρατος ἦρχε ᾿Αθηναίων, οὔτε τιμὰς τὰς ἐούσας συνταράξας οὔτε θέσμια μεταλλάξας, ἐπί τε τοῖσι κατεστεῶσι ἔνεμε τὴν πόλιν κοσμέων καλῶς τε καὶ εὖ.

[Wounding himself and his mules, he drove his carriage into the agora with a tale that he had escaped from his enemies who, he said, would have slain him as he was driving into the country. So he asked the people to give him a guard to protect his person; for he had won himself a reputation in his command of the army against the Megarians, when he had taken Nisaea and had performed other great deeds. Thus the Athenian *demos* was deceived and gave him some men chosen from among the townsmen; these men did not become Pisistratus' spear-bearers but his club-bearers—for those who followed behind him bore wooden clubs. These men, joining in rebellion with Pisistratus, took the Acropolis. In this way, Pisistratus came to rule the Athenians and he

---

33. On the debate over the number of Pisistratus' attempts at the tyranny, see Rhodes 1981, 15–30; Jacoby 1949, 152–68.

neither disturbed the existing laws nor changed the order of offices, but he governed the city according to its established laws and ordered it fairly and well.] (1.59)

This passage contains three related and recurring topoi in the account of the Athenian tyrant: the representation of his career as a series of staged events, the representation of his ability to deceive the Athenian citizenry, and the representation of the Athenians' ambivalence toward their role in aiding and abetting the tyranny. This ambivalence, expressed in Herodotus' assertion that Pisistratus governed according to the established laws, is not simply explained by its place within a larger tradition about tyranny in general, however. Nor is it to be taken at face value, that is, as a simple statement of historical fact. Rather, that larger tradition is the product of Athenian sources and is therefore predicated on the ambivalence that characterizes the Athenian example.

In the *Politics,* Aristotle provides perhaps the best commentary on the assumptions that produce and perpetuate this ambivalence (1313a34–1316a1). According to Aristotle, "tyrannies are preserved in two extremely opposite ways." The first, exemplified by Periander of Corinth and tyranny under the Persian ἀρχή, or empire, is the "traditional way and the one according to which most tyrants exercise their authority." It is characterized by harsh measures designed to maintain an apathetic and servile population; Aristotle specifies again that these are the measures of "Persian and barbarian tyranny, for all exercise the same sort of power" (1313a34–35; 1313a35–36; 1313b9–10).[34] In Aristotle's scheme, this first type of barbarian tyrant aims at three things.

εἰς οὓς μὲν οὖν ὅρους ἀνάγεται τὰ βουλεύματα τῶν τυράννων, οὗτοι τρεῖς τυγχάνουσιν ὄντες· πάντα γὰρ ἀναγάγοι τις ἂν τὰ τυραννικὰ πρὸς ταύτας τὰς ὑποθέσεις, τὰ μὲν ὅπως μὴ πιστεύωσιν ἀλλήλοις, τὰ δ' ὅπως μὴ δύνωνται, τὰ δ' ὅπως μικρὸν φρονῶσιν.

---

34. Cf. Herodotus *Histories* 3.80, where Otanes describes the harsh rule of the model barbarian tyrant. For a discussion of Herodotus' assessment of tyrannical rule, see Hartog 1988, 325–39.

[These are the three aims to which the plans of tyrants are directed; for all the measures taken by tyrants one might class under the following principles—those that are designed to prevent mutual trust, those that are designed to prevent power, and those that are designed to diminish ambition.] (1314a25–29)

In contrast to this mode of tyrannical rule, Aristotle describes another in which the tyrant pretends to be a kind of benevolent monarch.

ὁ δ' ἕτερος σχεδὸν ἐξ ἐναντίας ἔχει τοῖς εἰρημένοις τὴν
ἐπιμέλειαν. ἔστι δὲ λαβεῖν αὐτὸν ἐκ τῆς φθορᾶς τῆς τῶν
βασιλειῶν. ὥσπερ γὰρ τῆς βασιλείας εἷς τρόπος τῆς φθορᾶς τὸ
ποιεῖν τὴν ἀρχὴν τυραννικωτέραν, οὕτω τῆς τυραννίδος
σωτηρία τὸ ποιεῖν αὐτὴν βασιλικωτέραν, ἓν φυλάττοντα
μόνον, τὴν δύναμιν, ὅπως ἄρχῃ μὴ μόνον βουλομένων ἀλλὰ
καὶ μὴ βουλομένων. προϊέμενος γὰρ καὶ τοῦτο προΐεται καὶ τὸ
τυραννεῖν. ἀλλὰ τοῦτο μὲν ὥσπερ ὑπόθεσιν δεῖ μένειν, τὰ δ'
ἄλλα τὰ μὲν ποιεῖν τὰ δὲ δοκεῖν ὑποκρινόμενον τὸν βασιλικὸν
καλῶς.

[The other [sort of tyranny] tries to operate in a manner almost the opposite to those that have been mentioned. And it is possible to ascertain this from the fall of monarchies. For just as one way of destroying a monarchy is to make the government more like a tyranny, so one way of securing a tyranny is to make it more like a monarchy. In this way, by protecting only his power, he rules not only over those who consent but also over those who do not. For if the tyrant gives up ruling over those who do not consent to his rule, he also gives up being a tyrant. But this must always remain a principle [of such a tyrant], that he play the royal role well [ὑποκρινόμενον τὸν βασιλικὸν καλῶς] in all his other actions—both those that he does and those that he seems to do.] (1314a31–40)

The defining characteristic of this manner of tyranny is its reliance on pretense or role playing, specified by Aristotle as "playing the royal role well" (ὑποκρινόμενον τὸν βασιλικὸν καλῶς).[35] The disjunction

---

35. Cf. Plato *Republic* 577b–579c.

between what such a tyrant is and what he appears to be is made
more explicit when Aristotle discusses the importance of military
valor in this tyrant's self-presentation.

καὶ [δεῖ] φαίνεσθαι μὴ χαλεπὸν ἀλλὰ σεμνόν, ἔτι δὲ τοιοῦτον
ὥστε μὴ φοβεῖσθαι τοὺς ἐντυγχάνοντας ἀλλὰ μᾶλλον
αἰδεῖσθαι· τούτου μέντοι τυγχάνειν οὐ ῥᾴδιον ὄντα
εὐκαταφρόνητον, διὸ δεῖ κἂν μὴ τῶν ἄλλων ἀρετῶν ἐπιμέλειαν
ποιῆται ἀλλὰ τῆς πολεμικῆς, καὶ δόξαν ἐμποιεῖν περὶ αὑτοῦ
τοιαύτην·

[It is necessary that he appear to be not harsh but dignified and
that he do this so that he inspires not fear but rather respect in
those who encounter him, though this is not easy to achieve for
a contemptible person; therefore it is necessary that even if he
pays no attention to other sorts of virtues, he must pay attention to military valor and make himself a reputation in this.]
(1314b18–23)

Verbs meaning "to seem" (δοκέω) and "to appear" (φαίνομαι) pre-
dominate in this description of the tyrant who can seem to be worthy
of respect even though he may be a contemptible person. While there
is little attention paid to how this sort of tyranny actually differs from
the benevolent monarchy it imitates, Aristotle insists that the success
of the second sort of tyrant depends on his ability to pretend to be
what he is not, and crucial to this successful pretense is the ability to
establish a reputation (δόξα) for military valor. The nature of this
reputation is suggested at *Politics* 1315b28–29, where Aristotle says
that Periander ruled for a long time because he was "tyrannical but
warlike" (Περίανδρος δ᾽ ἐγένετο μὲν τυραννικός, ἀλλὰ πολεμικός).
The contrast implies that tyrants are not usually or rightly defined as
warlike. But Periander, of course, exemplifies the first sort of tyrant
(cf. 1313a37–39), who, to keep his subjects occupied, is a "warmon-
ger" [πολεμοποιός] (1313b28). The seeming contradiction can be explained by the further implication that true martial valor (as opposed
to simply waging war to keep people busy) is a positive trait that
tyrants do not usually possess. And this seems to be the case for both
types of tyrants; the second type of tyrant needs a reputation for

martial valor, but this reputation too, like his imitation of a benevolent monarch, is only a pretense.

Aristotle's detailed discussion of these two sorts of tyranny summarizes the ambiguous nature of tyranny in Athenian political and civic discourse, including the way in which martial valor is a factor in that ambiguity. More specifically, it helps to contextualize the paradoxical quality of the Athenian tyranny, or rather to explain why the Athenians in Herodotus' account seem to be ruled and yet not ruled by the tyrant. Given the two sorts of tyrants in Aristotle's treatise, Pisistratus is the second, untraditional sort, who, insofar as he is said to have kept the established laws or customs, succeeds in the pretense that he is not a tyrant. In the list of historical examples following his lengthy description, Aristotle notes that Pisistratus "submitted to a summons for a trial before the Areopagus" (1315b22–23), implying that the Athenian tyranny lasted as long as it did because Pisistratus did not seem to be above the law. He also notes that several other tyrannies were long lasting because the tyrant treated his subjects with moderation and observed the laws (as in the case of Orthagoras; see 1315b16–17) or because he was warlike and looked after the interests of the people (as in the case of Cleisthenes and Periander; see 1315b17–19, 29–30). While the historical examples are too general to do justice to the detailed treatment of the monarchlike tyrant that precedes them, it is curious that Aristotle does not use Pisistratus as the primary example of his second sort of tyrant, especially given the Herodotean narrative of the Pisistratid tyranny, with which Aristotle was familiar. But this too is perhaps revelatory of an ambivalence toward the Athenians' role in the tyranny. Aristotle's famous description of Pisistratus in the *Athenaion Politeia* as an "extreme advocate of the people" [δημοτικώτατος] (14.1) is another expression of this ambivalence insofar as it signifies not so much a political fact as the representation of a political past in which the tyranny, in Aristotle's time, is described retrospectively in terms of the later democracy.[36]

To view Herodotus' account of Pisistratus in the light of Aristotle's discussion of tyranny may seem anachronistic. But Aristotle's views

---

36. Euripides' statement at *Frogs* 952 that the freedom of speech he allows his dramatic characters is "democratic" (δημοκρατικὸν γὰρ αὖτ᾽ ἔδρων) is one example of the lexicon of democracy in use in the fifth century.

presumably developed out of long-standing cultural debates about tyrannies and tyrants that necessarily included the Pisistratids. In other words, the philosopher's views are unique neither to him nor to his time. Aristotle's description of tyranny in fact illuminates Herodotus' story of Pisistratus' successfully fraudulent wounds. By suggesting that the Athenians did not overtly cooperate with Pisistratus, the story helps us to formulate a discourse of Athenian tyranny in which the Athenians are implicitly excused for accepting a tyrant as their leader: the reason they played the part he wanted them to play was because he played his part so well. The Athenians can be described in this episode as willing participants in a spectacle that, more powerful than physical or military force, gave the illusion of public consent.[37] But at the same time, Pisistratus' act indicts the Athenians for their gullibility, a gullibility that Herodotus makes more explicit in the episode in which the tyrant is aided by a false Athena (discussed later in this chapter). In sum, we have a story that, on the one hand, condemns the Athenians for accepting and even aiding the tyrant in executing his fraudulent and forceful takeover (they even give him a bodyguard) and, on the other hand, excuses them by reporting that Pisistratus "neither disturbed the existing laws nor changed the order of offices, but governed the city according to its established laws and ordered it fairly and well." The theatricality of this event—its representation of the tyrant's theatrical body and scripted speech (i.e., the assertion imputed to Pisistratus that he was fleeing his enemies [ὡς ἐκπεφευγὼς τοὺς ἐχθροὺς])—illustrates the contested status of the tyrant in Athenian history and the broader applicability of theater-like practices in the context of Athenian political self-representation.

The ruse of self-mutilation—here the mark of what I am calling Pisistratus' theatrical body—is not unique to the Athenian tyrant, however, and comparison with a similar story in Herodotus puts his entry into Athens into a larger cultural perspective. In book 3 of the *Histories*, Herodotus tells the gruesome story of Zopyrus, a high-ranking Persian

---

37. Cf. de Ste. Croix 1981, 301: "In fourth-century Athens even would-be oligarchs found it politic to *pretend* that they too wanted democracy" (emphasis added). The practice of attaching liturgies to the most important magistracies is one of the important ways in which democracy in fourth-century Athens was in reality rule by the most wealthy. See de Ste. Croix 1981, 305–6, on Aristotle *Politics* 1321a31–42.

who mutilates himself as part of a plan to capture Babylon (3.153–60). In considering these two stories together, I am relying neither on the chronological priority of Darius' capture of Babylon nor on any argument about the order in which the books of Herodotus' text were composed. I am suggesting that by virtue of their similarities, these accounts constitute what Homeric scholars would call a type-scene and what I am calling a theater-like type-scene.[38]

After cutting off his ears and nose and scourging himself, Zopyrus enters Babylon and convinces the Babylonians that he was disfigured by Darius because he had advised the king to quit the siege of their city. The Babylonians are persuaded by his appearance and assent to his request for a body of troops (ἐδέετο δὲ στρατιῆς, 3.157.2). Finally, Zopyrus achieves his goal of allowing Darius to enter the city and subdue it, and Herodotus reports that as a result of his exploit, Zopyrus was held in great esteem by the king (3.160). The story of Zopyrus illustrates an extraordinary act of self-mutilation and presents what might be called a hyper-real theatrical body, insofar as Zopyrus incurs "real" wounds for the purpose of playing the role of an ill-treated underling. Of course, barbarian despots are well known in Herodotus for mutilating their enemies.[39] To Darius' inquiry about who is responsible for his wounds, Zopyrus replies, "There is no man except yourself who has the power to treat me in such a way—no stranger has done this, but I myself did it because I consider it a terrible thing for Assyrians to laugh at the Persians" (3.155.2). Darius responds that Zopyrus has committed a most shameful act and that he must have been out of his mind to have done it (κῶς οὐκ ἐξέπλωσας τῶν φρενῶν σεωυτὸν διαφθείρας, 3.155.3). The king's response registers the fact that self-mutilation is unusual even among barbarians. In general, Herodotus' narrative exemplifies the cruelty of the barbarian despot, the extreme loyalty he can claim from his sub-

---

38. On the Homeric type-scene, see Nagler 1974; Edwards 1992. Cf. Barthes 1982a. On Herodotus' account of the revolt of Babylon and its capture by Darius, see How and Wells 1968, 1:299–300. They discuss the possibility that the capture of Babylon that Herodotus recounts in book 3 belongs not to Darius but to Xerxes in 478 B.C.E.

39. See Hall 1989, 158–59 and, on eunuchs, 209–10; see also Hartog 1988, 333–34. Other examples of barbarian despots who mutilate their enemies are found at Herodotus *Histories* 3.69, 3.79, 7.238, 8.90.

jects, and the uniqueness of self-mutilation in the *Histories*. The meaning of Pisistratus' self-mutilation in the history of Athenian civic identity can be contextualized within these related themes.

Like Zopyrus, Pisistratus enters a city and, calling attention to his supposed wounds, asks for military aid against an imagined enemy.[40] The principal difference between these two episodes, of course, is that whereas Pisistratus claims he has sustained his "wounds" in a military skirmish with his enemies, Zopyrus claims that he has been mistreated by his king. The false stories given out by Zopyrus and Pisistratus thus attest to culturally specific prejudices. Pisistratus' story relies on the Greek privileging of martial valor, validated by the Herodotean narrator when he mentions Pisistratus' reputation as a general in the war against the Megarians.[41] The story of his nonexistent enemies indicates that he is deserving of the Athenians' aid precisely because of his military reputation, the sort of reputation Aristotle says is essential for the tyrant who pretends not to be a tyrant (*Politics* 1314b22–23).[42] Zopyrus' story relies on the common account of unjust and cruel punishment at the hands of a barbarian despot. Thus these acts of self-mutilation differ both in degree and in kind, differences that—from the Greek point of view, of course—distinguish the barbarian from the Greek.

A critical feature of this distinction is the overtly theater-like nature of Pisistratus' act of self-mutilation in comparison with that of Zopyrus. While there can be no doubt that Zopyrus really disfigured himself in Herodotus' narrative, Pisistratus' wounds seem superficial at best. Herodotus says only that he "wounded himself" (τρωματίσας ἑαυτόν, *Histories* 1.59.4), and the historian offers no detailed description of what those wounds looked like or how serious they might have been. This lack of elaboration can be explained in a variety of ways, but one of the conclusions to which it leads is that the tyrant's wounds were the sort that could give the appearance of injury without being truly grievous or disfiguring. One might also conclude, again by comparison with Zopyrus, that only a barbarian would be

---

40. Cf. ἐδέετό τε τοῦ δήμου φυλακῆς (Herodotus *Histories* 1.59.4) with ἐδέετο δὲ στρατιῆς (3.157.2).

41. But cf. Plutarch's account of the war against the Megarians (*Life of Solon* 8.4–6), where Pisistratus' participation is less than clear.

42. Cf. Aristotle *Politics* 1279a39–b3.

capable of such actual self-brutalization. At the same time, the noticeable absence of any detailed description of Pisistratus' wounds suggests that it took less (in terms of a "reality effect") for Pisistratus to convince the Athenians to do what Pisistratus wanted than it did for Zopyrus to convince the Babylonians to do what Zopyrus wanted. And precisely because Herodotus implies that Pisistratus' wounds were superficial, the tyrant's effect on the citizens he would dupe is more astounding. Zopyrus is given a bodyguard by the Babylonians, but he must ultimately admit Darius and the Persian army into the city to achieve his aim of subduing it. In comparison, Pisistratus is given a bodyguard by the Athenians but does not need to call in an army to gain control over the city. And because the constitution and strength of his bodyguard is less than clear in the text (see discussion later in this chapter), the superficiality of Pisistratus' wounds in comparison with those of Zopyrus seems inversely proportional to his power in the city. Or, to put the matter another way, the very superficiality of his "wounds" ironically works to prove his real power over the citizens. Insofar as Pisistratus plays what might be called an Athenian version of the barbarian Zopyrus, that power is achieved by virtue of the fact that his political persona is a powerfully effective theatrical persona.

This theatrical persona is even more explicitly represented in Plutarch's later account of Solon's opposition to Pisistratus' motives and means. In the narratives of competition between Solon and Pisistratus, Solon generally represents the conservative soldier-citizen who relies on face-to-face speech and man-to-man combat in doing his civic duty. In contrast, as Plutarch recounts, Pisistratus can only try to play the part of a hero.[43]

Ἐπεὶ δὲ κατατρώσας αὐτὸς ἑαυτὸν ὁ Πεισίστρατος ἧκεν εἰς ἀγορὰν ἐπὶ ζεύγους κομμιζόμενος, καὶ παρώξυνε τὸν δῆμον ὡς διὰ τὴν πολιτείαν ὑπὸ τῶν ἐχθρῶν ἐπιβεβουλευμένος, καὶ πολλοὺς εἶχεν ἀγανακτοῦντας καὶ βοῶντας, προσελθὼν ἐγγὺς ὁ Σόλων καὶ παραστάς, "Οὐ καλῶς," εἶπεν, "ὦ παῖ

---

43. On the problems of chronology, see Rhodes 1981; Freeman 1926, 153–55. Rhodes (202) states: "It is possible that Solon lived to 560/59 and witnessed Pisistratus' first *coup*, and fr. II may confirm this; otherwise nearly all is probably invention."

Ἱπποκράτους, ὑποκρίνῃ τὸν ῾Ομηρικὸν ᾿Οδυσσέα· ταῦτα γὰρ
ποιεῖς τοὺς πολίτας παρακρουόμενος οἷς ἐκεῖνος τοὺς
πολεμίους ἐξηπάτησεν, αἰκισάμενος ἑαυτόν." ἐκ τούτου τὸ μὲν
πλῆθος ἦν ἕτοιμον ὑπερμαχεῖν τοῦ Πεισιστράτου, καὶ
συνῆλθεν εἰς ἐκκλησίαν ὁ δῆμος.

[When Pisistratus had wounded himself and had come into the
Agora riding in a chariot, and intending to provoke the demos
with the charge that he had been plotted against by his enemies
on account of his political opinions, he caused many of the people
to be angry and to shout out. But Solon drawing near stood beside
him and said, "O son of Hippocrates, you are not playing
[ὑποκρίνῃ] the Homeric Odysseus well; for when he maltreated
himself it was to deceive his enemies, but you do it to lead your
fellow citizens astray." After this the multitude was ready to fight
for Pisistratus, and the people met together in a general assembly.] (Plutarch *Life of Solon* 30.1)

Plutarch's account represents another retrospective position (i.e.,
like that of Herodotus or Aristotle) from which to view the tyrant's
persistent reputation for theater-like display. As such, it functions
within what Joseph Roach calls a "genealogy of performance," where
the definition of performance combines notions of substitution and
repetition that take bodily form. A past that is represented as a series
of such substitutions and repetitions necessarily jeopardizes the
search for the origins of cultural practices, including history as an
inscription of that search. According to Roach, "genealogies of performance document—and suspect—the historical transmission and dissemination of cultural practices through collective representations."[44]
In Plutarch's account, the cultural practices under scrutiny are bodily
substitution and repetition themselves, in which the "wounded"
Pisistratus takes on the role of the "Homeric Odysseus" and the Athenian Agora is turned into a theatrical space.[45] Genealogy and theatri-

44. Roach 1996, 25, following the work of Foucault and Jonathan Arac. Cf.
Roach's p. 6: "[T]he relentless search for the purity of origin is a voyage not of
discovery but of erasure."
45. See Kolb 1981. On Odysseus as the locus classicus of the king disguised as a beggar, see my discussion in chap. 3.

cality are explicitly linked in this episode in the reference to a heroic lineage, that is, a lineage in which the epic heroes (like Odysseus) are a conventional source of cultural reenactment. The reference to Pisistratus as his father's son ("O son of Hippocrates") testifies to that linkage not only in terms of individual identity but also in terms of textual traditions, since patronymics are a common rhetorical device in epic; in this latter sense, Solon himself is presented as an epic speaker. The notion of theatricality in this scene comprises acts of bodily substitution and verbal repetition (including first-person quotation) in the process of re-animating both the epic hero (played by Pisistratus) and the epic poet (played by Solon).[46]

In reporting Solon's comparison of Pisistratus to Odysseus, Plutarch is referring to the episode in the *Odyssey* where Helen tells the story of Odysseus' infiltration among the Trojans.

αὐτὸν μιν πληγῇσιν ἀεικελίῃσι δαμάσσας,
σπεῖρα κάκ' ἀμφ' ὤμοισι βαλών, οἰκῆϊ ἐοικώς,
ἀνδρῶν δυσμενέων κατέδυ πόλιν εὐρυάγυιαν·
ἄλλῳ δ' αὐτὸν φωτὶ κατακρύπτων ἤϊσκε
δέκτῃ, ὃς οὐδὲν τοῖος ἔην ἐπὶ νηυσὶν Ἀχαιῶν.
τῷ ἴκελος κατέδυ Τρώων πόλιν, οἱ δ' ἀβάκησαν
πάντες· ἐγὼ δὲ μιν οἴη ἀνέγνων τοῖον ἐόντα.

[He flagellated himself with degrading strokes, then threw
a worthless sheet about his shoulders. And looking like a servant,
he crept into the wide-wayed city of his enemies,
concealing himself in the likeness of another man,
a beggar, not the sort of man he was beside the ships of the
Achaeans.
In this likeness he crept into the city of the Trojans, but they were
all
speechless; I alone recognized him as he was [in this disguise].]
(*Odyssey* 4.244–50)

In Solon's comparison, Pisistratus imitates Odysseus' playing the part of the wounded beggar but does not play his part well (οὐ καλῶς),

---

46. On direct quotation, see chap. 2.

because he plays it before the wrong spectators, that is, before his fellow citizens instead of his acknowledged enemies.[47] Nonetheless—and this point is the basis of Solon's quarrel—Pisistratus' role playing is successful in that he duped the Athenians, just as Odysseus' role playing was successful in that he evaded recognition by the Trojans. In both cases, the citizens act in accordance with the theater-like scene in which they are cast—but with a difference. In Homer, the Trojans' failure to recognize Odysseus for the "man he was beside the ships of the Achaeans" [ὃς οὐδὲν τοῖος ἔην ἐπὶ νηυσὶν 'Αχαιῶν], is rendered as a speechlessness that compromises their defenses (οἱ δ' ἀβάκησαν πάντες). In Plutarch, the Athenians not only recognize Pisistratus but are even prepared to fight his putative "enemies" (τὸ μὲν πλῆθος ἦν ἕτοιμον ὑπερμαχεῖν τοῦ Πεισιστράτου). But this obvious difference between Odysseus' effect on the Trojans and Pisistratus' effect on the Athenians only emphasizes how Solon's comparison implicitly likens the fighting spirit of the latter to the inactivity of the former, a likeness based on the proposition that both responses on the part of the citizens pose a risk to their respective cities (Troy and Athens).

The Trojans, of course, are unambiguously Odysseus' enemies, just as the Babylonians were Zopyrus' enemies. And as Solon remarks, Pisistratus should play the wounded victim for his enemies (as do Odysseus and Zopyrus) but instead plays it for his fellow citizens. Another way of understanding this difference between the stories is to note that whereas Odysseus' and Zopyrus' disguises enable their roles as theater-like outsiders, Pisistratus' self-inflicted wounds enable his role as a theater-like insider. I take this sociopolitical relationship between the disguised and/or deceptive role player and his intended audience to be central to the concept of the theater-like; we might refer to this relationship as the "recognition factor." In general terms, formal dramatic performance—such as that in fifth-century Athens—can be described as a presentation of disguise and scripted speech that operates within a discrete cultural context defined more specifically by the presence of an audience of cultural literates. Such

---

47. By Plutarch's time, the meaning "to act in the theater" was well established for ὑποκρίνω. Cf. Aristotle On Rhetoric 1403b23.

an audience recognizes the culture-specific signs of scripts and disguises enacted for their benefit. More concretely, culturally literate
spectators are defined by their ability to see beneath the actor's costume and mask.[48]

In the scene from the *Odyssey* to which Solon refers in Plutarch's
text, Helen can be said to exemplify this sort of culturally literate
spectator when she alone recognizes the disguised Odysseus in Troy.
By contrast, the Trojans, who fail to recognize Odysseus for who he is
(like the Babylonians who fail to recognize Zopyrus for who he is), are
illiterate spectators. They are not privy to the cultural knowledge that
allows Helen to recognize her countryman in disguise; in this instance, their position as cultural outsiders is in fact defined by their
failure to do so. It should be noticed, however, that the response of
both the literate and the illiterate spectator is inaction; in both cases
they watch and say nothing (οἱ δ᾽ ἀβάκησαν πάντες)—at least in
principle. But in the case of the Trojans, their inaction is a consequence of their failure to see behind the disguise and has serious
negative consequences for their city. This distinction between literate
and illiterate spectators is ambiguously played out in the Pisistratid
narratives. The Athenians are obviously Pisistratus' fellow citizens,
with the implication that they would (or should) recognize Pisistratus'
ploys as ploys; in Plutarch's account Solon is the model citizen who
clearly recognized them as such. But unlike Solon, the rest of the
Athenians behave like illiterate spectators, since their failure to act
against the tyrant is a function of their failure to recognize his theater-
like act.

This failure is epitomized in the bodyguard that Herodotus says the
demos provided Pisistratus (ὁ δὲ δῆμος . . . ἔδωκέ οἱ τῶν ἀστῶν καταλέξας ἄνδρας, *Histories* 1.59). Ostensibly intended to protect the tyrant
from his nonexistent enemies, this bodyguard is deployed against the
Athenians themselves: Pisistratus subsequently takes the Acropolis
with these men.[49] Although Herodotus refers to the bodyguard simply

---

48. See Elam 1980, 101–2, on the relevant notion of "possible worlds."

49. It does not seem to matter here whether we differentiate between the
demos (as the "common people") and the elites. Cf. *Life of Solon* 30.1, where
Plutarch has Solon differentiate between economic classes, that is, between

as a guard (ἐδέετό τε τοῦ δήμου φυλακῆς τινος πρὸς αὐτοῦ κυρῆσαι,
1.59), both Aristotle (*Athenaion Politeia* 14.1) and Plutarch (*Life of Solon*
30.2) refer to it more pointedly as a "guard for his body" [φυλακὴ τοῦ
σώματος].[50] While the phrase may be conventional, this later tradition
emphasizes the tyrant's body and focuses narrative attention on what
it means to guard that body—from whom, under what circumstances,
and by what means. In short, the story of the bodyguard is a narrative
distillation of the effect of the display of the tyrant's body, here the
effect of his false wounds, on the citizens.

While Plutarch implies that this bodyguard was a formidable force,
his source, Herodotus (*Histories* 1.59), is decidedly more vague about
its size and disposition. According to Plutarch (*Life of Solon* 30.2),
although Ariston originally made a motion that Pisistratus be allowed
a bodyguard of fifty club-bearers, the Athenians subsequently passed
a decree that allowed him as many as he wished.[51]

ὁρῶν δὲ τοὺς μὲν πένητας ὡρμημένους χαρίζεσθαι τῷ
Πεισιστράτῳ καὶ θορυβοῦντας, τοὺς δὲ πλουσίους
ἀποδιδράσκοντας καὶ ἀποδειλιῶντας, ἀπῆλθεν εἰπὼν ὅτι τῶν
μέν ἐστι σοφώτερος, τῶν δὲ ἀνδρειότερος· σοφώτερος μὲν τῶν
μὴ συνιέντων τὸ πραττόμενον, ἀνδρειότερος δὲ τῶν συνιέντων
μέν, ἐναντιοῦσθαι δὲ τῇ τυραννίδι φοβουμένων. τὸ δὲ ψήφισμα
κυρώσας ὁ δῆμος οὐδὲ περὶ τοῦ πλήθους ἔτι τῶν κορυνηφόρων
διεμικρολογεῖτο πρὸς τὸν Πεισίστρατον, ἀλλ᾽ ὅσους ἐβούλετο
τρέφοντα καὶ συνάγοντα φανερῶς περιεώπα, μέχρι τὴν
ἀκρόπολιν κατέσχε.

[When he [Solon] saw that the poor were anxious to gratify
Pisistratus and were cheering him on, while the rich were evading him because they were afraid, he left saying that he was
wiser than some and more manly than others—wiser than those

---

the poor (τοὺς μὲν πένητας) and the wealthy (τοὺς δὲ πλουσίους); his point is
that neither was able to withstand the tyrant.
    50. Cf. Plato *Republic* 566b5–8, where Socrates refers to the tyrant's plea for
a bodyguard.
    51. Cf. Polyaenus Historicus (second century C.E.) 1.21.3 and the scholium
on Plato *Republic* 566b, where the club-bearers are said to have numbered
three hundred.

who did not understand what was being done, and more manly than those who understood what was happening but were nevertheless afraid to oppose the tyranny. So the people [ὁ δῆμος] passed a decree and no longer held Pisistratus to a strict account of the number of his club-bearers but allowed him to keep and lead about in the open as many as he wished, until he took the Acropolis.] (Plutarch *Life of Solon* 30.3)

It is telling that neither Herodotus nor Plutarch indicates against whom Pisistratus and this bodyguard contended or by what methods or means they took the Acropolis. But whether that bodyguard consisted of fifty or three hundred men, it was appointed or chosen by the Athenian demos from among the citizen body. Again, this uncertainty in the sources about the size and purpose of the tyrant's bodyguard has to do with the question of Athenian complicity in his takeover.[52] In this instance that question is framed by the citizens' potential failure to be ἀνδρεῖοι, a failure made explicit in Solon's claim that he is "more manly" (ἀνδρειότερος) than his fellow citizens because of his opposition to the tyrant. Here Solon is positioned as a model literate spectator whose ability to see beneath the surface of the tyrant's deceptive activities, that is, his ability to recognize and refute the tyrant's theater-like acts, is a sign of his (Solon's) manliness. In contrast to him are those Athenians who also knew what was happening (τῶν συνιέντων) but were afraid to do anything about it.[53] In this complex narrative, with its blurring of the Athenians' role as agents or victims, spectatorship is implicated in a con-

52. McGlew (1993, 74–76) argues that the club is traditionally used "to correct and reform" and that it functions as a symbol of retribution for the tyrant. McGlew seems to take the account at (historical) face value, however, rather than a narrative of Athenian self-representation.

53. Perhaps it is in light of the Athenians' potential failure to be "manly" that we can understand the remark in Herodotus that Pisistratus' bodyguard was made up of club-bearers (κορυνηφόροι) instead of spear-bearers (δορυφόροι, *Histories* 1.59). Spears are routinely used in military operations, whereas clubs are uncommon. And when clubs are military weapons, they are usually inferior to spears. Cf. the story of Areïthoös (*Iliad* 7.136–47), called the "club-bearer" (κορυνήτης), who is killed by the spear of Lykourgus. Boardman (1972, 62), cited by Rhodes (1981, on *Athenaion Politeia* 14.1), describes Pisistratus' club-bearers as "more like riot police than military."

flict over political identity and martial prowess with Solon's conventional and individual manliness on one side of the conflict and Pisistratus and his club-bearers on the other.

For even though Plutarch says that the Athenians were "ready to fight on behalf of Pisistratus" (τὸ μὲν πλῆθος ἦν ἕτοιμον ὑπερμαχεῖν τοῦ Πεισιστράτου) (30.2), this testament to their martial readiness falls flat in light of the assessment of the situation that he attributes to Solon, namely, that the Athenians were too afraid to oppose the tyrant. In other words, their readiness to fight for Pisistratus is subverted in the text by Solon's statement that they were too afraid to fight against him. We know, moreover, that the enemies against whom the Athenians would ostensibly fight do not really exist, since we know that Pisistratus wounded himself. And while it might be objected that Solon is represented as a biased observer in the narrative, the narrator reports without comment that Solon saw (ὁρῶν) what the Athenians were about and thereby authorizes the truth or accuracy of Solon's point of view. Coming just before mention of the decree that allowed Pisistratus a larger bodyguard, Solon's observations about the Athenians' temerity seem to be offered as a means of explaining that decree.[54] But here again the logic is elusive, since it does not follow from Solon's characterization of the Athenians that Pisistratus would require a larger bodyguard or that a legal decree would be necessary for him to get one. And again, those enemies from whom Pisistratus ostensibly needs protection are left out of the explanation. The conclusion that emerges from the account is that fighting on behalf of the tyrant is equivalent to a kind of shadowboxing and that the martial prowess of the Athenians is as insubstantial as that of Pisistratus' enemies.

In this respect it is useful to recall Aristotle's second sort of tyrant, who, though he does not need to, keeps up the appearance of military readiness and of obeying the laws of the land. The complacency and complicity of the Athenians are demonstrated in Plutarch's narrative by the implication that they too are only keeping up the appearance of acting in accordance with the requirements of martial valor and legal

---

54. Cf. Aristotle *Athenaion Politeia* 14.2. Plutarch's version is thought to be the older and "appears to be the version behind *A.P.*'s allusion" (Rhodes 1981, ad loc.).

precedent. These conclusions are in fact summed up in Plutarch's account of Pisistratus' effect on Solon.

οὐδενὸς δὲ προσέχοντος αὐτῷ διὰ τὸν φόβον ἀπῆλθεν εἰς τὴν οἰκίαν τὴν ἑαυτοῦ, καὶ λαβὼν τὰ ὅπλα καὶ πρὸ τῶν θυρῶν θέμενος εἰς τὸν στενωπόν, "Ἐμοὶ μέν," εἶπεν, "ὡς δυνατὸν ἦν βεβοήθηται τῇ πατρίδι καὶ τοῖς νόμοις." καὶ τὸ λοιπὸν ἡσυχίαν ἦγε, καὶ τῶν φίλων φεύγειν παραινούντων οὐ προσεῖχεν, ἀλλὰ ποιήματα γράφων ὠνείδιξε τοῖς 'Αθηναίοις·
Εἰ δὲ πεπόνθατε δι' ὑπτέρην κακότητα,
μή τι θεοῖς τούτων μῆνιν ἐπαμφέρετε
αὐτοὶ γὰρ τούτους ηὐξήσατε ῥύματα δόντες,
καὶ διὰ ταῦτα κακὴν ἔσχετε δουλοσύνην.

[No one supported him [Solon] on account of fear, and so he went to his own house, took his arms, and after he placed them in front of his doorway, lamented, "I have done all I can to help my country and its laws." From that time on he lived in quiet retirement, and when his friends urged him to flee, he paid no heed but kept on writing poems, in which he reproached the Athenians:

If you now suffer grievously on account of your evil ways,[55]
Do not throw your anger back at the gods for this,
For you yourselves increased his powers by giving him these men,
And on account of this you are in evil slavery.]

(30.5–6; cf. Aristotle *Athenaion Politeia* 14.2)

In this account, Solon implicitly advocates armed combat with Athens' enemies in which real wounds are sustained, in contrast with Pisistratus, who fights a fictitious enemy and wounds himself to deceive his fellow citizens. Solon's military ethos is based on action undertaken by fellow soldier-citizens against an enemy, the sort of action he fails to muster against the tyrant "on account of [the citizens'] fear" [διὰ τὸν φόβον]. Pisistratus' ethos is based on the perpetration of a fraud, with the result that he effectively neutralizes the

---

55. κακότητα can also be translated as "cowardice." See LSJ I.

citizens' resistance so that even Solon, his most ardent opponent, is forced to go home, give up his arms, and live in "quiet retirement" [ἡσυχία]. In a relevant passage, Herodotus offers a general indictment of tyranny in Athens by explaining that the increasing military might of the Athenians is the result of their ridding themselves of their tyrants (*Histories* 5.78).

In chapter 2, I argued that just as face-to-face speaking is analogous to man-to-man combat in the epics, writing as mediated speech is analogous to archery, in which men fight from a distance. In Plutarch's account of Solon and Pisistratus, this equation of competing martial and communicative practices is illustrated when the tyrant forces the lawgiver out of the public space of man-to-man speaking and military action. Solon leaves his arms "in front of his doorway" [πρὸ τῶν θυρῶν] and enters a domestic space (εἰς τὴν οἰκίαν) where he occupies himself with writing poems (ποιήματα γράφων). As the occupation of his "quiet retirement" [ἡσυχία], writing poetry is arguably an inferior substitute for Solon's former military life—a life attested to by the reference to his "arms," or ὅπλα. Solon's explicit transformation from fighter to writer can be ultimately attributed to Pisistratus' activities, the full effect of which is made clear in Plutarch's concluding remarks.

οὐ μὴν ἀλλ᾽ ὁ Πεισίστρατος ἐγκρατὴς γενόμενος τῶν
πραγμάτων οὕτως ἐξεθεράπευσε τὸν Σόλωνα, τιμῶν καὶ
φιλοφρονούμενος καὶ μεταπεμπόμενος, ὥστε καὶ
σύμβουλον εἶναι καὶ πολλὰ τῶν πρασσομένων ἐπαινεῖν.
καὶ γὰρ ἐφύλαττε τοὺς πλείστους νόμους τοῦ Σόλωνος,
ἐμμένων πρῶτος αὐτὸς καὶ τοὺς φίλους ἀναγκάζων·

[But when Pisistratus had taken control of the government, he so
won over Solon by honoring him and showing him kindness
and seeking him out that Solon actually became his advisor and
praised many of the things he did. And Pisistratus even
retained most of Solon's laws, observing them first himself, and
forcing his friends to do so also.]

(Plutarch *Life of Solon* 31.1)

Solon's recognition of and active opposition to the tyrant are shown to be only temporary. He eventually succumbs and, like the

rest of his fellow citizens, becomes a passive spectator (even an advisor, or σύμβουλον) in the Athenian theater of tyranny. In McGlew's
terms, this transformation is the source of Solon's "personal tragedy,"
but we need not appeal to Solon's biography to see that this story
again illustrates the confused shifting in the sources between Athenian opposition to and complicity with the tyrant. It is noteworthy too
that the Athenian lawgiver occupies a similarly ambiguous position in
this account and that his acquiescence to the tyrant can also be construed as validating the Athenians' failure to resist tyranny. According to McGlew (1993, 122), "Plutarch probably shaped his description
of Solon's last years to strengthen his view that Solon was not quite
the enemy of tyranny that he should have been, and thereby to explain Solon's political failings by reference to his personal character."
But Plutarch's text is less about his chastisement and redeeming of
Solon as a historical agent than it is a representation of early Athenian
history that both declares a fascination with tyranny (and the tyrant)
among sixth-century Athenians and effectively exculpates their fifth-
century "democratic" ancestors. This larger view is taken through the
retrospective lens of Plutarch but is not limited to Plutarch's personal
assessment of Solon. Whatever Solon actually did or did not do and
whatever Plutarch may have thought about Solon's political activities,
Plutarch's narrative—especially Solon's reference to the tyrant playing the epic hero—demonstrates how theater-like activities in Athenian political history reveal a conflict between the preservation and
loss of an idealized masculine identity. The representation of events
like those in which Pisistratus is involved illustrates both that political
history is a history of "great men" and that, as objects of desire within
that history, such men need to be continually reinvented. The reason
Herodotus gives pride of place to the Pisistratids in the early history
of Athens while he virtually erases Solon from that history might have
something to do with the role that Plutarch subsequently gives to
Solon in Pisistratus' success.[56] If for no other reason, the historian's
silence protects Solon from any hint of complicity in the tyranny and
preserves him as a model of Athenian civic virtue, the role he also
plays in Herodotus' chronologically impossible Croesus episode.

---

56. McGlew (1993, 111–23) discusses Solon's laws in relation to the establishment of the tyranny; one of his aims is to absolve Solon of blame for
Pisistratus' success.

My purpose here is not to second-guess Herodotus' motives, however, but to articulate the meaning of theater-like events in the early
history of Athens. Toward this end, Solon's contention in Plutarch's
account that he was "wiser than those who did not understand what
was being done, and more manly than those who understood what
was happening but were nevertheless afraid to oppose the tyranny"
(*Life of Solon* 30.3) can be compared with Gorgias' description of the
complicity that is necessarily required of spectators at a tragic performance (also preserved by Plutarch). Together these passages illustrate
the opposition between the manliness that distinguishes Solon (if
only ideally and temporarily) in the theater of tyranny and the behavior that defines the dramatic spectator in the Theater of Dionysus (at
least according to Gorgias).

ἤνθησε δ᾽ ἡ τραγῳδία καὶ διεβοήθε, θαυμαστὸν
ἀκρόαμα καὶ θέαμα τῶν τότ᾽ ἀνθρώπων γενομένη καὶ
παρασχοῦσα τοῖς μύθοις καὶ τοῖς πάθεσιν ἀπάτην, ὡς
Γ. φησίν, ἣν ὅ τ᾽ ἀπατήσας δικαιότερος τοῦ μὴ
ἀπατήσαντος καὶ ὁ ἀπατηθεὶς σοφώτερος τοῦ μὴ
ἀπατηθέντος. ὁ μὲν γὰρ ἀπατήσας δικαιότερος ὅτι τοῦθ᾽
ὑποσχόμενος πεποίηκεν, ὁ δ᾽ ἀπατηθεὶς σοφώτερος·
εὐάλωτον γὰρ ὑφ᾽ ἡδονῆς λόγων τὸ μὴ ἀναίσθητον.

[Tragedy was growing and being celebrated as something
    wonderful to hear and see by the men of the time, insofar as it
    added the element of deceit to the events recorded in myth. As
    Gorgias said, "The one who deceives is more just than the one
    who does not, and the one who is deceived is wiser than the
    one who is not deceived. The deceiver is more just because he
    has done what he has promised, while the one deceived is
    wiser because to be easily taken in by the pleasure of words is a
    sign of good sense."][57]
                    (DK 82.B23 = Plutarch *Moralia* 348c)

---

57. The translation is free, but I believe it gives the right meaning. Cf. the
translation provided in DK: "Die Tragödie *bewirkt durch die Darstellung der
Sagenstoff und der Leidenschaften* eine Täuschung, bei der der Täuschende
gerechter ist als der nicht Täuschende und der Getäuschte klüger als der nicht
Getäuschte." Cf. *Dissoi Logoi* DK 90.1.6, dating to around 400 B.C.E., for a
similar sentiment.

The preceding passage might be considered nothing more than an example of sophistic rhetoric; Dover (1993, 31–32) notes that, like DK B11.9, it too may have been "only incidental to the theme of its context."[58] Nonetheless, as Dover also concedes, it offers "some interesting observations on the 'deception' essential to tragedy." Thus, even if it remains uncertain whether Gorgias produced a "serious theory" of tragedy,[59] the epigram can be included among—even if it is not equivalent to—the more extended or "serious" critiques of theatrical or mimetic performance found in Plato and Aristotle.[60] What I have translated as the "element of deceit" [ἀπάτη] in Plutarch's introduction to Gorgias' statement is offered as an essential and necessary part of tragic performance and seems to refer to the aural and visual enhancement of the stories from myth (ἀκρόαμα καὶ θέαμα) by means of the conventions of the stage. Gorgias is presumably talking about the tragic spectator (the deceived) and the tragic playwright or actor (the deceiver). Accordingly, the more just playwright or actor is the one who "does what he has promised" insofar as he succeeds in deceiving the spectator, and the more wise spectator is the one who allows himself to be so deceived. We can call this passage an ancient formulation of the literate spectator, someone who knows that a "deceptive" drama is being enacted for his benefit—and for his pleasure.

Although the terms of the comparisons attributed by Plutarch to Gorgias and to Solon are not identical, they are complementary. Each begins with a general but double comparative statement (including

---

58. Despite various attempts to prove the contrary, there is no convincing evidence that Gorgias was especially interested in tragedy in general or in any play or playwright in particular. Gorgias is said to have first gone to Athens in 427 B.C.E. (Diodorus 12.53), but it is not known what plays were performed in the spring of that year, nor is it likely that he was in Athens at the time of the tragic festival. The only evidence that suggests that he had knowledge of a particular play is Plutarch's statement (DK 82.B24) that he called Aeschylus' *Seven against Thebes* "full of Ares." But Aeschylus, as a character in Aristophanes' *Frogs* (1021), makes this same observation about his own play, which makes Plutarch's attribution less than reliable. In short, the fragment preserved by Plutarch remains without a clear context.

59. See Lucas 1968, xx.

60. Cf. Aristotle's assessment of μίμησις in the *Poetics*, esp. 1448b4–19. The pleasurable effect that Gorgias implicitly gives to ἀπάτη (inferred from ἡδονὴ λόγων) can be equated with that which Aristotle gives to μίμησις.

σοφώτερος), which is then followed by an explanation of the terms of the comparisons. In *The Life of Solon*, Solon compares himself with those Athenians who were deceived by the tyrant when he played the role of Odysseus and contends that he is wiser and more manly than they, presumably because he was not deceived. In the epigram attributed to Gorgias, the phrase translated as "to be easily taken in by the pleasure of words is a sign of good sense" more accurately says "to be easily taken in by the pleasure of words does not indicate a lack of sense or sensitivity." The litotes suggests the existence, or at least the possibility, of the counterclaim, namely, that "to be easily taken in by the pleasure of words" was considered a sign of poor sense. This counterclaim is in a sense the basis of Solon's claim to be more wise and more manly than the Athenians, a claim based on the fact that the Athenians were taken in by the tyrant's words to such a degree that they believed his playacting was real. In sum, for Solon, the wiser and more manly man (or, more specifically, the wiser or more manly citizen) is whoever is not taken in by Gorgias' "element of deceit." Such a person knows deception from reality, as explained by the example of someone who knows the difference between a would-be tyrant trying to play Odysseus and a wounded citizen in need of protection. The Athenians in Plutarch's account should have been wise enough to know one from the other (as Solon says). These comparisons certainly do not prove that Plutarch had Gorgias in mind when he wrote about Solon (although he may have) but can nonetheless help us locate the story of Solon and Pisistratus within a Greek tradition of theoretical approaches to formal theatrical performance. Gorgias' definition of tragedy offers a positive appraisal of dramatic deception in which literate spectators enjoy being deceived and enjoy knowing that they are being deceived, in contrast to Plutarch's representation of the Athenians as illiterate spectators who effectively become slaves in the theater of tyranny. It is perhaps predictable that a sophist is credited with providing a defense of theatrical performance as a form of deception. The battle between sophists and statesmen, exemplified in the works of Plato, here finds expression in Gorgias' and Solon's opposing viewpoints on the matter of deceptions and impersonations in the city.

I have suggested that Herodotus' account of Pisistratus' first attempt at tyranny, together with Plutarch's later elaboration of that attempt, focuses attention on the physical presence of the tyrant, or rather on how watching him has the potential of neutralizing manly action in the city. This neutralization is obviously the effect he has in Plutarch's account of Solon. In Herodotus' narrative of the tyrant's second attempt at becoming tyrant of Athens—the famous Phye episode—we find the same effect at work.[61]

Megacles sent a message to Pisistratus asking if he wished to take his daughter as wife with a view toward taking the tyranny. Pisistratus accepted this offer and agreed to its terms, and they devised a plan for his return. This was a most foolish plan, I think, especially since they devised it to be perpetrated on the Athenians, who are considered to be the foremost of the Greeks in cunning, since from very early times the Hellenic race has been distinguished from the barbarian by its greater cleverness, and freedom from silly foolishness. In the Paeanian deme was a woman named Phye. She was three fingers short of four cubits tall and in other respects fair to look on. They equipped this woman in full armor, put her in a chariot, and having arranged the show to best advantage, sent heralds before them and themselves marched in the city. When the heralds came into the city, they announced what they had been told, saying the following: "Oh Athenians, receive Pisistratus with equanimity, for Athena herself has given honor to him and is leading him into her own citadel." The heralds announced these things throughout the city, and right away the report came to the country districts that Athena was leading back Pisistratus. The people in the city were persuaded that the woman was the goddess herself, and they worshiped this mortal woman and took back Pisistratus. (Herodotus *Histories* 1.60)

In an important and influential article, W.R. Connor suggests that this episode references certain established formal processions or "arrival ceremonies" and that it enacts "a pattern of praise in which a

---

61. Cf. Herodotus *Histories* 4.180. Cf. Sissa 1990, 344, on the Ausean women.

young woman is likened to a goddess."⁶² These conclusions are both appealing and problematic. As an illustration of the latter claim, Connor refers to the example of Odysseus when he praises Nausicaa by likening her to a goddess (*Odyssey* 6.149–55).⁶³ But while the rather clinical physical description of Phye indicates that she was a plausible stand-in for Athena, the text does not clearly evoke Connor's "verbal pattern of praise"; Phye is not overtly praised in Herodotus' narrative, nor likened to a goddess in the same way in which Odysseus likens Nausicaa to one.⁶⁴

What distinguishes Phye's theater-like impersonation is the overtly political purpose for which it is enacted and, more specifically, the fact that it is preparatory to the reinstatement of the tyrant in Athens. Consequently, this purpose necessarily mocks or makes a parody of any religious procession to which it may be compared, especially when Herodotus reproaches the Athenians for being no smarter than barbarians because, as a result of Phye's impersonation, they reinstate Pisistratus as tyrant.⁶⁵ The grammatical con-

---

62. Connor 1987, 42–44. Connor also discusses the various arguments for and against the historicity of the episode. Cf. How and Wells 1968, ad loc. See also Sinos 1993.

63. Odysseus says to Nausicaa, "I liken you most to Artemis, the daughter of great Zeus, for beauty, figure, and stature" [Ἀρτέμιδι σε ἐγώ γε, Διὸς κούρῃ μεγάλοιο, / εἶδός τε μέγεθός τε φυήν τ᾽ ἄγχιστα ἐίσκω] (*Odyssey* 6.151–52).

64. As an example of a relevant religious procession, Connor mentions one in honor of Artemis in which a young girl, dressed like the goddess, takes a leading role (Xenophon of Ephesus *An Ephesian Tale* 1.2). But the differences between this account of a procession in honor of Artemis and Herodotus' account of Phye only serve to demonstrate how the latter does not seem to describe a communally sanctioned religious event. The late date of the novel and its possible reliance on Herodotus as a source should also be considered. Cf. *An Ephesian Tale* 2.9, in which Antheia is married to a goatherd, with Herodotus *Histories* 1.107, the story of Mandane's marriage to Cambyses.

65. Aristotle (*Athenaion Politeia* 14.4) says that Pisistratus was brought back ἀρχαίως καὶ λίαν ἁπλῶς, translated by Rhodes (1981, ad loc.) as "in a primitive and excessively simple manner." Aristotle is obviously varying Herodotus' account of the Athenians' gullibility by locating it in some earlier stage of social development (his ἀρχαίως seems to be a revision of Herodotus' ἐκ παλαιτέρου). And while Aristotle does not say that the Athenians are engaging in barbarian-like behavior, he does say that they "received [Pisistratus] back in a fawning manner" [προσκυνοῦντες ἐδέχοντο].

struction of the sentence that reports this outcome, namely, that the Athenians "worshiped the mortal woman and took back Pisistratus" [προσεύχοντό τε τὴν ἄνθρωπον καὶ ἐδέκοντο Πεισίστρατον], marks the similarity of these two events, so that worshiping the mortal woman is equated with taking back a tyrant; both actions result from public spectacles and deceptions. In short, if we compare Pisistratus' overtly fake Athena to a solemn religious procession that "enacts a pattern of praise," Pisistratus' procession becomes a political tour de force.[66] In this sense it is difficult to agree with Connor's conclusion (1987, 46) that the "procession of Pisistratus and Phye [is an] elo-quent . . . expression of the closeness between Pisistratus and the residents of Attica at this point in his career."

At the same time, Connor (among others) notes the obvious theatri-cality of the episode but he appeals to historical reality in a curious displacement of the Herodotean narrative.

> The citizens are not naive bumpkins taken in by the leader's manipulation, but participants in a theatricality whose rules and roles they understand and enjoy. These are alert, even sophisti-cated, actors in a ritual drama affirming the establishment of a new civic order, and a renewed rapport among people, leader and protecting divinity. (Connor 1987, 46)

This dominant view of the narrative exemplifies once again the persis-tent nostalgia that guides the reception of theater-like events in Greek culture. In this case, that nostalgia can account for the fact that Con-nor's picture of civic harmony achieved through a theatricalized disci-pline (or "rules") is painted at Herodotus' expense. For if we find Herodotus guilty of underestimating "the popularity of Pisistratus, and the spontaneity and enthusiasm for his return," as Connor claims, we also have to say that Herodotus misunderstood the force of

---

66. That "divine dress" was used by both men and women on cult occa-sions is also not clearly relevant for the Phye episode; see Connor 1987, 45–46 with n. 25. As Connor points out "although there was a cultural pattern among the Greeks of dressing as a divinity on certain ceremonial occasions, Pisistratus did not use it." Instead of presenting himself in the guise of a god, he plays a subordinate role to his "Athena." Cf. Sinos 1993.

the pseudoreligious procession for which Connor argues.[67] And if such religious processions were current in the fifth century, we have to ask why Herodotus would be "carried away by his amusement that the Athenians, who in his day made pretensions to the greatest urbanity and sophistication, acted so differently in an earlier period" (Connor 1987, 47). That is, we have to ask why Herodotus would be so naive as not to recognize or admit to the shared complicity of citizens who were not, in Connor's words, "naive bumpkins" but were, in my words, literate spectators.

My point is that Herodotus' narrative more convincingly conveys an ambiguity about tyranny in Athens than praise of a new civic order.[68] And I maintain that this ambiguity is directly attributable to the theatricality of the episode as Herodotus describes it. From this point of view, it is unnecessary to assume that the historian misunderstood the tyrant's role in adapting a formal religious procession. Rather, similar to his story about Pisistratus' self-inflicted wounds (*Histories* 1.59), Herodotus has given us another story about the tyrant's theater-like persona. In fact, here the narrative makes more overt reference to all the requirements of formal theatrical performance: actors, costumes, props, and a script. Within that narrative, the nascent foundations of Athenian democracy are presented as provisionally at risk, and theatrical tactics, this time enacted by a woman under the direction of the tyrant, are the instruments by which that risk is introduced into the polis.[69] Connor is right to stress that the narrative presents Pisistratus as making what must be considered a formal entrance into the city. And like the entrance he is said to have made in his first attempt at the tyranny, this one too posi-

---

67. Connor 1987, 46. Cf. Sinos 1993, 87: "Herodotus makes it very apparent that the Athenians accepted [Pisistratus'] manifestation of divine support simply because they wanted to believe in the illusion he presented to them." Sinos' conclusion, like Connor's, is problematic because it is based on what the Athenians actually believed or wanted to believe. Jacoby (1949, 168) calls the story of Phye "society gossip."

68. Connor (1990) argues, however, that the City Dionysia was founded not by Pisistratus but as a festival in celebration of "civic freedom" from a tyranny that had become harsh under Pisistratus' sons.

69. Cf. *Lysistrata* 631, where Greek men associate women with pretenders to tyranny. See Foley 1982–83, 10.

tions the Athenians as spectators.[70] But in this case the tyrant's success is achieved not only by means of the public display of his own body but also by the additional spectacle of a woman disguised as a goddess.[71]

The effect of this particular spectacle is specified as gullibility in Herodotus' narrative because the Athenians believed that Phye was the goddess herself. This gullibility, he says, is more naturally suited to barbarians, who are neither as clever nor as wise as the Athenians.[72] Here we might recall the story of Zopyrus among the Babylonians, who, as illiterate spectators, took his disfigurement at face value. Or we might recall the story of Solon, who deemed himself more wise than those Athenians who did not see through Pisistratus' deceptions. In doing so we can appreciate the fact that Herodotus' story of Phye and her reception is one of a set of narratives that feature theater-like events in the presence of literate or illiterate spectators, events that are clearly focused on questions of political and gender-specific identity. In the presence of Phye-Athena, the Athenians exhibit the slavishness that, according to Aristotle, for example (*Politics* 1252b7–9, 1255a29–35), is natural to barbarians; one of the essential differences between Greeks and barbarians is that the latter are made to be mastered and specifically to be the subjects of a tyrant.[73] As Athena, Phye appealed to Athenian civic identity, including the religious foundations of that identity.[74] But because the Athenians' reaction to this Athena is construed by Herodotus as antitheti-

---

70. Cf. Plutarch *Life of Camillus* 7.1, where Camillus is reproached for his pride and arrogance and for overstepping the boundaries set for the magistrates of the Republic; he is said to have gone through the streets of Rome in a chariot drawn by four white horses. On this topic, see Affortunati and Scardigli 1992, 118. Cf. Mullaney 1983, 45–48, for a relevant discussion of Henry II's royal entry into Rouen in 1550.

71. Cf. the story of Gyges discussed in chap. 3. See also Case 1985, 320–22, on the role of Athena in Athenian civic ideology.

72. Cf. Euripides *Iphigenia at Aulis* 1400–1401. See also de Ste. Croix 1981, 416–18; Konstan 1987.

73. Cf. *Politics* 1313b36–37, where Aristotle says that "slaves and women do not plot against tyrants," thereby equating all three.

74. Seltman (1933, 48–51 ff.) suggests that Pisistratus is to be credited with creating a national symbol when he introduced Athena's owl on Greek coinage. But cf. Frost 1985, 65–66.

cal to what it means to be Athenian, Pisistratus' appropriation of the goddess is presented as an instance of using culture against itself. Instead of marshaling the Athenians in defense of their city, this Athena makes them behave like unwarlike barbarians.[75] The quality of deceit that defines feminine subjectivity, especially in terms of feminine adornment, is deployed here with the result that even "Athena" nullifies the political and martial responses of her citizens.[76] It may be objected that Phye's Athena costume is not exactly "female adornment," since the armor (πανοπλία) she is described as wearing is, strictly speaking, male attire. But her armor is part of an overt disguise, so its meaning in the customary context of normative masculine identity is compromised, especially because it functions in the service of verifying a false Athena. As the symbol of Athenian civic identity, the warrior-goddess born from Zeus' head represents above all else the privileging of masculine virtues and attributes and the disavowal of feminine subjectivity and agency. In the theater of tyranny, however, she signifies feminine treachery that (in Herodotus' terms) results in the Athenians' barbarian-like submission to the tyrant; she turns her citizens into passive and illiterate (i.e., gullible) spectators.

This narrative of tyranny as an absence of political and martial activity, that is, as a narrative in which citizens forfeit their active participation in civic life as a result of viewing the public spectacle of tyranny, continues in Herodotus' and Aristotle's accounts of Pisistratus' third attempt to gain power. It is reported that as a prelude to that attempt, and as a means of solidifying a joint venture, Pisistratus agreed to marry Megacles' daughter.[77] According to Herodotus, Pisistratus did not wish to have children with this woman and so had intercourse with her "not according to custom" (ἐμίσγετό οἱ οὐ κατὰ

---

75. Boardman (1972) believes that Phye recalls Athena's introduction of Herakles to Olympus by chariot and points to the popularity of Heracles in Athenian art of the period as circumstantial proof. Although convincingly discounted by Shapiro (1989, 15), the idea of a Pisistratus-Heracles suggests a conception of the tyrant that combines the traits of hypermasculinity and effeminacy that describe the mythological hero. Cf. Frost 1985, 63; Loraux 1990.

76. On the relationship between feminine adornment, deception, and compromised masculinity, see chap. 3.

77. Cf. Rubin 1975 on the politics of exchanging women.

νόμον, *Histories* 1.61.4); Aristotle simply says that he did not live with her (*Athenaion Politeia* 15.1). Whatever the case, this anecdote conveys another kind of uncertainty about Pisistratus, namely, uncertainty about his sexual proclivities. His body is implicitly subjected to the sort of sexual scrutiny that looks negatively or at least suspiciously on his masculinity. As a result of this affront to Megacles' daughter (or rather to Megacles), the political factions split once again; Pisistratus leaves Athens to secure money and mercenary soldiers and then returns. In addition to making a point of the ambiguous nature of Pisistratus' sexuality and of Pisistratus' role as a single actor (the coalition with Megacles does not work out), this story also takes its place in the continuing saga of the tyrant's ability to nullify or neutralize the Athenians' martial prowess.

> The Athenians from the city had just finished their midday meal, after which some of them were engaged in playing dice, while others were sleeping, when Pisistratus, with his troops, fell on them and put them to the rout. As soon as the flight began, Pisistratus came up with a most wise plan, whereby the Athenians might be induced to disperse and not unite in a body anymore. He mounted his sons on horseback and sent them on in front to overtake the fugitives, exhort them to have confidence (θαρσέειν), and return each man to his home. The Athenians took the advice, and Pisistratus became for the third time master of Athens, with the help of many mercenaries and an abundance of cash. (Herodotus *Histories* 1.63)

Herodotus maintains later that some Athenians fell in the battle while others fled with the Alcmeonids. But the account still reveals the ambivalence that characterizes the Athenian representation of the tyranny in general. In this story the Athenians are caught unprepared; instead of being ready to resist, they are found sleeping or playing dice. And although a battle seems to have been fought, the Athenians are defeated and are finally persuaded to give in to the tyrant and his sons by nothing more than an exhortation to "have confidence" (or "take heart" [θαρσέειν]).

Aristotle follows Herodotus in his story of Megacles' daughter and Pisistratus' exile and return but gives a different account of Pisistratus' means of success. But in his account too the Athenians' failure to mount a defensive against the tyrant is a dominant theme.

> After winning the Battle of Pallene, [Pisistratus] seized the city and took the people's arms away from them; now he held the tyranny firmly, and he took Naxos and appointed Lygdamis ruler. The way in which he took the arms away from the people is this. He made an armed muster at the Temple of Theseus, and he attempted to hold an assembly of the people. He lowered his voice a little, and when the people said that they could not hear him, he told them to advance toward the gate of the Acropolis so that he could make himself heard by shouting. And while he was making his speech, men who had been appointed to the task gathered up the people's arms. After they had shut them up in the neighboring buildings of the Temple of Theseus, they came to Pisistratus and indicated to him that the task had been carried out. When he had finished the rest of his speech, he told the people that it was unnecessary to wonder at or to be disturbed by what had happened to their arms, to go home and occupy themselves with their private business, and that he himself would take care of all public business. (Aristotle *Athenaion Politeia* 15.3–6)

Aristotle explicitly says that this time Pisistratus attempted to overpower the Athenians by force (πρῶτον ἀνασῴσασθαι βίᾳ τὴν ἀρχὴν ἐπεχείρει). But while his forces (i.e., the Thebans and Lygdamis of Naxos) are victorious in a Battle at Pallene, the details of the Battle are passed over, and its relationship to Pisistratus' success in Athens is not clearly spelled out.[78] The narrative implies that the tyrant was able to take the city and confiscate the arms of the citizens as a result of this victory (νικήσας δὲ τὴν ἐπὶ Παλληνίδι μάχην καὶ λαβὼν τὴν πόλιν καὶ παρελόμενος τοῦ δήμου τὰ ὅπλα). The paratactic compounding of participles, however, fails to give a clear sense of the causal relationship between these events, and there are no clues as to how or against

---

78. There is some uncertainty as to whether this means that there was a battle in the deme of Pallene, which lay northeast of Athens, or in the temple of Athena Pallenis between Marathon and Athens (as Herodotus *Histories* 1.62 says). See Rhodes 1981, ad loc.

whom Pisistratus and his forces won the battle or took the city. Uncertainty about the cause and effect relating to these events is also suggested in the lack of clearly delineated factions or class affiliations within the city. Instead, the narrative focuses on Pisistratus' disarming of the demos.[79]

Pisistratus is said to have initiated his plan by holding an armed muster (ἐξοπλασία) in the city. But this action follows a strange logic: if he intended to take the city by force, why would he hold an armed muster and thereby provide the perfect opportunity for an Athenian counterattack? My intention here is not to second-guess the logic of the events, however, but to point out the way in which the narrative of those events raises the question of Athenian complicity in the tyranny. Once again the locus of the tyrant's power in Athens is not so much his army as it is his own bodily presence. He is able to disarm the citizens because, to hear him better, they have moved closer to him and further away from their weapons.[80] As the immediate cause that draws the Athenians up to the Acropolis, the tyrant's voice seems to speak that pleasurable speech (ἡδονὴ λόγων) that Gorgias says is necessary to a successful dramatic performance.

The tyrant's theater-like presence in the account of Athenian political history and identity emerges again in Plutarch's continuing tale of Solon and Pisistratus. According to Plutarch, Solon was intent on encouraging the Athenians to continue their fight against the Megarians for control of the island of Salamis (*Life of Solon* 8.1–6). To effect

---

79. Cf. Winkler 1990a. In an earlier version of this article (Winkler 1985, 45–46), Winkler suggests that the stories about Pisistratus disarming the citizens and protecting himself by a personal bodyguard of armed men preserves a connection between ephebic training and choral dancing.

80. The meaning of ἐχάλασεν, which I have taken to mean that Pisistratus lowered his voice, is somewhat unclear. Nevertheless, the problem is that the Athenians cannot hear him well enough. Thucydides (*History* 6.56.2) claims that the citizens carried arms to take part in the Panathenaic procession. Thucydides' story of Alcibiades' attempt to win admittance into the Sicilian town of Catana (415 B.C.E.) provides a useful parallel. The Catanians would not receive the Athenian army into their town but invited the generals to come in and to say what they wanted (*History* 6.51; cf. 6.53). Alcibiades, like Pisistratus, so completely engaged their attention that they were oblivious to what was going on around them and, as a result, allowed the enemy army to enter their city. See Ostwald 1986, 321–26, on the suspicion that Alcibiades aimed at tyranny (e.g., at *History* 6.15.4).

this goal, Solon went into the marketplace pretending to be insane
(ἐσκήψατο μὲν ἔκστασιν τῶν λογισμῶν), and sang a song in favor of
renewing the war. Of those in his audience, it is said that "Pisistratus
in particular urged and incited the citizens to obey" (8.3) and that as a
result the people decided to renew the war. At first glance, this episode seems to counter the claim that one of the recurring motifs in the
Pisistratus narratives is the tyrant's failure to inspire martial prowess
in the Athenians, exemplified most obviously by their failure to expel
the tyrant himself. But even here, where what is at stake is Pisistratus'
ability to provoke the citizens to go to war against external enemies,
our confidence in that ability is dampened by the description of the
ensuing campaign.

> The popular account of this campaign is as follows. Having
> sailed to Cape Colias with Pisistratus, and having found all the
> women there performing the customary rites to Demeter, [So-
> lon] sent to Salamis a trustworthy man who pretended to be a
> deserter. And this man told the Megarians that if they wished to
> capture the leading women of Athens, they should sail to Colias
> with him as quickly as possible. The Megarians were persuaded
> and sent men in his ship. When Solon saw the ship sailing back
> from the island, he ordered the women to withdraw and di-
> rected those of the younger men who were not yet bearded,
> once they had put on the garments, headbands, and sandals
> that the women had worn and had taken up concealed weap-
> ons, to play and dance on the seashore until the enemy had
> disembarked and the ship was captured. His orders were carried
> out, and the Megarians, led on by the spectacle [τῇ ὄψει], landed
> their ship nearby and leapt out to attack the women, vying with
> one another. The result was that not one man escaped but all of
> them were killed, and the Athenians at once set sail and took
> possession of the island. (8.4–6)

As Nilsson explains, chronology makes it unlikely that this joint
venture by Pisistratus and Solon ever took place.[81]

---

81. Nilsson is referring to Solon's role in Plutarch's account of Pisistratus'
first takeover in 561 B.C.E. (*Life of Solon* 30 and 31). Cf. Herodotus *Histories* 1.59
and Aristotle *Athenaion Politeia* 14.1.

For chronological reasons it is impossible that Solon was leader of a warlike enterprise at the same time when Pisistratus was able to do so and had acquired political influence. Pisistratus died in 525 B.C. and was probably born about the year when Solon was archon, 594 B.C., and when Pisistratus seized the power in 561 B.C. Solon was an old man who was unable to fight. (Nilsson 1951, 27)

Precisely because of this chronological improbability (acknowledged by Aristotle at *Athenaion Politeia* 17.2), the role that Plutarch somewhat halfheartedly gives to Pisistratus requires explanation. This halfheartedness—we are not told anything about Pisistratus except that he urged the citizens to obey Solon and accompanied him to Cape Colias—may in fact reflect that improbability; it betrays a reticence about the part Pisistratus played in these events, which is tantamount to acknowledging the implausible down-dating. Why then does Plutarch include Pisistratus in this story, if the tyrant is clearly and chronologically out of place and if the part he plays is minimal?

Given the related problems of chronology and purpose, Pisistratus' appearance in the wings of the narrative emphasizes the contrast between his theater of tyranny and Solon's engagement in "real" military action. The devices Solon uses to defeat the Megarians are similar to those Plutarch says Pisistratus uses to win over the Athenians. Solon's feigned madness, the pretend deserter, and the young warriors disguised as women are similar to Pisistratus' pretenses, that is, his false wounds and his false Athena. But whereas Pisistratus' theater-like activities result in the inaction and passivity of the Athenian citizens, Solon's deceptions lead to a complete military victory over Athens' enemies (ἁμιλλώμενοι πρὸς ἀλλήλους, ὥστε μηδένα διαφυγεῖν, ἀλλὰ πάντας ἀπολέσθαι, 8.6).[82] The account of Solon and Megara may thus be said to provide a positive tale of manhood achieved, to counteract the negative tale of manhood lost in the theater of tyranny at Athens; here as elsewhere, Solon assumes

---

82. The presumed desire of the Megarians to kidnap the women of Athens can be compared to Herodotus' account of stolen women in early rivalries between Greeks and barbarians (*Histories* 1.1–5).

the role of an anti-Pisistratus. But at the same time, that Pisistratus supports Solon's venture puts that venture—with its Pisistratean elements—under suspicion.

In fact, the appeal to the Athenians' martial prowess in this story seems misplaced when we think of those soldiers cavorting as women on the shore at Colias. The center of attention in this scene, however, is the transformation or transition from the appearance of women with their hidden weapons (ἐγχειρίδια κρυπτά, 8.5) to the appearance of ruthless fighters who will not leave one enemy soldier alive.[83] For all intents and purposes, this transition enacts a successful ephebic moment in which the acquisition of masculine identity is manifested in martial success. It is a moment that necessarily requires a previous moment of uncertainty, a demonstration of what is at stake in failing to make the transition. In Plutarch's account, this moment of uncertainty is clearly specified in the warriors' wearing of women's clothing and, as such, can be read as an ironic counterexample to Herodotus' story of Phye. Under Solon's instruction the Athenians wear women's clothing to defeat their enemies; under the tyrant's instruction a woman wears warrior's armor to lure the Athenians into inaction.[84] As part of the Solonic legacy, we are led to expect that the Athenian youth will pass through their moment of uncertainty and fight and win like men. Or, to put it another way, making the Athenian boys put on women's clothing only emphasizes their subsequent transformation into fighting men and contrastively suggests the arrested masculinity of the Athenians under the spell of the tyrant and Phye.[85]

In his culminating account, Plutarch says that after Solon made his

---

83. See chap. 3 on the transition from being armed to being unarmed in the epic. See chap. 5 on the concept of femininity as disguise.

84. In his account of the ephebic institution, Vidal-Naquet (1986, 115) notes that Athena Skiras "seems to have been linked significantly with the custom of dressing up" and refers to Plutarch's account of the capture of Salamis; Salamis is otherwise known as Skiras. He does not stress the important transition in which boys disguised as women become ruthless warriors in the narrative, however. Cf. Aristophanes *Lysistrata* 46–52, where male actors (ephebes?) dressed as women discuss how women's clothes can make friends out of male enemies. I discuss this passage in chap. 3.

85. Pisistratus is reported to have been a descendant of Melanthos, the deceptive figure who stands behind the aetiological myth of the ephebic institution. See Nilsson 1951, 61–63; Frost 1985, 69–70.

laws, he left Athens for ten years, but that soon after his return, he again met Pisistratus, who was especially genial toward him.

Pisistratus was flattering and pleasing in his manner of conversation; he was ready to help those who were poor, and he was reasonable and moderate toward his enemies. Those things that he did not possess by nature he imitated (μιμούμενος), and he won more confidence thereby than those who actually possessed them. In this way he appeared to be a cautious and order-loving man especially fond of equality and to take it badly if someone disturbed the existing order and aimed at revolution. On these points he deceived most people. But Solon quickly saw his character and first perceived his enterprise [i.e., Pisistratus' desire to be tyrant]. (Plutarch *Life of Solon* 29.2–3)

The assertion that Pisistratus could imitate (μιμούμενος) those virtues that had been denied to him by nature and that he deceived the majority of the people makes him an excellent candidate for Aristotle's second sort of tyrant.[86] But the more pertinent significance of the story becomes apparent in the account of Solon and Thespis that immediately follows, in which an implicit contrast is made between Pisistratus, who only appears to possess certain virtues by nature (φύσει, 29.3), and Solon, who does possess virtues by nature (φύσει, 29.4).

Thespis was beginning to develop tragedy, which attracted many people because of its novelty, although it had not been made a matter of competitive contest. Solon, being a man who was by nature fond of hearing and of learning and who even more in his old age passed his time with leisurely amusement and even, by God, with wine and song, went to see Thespis himself acting in a play, as was the custom of the ancient poets [?]. After the spectacle, he called out to Thespis and asked him if he was not ashamed

---

86. On the Platonic critique of dramatic mimesis (*Republic* 394b5 ff.), see chap. 5. Sörbom (1966) discusses the association of "*mimesis* words" with early dramatic performance (Sicilian mime) and the connection between these words and "deliberate behavior intended to deceive" both in the fifth and fourth centuries. Plutarch, writing much later, may be calling forth the pregnant meaning of the verb *mimeomai*, that is, "to be deliberately and dramatically deceptive."

to tell so many lies in front of such a number of people. When Thespis answered that it was not terrible to speak and to do such things in a play [μετὰ παιδιᾶς], Solon struck the ground sharply with his staff and said, "Soon we shall find this kind of play in our everyday affairs (ἐν τοῖς συμβολαίοις) if we give it so much honor and praise." (29.4)

The entry of Thespis into the narrative of Pisistratus and Solon follows on the description of Pisistratus' deceptive character and precedes the story in which Solon berates Pisistratus for playing the Homeric Odysseus badly. In this arrangement of episodes, Plutarch uses the behavior of Pisistratus to illustrate what he says Solon believes tragedy to foster, namely, deceptions and lies in everyday social intercourse (ἐν τοῖς συμβολαίοις, 29.4). It is implied that both Thespis and Pisistratus are problematic figures in the city because they deal in appearances rather than reality and, more to the point, that the Athenian spectator is vulnerable to the deceptions of the actor in the same way that he is vulnerable to the deceptions of the tyrant. In his criticism of Thespis, Plutarch's Solon (like Plato's Socrates) relies on the equation of "lying" on stage with lying in the city. In doing so, he must envision the Athenians as illiterate spectators who see no difference between dramatic events and political events and who act as if the former were the latter. My point is again not to prove what Solon actually said or did but to understand how a narrative that brings together Solon, Thespis, and Pisistratus defines the theater of tyranny in terms of an essential conflict between the lawgiver and the tyrant, that is, between the model soldier-citizen and the model anticitizen. But what matters most, of course, is the representation of the Athenian demos, who, as the principal spectators in this theater, reflect that ambivalence in their own oscillation between soldier-citizens and anticitizens.

This ambivalence finally extends to the complex account of Athens' liberation from tyranny. On the one hand, there is the tradition of tyrannicide, what Jacoby calls the "official version," in which Harmodius and Aristogeiton are made heroes for having liberated Athens from tyranny by murdering Pisistratus' son Hipparchus.[87] On the

---

87. Thucydides *History* 6.54–59. Cf. Plato *Symposium* 182c5–7.

other hand, according to Thucydides, the murder was the result of an erotic affair (ἐρωτικὴν ξυντυχίαν, *History* 6.54) and was not politically motivated; in other words, Hipparchus was not killed because he was tyrant. In fact, Thucydides says that *Hippias* was tyrant at the time of the murder (6.54.2, 6.55.1–4) and that the liberation of Athens was achieved only in the fourth year after the murder of Hipparchus, when the Spartans and the exiled Alcmeonids forced Hippias to leave Athens (ἐχώρει, 6.59.4; cf. Herodotus *Histories* 5.62–65 and Aristotle *Athenaion Politeia* 18.1–19.6). In chastising the Athenians for not giving "an accurate account about their own tyrants," Thucydides acknowledges the persistence of the so-called official version (*History* 6.54.1).[88]

We have, then, two rival accounts of Athenian liberation from tyranny: Jacoby's so-called official version of the tyrant's murder and the counterversion of the tyrant's expulsion. While both seem to have had wide currency in the fifth century, the opinion that the former is the official version is verified by the fact that the tyrannicides were said to have been commemorated by statues and by other extraordinary honors and privileges accorded their descendants.[89] And it is clear that this overt public recognition of the heroic story of Harmodius and Aristogeiton validates martial valor as an enduring principal of Athenian identity. McGlew (1993, 155) concludes that, "The Athenian heroization of Harmodius and Aristogeiton itself answered Herodotus's criticism of the Athenians' passivity toward the Peisistratids." For while the counter or unofficial version may be flattering to the Alcmeonids (because it makes them the liberators of Athens), it also admits the need for Spartan assistance against the tyrants.[90] It therefore represents a diluted version of the Athenians' responsibility for bringing about their own liberation.[91] In the end, these two conflicting versions

88. See Jacoby 1949, 159.
89. See Jacoby 1949, 159–60 with n. 52; Rhodes 1981, 289, 308; McGlew 1993, 153.
90. See Jacoby 1949, 158–65; Rhodes 1981, 190, 230.
91. These competing narratives of Athenian liberation may be relevant to the history of ostracism in Athens. According to Aristotle, ostracism was instituted to rid the city of would-be tyrants and was originally used against the "friends of the tyrants" [τοὺς τῶν τυράννων φίλους] (*Athenaion Politeia* 22.6). It is unclear, however, whether ostracism was instituted at the time of the Pisistratids or at the time when it was supposedly first used (i.e., against

of liberation constitute yet another instance of the defining characteristic of the Athenian theater of tyranny, namely, ambivalence expressed in terms of the culture- and gender-specific protocols that determine civic identity.

Writing about Athenian myths of autochthony, Nicole Loraux states that "mythical schemes legitimate and model civic experience."[92] While the stories about Pisistratus are not precisely mythical, they constitute a myth of Athenian political history in which civic experience is modeled on theatrical performance. As Aristotle makes clear, the tyrant in Athenian culture is the symbol of political ambiguity precisely because he can seem not to be a tyrant. And this ambiguity, embodied in the presence of the tyrant in Athens and in the sources that record that presence, is expressed in the persistent question of Athenian complicity in his actions. That question, in turn, is a matter of the integrity (or the lack thereof) of the normative masculine subject, whose principal attributes are martial valor and the kind of wisdom that defines the literate spectator. In the final analysis, the representation of the theater of tyranny in Athens distances the Athenians from the implied reality of their city under the sway of a tyrant. For if the tyranny can be conceived of as a kind of theatrical performance in which the Athenians play the role of spectators, they can be excused for being participants in a past that is so incompatible with the masculinist ideology of fifth-century Athens—incompatible, for example, with the Athens of Pericles' funeral oration.[93] Thus the theater of tyranny is perhaps the most conspicuous expression of theater-like activities as the product of cultural and political nostalgia. We see in these narratives an attempt to preserve a valorized masculine identity in the face of theatrical practices that are construed as tyrannical. When the Athenian citizen takes his place in this theater,

---

Hipparchus, son of Charmus). Cf. Androtion (fourth century B.C.E.) frag. 6 (Jacoby), cited by Rhodes (1981, 267) as Aristotle's source. On the dating of the institution of ostracism, see Ostwald 1955, 107–10; Thomsen 1972. Ostwald's argument is summarized and critiqued by Rhodes (1981, 220–22). Cf. Ostwald's discussion (106–10) of the ἄτιμος individual, or "outlaw"; the term ἄτιμος is used by Aristotle to describe a legal indictment against a person aiming at tyranny (*Athenaion Politeia* 16.10).

92. Loraux 1981, 35.

93. See Loraux 1986, chap. 6.

his role as spectator signifies both the end of manly action in the city and the implicit desire for its return, that is, for the reassertion or reanimation of a Solonic version of manhood. And because the theater of tyranny is the product of a culture in which formal theatrical performance—what Solon calls "to tell . . . lies in front of . . . a number of people"—has become a public institution, this formulation raises the question of how that institution is incorporated into Athenian political and civic ideology. More specifically, it invites us to ask whether the Athenian spectator in the theater of tyranny can be productively compared with the Athenian spectator in the Theater of Dionysus. This question is the focus of the following chapter.

5

The Theater of Dionysus

The meaning of spectatorship as a theoretical and historical practice in fifth-century Athens cannot be detached from its meaning in Greek history and culture in general. At the same time, however, it is obvious that spectatorship has a special significance in the context of the Theater of Dionysus. In this context, the spectator becomes explicitly defined as a category of analysis and is particularized within Athenian civic ideology and the history of the European theater. The development of that definition may again be understood in terms of the ritual origins of Greek drama or in terms of historical personages and events—for example, in terms of the stories told about Thespis or Solon. But as I have suggested, any explanation of the theatrical experience in ancient Greece that appeals to strictly empirical evidence (whether explicitly or implicitly) is problematic at best. We can say that as a cultural phenomenon whose meaning develops over time, theatrical performance in Athens—including the idea of the theatrical spectator—has something to do with Dionysus. But this premise is also problematic, since it is difficult to say what, if anything, is uniquely "Dionysiac" about drama as a genre or about the spectator's experience of dramatic performance.[1] Still, we can proceed from the

---

1. Else (1965, 30) maintains that "there is no plausible reason to believe that tragedy was ever Dionysiac in any respect except that Pisistratus attached it, once and for all, to his festival of the Greater Dionysia [in 534 B.C.E.]." Zeitlin (1990a, esp. 66–67) stresses the limitations of understanding tragedy in terms of "ritual logic." In contrast, Seaford (1994, esp. chaps. 7 and 8) offers the most extended recent argument for the importance of Dionysiac cult and ritual in the origin and development of Athenian drama. Goldhill (1990) argues that many of the plays have in them what might be called Dionysiac elements, since they "subvert the city's order." Connor (1990) argues that the City Dionysia celebrates a new civic order and "civic freedom" from the Pisistratid tyranny, and he implies that there is something Dionysiac in this expression of freedom.

plausible hypothesis that the experience of the theater named after Dionysus is somehow related to the god's role in Greek culture at large.

If we reject strictly historical and/or ritual explanations of that relationship, however, the question of the god's role in the political, ideological, and theatrical life of Athens may seem arbitrary. Why ask about a divinity's meaning in the context of any cultural institution if neither religious practice nor historical circumstance can provide a satisfactory answer? The question becomes less arbitrary and more productive, however, if we begin by considering Dionysus in the broader context of the ethnographic accounts of his entry into and subsequent effect within Greek and Athenian culture. Such an approach can provide a less contingent and more appropriately secular understanding of the god as a product of Athenian self-representation in general and of his role in the theater as a cultural and civic institution in particular. By reference to the general and the particular, I do not mean to suggest that there is a chronological relationship between them, that is, that the former necessarily precedes and determines the latter. Rather, they operate synchronically within a tradition that, like that of the Pisistratid legacy, finds its definitive expression in fifth-century Athenian sources. While references to the god appear in the Linear B tablets and in Homer, and while visual images of Dionysus are numerous throughout the archaic and classical periods, the theatrical Dionysus—the Dionysus who is associated with formal theatrical production and who appears as a dramatis persona on the Athenian stage—is a fifth-century Athenian phenomenon.[2]

Dionysus' long-standing association with drama in Athens and its environs is well established, whether or not we credit the Pisistratids with its inception in the middle of the sixth century. To understand

---

2. Dionysiac ritual is not attested in historical times, although other similar cults—e.g., that of Sabazius and the Thracian Dionysus—are. See Lucas 1968, 281. On the prehistory of Dionysus, see Burkert 1985, 161–63. On his appearance on the Linear B tablets, see Chadwick 1976, 99–100. On the prevalence of images of Dionysus on Attic vases in the sixth century, see Shapiro 1989, chap. 5. Carpenter (1986, xv) contends that "the major developments in the early iconography of Dionysos are Attic inventions." See also Frontisi and Lissarrague 1990, esp. 232 with nn. 109 and 110. On the general attributes of Dionysus, see Oranje 1984, 101–13, esp. 110–11.

that association, we need not imagine some originary or founding moment—although, as I have suggested, it is important to recognize the motivation for doing so. I propose instead to work toward an understanding of what might be called that association's culminating expression late in the fifth century, namely, the presentation of the god as a character in Euripides' *Bacchae* and Aristophanes' *Frogs*. I begin with the assumption that this presentation is imbedded— however ambiguously—within a larger tradition, beginning with the Homeric poems, in which Dionysus is called the "maddened one" (μαινομένοιο Διωνύσοιο, *Iliad* 6.132) and in which are "maddened" not only the god himself but those mortals with whom he comes into contact. Taking the Homeric epithet as epitomizing Dionysus' reputation in Greek culture over time, I want to begin by asking what Dionysiac madness and, more generally, the Dionysiac experience mean in that larger context and what they mean for our understanding of theatrical production in Athens.

While Dionysiac madness can take many mortal forms, it generally describes both the punishment for failing to worship the god and the ecstatic expression of his worship: *mania* is the condition attributed both to the believer and to the nonbeliever. This predicament demonstrates a dominant feature of the Dionysiac experience, namely, that the god poses an inescapable threat to the norms by which Greek culture defines itself as rule-governed and homogeneous, that is, as sane. But madness is not to be disassociated from the other attributes that are characteristic of the god, namely, his foreignness and his femininity.[3] Exemplified in the maenads, all three attributes are argu-

---

3. Dionysus becomes orientalized probably sometime in the sixth century; the process is perhaps the result of syncretism with eastern gods, such as Sabazius. On Dionysus' foreign origins, see Segal 1982, 118–24; Dodds 1966, on *Bacchae* 453–59. Cf. Herodotus' story of Melampus (*Histories* 2.48–49), who is said to have introduced the worship of Dionysus into Greece from Egypt. Hartog (1988, 75–84) discusses Dionysus' genealogy in Herodotus. See also Bernal 1987, 113, on Plutarch's attack against Herodotus for being a "lover of barbarians" [φιλοβάρβαρος] (*Moralia* 857a). Vernant (1985) figures Dionysus as the incarnation of the other, which permits the "possibility of a joyous alterity." Cf. Laporte 1969, 57: "The tale of Apollo and Marsyas suggests the Greek effort to suppress the disturbing power of a foreign, 'barbarian,' intruder." In summing up his account of Cambyses' madness, Herodotus maintains that a madman is a man who does not recognize the danger of cultural

ably the most descriptive features of Dionysus in the Greek historical and literary sources. The common denominator shared by all is the threat they potentially pose to the undisputed integrity and dominance of the masculine subject. For in a culture that privileges that subject, the true victims of Dionysiac madness, or at least the victims who count, are males (like Pentheus in the *Bacchae*).4 Our task is to discover how these attributes of the god—as afflictions—are also relevant for understanding theatrical experience in Athens as part of a nostalgic cultural project in the service of preserving that subject.

The Dionysiac narrative of madness, foreign intrusion, and feminine power can be documented in the ethnographic or historical accounts of Dionysus' introduction into Greece and Athens. That he must be introduced, that he comes from beyond the borders of the Greek world, is of course the first proof of his foreign or marginal status. In the metaphors of modern medicine—metaphors that also operate in the ancient sources—Dionysus enters Greece like a disease that requires a cure.5 The accounts of his introduction are found in a variety of sources and certainly do not add up to anything like a consistent tradition; their anecdotal quality may also be found wanting. But

---

chauvinism (*Histories* 3.38): Cambyses' madness is the result of his failure to give proper respect to the Egyptian god Apis. Herodotus' assessment of Cambyses, the Persian or barbarian madman par excellence, illustrates the way in which the behavior of a madman is figured both as the failure to incorporate a foreign divinity and as antithetical to Greek cultural and political norms. On Cambyses, see Munson 1991. In the *Bacchae*, Pentheus' failure to give proper due to Dionysus is characterized by Tiresias as madness (μαίνῃ γὰρ ὡς ἄλγιστα, 326). Kadmeian Ino is reported to have raised Dionysus like a daughter (Apollodorus 3.4.3; cf. Oppian *Kynegetika* 4.237–77). These references are cited in Olender 1990, 100 n. 94. The "effeminate" Dionysus of Euripides' *Bacchae* is discussed later in this chapter.

4. This fact does not mean that Agave's suffering is without meaning, only that the consequences of her suffering are focused on her male kin. Zeitlin (1990a, 66) notes that "in the divine world it is, for the most part, feminine agents who, in addition to Dionysos, inflict men with madness—whether Hera, Aphrodite, the Erinyes, or even Athena, as in Sophokles' *Ajax*."

5. See, for example, Pentheus' assertion that there is nothing "healthy" in the rites of Dionysus (οὐχ ὑγιὲς οὐδὲν ἔτι λέγω τῶν ὀργίων, *Bacchae* 262). Zeitlin (1982a, 134), referring to I. Lewis (1971), notes that "the cultural idiom of an 'illness' that requires a 'cure' [is] especially useful for examining Dionysiac ecstatic experience."

anecdotes are not simply the marginalia of history.[6] Moreover, the stories of Dionysus' entry into Greek civic space contain significant similarities, the most persistent of which is the tale of opposition to the god, although this tale too takes various forms.[7] I begin with two stories from Herodotus' Scythian *logos* that are particularly instructive because they are situated in a barbarian, or non-Greek, context where Greek resistance to Dionysus is transferred onto the Scythians. These stories reveal more about the meaning of that resistance and about its relation to Greekness as a gender- and culture-specific construct than they do about barbarian beliefs or customs.

The first story is about the Scythian king Scyles (Herodotus *Histories* 4.78–80). Born of a Greek mother, Scyles becomes the king of the Scyths but despises the Scythian way of life and prefers Greek customs. The narrative of this half-Greek, half-barbarian king speaks to the tenuous and unstable distinction between Greek and barbarian and, more specifically, to the meaning of Dionysus as emblematic of that uneasy distinction. The narrative also relies on the representation of what might be called culture-specific forms of disguise, specified in Scyles' exchange of Scythian customs and clothing for Greek counterparts. This element of disguise, employed in the context of forging a cultural identity or persona, makes the Scyles narrative an important example of theater-like practices. According to Herodotus, whenever Scyles entered the Greek town of the Borysthenites, he discarded his Scythian clothes and conduct to play the part of a Greek.[8]

εὖτε ἀγάγοι τὴν στρατιὴν τὴν Σκυθέων ἐς τὸ Βορυσθενεϊτέων ἄστυ (οἱ δὲ Βορυσθενεῖται οὗτοι λέγουσι σφέας αὐτοὺς εἶναι Μιλησίους), ἐς τούτους ὅκως ἔλθοι ὁ Σκύλης, τὴν μὲν στρατιὴν καταλίπεσκε ἐν τῷ προαστίῳ, αὐτὸς δὲ ὅκως ἔλθοι ἐς τὸ τεῖχος καὶ τὰς πύλας ἐγκληίσειε, τὴν στολὴν ἀποθέμενος τὴν Σκυθικὴν λάβεσκε ἂν Ἑλληνίδα ἐσθῆτα, ἔχων δ' ἂν ταύτην ἠγόραζε οὔτε δορυφόρων ἐπομένων οὔτε ἄλλου οὐδενός (τὰς

---

6. On the anecdote in historiography and in new historicism, see Fineman 1989, esp. 61–62.

7. See Dodds 1966, xxv–xxvi; Pickard-Cambridge 1968, 57–58; Parke 1977, 126. The tale of opposition to Dionysus begins with the epic story of Lycurgus at *Iliad* 6.130 ff.

8. See Hartog 1988, 62 ff.

δὲ πύλας ἐφύλασσον, μή τίς μιν Σκυθέων ἴδοι ἔχοντα ταύτην
τὴν στολήν), καὶ τἆλλα ἐχρᾶτο διαίτῃ Ἑλληνικῇ καὶ θεοῖσι ἱρὰ
ἐποίεε κατὰ νόμους τοὺς Ἑλλήνων. ὅτε δὲ διατρίψειε μῆνα ἢ
πλέον τούτου, ἀπαλλάσσετο ἐνδὺς τὴν Σκυθικὴν στολήν.

[Whenever [Scyles] came with his army to the town of the
Borysthenites (who, according to their own account, are colonists of the Milesians) he made it his practice, I say, to leave the
army before the city and, having entered within the walls by
himself, and having closed the gates, to exchange his Scythian
dress for Greek clothes, and in this attire to walk about the
marketplace, without guards or retinue. (The Borysthenites kept
watch at the gates so that no Scythian might see the king in this
attire.) Scyles, meanwhile, lived exactly as the Greeks and even
offered sacrifices to the gods according to the Greek rites. In this
way he would pass a month or more with the Borysthenites,
after which he would clothe himself again in his Scythian dress
and depart.] (4.78.13–25)

The narrative clearly divides the Greek and barbarian worlds into
two distinct spaces; the barbarian and nomadic Scyths are kept on the
outside of the city, while the Greek Borysthenites (colonists of the
Milesians) remain on the inside. When the half-Scyth, half-Greek
Scyles enters the city and closes the gates behind him, he effectively
cuts himself off from his barbarian warrior's life and, in doing so,
illustrates the cultural definition of the Greek city, including the activities and appearances that contribute to that definition. The city is
defined first of all as a confining and disciplinary space, one in which
even a nomadic Scyth conforms to the implicit codes of Greek civic
life—codes that are conspicuously manifested in Scyles' change of
costume. The story of Scyles thus neutralizes the implicit threat of
foreign or barbarian intrusion into Greek civic space. But it also enforces the notion that the cultural stability of the Greek city and its
citizens requires constant vigilance, especially if located in the Scythian hinterlands. That vigilance is manifested in the bodily presence of
the barbarian king, that is, by what he wears and the activities he is
seen to engage in while inside the city gates. The narrative thus intro-
duces the implicit assumption that Greekness is a set of bodily activities and behaviors that can be maintained within the spatial confines

of the polis. And the opposite assumption also obtains, namely, that outside these confines lies the possibility of reverting to a barbarian state, as does Scyles, who resumes his Scythian ways each time he leaves the town of the Borysthenites.

As Hartog convincingly argues, Herodotus' Scythian *logos* tells us more about the cultural prejudices of contemporary Greeks than it does about the Scythians. Consequently, this representation of the city reflects a Greek conception, partially displaced onto the character of the half-Greek Scyles. As a result, the narrative reveals an anxiety about confinement and conformity as necessary features of Greek civic life, ones in which secrecy and surveillance—in the form of guards at the gates (τὰς δὲ πύλας ἐφύλασσον)—are necessary for its preservation. The Borysthenites are to be on guard "so that no Scythian might see the king in this [Greek] attire" [μή τίς μιν Σκυθέων ἴδοι ἔχοντα ταύτην τὴν στολήν]. Here, Greekness is a function of disciplined watching aimed at stabilizing a potentially mutable identity.

This anxiety is manifested not only in the representation of urban space in the narrative but also in the person of Scyles' Greek mother, who "taught him the Greek language and letters" and whose upbringing is responsible for his preference for Greek ways (4.78.4–12).[9] In other words, the Greek city and the Greek mother are inextricably bound together. This linkage of maternity and citizenship has a significant referent in Athenian legal history, namely, the law of 451/0 that limited citizenship to persons with an Athenian mother and an Athenian father. Herodotus' *Histories* were familiar in Athens by 425, when they were parodied by Aristophanes in the *Acharnians* (515 ff.), and we know that the law was in effect down to 414, when it is mentioned in Aristophanes' *Birds* (1649–52).[10] But we need not appeal to Herodotus' biography, or rather to his knowledge of the citizenship law, to see that the story of Scyles and his Greek mother is symptomatic of an anxiety about citizenship that was current in fifth-century Athens.

---

9. The common link between Greek culture and the Greek language, reflected in the word *barbarian* itself, is expressed in this reference to Scyles' maternal education. See Slater 1968; Murnaghan 1992. In chap. 2, I discuss the association of writing (γράμματα) with women.

10. On the citizenship law attributed to Pericles, see Aristotle *Athenaion Politeia* 26.4; Plutarch *Life of Pericles* 37.3. For a general discussion of the law, see Patterson 1981.

This anxiety is expressed in a kind of civic essentialism—a manifestation of what Benedict Anderson has called the "remarkable confidence of community in anonymity"[11]—in which civic identity is contingent on the social repression of mothers and foreigners (or foreign
mothers). For the law was aimed primarily at those born of foreign
mothers, as Rhodes suggests.

> Before Pericles' law was enacted, any son of an Athenian father
> by a lawfully wedded wife (whether or not she was an Athenian)
> was a γνήσιος, a legitimate son who would be acknowledged as
> a citizen when he came of age and who could inherit his father's
> property. . . . Under the law μητρόξενοι [those born of foreign
> mothers] were denied citizenship.[12]

Rhodes also notes that according to the law, "a foreign man could
not become a citizen, acquire property in Attica or beget citizen sons,
by marrying an Athenian woman." In other words, the Athenian
male is affirmed as the principal arbiter of Athenian citizenship. Thus,
while the law may seem to legitimate the mother's role in guarantee-
ing the citizenship rights of her son, its effect is rather to restrict that
role—whether the mother is foreign or Greek. The law also places
restrictions on Athenian male citizens, of course, since they cannot
beget citizen-sons from foreign or noncitizen women. But the effect of
this restriction is to guarantee the homogeneity of the male citizen-
body to which foreign mothers pose a threat. I assume that it was
never the case that a foreign man could become a citizen by marrying
a citizen-woman. The point is that the law is explicit on this point;
both parents must be citizens. The story of Scyles is obviously not
about Athenian citizenship *per se*, but it is about a mother's failure to
make her son a "true" Greek and about her role as a source of barbarian intrusion into Greek civic space. The Athenian citizenship law
institutionalizes (and legitimates) this narrative of the mother's threat
to an immutable ethnic and civic identity by subjecting maternity to
the rule of law.

---

11. Anderson 1983, 36. Anderson makes this claim for the modern nation-
state, but the conditions that lead to the "origins of nationalism" as a modern
phenomenon (summarized on Anderson's p. 36) are arguably in place in fifth-
century Athens.

12. Rhodes 1981, on *Athenaion Politeia* 26.4.

The story of Scyles is a story about the limits of cultural and civic assimilation, in which Scyles' Greek mother is an ambiguous and insufficient guarantor of his Greekness. As mentioned earlier, anxiety over the preservation of Greek civic identity is presented in the narrative as the threat of barbarian intrusion—a threat ironically made possible by the fact that Scyles' mother is Greek and by the significant absence of a Greek father. Scyles' Greek mother also functions to define the Greek city as a domestic and feminine space where a dutiful son puts on the clothing in which his mother might have dressed him. In this sense, the failure of Scyles' Greek identity is enacted in the adoption of a maternal disguise, that is, a disguise that his mother implicitly provides and by means of which a barbarian can play at being a Greek.[13]

With this narrative of citizenship in mind, we come to what is perhaps the most remarkable of Scyles' preferences for Greek customs, namely, his desire to be initiated into the rites of the Bacchic Dionysus. According to Herodotus, this desire is anathema to the rest of the Scythians.

Σκύθαι δὲ τοῦ βακχεύειν πέρι Ἕλλησι ὀνειδίζουσι· οὐ γὰρ φασι οἰκὸς εἶναι θεὸν ἐξευρίσκειν τοῦτον ὅστις μαίνεσθαι ἐνάγει ἀνθρώπους. ἐπείτε δὲ ἐτελέσθη τῷ Βακχείῳ ὁ Σκύλης. διεπρήστευσε τῶν τις Βορυσθενειτέων πρὸς τοὺς Σκύθας λέγων· Ἡμῖν γὰρ καταγελᾶτε, ὦ Σκύθαι, ὅτι βακχεύομεν καὶ ἡμέας ὁ θεὸς λαμβάνει· νῦν οὗτος ὁ δαίμων καὶ τὸν ὑμέτερον βασιλέα λελάβηκε, καὶ βακχεύει τε καὶ ὑπὸ τοῦ θεοῦ μαίνεται. εἰ δέ μοι ἀπιστέετε, ἕπεσθε, καὶ ὑμῖν ἐγὼ δέξω. εἵποντο τῶν σκυθέων οἱ προεστεῶτες, καὶ αὐτοὺς ἀναγαγὼν ὁ Βορυσθενείτης λάθρῃ ἐπὶ πύργον κατεῖσε. ἐπείτε δὲ παρῆιε σὺν τῷ θιάσῳ ὁ Σκύλης καὶ εἶδον μιν Βακχεύοντα οἱ Σκύθαι, κάρτα συμφορὴν μεγάλην ἐποιήσαντο, ἐξελθόντες δὲ ἐσήμαινον πάσῃ τῇ στρατιῇ τὰ ἴδοιεν.

[The Scythians censure the Greeks for engaging in Bacchic frenzy, for they say that it is not fitting to imagine a god who drives men

---

13. It is true that Scyles is only half barbarian. But, as I mentioned earlier, the fact that he is a Scythian king attests to the dominance of his barbarian status and is a necessary precondition of the argument that he only plays the role of a Greek by the temporary adoption of Greek clothes and behaviors.

to madness. So when Scyles had been initiated into the Bacchic rites, one of the Borysthenites went and said to the Scythians: "You laugh at us, Scythians, because the god takes hold of us and we succumb to Bacchic frenzy; but now this divinity has taken hold of your king, and he raves and is maddened by the god. If you don't believe me, follow me, and I will show him to you." The Scythian princes followed him, and the Borysthenite led them into the city and stationed them in secret on one of the towers. When Scyles passed by with a band of initiates and the Scythians saw him engaged in Bacchic revel, they counted it a great misfortune, and after they had departed, they told the whole army what they had seen.] (Herodotus *Histories* 4.79.9–22)

Because women are the more frequent practitioners of Dionysiac frenzy in Greek cultural discourse, Scyles' Bacchic revels make him conspicuous not only in the eyes of the Scythians but also, it might be assumed, in the eyes of Herodotus' Greek readers.[14] In other words, the Scythians' opposition to Dionysus and his frenzy is a displacement of the Greeks' own opposition to the god. As a function of that displacement and by means of an inversion of narrative elements within it, Scyles plays the role of a barbarian Pentheus who, instead of opposing Dionysus, is an enthusiastic initiate.[15] In fact, this story is striking for the number of features it shares with the plot of Euripides' *Bacchae.* That the publication of the *Histories* predates the production of the *Bacchae* is not necessarily significant, since plays about Pentheus predate the *Bacchae:* the point is not that the Scyles episode is modeled on the *Bacchae* but rather that it contains similarities with the story of

14. The uniqueness of Scyles' desire is noted in the third edition of the *Oxford Classical Dictionary* (1996), under the entry for "Dionysus": "The practitioners of *bakcheia* were usually women; the exception is Scyles, the 'mad' Scythian king who danced through the streets of Olbia—an early centre of the Dionysus cult—as a *bakchos.*" Cf. Dodds 1966, on *Bacchae* 761, for the story of "the Macedonian king who used women dressed as maenads to frighten an invading army" (Polyaenus *Strat.* 4.1; scholium on Persius 1.99). Cf. Zeitlin 1990a, 75.

15. See Hartog 1988, 214, on the "principle of inversion" in Herodotus, which "is a means of communicating otherness, by making it easy to apprehend that in the world in which things are recounted it is just the same except that it is the other way around."

Pentheus as it is best preserved in that play.[16] As is true for Pentheus, Scyles' death is linked to the fact of his kingship and his Bacchic madness. Both kings become objects of derision after an exchange of gender- or culture-specific clothing; their palaces are destroyed by what appears to be numinous agency; and each is killed and beheaded by a member of his own family.

The most remarkable episode in the *Bacchae* takes place when Pentheus puts on the maenad's costume while under the "spell" of Dionysus, a "spell" that may be better described as the disciplining gaze of the effeminate god (Euripides *Bacchae* 918 ff.). For Dionysus' power over Pentheus is a kind of *paideusis;* he gives him detailed instructions about how to look and act like a maenad. We can compare this *paideusis* to that which Scyles' mother implicitly provides in Herodotus' narrative and which also results in a change of clothes, or, more precisely, in Scyles putting on a kind of costume. Indeed, Scyles' Dionysiac madness and his Greek costume occupy similar visual fields in Herodotus' narrative; the sight of each is anathema to the Scythians. If, as is commonly argued, Pentheus' dressing in a maenad's costume in the *Bacchae* reflects a rite of investiture, Scyles' dressing in Greek clothes in Herodotus presents a variation on this theme.[17] Scyles playing the Greek is not the same thing as Pentheus playing the maenad, but both incidents of dressing up occur in the context of Dionysiac experience. Scyles' Dionysiac frenzy is the culminating expression of his Greek persona. In general terms, that frenzy and that persona have in common their status as temporary transformations. In her study of madness in Greek literature and culture, Ruth Padel suggests "an overriding Greek sense that madness is temporary";[18] perhaps the most vivid expression of this "Greek sense" is the transitory nature of Agave's Dionysiac frenzy in the *Bacchae.* Like

---

16. See Hartog 1988, 8; Dodds 1966, xxviii.

17. See Dodds 1966, xxvii–xxviii. Seaford (1981, 258–61), who believes that Pentheus' disguise in the *Bacchae* "serves no purpose in the story," concludes that it must therefore be a given of Dionysiac initiation. See now Seaford 1994, 272–74. Pentheus' wearing of women's attire is meaningful even without reference to actual ritual practice, however, and can be discussed in terms similar to those I mentioned in chap. 3 with respect to the adornment of Odysseus. The disguise is not "only fleetingly motivated" by Dionysus' desire to make Pentheus a laughingstock in Thebes, as Seaford contends.

18. Padel 1994, 30.

his Dionysiac frenzy, Scyles' Greekness is only temporary, since he effectively puts it on and takes it off as he enters or departs from the Greek city.

Thus, like Pentheus' maenad persona, Scyles' Greek persona is a conspicuous example of how Dionysiac madness is homologous with theater-like impersonations in Greek cultural discourse. Dionysiac madness is manifested in publicly recognized acts of disguise or impersonation, acts that once again testify to the notion of femininity as disguise, as I have discussed it in chapter 3. The tales of resistance to such displays, whether to Dionysiac frenzy or to dramatic mimesis (as in Plato), are waged against a common enemy, namely, the possibility that Greekness, which is coextensive with an idealized masculine subjectivity, is only the effect of bodily dispositions and activities and, conversely, that bodily dispositions are finally insufficient guarantors of a stable core of masculine identity. In the *Bacchae*, this possibility is vividly enacted in the *sparagmos*, or ritual dismemberment, of Pentheus; in the Scyles episode, it is similarly figured in the overthrow and beheading of the king (Herodotus *Histories* 4.79.13–14). But these gruesome events are only the final effects of a more significant social scrutiny. Dressed as a Greek and raving in Bacchic frenzy, Scyles is laughable in the eyes of his army (Ἡμῖν γὰρ καταγελᾶτε, ὦ Σκύθαι); dressed as a maenad and under the spell of Dionysus, Pentheus is laughable (γέλωτα, 854) in the eyes of his citizens.[19] This public ridicule, expressed in terms of the martial and political failure of the disguised male, is a defining feature of the Dionysiac experience.

The second instructive story from Herodotus' Scythian *logos* is less "dramatic" but provides another instance of the relationship between Dionysiac experience and the instability of Greek masculinity. Herodotus explains why the Geloni, another Scythian people, worshiped the god.

---

19. Euripides *Bacchae* 854. I disagree with Seaford (1981, 258 n. 57), who, following Dodds, believes that this line contradicts *Bacchae* 841, in which Dionysus tells Pentheus that he will lead him through deserted streets. The ostensible contradiction is explained by the different addressees: the later statement is addressed to the chorus after Pentheus has left the stage and can indicate what the god actually intends to do; the earlier one is addressed to Pentheus and can be explained as part of the god's inducement to get the king to put on the maenad's costume.

ἔστι γὰρ δὴ αὐτόθι Ἑλληνικῶν θεῶν ἱρὰ Ἑλληνικῶς
κατεσκευασμένα ἀγάλμασί τε καὶ βωμοῖσι καὶ νηοῖσι
ξυλίνοισι, καὶ τῷ Διονύσῳ τριετηρίδας ἀνάγουσι καὶ
βακχεύουσι, εἰσὶ γὰρ οἱ Γελωνοὶ τὸ ἀρχαῖον Ἕλληνες, ἐκ τῶν
δὲ ἐμπορίων ἐξαναστάντες οἴκησαν ἐν τοῖσι Βουδίνοισι· καὶ
γλώσσῃ τὰ μὲν Σκυθικῇ, τὰ δὲ Ἑλληνικῇ χρέωνται.

[There [in the city of the Geloni] are temples built in honor of the
Greek gods and adorned after the Greek fashion with images,
altars, and shrines, all in wood. There is even a festival, held
every third year, in honor of Dionysus, at which the Geloni fall
into the Bacchic fury. For the Geloni were Greeks in ancient
times, who, being driven out of the markets along the coast,
established their homes among the Budini. They use a language
half Greek and half Scythian.] (Herodotus *Histories* 4.108)

Herodotus mentions that the Geloni worshiped other gods of the
Greek pantheon, but Dionysus is singled out among them as the god
whose worship must be explained by appeal to the Geloni's Greek
ancestry. The result is an overdetermined insistence on Dionysus'
Greek origins, for the reference to the Geloni's Greek origins only begs
the question of Dionysus' foreign ones; or rather, it draws attention to
the absence of the god's foreign ancestry in the narrative (cf. Herodotus' story of Melampus at 2.48–49). In the end, the reference to the
Geloni's Greekness explains their current customs by insisting too
much on Dionysus' Greekness. In this way, Herodotus' narrative testifies not simply that Dionysus became a signifier of Greekness over
time, as Hartog suggests, but that the problem of Dionysus' Greekness
is the problem of cultural homogeneity and conformity in conflict with
cultural assimilation.[20] While Dionysiac frenzy is presented as proof of
the Geloni's Greek ancestry (and might be cited as proof of Scyles'
Greek ancestry as well), it is also ironically the proof of the contested
nature of that ancestry. In the ethnological record, then, Dionysus may
be a signifier of Greekness, but he is a signifier that simultaneously
denies confidence in the stability of Greek identity.
    The representation of Dionysiac experience in these ethnographic

---

20. Hartog 1988, 79.

narratives turns on the question of Greek identity—including the masculine virtues that implicitly guarantee that identity. And that question resides within the related question of resistance to the god who represents above all else the possibility that any culture- or gender-specific identity is tenuous and temporary. This narrative of resistance finds expression in a uniquely Athenian context in an anecdotal account of the institution of the phallic procession provided by a scholiast on Aristophanes' *Acharnians*.[21] The scholiast seems to be conflating and embellishing two traditions preserved in Herodotus. In the first, the phallic procession associated with Dionysus' worship is said to have been introduced into Greece from Egypt by Melampus (Herodotus *Histories* 2.49). In the second, Herodotus tells how the "Athenians were the first of all the Greeks to make their statues of Hermes with an erect phallus," a practice that he says they learned not from the Egyptians but from the Pelasgians (2.51). The early history of the phallic procession associated with Dionysus and its relationship to the phallic herms may never be sorted out, nor may the problem of the scholiast's sources.[22] Nonetheless, both the scholiast and Herodotus preserve a tradition that focuses attention on a special, if not unique, relationship between Dionysus and the Athenians, a relationship manifested in the Athenians' initial resistance to the god and in the subsequent public display of the phallus in his honor.[23]

---

21. On the evidence for the phallic procession, see Pickard-Cambridge 1968, 62; Nilsson 1967, 590–91.

22. Hermes and Dionysus are regularly associated in Greek literature and art. Cf. Burkert 1985, 222: "Dionysos himself may be set up as a herm; even in antiquity interpretation often seems unsure whether it is Hermes or Dionysos that is represented, and in many cases the problem remains the same for modern interpreters; the lines separating the two figures become fluid."

23. The story preserved by the scholiast also brings to mind the well-known story of the dismemberment, or *sparagmos*, of Osiris, the Egyptian counterpart of Dionysus, in which the god's lost penis is replaced by the phallos as "a symbol, a simulacrum, the signifier of rejuvenation and sexual pleasure" (Goux 1992, 42). See also Griffiths 1970, on Plutarch *Moralia* 364f5–7. Seaford (1994, 282–84) discusses dismemberment as a shared feature in the myths of Dionysus and Osiris but does not discuss Plutarch's text or the phallic processions in this context. The scholiast's vague reference to a "certain mystic rite" [κατά τι μυστήριον] may refer to a rite relating to the dismemberment of the god and the loss of his penis. Perhaps Herodotus' reluctance to mention the name and describe the sufferings of Osiris at *Histories* 2.171

At this point in the play, Dicaeopolis is leading a procession in honor of Dionysus and instructs his slave Xanthias to "hold the *phallos* straight." To explain Dicaeopolis' command, the scholiast tells the following story.[24]

The *phallos* was a long wooden pole, on the top of which was hung an object of reverence made out of leather. The *phallos* was instituted in honor of Dionysus in accordance with a certain mystic rite. The following story is told about this *phallos*. Pegasus, an Eleutherian (Eleutheria is a city in Boeotia), stole the statue in honor of Dionysus and came into Attica. The Athenians, however, did not receive the god with honor. But the god did not let those who had planned such things get away without paying a price. On account of the god's wrath, a disease attacked the genitals of the men and caused incurable suffering. They say that since the disease was stronger than every human magic and artifice, envoys were sent with all haste [to Delphi?]. When they returned, they said that there was only one cure, namely, that the Athenians should accept the god with every honor. The Athenians were persuaded by what they said and constructed *phalloi* privately and even in public, and with these they celebrated the god, establishing this as a reminder (ὑπόμνημα) of their suffering. But perhaps this is because Dionysus is the god who causes the begetting of children. For he is the founder of enjoyment and of wine, which increases sexual desire. Therefore even Laius, having surrendered himself to wine, begot a child after "falling into a Bacchic frenzy" [Euripides *Phoenissai* 21]. For the *phallos* is the penis. (scholium on *Acharnians* 243)

In the scholiast's first version, the genital disease with which Dionysus infects the male population of Athens can be said to be analogous

---

can be explained by this particular manifestation of his suffering. The satyr figure, so often included in the *thiasos* of Dionysus in the visual and literary sources, may be another manifestation of phallic display as a compensatory gesture in the context of Dionysiac experience. On satyrs, see Lissarrague 1990.

24. The *Acharnians* was produced in 425 B.C.E. The scholia may date to as early as the fourth century.

to the frenzied madness he more commonly visits on women in other cities in the mythological tradition (Thebes, Orchomenos, Argos, Tiryns).[25] Here that madness is replaced by and implicitly equated with a particular kind of masculine suffering in Athens, expressed in terms of genital health and, by extension, of sexual potency. As a compensatory gesture in the scholiast's story, the phallic procession is symbolically appropriate; the Athenian citizens' incurable suffering is implicitly cured by the public display of what, in effect, they were at risk of losing.[26] While not to be equated with the presentation of male nudity discussed in chapter 3, this account of the public exposure of the phallus operates in a similar cultural register. The phallic procession puts the male citizens of Athens in the position of spectators who must witness this reminder (ὑπόμνημα) of their suffering, symbolized but also neutralized in the public and hyperbolic display of the male genitalia.[27]

But the scholiast offers another *aition* for the phallic procession, namely, that it may have been instituted because Dionysus is responsible for sexual reproduction. This alternative version indicates either a lack of faith in the credibility of the story of punishment and cure or some hesitation about making the Athenians protagonists in such a story. In either case, the scholiast's two versions communicate a compulsion both to blame and to praise Dionysus, to find good and evil in the god who in the *Bacchae* calls himself "the most terrible and the most gentle to mankind" (860–61).[28] Thus, while the alternate version

---

25. See Burkert 1983, 168–76.

26. The scholiast implies that this public display was a particularly Athenian innovation (οἱ ᾿Αθηναῖοι φαλλοὺς ιδίᾳ τε καὶ δημοσίᾳ κατεσκεύασαν). See Denniston 1934 on τε κάι.

27. Cf. Freud's description ([1922] 1940, 213) of the effect of the Medusa: "I defy you. I have a penis!"

28. Cf. Seaford 1981, 261, on this passage: "Dionysus is for mankind in general ἡπιώτατος (cf. 272–85), but for his initiands, in the ritual of initiation (ἐν τέλει), δεινότατος, because they will undergo the terrors of a ritual death." Seaford (1994, 363–67) finds the resolution of this Dionysiac ambiguity in the benefit the god ultimately bestows on the polis: "For the Dionysos of the fifth stasimon [of the *Antigone*] is the civic god who in tragedy after tragedy presides over the self-destruction of ruling families of the mythical past, to the benefit of the polis, the god who has thereby indeed put an end to that introversion and autonomy of the family which gave rise to tragic conflict." For a critique of this conclusion, see Griffith 1995.

may be meant to inspire greater confidence in its veracity, it is more successful as an expression of the ambivalence that characterizes Dionysus' reception in the Athenian context.

In fact, the alternate version is not a straightforward reference to the beneficent effects of Dionysiac frenzy, since the scholiast offers the example of Laius in Euripides' *Phoenissai* as a testament to the potency of men who give themselves over to the god of wine. For the son whom Laius begets while in that Bacchic frenzy grows up to be his father's murderer and the sexual partner of his own mother. Similar to the state of affairs in the *Bacchae*, this reference to the story of Oedipus indicates how acquiescence to the god can be mortally dangerous for men. Whether we prefer (along with the scholiast) to explain the phallic procession as a means of invoking the power of the god, either to cure a genital disease or to insure fertility, each explanation gives voice to a potential threat to the Athenian male as a social and sexual subject, a threat answered by the compensatory gesture of the phallic procession. But the scholiast's reference to a play (the *Phoenissai*) to exemplify his point is of particular interest. For in making that reference, he demonstrates how the effect of Dionysiac frenzy is best represented through the experience of a dramatic performance. That the example of Laius undermines his point—or at least that it renders problematic his tale of sexual potency—proves the power of this representational strategy and demonstrates the equation of Dionysiac experience with theatrical experience in Athens. It also demonstrates how the uncertain status of masculine prerogatives, expressed in Laius' Bacchic frenzy, is a principal element in that equation. And while the phallic procession in honor of Dionysus is not itself a theatrical event, it has become one in the context of the *Acharnians*, where holding the *phallos* straight or erect (ὀρθός) is difficult at best.[29] In sum, this scene in the *Acharnians*, together with the scholiast's testimony, speaks to a homology between theatrical performance and Dionysiac experience based on a shared narrative of masculine vulnerability.

Madness (μανία) is the most distinguishing element in ethnographic and historical accounts of Dionysus in Greece, and the mean-

---

29. Aristotle (*Poetics* 1449a11) says that comedy originated in phallic songs.

ing of that madness can be found in gender- and culture-specific anomalies.[30] More specifically, it can be found in the equation of madness with a breakdown of cultural norms and/or with physical debilitation and impotence. We may be inclined to limit this equation to its mythological context, that is, to see it simply as a function of mythological thought preserved in Greek ethnography and anecdotal history. But it also has currency in the context of contemporary social relations.[31] According to [Demosthenes], for example, a man could be considered incompetent before the law because of "being out of his mind by reason of old age, drugs, or disease, or by reason of a woman's persuasion [γυναικὶ πειθόμενος], or if he is held under constraint or imprisoned."[32] While madness has several causes here, the effects of old age, drugs, and disease are physiological and, to some extent, unavoidable. A woman's persuasion is obviously a different sort of thing, and we might wonder why it is included in this list. But just as obviously, its inclusion did not seem out of place to [Demosthenes] or, presumably, to his audience. Indeed, the legal context only emphasizes the normative connection made here between madness, disease, confinement, and women in public discourse. And again it should be stressed that *men* are the victims of this female-inspired madness and, moreover, that, as victims, their incompetence before the law makes them like women, whose legal rights are similarly limited. According to Lacey, a man "would be disbarred from disposing of his property, or from any valid legal act if he were out of his mind."[33] Here the legal punishment for being mad is essentially the same as the punishment for not having two Athenian parents under

---

30. The lexicon that comprises "madness" (e.g., μανία, λύσσα) does not seem to distinguish between a generalized sort of madness and Dionysiac madness or ecstasy, except in the case of *baccheia* (βαχχεῖα) and related words. Cf. *Bacchae* 305, μανία Διονύσου πάρα; cf. also *Bacchae* 850–53. For a discussion of the Greek lexicon of madness connected with Dionysus, see Padel 1994, 23–33. Cultic inscriptions are apparently limited to "the technical language" of *bakcheia* and *bakcheuein* (*OCD*, 3d ed., p. 480).

31. On mythological narratives as expressive of social structures, see the standard article by Lévi-Strauss (1963b).

32. See Lacey 1968, 125 with n. 3, on the law quoted in [Demosthenes] 46.14. See also Segal 1978; Zeitlin 1990a, 65–66.

33. Lacey 1968, 125.

the citizenship law of 451/0; under this regime, the foreigner, the
madman, and, by extension, the woman are effectively classified together as noncitizens.[34] In this legal context, then, and by the fourth
century, madness is part of a tradition of social incompetence and
subservience that can be used to explain the loss of masculine virtues
and prerogatives. As a particular sort of madness, Dionysiac frenzy
represents perhaps the most conspicuous public demonstration of
that potential loss—whether we think of it as an actual ritual practice,
as part of a narrative or mythological tradition, or as both. Such frenzy
is certainly not without its own sources of power, as the examples of
Agave's strength in hunting and the magical abilities of the maenads
in the *Bacchae* prove.[35] But the greater the frenzy is—whether it is
inflicted on women or men (with Pentheus as the exemplar)—the
greater is the threat to the normalizing power of masculine control
over the body and in the city.

I have suggested that Dionysiac madness and theatrical or theater-
like practices in Greek cultural discourse are homologous insofar as
they both undermine confidence in a stable core of masculine identity.
This lack of confidence can explain both the general narrative of resistance to Dionysus in Greek texts and the narrative of resistance to
dramatic impersonation that governs Plato's critique of tragedy and
comedy in the *Republic*. Although Dionysiac madness does not figure
in Plato's condemnation of dramatic mimesis, Socrates' specifically
cautions the guardians against imitating madmen, worthless men,
and women—all of whom he effectively puts into a single category.

οἶμαι δὲ οὐδὲ μαινομένοις ἐθιστέον ἀφομοιοῦν αὑτοὺς ἐν
λόγοις οὐδε ἐν ἔργοις˙ γνωστέον μὲν γὰρ καὶ μαινομένους καὶ
πονηροὺς ἄνδρας τε καὶ γυναῖκας, ποιητέον δὲ οὐδὲν τούτων
οὐδὲ μιμητέον.

[And I think that [the guardians] must not get into the habit of
likening themselves to madmen in word or deed; they must
know about madmen and about worthless men and women, but
they must neither do any of these things nor imitate these sorts.]
(*Republic* 396a2–6)

---

34. See my discussion of Pericles' citizenship law earlier in this chapter.
35. On maenads and maenadism, see Henrichs 1978.

Similar to Demosthenes' discussion of legal precedent, this reference to madmen (μαινομένους) is part of a discussion of how men
ought to behave in the city or, more generally, of what sorts of men are
to be included in the classification of citizen. Of course, Plato's description of the polis in the *Republic* is not a window onto Athenian social
reality, but it overtly situates the meaning of madness within the context of dramatic impersonation as a civic practice in Athens. What
constitutes the danger of a legally defined madness in Demosthenes—
madness that can be the effect of a woman's persuasion—becomes the
danger of a necessarily restricted kind of impersonation in Plato. In
general, the easy and perhaps familiar assimilation of madmen, worthless men, and women in Plato's text demonstrates that madness as a
generic concept (if not a specifically Dionysian one) can be naturalized
within a critique of dramatic impersonation insofar as it undermines
the dominant position of the model soldier-citizen. Such impersonations, says Socrates, are dangerous, because if they are continued
from childhood they can "settle into habits and become nature in body,
voice, and thought" (ἐὰν ἐκ νέων πόρρω διατελέσωσιν, εἰς ἔθη τε καὶ
φύσιν καθίστανται καὶ κατὰ σῶμα καὶ φωνὰς καὶ κατὰ τὴν διάνοιαν,
395d1–3). Here Plato clearly articulates the premise that internal dispositions, those dispositions that constitute a core of essential and normative masculinity, are not natural but may become naturalized as the
effect of bodily acts or impersonations.[36]

In the context of Plato's attack on mimesis in general and on dramatic mimesis in particular, the negative corollary between madmen
and women implicitly makes reference to the dramatic convention of
imitating or impersonating women on the Attic stage; that is, it suggests that actors who impersonate women act like madmen.[37] The most
conspicuous manifestation of this equivalence occurs in Greek drama
itself. In the *Bacchae*, Dionysus is the agent of Pentheus' madness, and
that madness—in a parodic representation of the male actor playing a
female persona—is the precondition of the king's transvestitism. In

---

36. Aristotle's statements at *Poetics* 1448b4–8 use much the same language
as Plato's at *Republic* 395d2–3. "Imitation," says Aristotle, "is natural in humans from childhood" [τό τε γὰρ μιμεῖσθαι σύμφυτον τοῖς ἀνθρώποις ἐκ
παίδων ἐστί]. See chap. 1.

37. Cf. Padel 1994, esp. 32–33: "It is the activity [of madness], the verbs,
that matter."

other words, the consummate expression of Dionysiac madness in the *Bacchae* can be said to illustrate Plato's condemnation of the imitation of madmen and women in the *Republic*, even though Plato makes no direct reference to the *Bacchae*. In more general terms, Plato's critique of dramatic mimesis establishes a category of analysis comprised of dangerous acts of impersonation, acts that constitute public displays of madness, worthlessness, and femininity. The danger inherent in such acts, whether they occur in the theater or in the city at large, is again the threat they pose to the integrity of the masculine subject as a soldier-citizen (exemplified by Plato's guardian).

As I mentioned at the beginning of this chapter, the *Bacchae* and the *Frogs* provide the most sustained demonstrations of this threat in the context of the theater as the special domain of Dionysus. As plays about the god's effect in the city and about bodily mimesis or impersonation as a vehicle of that effect, both plays show how spectatorship and impersonation as formal practices in the theater have analogs in social or political practices in the city at large. And as the plots of the plays make clear, as the architectural contiguity of theater and city confirm, and as Plato later attests in the *Republic*, these two spaces are not mutually exclusive in Athenian civic ideology.[38] That both the *Bacchae* and the *Frogs* were produced at the end of the fifth century provides the general historical background for this proposition. Of course, it may simply be coincidental that two plays about Dionysus were produced near the time of the collapse of Athenian military and political hegemony in 404 B.C.E.[39] Nonetheless, the plays

---

38. Méautis (1934) compares the *Frogs* with Cratinus' earlier *Dionysalexandros*, which he dates to 430 B.C.E. (Cratinus frags. 39–51 with *POxy.* 663). According to Méautis, Dionysus is disguised as Paris in the play and makes the fatal judgment that leads to the Trojan War. Méautis (465–66) also discusses the hypothesis of the play, in which Dionysus (as the cause of the Trojan War) is compared with Pericles (as the cause of the Peloponnesian War); Dionysus is handed over to the Greeks at the end of Cratinus' play, and Méautis surmises that the playwright is advocating giving over Pericles to the Spartans. According to the hypothesis, affairs in the city are overtly equated with plots in the theater. Cf. Thucydides *History* 1.127.

39. The *Frogs* was produced during the Lenaea in 405 B.C.E., the *Bacchae* during the Greater Dionysia a year or two before. Segal (1961, 227) offers the hypothesis that Aristophanes' "central image [in the *Frogs*] itself reflects his deeper awareness of the inevitability of the approaching collapse of Athens."

must be contextualized within the panorama of political and military events between the end of the Persian Wars and the end of the Peloponnesian War, a period that roughly corresponds to that between the first and final dramatic performances at the City Dionysia.[40] At stake at the end of this period is the political survival of the city and the ideological survival of the soldier-citizen who stands in a metonymic relationship to the city. The point of contextualizing the plays in this way is not to argue about references to actual historical events—that is, the point is not to argue that literary or dramatic texts necessarily "reflect" actual social or historical reality—but to stress the immediacy and predominance of a martial ethos in Athens at the time of their production.[41]

The details of that ethos are not easily articulated. In her study of the military funeral oration in the fifth and fourth centuries, however, Nicole Loraux describes that genre's representation of a homogeneous "Athenian warrior group."

> Now, in the funeral oration, the Athenians, interchangeable and anonymous, are so many replicas of a single, implicit model, that of the hoplite, whose constricting ethic they observe: in the epitaphioi there are no oarsmen or archers, only Athenians. (Loraux 1986, 278)

Loraux thinks this unifying hoplite model is "no doubt democratic," and it may well have operated in Athenian democratic ideology as part of the concept of isonomia, or the equality of political rights. As Loraux also explains, the military code prevalent in the fifth century and verified in the figure of the hoplite was also necessarily oppositional and superior to all that was designated feminine by nature.[42]

Other plays about Dionysus are attested both earlier and later than the *Bacchae* and the *Frogs*. See Dodds 1966, xxviii–xxxiii.

40. See Pickard-Cambridge 1968, 71–72. The dating and civic context of the earliest tragic performances are uncertain.

41. See the brief historical summary in Stanford 1968, xiv–xv. More recently, see Dover 1993, 4–5.

42. Loraux 1986, 147.

In a military speech, which uses *arete* [excellence] and *andreia* [manliness] without distinction to designate the highest worth, there is little room for a female virtue, except to define it as the reverse of male virtue. Thus, after reminding the sons and daughters of the dead that the first imperative is, for the *aner*, always to go beyond himself, Pericles asks the women not to prove inferior to their natures: *physis*, a starting point for the men, is, then, for women, an end, inscribed in them as a norm. Similarly, the word *doxa* has meaning only in a male world in which renown is the highest reward; female glory—a contradiction in terms—consists on the contrary in not speaking of oneself. (278–79)

This appeal to an imagined community based on manly excellence in military action must have come under stress during the twenty-five-year Peloponnesian War, that is, from the ostensible date of Pericles' funeral oration to the production of the *Bacchae* and the *Frogs*.[43] Thucydides' history of that war, probably published around 404, gives the details of this warrior ethos in crisis.[44] Loraux argues that within that history, the funeral oration "represents for Thucydides a symbol of the greatness of Athens, destined to ward off in advance any account of its failure."[45] I am not entirely convinced that the oration could "ward off in advance" Thucydides' subsequent account of Athenian failure, but Loraux is right in pointing out that the historian has set up at the beginning of his account an idealized version of Athens and its citizens that he cannot maintain to its end.

In the context of this impending failure, the valorization of the hoplite warrior is part of the nostalgic enterprise of Athenian self-representation. Based on a code of elite manly virtue,[46] this hoplite becomes fused with the epic or legendary hero in the *Frogs*, where that fusion is a principal source of the play's comic business. This fusion is most vividly represented in Aeschylus' claim to have be-

---

43. Cf. Anderson 1983. On the concept of an "imaginary Athens," see Loraux 1986, 328–39.

44. See Finley 1967, 2.

45. See Loraux 1986, 289–91, on the "homological relationship that has often been observed between the epitaphios and [Thucydides'] work as a whole."

46. On the prominence of elite families and values during the democracy, see Griffith 1995, 65–72.

queathed to Euripides an audience that "breathed spears and helmets and white-crested plumes, greaves and darts and hearts made of sevenfold oxhide" (*Frogs* 1016–17). While Aeschylus' boast is certainly not to be taken at face value or as reflecting any social reality, it does reflect the currency of epic exemplars in contemporary military rhetoric.[47] Expressed in terms of the accoutrements of the epic hero—his weapons and armor—Aeschylus describes an idealized warrior both for the audience he claims to have created and for the audience watching Aristophanes' play; indeed, these audiences are one and the same. But it is important to note that the equation of the hoplite with the heroic warrior in the late fifth century occurs when the hoplite is no longer the principal figure in Athenian military strategy.[48] In other words, the fusion of hoplite and hero (and audience member) represents the lost and longed-for dominance of an elite masculine ethos defined in terms of martial virtue. In this sense, the hoplite warrior— like the epic hero—has become the equivalent of a dramatic character, as Aeschylus' bequest suggests.

This notion of military virtue as a theater-like act may help to explain the role played by the ephebes, or young warriors of Athens, in accounts of the history of the Greek theater. As Jack Winkler has argued, male citizens established the tragic contests in Athens, and tragedies were produced and performed by male citizens for male citizens. Those citizens were marshaled together in a "quasi-official gathering" and were perhaps seated in the theater according to tribal

---

47. The word used by Aeschylus for "helmet" is the epic τρυφάλεια; the adjective ἑπταβοείους, "sevenfold oxhide," is used by Homer to describe the shield of Ajax (e.g., at *Iliad* 7.220).

48. I want to thank an anonymous reader of my manuscript for this book for making this important point. On the decline of hoplite warfare during the Peloponnesian War, cf. Hanson 1989, 39: "By the late fifth century, the Athenians, in hopes of spreading their untraditional ideas about the avoidance of hoplite battle on the plains, sent out corps of 'long-wall builders' to other cities. . . . Consequently, there was less chance now that a single, simple clash of Spartan and Athenian infantry would be the decisive factor in determining the outcome of a war between the two states; throughout Greece the old way of massing in formation to decide a conflict on the battlefield was nearly forgotten." Hoplite warfare was used during the Peloponnesian War, that is, at the Battle of Mantinea, but the Athenians relied on their fleet. See now Hanson 1996.

and military organization.[49] As part of this display of masculinity and militarism, the ephebes were accorded special prominence at the City Dionysia, beginning with their "reenactment of the advent of Dionysos" from Eleutherai.[50] Although the ephebic inscriptions that provide the evidence for this reenactment, or εἰσαγωγή, are late (between 127 and 106 B.C.E.), the practice may predate the inscriptions, as Pickard-Cambridge explains.

> The enactment of the god's advent does not look like an afterthought and probably goes back to the earliest days of the festival when, after his first cold welcome, it was desired to make amends by doing him special honor. (Pickard-Cambridge 1968, 60)

Whether or not this enactment "goes back to the earliest days of the festival," it makes us ask why the ephebes should comprise Dionysus' special entourage. It may be that the Athenians desired to make amends for Dionysus' "cold" reception, as Pickard-Cambridge suggests. But this reading only begs the question of why the ephebic procession should perform that particular function. If it is part of the tradition of the god's cold reception, the ephebes' reenactment can be compared to the phallic procession as it has been discussed earlier in this chapter. Both processions act as defensive activities in the face of Dionysus' potentially dangerous entry into the city. The young warriors, who represent the continuity and preservation of an elite warrior class (and by extension the preservation of the city), escort but also hold in check the god, by means of their physical and symbolic presence. In more general terms, the theatrical space and the dramatic festivals are themselves constituent of this disciplinary regime, and the foreign god is defined by his need to be constrained by Greek institutions. Here we can recall how the city of the Borysthenites is depicted as a disciplinary space in Herodotus' Scyles narrative. It may also be that the ephebes, who occupy a tenuous position between boyhood and manhood, are Dionysus' special companions because he too is a liminal figure; in the mythological and visual traditions, the god is often represented as an ephebic type.[51]

---

49. See Winkler 1990a, 22. See also Pickard-Cambridge 1968, 264–65.
50. See Winkler 1990a, 37.
51. See Dodds 1966, on *Bacchae* 453–59. See also Winkler 1990a, 35–37.

But wherever we wish to lay the emphasis in explaining the ephebic procession, it suggests that the meaning of Dionysus as the god of the theater cannot be disassociated from the ideology of Greek masculinity and militarism.

Simon Goldhill's discussion of the preplay ceremonies at the Greater Dionysia provides additional evidence for the notion that theatrical experience in Athens is part of a system of preserving a normative Greek masculinity. Goldhill discusses the parade of war orphans in full armor, the display of the foreign tribute, the crowning of deserving citizens and foreigners, and the possible active involvement of the ten generals, or *strategoi*. But despite his conclusions about the tension between the "public display of the success in military and political terms of the city" and the tragic texts, which often undermine that success, it must still be asked why the overt display of achieved manhood (especially the parade of the young men in armor) should necessarily be connected with the great dramatic festival.[52] Granted, the Greater Dionysia was "open to the whole Hellenic world" and gave perhaps the widest scope to such a display.[53] But this argument does not provide a completely satisfactory answer to our question. Nor is it enough to agree with Goldhill that some extant plays (i.e., *Ajax, Philoctetes*) are concerned with an ephebe (ἀνδρόπαις ἀνήρ) in the process of achieving adulthood.

The foundational narratives of the ephebic institution demonstrate how the display of the young male body as a militarized body is embedded in the discourse of Athenian political and social life. Vidal-Naquet argues that these narratives predate the institution of the ephebia itself and that similar myths and practices are also in evidence in other parts of Greece (e.g., Sparta).[54]

---

52. See Goldhill 1990, 102. Cf. 125 n. 83: "The assumption of full armor . . . is a significant gesture in marking [the conclusion of ephebic status], since the ephebe is conceived of as lightly armed specifically in contrast with the panoply of the hoplite. In the theater, they appear as *andres politai*, 'adult male citizens,' for the first time (in full armor)." The parade of the war orphans "appears to have been abolished at some time in the fourth century" (Pickard-Cambridge 1968, 59 with n. 2).

53. The quote is from Pickard-Cambridge 1968, 58.

54. Vidal-Naquet 1986. See also Goldhill 1990; Winkler 1990a; Mason 1984, 51–57.

Everyone would now agree that the ephebia of the fourth century B.C. had its roots in ancient practices of "apprenticeship,"
whose object was to introduce young men to their future roles as
citizens and heads of families, that is, as full members of the
community. This membership also included membership in the
hoplite ranks. (Vidal-Naquet 1986, 106)

The aetiological myth of the ephebic institution (and the Apatouria)
tells the story of a young man who bests an enemy by means of a trick.
In this well-known story, Melanthos the Athenian (the Black One) is to
fight a *monomachia*, or single combat, in a border dispute between the
Athenians and the Boeotians.[55] He overcomes his enemy by shouting
out to him, "Xanthos, you do not play according to the rules; there is
someone at your side." When Xanthos turns to see who is beside him,
Melanthos kills him and subsequently becomes king of Athens. According to another version, Melanthos disguises himself as a peasant, is
killed, and thereby ensures the safety of Athens.[56] The point of Vidal-
Naquet's inquiry into this aetiological myth is to determine why the
ephebes should be "offered a model of behavior contrary to that which
they swear in their oath to observe." He continues, "We have single
combat and trickery contrasted with fair hoplite fighting on even
terms."[57] The narrative locates the young man on the outskirts of town
(the ἐσχατιά); he is also associated with foreigners or noncitizens.[58] As

---

55. Nilsson (1911) argues that the story of the black hunter, linked with the
worship of Dionysus, was one of the earliest forms of tragedy. See also Farnell
1909a, 1909b.

56. See *FGrH* 3b Supp. 2:50 (on 323a F 23), cited by Vidal-Naquet (1986).

57. See Vidal-Naquet 1986, 109–11 and the sources cited there. Burkert
(1985, 262) explains how the Spartan youth in preparation for elite adulthood
had to spend time as robbers and feed themselves by theft. Odysseus'
strategem for overcoming the Cyclops by getting the monster drunk and
calling himself "Nobody" (*Odyssey* 9.345 ff.) also comes to mind. Cf. the story
of the young Philios who slew a lion by means of a trick (ἀπάτη); he made it
drunk. The story is found in Antoninus Liberalis *Metamorphoses* 12 (cited by
Vidal-Naquet [1986, 119]).

58. See Aeschines *On the Embassy* 167–68; Plato *Laws* 6.760b; Thucydides
History 4.67–68 and 8.92.2. These sources are cited by Vidal-Naquet (1986,
107). Telemachus emulates the model provided by his father and is expected
to take his father's place. His voyage to Pylos and Sparta, for example, reca-
pitulates Odysseus' voyages and positions Telemachus as a περίπολος whose

Vidal-Naquet observes, the ephebe is a περίπολος, or a young man in transition—one who, prior to becoming a fully recognized citizen, the married head of a family, and a hoplite, temporarily occupies a marginalized social position.[59]

But what seems obvious is that in the "model of behavior" offered the ephebe, he is required to play the role of the deceptive stranger or foreigner before he can become a lawful citizen and warrior. We might even suggest that this model of behavior is exemplified by Dionysus in the *Bacchae* when he plays the role of the Lydian stranger before he can be recognized as a god. The transvestitism that takes place in festivals celebrating the political and martial coming of age of the male citizen also attests to the importance of theater-like practices in this process. As part of the Oschophoria, for example, a procession was led from a temple of Dionysus to the shrine of Athena Skiras (Athena of the Suburbs, or Outland) by two boys dressed as girls (see Plutarch *Life of Theseus* 23).[60] What Vidal-

---

return to Ithaca sets him up for the assumption of his rightful claim to the kingship. See Murnaghan 1987, 34–35 with nn. 22 and 23.

59. Although Odysseus is not a young man when he returns to Ithaca, his story has some close parallels with the ephebic narratives. He is in many senses a περίπολος who has returned to his city after a long excursion abroad. He plays the role of an outsider (from Crete), and it is by means of a trick (his disguise) that he claims his place as a citizen, the head of his family, and king. Before he engages the suitors, Odysseus will string the bow that he was given while still a child (παιδνὸς ἐών, *Odyssey* 21.21). His subsequent defense of himself with its arrows (before he is armed to the teeth; see 22.105 ff.) demarcates the transition from ephebic hunter to hoplite fighter, as Vidal-Naquet (1986, 117–22) describes it. Also relevant is Odysseus' defeat of the treacherous Melanthius (son of Dolios, i.e., son of Tricky) at *Odyssey* 22. Cf. Pindar *Pythian Odes* 4.233–34, where, although Jason does not put on a disguise, his reliance on Medea's foreign witchcraft suggests that the negative influence of women also operates in narratives of precitizenship or noncitizenship or that insofar as a man's political position is at risk, that risk is associated with foreigners, beggars, tricksters, and women. See chap. 4 on this phenomenon in the Pisistratid narratives. The story of Pentheus in the *Bacchae* may be said to be a narrative of transition gone wrong.

60. Vidal-Naquet (1986, 116) notes: "It is well known that in archaic Greek societies, as well as in other societies, dressing up as a woman, as in the procession at the Oschophoria, was a means of dramatizing the fact that a young man had reached the age of virility and marriage. The classic example in Greek mythology is the story of Achilles on Skyros, dressed up as a girl but

Naquet (1986, 114) calls the "law of symmetrical inversion" is a complex relationship between gender and disguise that, in Butler's phrase (1990, 273), activates the potential failure to "do one's gender right." In this sense, the aetiological myths and rituals connected with the ephebic institution and attached to the Greater Dionysia coalesce around the potential failure to achieve a normative Greek manhood defined in culture- and gender-specific terms.

Thus one way of understanding the discourse of manhood in the context of the Attic theater is to suggest that the overt display of idealized manly virtues and successes in the ephebic procession and in the preplay ceremonies testify to a desire to imitate what is no longer to be seen in the "real life" of the city. In other words, imitation or impersonation is a compensatory gesture. Here the escorting of the god of the theater is paradigmatic of a theater-like event. Another way of understanding the phenomenon is to suggest that the loss of those manly virtues is implicit in the very production of the plays to follow, not only in the context of particular plots (as Goldhill argues), but also in terms of the formal conventions of the theater. For the plays present male bodies as theatrical bodies, that is, as bodies that implicitly allude to the unstable nature of an internal and unchanging essence of masculine identity. Thus the display of citizen boys in full armor, like the procession of the ephebes, counteracts the display of the actors in their theatrical disguises.[61] Insofar as those boys have shed the taint of deception and subterfuge associated with ephebic training and the

---

unable to control himself at the sight of a weapon." See Burkert 1985, 260–64; Ferrari 1993, 104–5. Significantly it is at this festival that, in Aristophanes' *Ecclesiazousae*, Praxagora and her girlfriends decide to dress as men and take the mens' places as voting citizens in the *ecclesia*. This mock transformation operates on two levels in the play, since the women, who are played by men, disguise themselves as men.

61. Ephebic or initiatory rites often included nudity. Burkert (1985, 261) suggests that "their sporting [?] nakedness contrasts with the girlish clothing of the younger boys." On idealized male nudity, see my chap. 3. Winkler (1990a, 43) argues that the tragic choristers were ephebes. Since the tragic choruses are often made up of marginalized persons—slave women, prisoners of war, old men—who admonish and advise the main actors, two conclusions present themselves. First, the ephebes are purposely miscast in the roles they play; second, they perform a scrutinizing function that perhaps reflects their newly acquired role as male soldier-citizens.

transition to full adult manhood, they serve to defuse the threat of compromised male identity that, beginning with the epic, the disguised or adorned male body can signify.[62] They are *real men* (in both senses of the phrase) who stand up to the compromised or less than real men on stage (whether they play the roles of male or female personae). In the world of the theater, the ephebes are antiactors.

The god of the theater is the god whose actions and attributes focus attention on the essential but arduous cultural task of preserving a normative Greek identity and masculinity. This focus comes into view in a variety of texts and contexts but is most conspicuous on the Attic stage itself, where Dionysus plays his part in the *Bacchae* and the *Frogs*. I want to turn to these plays now and to the figure of Dionysus on stage as the embodiment of dramatic performance as a nostalgic project. I do not intend to offer a comprehensive reading of each play; my debt to the many excellent studies that already exist will be obvious. Instead, I will focus on how each play contributes to our understanding of theatrical performance in Athens and on the related fears and desires inherent in opposing or embracing the god of the theater. Within their status as plays, the *Bacchae* and the *Frogs* also focus attention on the position of the Athenian citizen as a dramatic spectator and on what that position means in the ideology of Greek identity and masculinity. The premise of the *Bacchae* sets the stage for these foci: Dionysus has come to Thebes in the shape of a mortal to prove himself the son of Semele and a god.[63] From the start the play is a vehicle for examining the god's entry into Greek civic space. Similar to Scyles' shifting identity, Dionysus' identity is figured first of all through his mother and is then visualized in an act of disguise or impersonation.

ὧν οὕνεϰ' αὐτῷ θεὸς γεγὼς ἐνδείξομαι
πᾶσίν τε Θηβαίοισιν. ἐς δ' ἄλλην χθόνα,
τἀνθένδε θέμενος εὖ, μεταστήσω πόδα,
δειϰνὺς ἐμαυτόν· ἢν δὲ Θηβαίων πόλις

---

62. Cf. chap. 3 on the adorned body of Odysseus.

63. Cf. the Dodds' 1966 introduction to the *Bacchae* for a summary of scholarly debates over the play, which he characterizes as a "topical yet deeply traditional miracle-play, 'old-fashioned' in style and structure as in the incidents it depicted, yet charged with emotion." More recently, see Segal 1982; Zeitlin 1990a; Foley 1985.

ὀργῇ σὺν ὅπλοις ἐξ ὄρους Βάκχας ἄγειν
ζητῇ, ξυνάψω μαινάσι στρατηλατῶν.
ὧν οὕνεκ᾽ εἶδος θνητὸν ἀλλάξας ἔχω
μορφήν τ᾽ ἐμὴν μετέβαλον εἰς ἀνδρὸς φύσιν.

[For these reasons I shall show him [Cadmus]
and all the Thebans that I am a god. Then, after being
well established here, I will march into another land
and reveal myself. If Thebes, in anger,
seeks to go in arms and drive the Bacchae
from the hills, together with the maenads I will engage them in
    battle.
For these reasons I have taken on the appearance of a mortal
and have changed my shape to fit the nature of a man.]
                                        (*Bacchae* 47–54; cf. 4)

In these lines and those that precede them, emphasis is divided
between Dionysus' disguise as a Lydian stranger and his desire to be
revealed as a god, between what he says he is and what he appears to
be (cf. ἐμφανής, 22; φανέντα, 42). And this emphasis encourages us—
as it has others—to ask why the disguise is necessary. E. R. Dodds
has discussed what has seemed to be the unnecessary repetition in
lines 53–54 and comments that there is a "good practical reason for
the repetition, in the necessity for making it quite clear to the audience that the speaker, whom they accept as a god, will be accepted as
a man by the people on the stage." Dodds goes on to speculate, as
have other commentators, that this "motive might of course have led
an actor to interpolate the lines."[64] Dodds' appeals to practical necessity and an actor's interpolation make sense but also suggest a more
complex reading of the prologue and the god's disguise.

In the first place, it is obvious that the plot of the *Bacchae* assumes a
distinction between the actor's role as the god and his role as the god
disguised as a man. Such a distinction would presumably require not
only verbal clues but visual ones, that is, the semblance of a mortal
disguise concealing an immortal form.[65] The *Frogs* also plays on this

---

64. Dodds 1966, ad loc.
65. See Foley 1985, 246–48.

visual predicament, by means of the costume exchanges between Dionysus and his slave Xanthias. Visual clues, of course, are only available to us in textual references to costuming conventions or in ostensible depictions of dramatic performances on vases. The picture provided by these sources is often less than clear, but a Lydian man would presumably be recognizable by a typical style of dress. Relying on the reports of others, Pentheus refers pejoratively to the stranger as a "wizard conjurer" (*Bacchae* 234), and we can infer that such a person would have worn a unique sort of costume. But as Pentheus' own descriptions of the stranger's physical characteristics reveal (233–38 and 453–59), this costume did not in fact conceal those feminine attributes so commonly associated with Dionysus outside Euripides' play, both prior to and during the fifth century.[66] Rather, the Lydian disguise only seems to accentuate these attributes. Thus the potential confusion, implicit in Dodds' discussion, between the god disguised as a mortal and the god himself arises in part because feminine features are the visible characteristics of both. The effect of this confusion is that the practice of disguise itself, exemplified both by 'Dionysus' disguise as the Lydian stranger and the disguise of the actor playing Dionysus, is associated with femininity.

In chapter 3, I argued that as a general rule disguise signifies the vulnerability of the masculine subject. Dionysus' role playing in the *Bacchae* illustrates this rule insofar as his disguise and his effeminacy are isomorphic. But at the same time, Dionysus is quite obviously *in*vulnerable in the play. This invulnerability does not quite mean, however, that his effeminacy is "on the side of femininity as power" and that Pentheus' effeminacy, made visually manifest by his maenad's costume, is "on the side of weakness."[67] Power and weakness are certainly in conflict in the play, but both are ultimately figured as masculine. What looks like feminine power, in other words, is really effeminacy as the mask of masculine weakness. Whether we

---

66. See Dodds 1966 on *Bacchae* 453–59. In the archaic and early classical periods, Dionysus is bearded; he seems to become more effeminate in the late fifth century.

67. Zeitlin 1990a, 64. But cf. Zeitlin's observation that "when [the male character] finds himself in a condition of weakness, he too becomes acutely aware that he has a body—and then perceives himself, at the limits of pain, to be most like a woman" (72).

are talking about the effeminacy of Dionysus, about his Lydian disguise, or about Pentheus in women's clothing, femininity is always a form of disguise—both in the fictional universe of the plot of the *Bacchae* and in the theatrical universe in which cross-dressed actors play female characters.[68] In other words, there is no essential femininity and no feminine power in the play; rather, femininity is a set of external, corporeal, and vestimentary attributes.[69] In this sense the feminine traits of the Lydian stranger/Dionysus signify the appearance of weakness as the vehicle of Dionysus' power—manifested first of all in his power over women. The visible feminine traits of the stranger-god, together with his effect on the women of Thebes, in fact motivate Pentheus' disastrous belief in his own moral and military superiority. Femininity as disguise thus signifies both the vulnerability and weakness of mortal males in the play and the power of the god of the theater.

To be revealed as a god, Dionysus must wear and then remove his disguise, no matter by what means this adjustment may have been executed on stage. As an actor playing a god who is playing a man in order to be revealed as a god, the theatrical body of Dionysus represents a complex embodiment of what Keir Elam refers to as the three distinct bodies on the dramatic stage: the fictional body of the

---

68. On the interplay of homoeroticism and dramatic transvestitism in the Elizabethan theater, see Case 1988, 21–27. Cf. Orgel 1989, 16: "But the argument against transvestite actors warns of an even more frightening metamorphosis than the transformation of the boy into a monster of both kinds. Male spectators, it is argued, will be seduced by the impersonation, and, losing their reason, will become effeminate, which in this case means they will lust not after the woman in the drama, which would be bad enough, but after the boy beneath the woman's costume, thereby playing the woman's role themselves. This fear, which has been brilliantly anatomized by Laura Levine, is so pervasive in the tracts, and so unlike modern kinds of sexual anxiety, that it is worth pausing over" (cf. Levine 1986). Foley (1982–83, 10 with n. 25) notes that "Greek men in drama fear feminization above all humiliations." Dover (1989, 76) says that "feminine clothes are unmistakably linked with passive homosexuality," but he does not discuss transvestitism as a theatrical convention.

69. Cf. Zeitlin 1990a, 87, noting Euripides' "greater interest in and skill at subtly portraying the psychology of female characters, and . . . his general emphasis on interior states of mind and on the private emotional life of the individual, most often located in the feminine situation."

dramatis persona, the physical body of the actor, and the virtual or ideal body of the actor as indicated in the text.[70] In the *Bacchae's* prologue and episodes—that is, up until his epiphany—Dionysus has what can be thought of as two fictional bodies in the play: that of the god and that of the god in disguise. In this respect, the bifocal situation I described in chapter 3 with respect to Odysseus and his beggar's disguise in the *Odyssey* also applies to the situation of Dionysus and his mortal disguise in the *Bacchae*. But the presence of the physical body of the actor in the latter sets up a different ontological regime. Because disguise is the sine qua non of dramatic performance, Dionysus' disguise indicates both the virtual body of the actor qua actor (the idea of the actor's body) and the physical body of the actor himself. And as a result of the unclear distinction between Dionysus in disguise and in propria persona, his appearance on stage simultaneously references the three constituent dispositions of Elam's theatrical body. Consequently, his appearance also testifies to the proposition that theatrical impersonation is antithetical to the notion of an essential and stable identity revealed on the surface of the body. Moreover, each of Dionysus' bodily dispositions or appearances (actor, foreigner, god) testifies to the proposition that effeminacy is the principal signifier of that antithesis.

But if femininity as disguise is the visual vehicle of Dionysus' persona and power in the *Bacchae*, then madness, or mania, is its most devastating effect. Dionysiac madness motivates the action of the play and is the contingent cause of the social and political destruction of Thebes. As I have already argued with respect to the Scyles narrative, the coincidence of disguise and madness is also a central feature of the theatrical experience as it is manifested in Euripides' play. As we have seen, Dionysiac mania can be the result both of a mortal's opposition to the god (as punishment) and of his absolute acquiescence to the god (as religious fervor or ecstasy); and both opposition and acquiescence have dangerous consequences for males. In the *Bacchae*, Pentheus' disguise as a maenad is the visual sign of both kinds of mania. His madness is proven by his opposition to the stranger and also by the fact that he puts on the maenad's costume. In general terms, the paradoxical meaning of Dionysiac mania in the *Bacchae* is expressed in

---

70. Elam 1984, 50.

the visual confusion that constitutes its principal symptom, and it is staged through Pentheus' disguise.[71] Dionysiac madness in the play is thus implicitly equated with the effect of dramatic impersonation not only on the characters in the play but also on the Athenian audience.

But the visual confusion that governs the plot is not only a symptom of madness. It is also the source of Pentheus' pleasure: in his maenad's costume, he takes sensual delight in imagining himself watching the "other" maenads on the mountain (*Bacchae* 918–70). It is also a source of pleasure for Agave, who takes pleasure in the belief that she has killed a lion cub (1168 ff.). As the experience of pleasure in the face of what are ultimately exceedingly painful events, the visual delusions of Pentheus and Agave anticipate Aristotle's discussion in the *Poetics* of the effects of imitation. As a prelude to his discussion of tragic imitation in particular, Aristotle suggests that "objects that in themselves we view with pain, we delight to contemplate when reproduced with minute fidelity, such as the forms of the most unworthy animals and of dead bodies" (*Poetics* 1448b10–14). According to Aristotle, the pleasure provided by the experience of a tragic performance is possible because imitation is necessarily not commensurate with real life. His reference to "forms of animals and dead bodies" seems an almost uncanny illustration of Agave's intense pleasure in what she thinks is the dead body of a young lion, until she recognizes it as the body of her own son (*Bacchae* 1167 ff.). I do not mean to suggest that this scene from the *Bacchae* is directly responsible for Aristotle's notion of the effect of dramatic mimesis in the *Poetics*. Rather, Aristotle's reference to a feeling of pleasure in the presence of painful sights helps us to understand theatrical experience in terms of unpredictable and even counterintuitive ways of seeing, ways of seeing in which what is seen registers a response that is opposite to what is expected. In this respect the visual effect of mimesis described by Aristotle has affinities with the effect of Dionysiac madness in Euripides' play. The effect of that madness in the *Bacchae* is to provide a pleasurable, if tenuous and temporary, freedom from the pain of recognizing the true causes and consequences of actions and commitments in real life, although "real life" is of course also an effect of

---

71. See also Seaford 1994, 299. The so-called palace miracle scene (*Bacchae* 585 ff.) also exemplifies the visual confusion in the play, since what actually happened on stage is unclear.

mimesis in the play. The difference is that, whereas Aristotle assumes on the part of the spectator a recognizable distinction between what seems real and what is real, Dionysiac delusion is produced out of an inability to make that distinction. That inability, as well as the related assumption that imitation can influence a man's character and behavior, informs Plato's attack on dramatic mimesis in the *Republic*.

It must be admitted, of course, that Aristotle's theory of mimetic pleasure implicitly refers to the effect of imitation on a "real-life" spectator and not to what happens between characters in a play. But this distinction between the two only helps to demonstrate that the theatrical bodies of Dionysus and Pentheus in the *Bacchae* operate within both the fictional world of the play and the notional world of the theater and that the effect of Dionysiac mania operates within both the fictional city of Thebes and the notional city of Athens.[72] I use the term *notional* here to refer to the spectator, the theater, and the city as concepts indicated in the text, in order to avoid the assimilation of dramatic characters to actual spectators, whose thoughts and feelings we cannot know in any reliable or significant sense. I want to suggest instead that the plot of the *Bacchae* imposes a theoretical link between what happens to the characters in the play and what happens to the spectators in the theater. This theoretical link forms the basis for the homology between Dionysiac experience and theatrical experience in Athens.

Like Pentheus and Agave, who are subject to the enforced madness of the god (*Bacchae* 32–33), the notional spectators in the Theater of Dionysus are participants in a distorted visual experience, guaranteed at the most obvious level by their very presence in the theater. With their attention directed at the stage, they are also necessarily distracted from engaging in actual social, political, or military activity.[73] In principle (if not in actuality) they assume a passive subject

---

72. Zeitlin (1990b, 130–39) argues that Thebes, considered Dionysus' native city, "provides a negative model to Athens' manifest image of itself with regard to its notions of the proper management of city, society and self. . . . Thebes is an 'anti-Athens.' "

73. Svenbro (1990, 371) writes: "The public—and already that of Thespis— is supposed to watch and listen, passively, for the most part (although not necessarily silently; we have anecdotes about audiences' vociferous reactions to performances)." Cf. Mulvey 1975, 16, on the character of Jeffries in Hitchcock's

position inimical to the elite masculine ethos that, from the time of the Greek epics, required men to be authentic speakers of words and doers of deeds. In this sense, dramatic spectators occupy a position analogous to the ideal (if not actual) position of women in Athenian society; like women, they are silent and inactive in a culture that demands action and speech defined by political and military service to the state (cf. Sophocles *Ajax* 293; Thucydides *History* 2.45; Aristotle *Politics* 1254b3–1277b25).[74]

Above all else, Pentheus' Dionysiac transformation in the *Bacchae* means his rejection of the warrior ethos to which he had been so fervently devoted before putting on the maenad's costume.[75] This devotion is illustrated when he calls for his arms (ὅπλα, *Bacchae* 809) just before Dionysus entices him to see the maenads and suggests that he wear the maenad's costume. Ὅπλον can mean "weapons" or "armor"; in the plural it is commonly used with the verb ἐνδύνω to mean "to put on one's armor."[76] Just as commonly, the verb means "to put on one's clothing," and its privileges of occurrence are principally with armor and clothing. Thus, while ἐνδύνω does not occur with ὅπλα in the *Bacchae*, armor and the maenad's dress constitute two terms in a complementary vestimentary discourse; in effect, Pentheus puts on female attire (θῆλυν ἐνδῦναι στολήν, 836; cf. 852–53) instead of taking up his weapons and putting on his armor. That the one form of dress is exchanged for the other is suggested more clearly in the interchange between the stranger/Dionysus and Pentheus just prior to the cross-dressing scene. Here Pentheus announces that he will either advance in arms against the maenads or be persuaded by the stranger's plan of disguise and subterfuge (840–61). Once he has put

---

Rear Window: "his enforced inactivity, binding him to his seat as a spectator, puts him squarely in the fantasy position of the cinema audience." Modleski (1988, 83), commenting on this same film, asks whether we might "not then say that spectatorship and 'narrativity' are themselves 'feminine' (to the male psyche) in that they place the spectator in a passive position and in a submissive relation to the text."

74. See Halperin 1990, 33–38, and Mason 1984, 23 ff., on the active-passive antithesis with respect to sex-gender roles in antiquity.

75. Cf. *Bacchae* 303, where Tiresias says that Dionysus, in Dodds' words, "is capable of injecting panic [*mania*] into armed and disciplined troops."

76. LSJ I.1. The verb is used of putting on clothing at *Iliad* 2.42 and of putting on armor at Herodotus *Histories* 7.218 (ἐνδύεσθαι ὅπλα).

on the fawn skin and taken up the thyrsus, Pentheus erroneously believes that he has superhuman strength: he thinks that he can lift Mount Cithaeron on his shoulders (945–51). But at the same time, he says that "one should not conquer women by force" and that he should spy on them instead by hiding among the trees (953–54).[77] In changing his costume, then, Pentheus exchanges the role of the face-to-face warrior-in-arms for that of a coward disguised as a woman; the ideal of martial valor as the essence of manliness is abandoned in an act of femininity as disguise.

In the world of the *Bacchae*, Dionysus' power over the actors as female dramatis personae together with the enforced transvestitism of Pentheus illustrate tragedy's most conspicuous illusionary feat, namely, its ability to make a man (the universal subject) look and behave like a woman (the universal other).[78] As I have suggested, femininity as disguise simultaneously signifies the vulnerability of mortal males and the power of the god of the theater. Dressed as a woman and under the compulsion of Dionysiac madness and delusion, Pentheus embodies both the tragic actor and the tragic spectator. Feeding on his hopes or desires (618), he wants above all else to watch the maenads from a safe distance. In fact, dressing as a maenad makes Pentheus' position as a spectator, or θεατής, possible; the former is a precondition for the latter, as Dionysus suggests.[79]

Πε. τίνα στολήν; ἢ θῆλυν; ἀλλ᾽ αἰδώς μ᾽ ἔχει.
Δι. οὐκέτι θεατὴς μαινάδων πρόθυμος εἶ.

[*Pe.* What sort of dress? A feminine dress? But shame takes hold of me.
Di. Then you no longer desire to be a spectator among the maenads.]

(828–30; cf. 811)

---

77. Cf. Agave's boast that the women have killed without weapons and with their bare hands (*Bacchae* 1207–10).

78. I mean that a male actor in a female role performs a more intense mimetic act than a male actor in a male role. The standard discussion of female subjectivity in Greek drama is Zeitlin 1990a; see, in particular, Zeitlin's discussion of the *Bacchae* on her pp. 63–64.

79. Cf. κατάσκοπος at *Bacchae* 916 and 956 and θεωρία at 1047.

In these lines, playing the woman is the precondition of watching a special kind of Dionysiac performance. Under the spell of Dionysus, a spell characterized by the victim's calmness, or ἡσυχία (622, 636),[80] and by his maenad's costume, the voyeuristic Pentheus "sees what it is necessary for him to see" (924) in a city that has been completely "Bacchanized" (1295). His position thus epitomizes the gender-specific prejudices that characterize the male as a spectator in Greek culture (θεατής); he plays the womanlike man who desires to look at other women. As I have argued in chapter 3, in this spectatorial system looking *like* a woman, being looked at *as* a woman, and being seen *by* a woman signify compromised masculinity; here the system incorporates another subject position, that of a male who watches women. And conversely, according to Dionysus, the maenads would kill Pentheus if they were to see him *as a man*.

Πε. τί δὴ τόδ'; ἐς γυναῖκας ἐξ ἀνδρὸς τελῶ;[81]
Δι. μή σε κτάνωσιν, ἢν ἀνὴρ ὀφθῇς ἐκεῖ.

[*Pe.* What is this? Am I to be ranked among women and apart from men?
Di. If you do not [wear the maenad's costume], they will kill you, if you are seen there as a man.]

(822–23)

It is in fact as a man, or rather as a man who is dressed as a woman, that the god finally brings Pentheus to the mountain and announces

---

80. On ἡσυχία and the debate over quietism in warfare, see Ehrenberg 1947. Cf. the Corinthians' speech on the difference between the Athenians and Spartans at Thucydides *History* 1.69–70. The Spartans are characterized by ἡσυχάζετε (1.69.13), in opposition to the Athenians. In Thucydides, ἡσυχία is part of a discourse of cultural difference, a discourse that defines non-Athenians against Athenians. See my chap. 4 for discussion of Solon's ἡσυχία.

81. The word τελέω (in line 822) means "to be an initiate," and specifically refers to being initiated into the mysteries of Dionysus at Herodotus *Histories* 4.79 and Aristophanes *Frogs* 357. Its use here seems to conflate Dionysiac initiation with gender instability. Cf. Dodds 1966, ad loc. The word τελεῖν means (1) "to pay taxes" (τέλη), (2) "to be classified for taxation," and (3) "to be classified" (generally); cf. Sophocles *Oedipus Tyrannus* 222, εἰς ἀστοὺς τελῶ.

his presence to the maenads (ἄγω τὸν ὑμᾶς κἀμὲ τἀμά τ̓ ὄργια/γέλων τιθέμενον, 1080–81). Here the meaning of femininity as disguise and as a futile gesture toward preservation in the ideology of Greek masculinity is most conspicuous. For as the eyes of the maenads become focused on Pentheus (1086–87), they see him neither as a man nor as a woman, but as a beast of prey, or θήρ (1108). In the end, Dionysiac madness entails a radical confusion of those ontological categories that, normative and hierarchical, are constitutive of Greek cultural identity. But I want to stress that Pentheus is at once a spectacle and a spectator and that this confusion (or fusion) of roles is the necessary precondition of his destruction. As the most conspicuous manifestation of that confusion, putting on the maenad's costume is not simply an act of cross-dressing; Pentheus takes on the persona of a woman when he puts on her clothes (925 ff.). I use persona here in the sense of a dramatic character to emphasize the difference between what is often assumed to be Pentheus' internalization of or identification with a feminine subjectivity through ritual activity and what I take to be theatrical rather than psychological.[82] In historical context, the fantastic and horrifying orgiastic rites and rituals described by the chorus and the messenger in the *Bacchae* and their effect on the characters are presumably far removed from Athenian familiarity with the god.[83] But whatever agency we ascribe to divinity in Greek society, or rather whatver agency we think the Athenian audience ascribed to the divinity of Dionysus, belief in such agency does not easily translate into the psychological state of the actors, characters, or audience members.[84]

Moreover, while *sparagmos*, or ritual dismemberment, would have been a commonly recognized element of the Dionysiac narrative in fifth-century Athens, Pentheus' dismemberment in the *Bacchae* is not simply the enactment of a moribund ritual.[85] Nor should we reduce Euripides' plot to a commentary on the introduction of eastern

---

82. On identification as a principle in psychoanalysis and performance theory, see chap. 1.

83. See Segal 1961, 218–21, on the contemporary cult practices associated with Dionysus.

84. Cf. Dodds 1951; Gould 1978.

85. On *sparagmos* and *omophagia* in Bacchic ritual, see Dodds 1966, xvi–xix. See Herodotus *Histories* 2.42 on the assimilation of Dionysus and the Egyptian Osiris. Plutarch (*Moralia* 358b3–8) tells the story of Osiris' *sparagmos*.

"mystery" gods, such as Sabazius, into Athenian religious life. As a theatrical practice, rather than a ritual one, Pentheus' bodily fragmentation is finally a horrific demonstration of the confused status of the theatrical body; when he is torn limb from limb, he loses his visual identity as a human, a man, and his mother's son. The act itself, of course, is reported by the messenger (1043 ff.), but it seems likely that its consequences were graphically displayed on stage at the end of the play and that Agave does attempt to piece Pentheus' body back together.[86] The staging of that futile attempt only magnifies the unstable predicament of the theatrical body by presenting it as a (male) body in pieces. Only the head of the king remains intact, containing those eyes with which he watched the maenads and that Agave did not see as the eyes of her son until it was too late (1265 ff.; cf. 1222).[87] And if this head is displayed as a mask with empty eye-sockets, it becomes a graphic emblem of the theatrical body as a body that lacks a unifying core of identity.

Judith Butler argues: "drag fully subverts the distinction between inner and outer psychic space and effectively mocks both the expressive model of gender and the notion of a true gender identity. . . . *In imitating gender, drag implicitly reveals the imitative structure of gender itself—as well as its contingency.*"[88] In the *Bacchae*, this "imitative struc-

---

86. On the textual difficulties of the play's ending, including the question of the *compositio membrorum*, that is, of whether Pentheus' limbs were recombined by Agave on stage, see Dodds 1966, on *Bacchae* 1300, 1329.

87. Seaford (1994, 300–301) argues that the play affirms "the transition to the salvation of the polis." The city is saved, argues Seaford, because "the *Bacchae* ends with dual benefit for the polis, the institution of the cult and the end of the royal household." This reading of the play and of the polis (in opposition to the royal house) may be in accord with contemporary Athenian ideology, but the distinction Seaford makes between a polis and a royal house is not so clear in the play: Thebes is called a polis, and Tiresias refers to the king as a citizen of the polis (πολίτης, *Bacchae* 271). As Seaford points out, the herdsman calls Pentheus too kingly (τὸ βασιλικὸν λίαν, 671). But the statement does not condemn kingship; in fact, it testifies to the herdsman's freedom of speech under a king who, in the next lines, says that it is not right to be angry with just men. There is no marked condemnation of the monarchy in Thebes or any indication in the play that another form of government (i.e., democracy) is superior. Cf. Griffith 1995 on the role of the elite in democratic ideology.

88. Butler (1990a, 137) cites Newton 1972. The emphasis is Butler's.

ture of gender" is emphasized in the distinction between seeing Pentheus as a man and seeing him as a woman (cf. *Bacchae* 223). As a general rule, theatrical performance focuses attention on the surface of the body as a precondition of producing the "effect of an internal core or substance" of a dramatic character.[89] In the case of Pentheus, this attention is expressed through his intense concentration on his own feminine appearance—on his hair, the drape of his hem, and the proper way to hold the thyrsus (925–44). For Dionysus, these are the signs that Pentheus has "changed his heart," that is, that his external appearance is expressive of his internal disposition. According to Dodds, the phrase μεθέστηκας φρενῶν (944) means "to change heart" but also hints that Pentheus is "out of his mind"; and as Padel points out, tragedy is very often concerned with the loss of or damage to the φρένες as a condition of madness.[90] Together effeminacy and madness are the means by which the god of the theater both disciplines and punishes Pentheus. And if we can say that the imitative structure of gender, witnessed in Pentheus' enforced effeminacy, reveals the imitative structure of the drama, both structures consign the consoling notion of an internal core of masculine identity to disillusion and disillusionment—a disillusionment is displaced onto and displayed as the disguise of femininity.

This play of illusion and disillusion that characterizes both the Dionysiac experience and theatrical experience in the *Bacchae* is also at work in Aristophanes' *Frogs,* produced around the same time or a little prior to the *Bacchae.*[91] Here the comic god of tragedy takes the stage as a spectator and a judge at a contest between the tragic poets Aeschylus and Euripides. This premise makes the *Frogs* the best evidence we have for understanding theatrical experience and the ideologies that inform that experience in fifth-century Athens. The play is built first of all on the notion of the theatrical text as a vehicle of desire and resurrection. Inspired by reading Euripides' *Andromeda,* Dionysus has developed an intense "desire for [the dead] Euripides" [πόθος

89. The quotation is from Butler 1990a, 136.

90. Dodds 1966, ad loc. Padel 1992, 20–23.

91. On the dating of two plays, see Segal 1982, 211–25; Hooker 1980; Dover 1993, 37–38. The relative chronology is uncertain, although Dover opts for the *Frogs* as the earlier play.

Εὐριπίδου] (*Frogs* 66–67).[92] To find his poet and bring him back to life, he will take a trip to the underworld dressed as Heracles, that is, in "a lion's skin over a yellow tunic with a club and buskin" (46–47).[93] The survival of Euripides' plays, it seems, is not enough; the plot is motivated by a nostalgic longing for the authentic body and voice of the dead Euripides.[94] But this longing for authenticity is belied by the comic Dionysus, who, as an indiscriminate user of disguises, will wear not only the lion skin of Heracles but—with equal enthusiasm—the clothes of his slave Xanthias. Preposterous disguises, social inversions, and the perversion of the tragic stage constitute the play's episodes and give the lie to the notion of a tragic poet who, according to Dionysus, can "save the city" (*Frogs* 1419–23). In other words, "serious" drama is set up as a vehicle for political and social salvation, only to be proven inadequate to the task; the comic plot finds its business in the nostalgic enterprise of the tragic plot.

Who or what is this comic Dionysus if not a parodic imitation of the tragic Dionysus? For the comic version of the god (including his role in satyr plays) is necessarily an approximation of the tragic model, so that the two avatars of Dionysus in these two plays constitute a kind of mimetic hierarchy, exclusive of their relative chronology. Dover notes, "Both Euripides and Aristophanes were working within the framework of traditional conceptions of Dionysos which are attested by literary and iconographic evidence."[95] These "traditional conceptions" may be explanatory of the similarities between the two plays but are ultimately as inadequate as the "origins" of cultural phenomena. What are the similarities between the Dionysiac experiences presented in the *Bacchae* and the *Frogs*, and what do those similarities mean? In both plays an effeminate Dionysus tries to prove himself a god (*Bacchae* 47; *Frogs* 631). In both, he assumes more than one role and convinces others to do the same. In both, possibilities for the exchange or blending of roles and for disguise are facilitated by kinship: Dionysus and Heracles are brothers; Dionysus and Pentheus are first cousins. And in both,

---

92. The lost *Andromeda* was produced in 412 B.C.E. See Lucian *On Writing History* 1 on the effect of the *Andromeda*. Cf. Aristophanes *Thesmophoriazousae* 1012 ff.

93. On Heracles, see Loraux 1990. See also Long 1986, 57 with n. 11. On Mesopotamian parallels to the myths of Heracles, see Burkert 1987, 14–19.

94. See chap. 2 on the significance of the living poet.

95. Dover 1993, 38.

Dionysus' actions have serious or potentially serious consequences for the social and political life of a city, that is, Thebes or Athens. Dionysus' Heracles disguise is of course an essential element in the *Frogs*, just as his disguise as a Lydian stranger is in the *Bacchae*.[96] The motivation for the disguise in the former is to facilitate Dionysus' journey to and return from the underworld, a journey that Heracles had previously made (*Frogs* 108 ff.).[97] Yet in the divine scheme of things Dionysus could presumably have gone to Hades and back in propria persona, that is, without the benefit (or burden) of what is obviously a marginally successful impersonation or mimesis (μίμησιν, 109).[98] While the Heracles disguise is provided with a plausible explanation in the plot, it does not seem to be motivated by anything in the mythological tradition; in other words, it does not function as part of a "traditional conception of Dionysus." One effect of this comic invention, of course, is to make the task of seeing or recognizing Dionysus in propria persona a featured element in the play, just as it is in the *Bacchae*. But the broader significance of this task is revealed in the initiates' song about the effeminate Callias, who also put on the lion's skin.

καὶ Καλλίαν γέ φασι
τοῦτον τὸν Ἱπποβίνου
κύσθου λεοντῆν ναυμαχεῖν ἐνημμένον.

[They say that Callias,
son of Horse Fucker,
went to sea after putting a lion's skin over his cunt.][99]

(432–34)

---

96. Taking the *Bacchae* as the earlier play, Segal (1961, 227–30) and Hooker (1980, 179–82) discuss specific allusions to the *Bacchae* in the *Frogs*.

97. The itinerary in the underworld may have been a standard feature of the Bacchic mysteries, as the text of the gold leaves from Hipponion-Vibo Valentia suggests. The text is translated by Burkert (1985, 293). See also Seaford 1994, 321; Tsantsanaglou and Parassoglou 1987 (cited by Seaford).

98. United in the promise of a "blessed afterlife," Dionysus and Hades appear to have been closely associated in the context of the ancient mysteries. See Heraclitus (DK 22.B15). On this topic, see also Burkert 1985, 290–95; Seaford 1994, 321–22.

99. On κύσθος as "cunt," see Henderson 1991, 130, 163. Henderson agrees with Bothe and Radermacher that the phrase should read κύσθῳ ναυμαχεῖν, meaning βινεῖν (fuck), with a "suggestion of mighty vessels circling and

As the reference suggests, the lion's skin is the predictable disguise of effeminate males like Callias and Dionysus.[100] In their disguises as Heracles, both are conspicuous examples of males for whom ἀνδρεῖα, or manliness, is a sham, a show, and a costume. By definition, putting on any disguise means concealing or transforming a prior visual identity. But at the same time, to the extent to which a disguise is recognized as such, it necessarily fails to finish its business of concealing or transforming; this is the paradox inherent in the notion of disguise. And putting on the lion's skin, whether it is over Dionysus' yellow tunic or Callias' κύσθος, has become emblematic of the fact that any disguise necessarily reveals more than it hides. This particular reference to the layering of visual identities in which the effeminate male is disguised as the Heraclean hypermale again gives the lie to the notion of an essential core of masculine identity; it makes gender part of an infinite regress whose core always remains just out of view. Moreover, the hypermasculine Pentheus in his maenad costume and the effeminate Dionysus in his Heracles costume enact a similar ontological and theatrical predicament. For if we can say that Pentheus' maenad costume and Dionysus' Lydian stranger costume in the *Bacchae* signify femininity as disguise, then Dionysus' Heracles costume in the *Frogs* is not so much a reversal of this phenomenon as it is a commentary on its power as a cultural trope. As a disguise, even Heracles' lionskin only reveals, rather than conceals, the effeminacy of its wearer, an effeminacy that itself is part of the theatrical performance.

When the wearer of the lion skin is the god of the theater and of tragedy, as Dionysus so obviously is in the *Frogs*, the theatricality of his disguise is beyond doubt. In fact, Dionysus' disguise can be understood as a kind of synecdoche for the dramatic genre as a whole. At the same time, the comic representation of the god of tragedy aligns him— perhaps even necessarily—with the tragic genre's negative ethical potential, exemplified by Euripides and his plays and reviled by Aeschylus. Indeed, Dionysus plays a triadic role in the play as the god of

---

colliding." In either case, the lion skin is a disguise for this effeminate male. Dover 1993 ad. loc. suggests "pussy-skin" for κύσθον λεοντῆν and argues that "Kallias wears a suitable trophy for his own 'conquests.'" Cf. Aristophanes *Birds* 286, where the female birds pluck out Callias' feathers.

100. Pisistratus is also thought to have identified himself with Heracles. See Boardman 1972, 1989.

tragedy, an effeminate Euripidophile, and a Euripidean character.[101] It should therefore come as no surprise when, at the end of the *Frogs*, Dionysus changes his mind—just as he changes his costumes—and chooses to bring Aeschylus, instead of Euripides, back to life. Motivated only by what his soul wishes (αἱρήσομαι γὰρ ὅνπερ ἡ ψυχὴ θέλει, 1468), his choice is based on a personal whim, much like his earlier desire for Euripides. In this universe where anarchy reigns and visual identity changes from minute to minute (especially in the early scenes with Xanthias), the two tragic playwrights are virtually interchangeable.[102] Dionysus' change of mind (or soul) at the end of the play is the culminating expression of a lack of faith in the notion of a stable internal identity. That lack of faith has in fact been projected from the outside to the inside, from the outer world of appearance to the inner world of the soul itself.

But this lack of faith, exemplified in the god's wish to resurrect Aeschylus, must also be situated in the context of the Aeschylean view of dramatic performance as it is represented in the *Frogs*. In general, that view is based on the twin principles of moral and martial superiority that Aeschylus says his plays inspired among men but of which Euripides' plays have made a mockery. Aeschylus says that, unlike Euripides, he did not turn good men into bad (ἐκ χρηστῶν καὶ γενναίων μοχθηροτάτους ἀπέδειξας, 1011). Nor did his plays "empty the wrestling schools and wear down the buttocks of stuttering boys" (1070–71; cf. 1087–88).[103] His heroes, he says, exemplified the conduct and ethical standards befitting the elite members of his audience. They spoke according to their lofty status and wore "grander" robes that fit their heroic stature, a "fit" that vouches for a natural correspondence between his characters, their speech, and their costumes (1058–62). As a result, and as mentioned earlier, the audience Aeschylus

---

101. Aeschylus' description of Euripidean characters at *Frogs* 1014–15 is a pretty good description of Dionysus in the play. See Michilini 1987, 127.

102. Segal (1961, 213) argues, however, that Dionysus "regains a sounder dignity" during the course of the play and that his choice of Aeschylus is indicative of an awareness "that comedy should be a reflection of the solidarity and secure firmness of the community." Cf. Heiden 1991, 97; Dover 1993, 42.

103. Stanford (1968, ad loc.) translates τὰς πυγὰς ἐνέτριψεν / τῶν μειρακίων στωμυλλομένων as "effeminized the youths with their babbling." Cf. Dover 1993, ad loc. For πυγίζω = *paedico*, see LSJ.

says he bequeathed to Euripides "breathed spears and helmets and white-crested plumes, greaves and darts and hearts made of seven-fold oxhide" (1016–17); everyone who saw his *Seven against Thebes* "wanted to be a mighty warrior" (ὃ θεασάμενος πᾶς ἄν τις ἀνὴρ ἠράσθη δάιος εἶναι, 1022). Here the epic lexicon of martial valor is appropriated by Aeschylus within the conservative narrative of the poet as teacher (cf. 1029 ff., 1053–56). As the agent of cultural preservation, he taught what was fitting and praiseworthy (χρηστά, 1054) and worked to replicate those masculine virtues in his audience. Aeschylus' didactic and ethical narrative thus exemplifies the difference between his mimetic regime and that of his rival playwright. More specifically, Aeschylus valorizes an unmediated form of mimesis in which the males in his audience will essentially become his idealized heroes as a result of watching his plays. In this regime, disguise is commensurate not with dissimulation—as, for example, in the case of Euripides' kings in rags (1060 ff.)[104]—but with replication in the service of a nationalist and masculinist ideology.[105]

Within such an ideology, Euripides' whores (πόρναι, 1043) and his kings in rags are suitable victims of Aeschylus' assault because neither are proper subjects for replication—the former because they are women, the latter because their deceptive rags subvert the ontological "fit" represented by Aeschylus' heroes in their grand robes.[106] As a negative example of the replicating power of the stage, Aeschylus says that the death of Euripides' Stheneboia caused "the noble wives of noble citizens" to drink hemlock (1050–51). Even the playwright is not immune: Dionysus implies that Euripides was cuckolded because he presented cuckolds on stage (1048). One of the underlying assumptions of Aeschylus' mimetic regime is that women (like those who drank hemlock) will imitate female characters while men will imitate male characters—in other words, that replication is gender-specific.[107]

---

104. For a discussion of Euripides' kings in rags, see chap. 3.

105. Zeitlin (1994, 178) notes how the shield scenes in Aeschylus' *Seven against Thebes* and Euripides' *Phoenissae* are evidence for this difference between Aeschylean and Euripidean theater.

106. No mention is made in the *Frogs* of Aeschylus' dangerous female characters (e.g., Clytemnestra) or of Euripides' praiseworthy ones (e.g., Alcestis). On the notion of an ontological fit, see chap. 3.

107. Cf. Agathon's speech at Aristophanes *Thesmophoriazousae* 146–52.

In addition to raising the question of whether or not women were in the audience in the Theater of Dionysus, this assumption ironically draws attention to the fact that male actors do imitate women when they play female characters on the Attic stage. As women, their disguises are analogous to the rags worn by Euripides' kings: both compromise the integrity and constancy of Aeschylus' idealized masculine subjects, whether on stage or off. The broader ethical effects of tragedy are thus illustrated in the distinction between clothing as disguise (including theatrical cross-dressing) and clothing as fitting or appropriate. In the end, the contest between Aeschylus and Euripides testifies to a nostalgic desire for an ethical seamlessness between the ideal male and the clothing he wears, a seamlessness that Euripides' plays subvert and that according to Aeschylus is consequently wearing thin in fifth-century Athens.

Based on the Aeschylean hypothesis that the tragic spectator will act the roles he sees, the disguises of Dionysus—now slave, now hypermasculine hero—give the possible subject positions assumable by that spectator; he can either indulge his nostalgia for an Aeschylean hero like Heracles or emulate the antiheroic shape-shifters of his contemporary Euripides. Of course, when we recall that Aeschylus had been dead for some fifty years at the time of the production of the *Frogs*, the contest and the desire to resurrect a dead poet are themselves only and obviously part of an act.[108] Within the fictional universe of the plot, moreover, Dionysus' failure as the Aeschylean hero type (except insofar as it is a comic success) undermines that playwright's faith in the ability of tragedy to make heroes out of tragic spectators (1013 ff.); even the god of tragedy cannot make a convincing show of old-style heroism. Nor is the pretense to such heroism any more socially redeeming than the pretense to slavery or poverty. The contest between Euripides and Aeschylus finally reveals the faded ideal of tragic heroism, represented in Dionysus' shifting personae and shifting allegiances and in the difficulty of distinguishing the god of tragedy dressed as a slave from a slave dressed as a hero (668–69).

In chapter 2, I argued that scripted speech is antithetical to face-to-face, or man-to-man, verbal exchange. In the *Frogs*, this antithesis is graphically illustrated by the fragments of tragic scripts that are constitutive of the comic script. This textual aggregation takes two forms:

108. See Michilini 1987, 58–59 with n. 29.

direct quotations from the prologues of known tragedies (1119 ff.) and lyric improvisations that caricature their tragic models (1330 ff.). Excerpted from their original texts and contexts, both forms are wantonly modified and made to suit the speaker's personal whim. For example, when Aeschylus tosses his famous phrase "he lost his little jar of oil" into Euripides' tragic scripts (ληκύθιον ἀπώλεσεν, 1200 ff.), he compromises the ostensible integrity and wholeness of those scripts. He also makes the comic script a vehicle for the indiscriminate use of metrical and grammatical filler. The result is what might be called the only verifiable example of tragicomedy in the corpus of Attic drama.[109] But more to the point, the hybrid script is analogous to the play's hybrid characters, Heraclesxanthias and Heraclesdionysus. Moreover, in the contest of theatrical words and phrases in the *Frogs*, it becomes clear that scripted speech (like those hybrid theatrical bodies) has no solid body and no ethical constancy.[110] Thus, when the chorus says at the beginning of the contest that the spectators are capable of making a judgment in the battle between the poets (πόλεμος, 1099) because they have fought in such battles before and because each one has his little book in hand (βιβλίον, 1114), the combined appeal to a fighting spirit, the authority of the text, and dramatic connoisseurship is belied by the comic plot and the comic text: having possession of a "little book" is about as reassuring as having lost a "little jar of oil."[111] In asserting that the dramatic spectator is up to the task of judging the contest, the chorus only raises the possibility that he may in fact not be up to it and that, like Dionysus, he too is a fickle judge.[112]

In the end, Dionysus' decision to resurrect Aeschylus is not indicative of the ethical or political efficacy of that playwright's mimetic

---

109. The term *tragicomedy* has often been applied to the late plays of Euripides. See Segal 1971; Burnett 1971, 84.

110. Cf. Wolin 1990, 8: "Innocence is regained by reducing existence to language and then reveling in a medium that appears pure, distorted only by 'mistakes' . . . in usage, not by the influences of class, wealth, or education."

111. On the reference to the "little book," see Dover 1993, 34–35; Stanford 1968, ad loc. Euripides' reputation for bookishness in the play (see *Frogs* 943 and 1409) contributes to the ambivalence toward scripted speech argued for here. See also Woodbury 1986.

112. Segal (1961, 214) believes that Dionysus "manages to remain a fair and impartial judge."

regime.[113] Based on a personal whim, that decision seems to be motivated only by the occasion it provides for Dionysus to indulge in a number of Euripidean parodies (1468 ff.). And these parodies in fact speak on behalf of the resurrection of Euripides; at least they suggest that his plays had a strong recognition factor and appeal among the members of Aristophanes' audience.[114] So although Dionysus' choice seems to validate Aeschylus' heroic ethos and his principle of individual martial valor, it really enforces a kind of aesthetic tyranny in which the god of tragedy simply gets his own way. It is also inimical to the ostensible impartiality adhered to in the judging of the dramatic contests in Athens and to the ostensible impartiality adhered to in the initiation rites of the Bacchic mysteries.[115] Thus, when Dionysus finally says that in choosing Aeschylus he has not acted shamefully "if it does not seem so to the spectators" (τί δ᾽ αἰσχρόν, ἢν μὴ τοῖς θεωμένοις δοκῇ, 1475), this parody of Euripides' *Aeolus* works on two levels.[116] First, we are reminded of Aristotle's assertion that tragic pleasure is compromised when poets follow the spectators' wishes and play into their weakness (τὴν τῶν θεάτρων ἀσθένειαν, *Poetics* 1453a30–35).[117] According to Aristotle, such plays—for example, those in which bitter enemies become best friends or in which no one is killed—are best suited for comedy (1453a35–38). This understanding of the comic plot must predate its formal expression in the *Poetics*,

---

113. Cf. Hooker 1980, 176–77, on the question of literary versus political merit in the contests between the poets. Hooker thinks that "Dionysus takes back Aeschylus not for his prowess in the poetic art but because of the political advice he is likely to give the city." Aeschylus does, of course, win the contest of the weighing of the words; that he would give good political advice is not at all clear in the text. For a different interpretation, see Segal 1961.

114. The play includes parodies of Euripides' *Hippolytus, Aeolus, Polyidus,* and *Phrixus.* See Dover 1993, 25 and 378–79.

115. On judging the tragic contests, see Pickard-Cambridge 1968, 95–99. Burkert (1985, 290–95) notes that behind the popular innovations pertaining to the cult of Dionysus, "there is clearly an impulse directed against the nobility, which comes from the lower classes of craftsmen and peasants from which the tyrants drew their support."

116. Cf. Spariosu 1991, 138.

117. Cf. Aristotle *Politics* 1341b9 ff. on pleasing the common crowd and 1342a19–20 on the two classes of audience.

as a reference in Plato suggests.[118] In any event, in choosing Aeschylus and abandoning his previously announced desire for Euripides, Dionysus both does what Aristotle says is best suited for the comic plot and, at the same time, seems to be playing to the spectators (τοῖς θεωμένοις) and to their nostalgic desire to bring back a lost heroic past.

Second, the parodic reference to Euripides' *Aeolus* reveals a critical and ideologically significant equivalence between dramatic spectators and those who commit shameful acts. In quoting the line, Dionysus substitutes τοῖς θεωμένοις [those who watch] for τοῖϛι χρωμένοις [those who do or act] in the original text. The original line "What is shameful if it does not seem so to the doers?" thus reads, "What is shameful if it does not seem so to the spectators?" Each question is problematic, of course, since both spectators and actors (χρωμένοι) pass judgment on their own behavior with no appeal to communal principles or rules of behavior.[119] Thus the parody compares these morally suspect actors to theatrical spectators; indeed, it is precisely in their role as spectators (θεωμένοι) that the Athenians' moral bankruptcy is made plain. In adapting this line to repudiate his previous desire for Euripides and in support of changing his mind in favor of Aeschylus, Dionysus succeeds in using Euripides against himself. The substitution of Aeschylus for Euripides again illustrates the mutability of the tragic script and the idiosyncratic nature of Dionysus' role as judge. Moreover, when he determines that the spectators find no shame in his decision, the implied passive reception of that decision is indicative both of the tyrannical nature of the god of tragedy, who rules by personal whim and pleasing the crowd, and of the abject position of the Athenians as spectators.

The *Frogs* offers a complex view of a city that needs a tragic poet when its only hope is to bring a dead one back to life. In the world of the comic play, and after twenty years of war, tragedy has become the dead art of dead poets, and Aeschylus' claims that his *Seven against*

---

118. See Plato *Laws* 659a–c, where the warning that judges should not acquiesce to the wishes of the audience implies that they were sometimes accused of doing so.

119. This line in Euripides' play "caused moral indignation in Athens" (Stanford 1968, ad loc.). Dover (1993) translates τοῖϛι χρωμένοις as " 'those who encounter it' (or '. . . deal with it')."

Thebes was "full of Ares" and that his plays made every man in the audience "eager to be a hostile warrior" (*Frogs* 1021–27) have a hollow ring. In its comic context, Dionysus' choice illustrates that Aeschylean heroism and militarism have become the stuff of hyperbole and parody. In the end, the mimetic reproduction of that past on the tragic stage (as in the *Seven against Thebes*) can only be a testament to the audience's nostalgic desire. At the end of the Peloponnesian War and in the midst of a political and military crisis, the question of reproducing that past and its warriors is simultaneously a question of the meaning of dramatic performance in democratic Athens.

M.H. Hansen notes, "political activity [in democratic Athens] can be divided into passive participation—that is, listening and voting—and active participation, which means proposing things and taking part in political argument: what the Athenians expected of the ordinary citizen was the former, . . . whereas active participation was left to those who might feel called to it."[120] Who is meant by "the Athenians" in this quotation begs the question of the distinction that Hansen is making but implies that the city's elite males were expected to be the active arbiters of the passive political role played by its ordinary citizens. The extent to which this hierarchical system was successfully coercive in fifth-century Athens is difficult to ascertain, but its persistence as an ideal seems to lie behind the complex fusion of political and theatrical discourses in the *Bacchae* and the *Frogs*. In both plays, the failed ideal of the elite or heroic warrior is figured in his role as a passive spectator.[121] This suggestion is based not on the political beliefs of Euripides or Aristophanes but on their respective presentations of the theatrical Dionysus; it is also situated within the larger perspective in which the god of tragedy and the tyrant credited with instituting the dramatic contests in Athens can be seen to be part of a similar discursive formation. Within the Theater of Dionysus, as it is presented to us in the *Bacchae* and the *Frogs*, the ordinary citizen of Athens is a dramatic spectator whose passivity and complicity are required by the dramatic mimesis. And within the city of Athens at

---

120. Hansen 1991, 306, cited by Griffith (1995, 66 n. 13).

121. Griffith (1995, 66 n. 13) suggests that "[i]n the early fifth century, the lines between passive and active participation were probably more sharply drawn than in the fourth, and the value of noble birth for election to office was still preeminent."

large, especially as it is represented in the *Frogs*, that citizen is also a
spectator who plays his part in a social and political drama, that is, in
the Athenian democracy. Both plays thus expose a system in which
the power of the demos or the male citizen body at large (δημοκρατία)
is part of an illusion born of pretense and passivity or, in Wolin's
phrase, is "a created world of images, sounds, and scenarios."[122]

The history of the theater in Greece, including the theater-like
scenes in the epics, the theatrical narratives of the Pisistratid tyranny,
and the dramatic plots of the *Bacchae* and the *Frogs*, is a history of the
mimetic and therefore unstable nature of a normative Greek masculinity. Embodied and made visible in vestimentary and ontological protocols, that identity also assumes internal dispositions that those protocols convey to the eye of a beholder. Codified in the representation of
the elite male warrior of the epics and adopted, if modified, in the
representation of the soldier-citizen of democratic Athens, these protocols require men to be authentic doers of deeds and speakers of
words. Within this cultural and historical panorama, the disguised, or
theatrical, body and mediated, or scripted, speech signal the possibility that identity—gender identity in particular—is a performance,
which like all performances requires spectators who will be taken in
by the act. In this context we are presented with the figure of Dionysus as the god of the theater and a dramatis persona. The force of that
presentation blurs the distinction between citizenship and spectatorship, between the city and the theater, and between acting like
men on stage and off. As a consequence, the Theater of Dionysus can
ultimately be understood as part of a disciplinary system aimed at
maintaining these distinctions (by exposing their mimetic possibilities) and at constraining the god who personifies their instability.

---

122. Wolin 1990, 27–28.

Epilogue: The End of Nostalgia

In *Cities of the Dead: Circum-Atlantic Performance,* Joseph Roach writes:

> Performance, in other words, stands in for an elusive entity that it is not but that it must vainly aspire both to embody and re-place. Hence flourish the abiding yet vexed affinities between performance and memory, out of which blossom the most florid nostalgias for authenticity and origin. (Roach 1996, 3–4)

Focused on performance practices in London in the eighteenth century and New Orleans in the nineteenth and twentieth centuries, Roach's formulation is also useful for understanding the performance history of classical Athens. In this book, I have argued that the theater and its critical discourses in ancient Greece—and, by extension, in the European canon—are forms of a cultural nostalgia. This model of cultural production, born from the desire to resurrect an idealized and ever receding past and the masculine subject who occupies and sanctions that past, is obviously tied to the notion of memory as Roach describes it. In the Greek context, the importance of memory for preserving the great deeds of the great men of the past has long been recognized as the enabling mechanism of the epic. But it is obvious that this act of preservation does not end with the epic. Nor is memory a disinterested human phenomenon. Rather, like the history it makes possible, memory is a function of selection and deletion. I have tried to show in this book that the Muses—the daughters of Greek cultural memory—are also daughters of desire and, more precisely, that desire and memory are the active agents of the Greek theater both as a collection of plots and as a history of social practices.

In temporal terms, both memory and desire allude to a perpetual looking back. Yet they are also predicated on a perpetual deferral—a deferrral of present time in the case of memory and of present satisfaction in the case of desire. But these rather abstract notions fail to address the more important and difficult issue of cultural specificity, that is, of how we come to understand memory and desire as the twin sources of particular forms of cultural production. In the ancient Greek context, desire and memory create and sustain what I have called the normative masculine subject of (Western) antiquity, whether as a figure in epic poetry, in monumental sculpture, in historical or ethnographic narrative, or in theatrical performance. And whether we take them to be the sources of specific forms of representation (like drama) or of social and academic practices, memory and desire are ideological, political, and gender specific. Thus, when I say that the Greek theater is an overtly disciplinary space, I am referring not only to its role in the preservation of a Greek style masculinity but also to its prominence in the history of classics as an academic discipline.

As the most highly prized examples of the "flowering" of Greek culture, the dramatic texts of fifth-century Athens have borne much of the burden of shaping and sustaining a narrative of the aesthetic, political, and cultural virtues of ancient Greece. The plots of individual tragedies and comedies are frequently cited as evidence for those virtues. But the representation of dramatic characters and their situations cannot be disengaged from the theatrical practices by which they become a form of public display and academic study. Those practices have a history that helps us to better understand both the dramatic plots and their civic context. I have argued that that history is produced in representations of bodily display in the epic, of tyranny in the early political history of Athens, and of the Dionysiac experience in Greece and Athens. There are certainly other scenes from the vast panorama of Greek antiquity that contribute to this history; the theater-like use of the first person in lyric comes immediately to mind.[1] But the aforementioned representations have seemed to me to be the most useful for illustrating the ways in which Greek self-representation is constituted in theater-like acts.

It has become a commonplace in American academic writing to assert that any account of cultural production must acknowledge the primacy of ethnicity, class, and gender. The challenge is to demonstrate how this primacy represents itself in a particular historical or cultural

---

1. See duBois 1996 for a relevant discussion of Sappho's poetic persona. See also Stehle 1997.

context. As I suggested in my introduction, critical accounts of the Greek theater assume a masculine subject who is perpetually at risk of losing his privileged position on the center stage of history. This risk is ancient and enduring. Framed by the philosophical discussions and criticisms of dramatic mimesis in the works of Plato and Aristotle, this risk gives rise to disciplinary regimes aimed at sustaining that privilege. In saying so, I do not mean to diminish the aesthetic significance of Greek drama but to focus more intently on the ideological factors that inform its production. I also want to suggest that the dominance of aesthetic judgments and the concomitant appeal to universal human values in the history of the Greek theater may be symptomatic of the relationship between memory and desire within that history. Within scholarly disciplines and practices, the ancient past is constructed out of the desire for universal essences embodied in a universal subject. Whether we view the Greek theater through the lens of Aristophanes' comic wit, Freud's Oedipal dream, or the history of Classical scholarship, all these lenses attest to the force of that desire.

In the history of the theater, memory and desire function much like Aristotle's *ethos* and *dianoia* in the *Poetics*. These inner and unseen dispositions prove that a person and a dramatic persona are of a "certain kind" (*Poetics* 1449b36–50a1) and are the means by which Aristotle fuses the social subject and the dramatic character so that drama (like real life) is an expression of a natural correspondence between internal dispositions and external actions. As I have suggested, the effect of Aristotle's argument is to diffuse the possibility, inherent in dramatic impersonation, that internal dispositions are only the effect of bodily or external acts. Thus, dramatic performance calls forth a normative social subject defined both by his innate Greekness and by his irrefutable masculinity (which for all intents and purposes are the same thing). Another way of putting the matter is to say that the alternative possibility, negatively embodied in the performances of Oedipus or Pisistratus or Dionysus, is the necessary precondition for defining that normative subject.

Roach's assertion that "[p]erformance . . . stands in for an elusive entity that it is not but that it must vainly aspire both to embody and replace" helps illustrate Aristotle's implicit fusion of the social subject and the dramatic character by means of a shared set of internal dispositions. More to the point, it suggests how memory, desire, and nostalgia function in the history of the Greek and European theater as a history of impersonations. Taking seriously the unique situation of theatrical performance as a predetermined and repeatable set of bodily acts and speech acts (at least in principle), dramatic impersonation holds out the possibility for embodying and replacing the elusive entity known as the ancient Greek. But like Dionysus' desire (πόθος) for Euripides and his *Andromeda* in the *Frogs*, the desire for that elusive entity only demonstrates that social subjects, like dramatis personae, lack a stable and immutable core of identity. For Dionysus' desire to embody and replace a lost "entity"—whether Heracles or Euripides or Aeschylus—is finally testament not to this immutable core but to its opposite. And here we come back to the heart of the matter as I have tried to present it in this book. If theatrical impersonation epitomizes the difficulty of establishing and maintaining a stable social and political identity, the desire within performance studies to preserve the "immediacy and evanescence" of the live (if not original) performance is the culminating expression of that difficulty.[2] The extent to which this desire is active in performance studies is the extent to which the ancient Greek theater is perceived to be its originary form.

I argued in chapter 1 that the theater is the negative corollary to Plato's ideal city, where impersonation is allowable only insofar as the best citizens perpetually impersonate (or replicate) themselves. Taking a longer view, the history of the Greek theater is a history of spectators who are determined to look back through time to see themselves as men and as Greeks. But as we have seen, spectatorship is problematic both as a theoretical and as a political practice. Defined by his passivity and inactivity, at least in principle, the spectator is defined by his failure to live up to the requirements of a normative masculinity. In Plato's regime, that passivity seems to encourage the citizen to engage in the indiscriminate imitations that Plato finds so dangerous in the city. In short, the spectator occupies a contradictory position in Greek cultural and theatrical discourses. On the one hand, he must keep his eyes focused on those repeated acts that implicitly guarantee the continuity and stability of a model social subject. On the other hand, he is open to the possibility of a liberating multiplicity of social identities. The legacy of the concept of Greek theater-like practices is the conflict between these two spectactorial and social

---

2. The quoted phrase is from Schechner 1986, 50.

systems, one normative and disciplinary, the other promiscuous and liberatory. Focused on establishing what Roach calls "authenticity and origin," the aim of the cultural nostalgia I have been discussing is part of the former disciplinary system. And memory and desire are arguably the internal dispositions that regulate that nostalgia. But as I have tried to show, the critical history of the Greek theater is founded on the proposition that internal dispositions may only be the effect of bodily acts. The search for authenticity and origins is therefore naturalized within that history, precisely because theatrical practices, illustrated by the multiplicity of impersonations I have discussed in this book, defy the belief that Greek ethnicity and masculinity can be guaranteed by a seamless series of repeated acts.

Bibliography

Affortunati, Monica, and Barbara Scardigli. "Aspects of Plutarch's *Life of Publicola*." In *Plutarch and the Historical Tradition,* ed. Philip A. Stadter, 109–31. London and New York, 1992.

American School of Classical Studies at Athens. *The Athenian Agora: A Guide to the Excavation and Museum.* 3d ed. Athens, 1976.

Andersen, O. "Thersites und Thoas vor Troia." *Symbolae Oliensis* 57 (1982): 7–34.

Anderson, Benedict. *Imagined Communities.* London, 1983.

Andrewes, A. "The Opposition to Perikles." *Journal of Hellenic Studies* 98 (1978): 1–8.

Arthur-Katz, Marylin. "Sexuality and the Body in Ancient Greece." *Metis* 4, no. 1 (1989): 155–79.

Austin, Norman. *Helen of Troy and Her Shameless Phantom.* Ithaca, 1994.

Bain, D. "Audience Address in Greek Tragedy." *Classical Quarterly* 25 (1975): 13–25.

Bakker, Egbert J. "Discourse and Performance: Involvement, Visualization, and 'Presence' in Homeric Poetry." *Classical Antiquity* 12 (1993): 1–29.

Barthes, Roland. "Introduction to the Structural Analysis of Narratives." In *A Barthes Reader,* ed. Susan Sontag, 251–95. Toronto, 1982a.

———. "The Reality Effect." In *French Literary Theory Today,* ed. T. Todorov, 11–17. Cambridge, 1982b.

Barton, I.M., ed. *Roman Public Buildings.* Exeter, 1989.

Bassi, Karen. "Helen and the Discourse of Denial in Stesichorus' Palinode." *Arethusa* 26 (1993): 51–76.

———. "Male Nudity and Disguise in the Discourse of Greek Histrionics." *Helios* 22 (1995): 3–22.

———. "Orality, Masculinity and Greek Epic." *Arethusa* 30 (1997): 315–40.

———. "The Somatics of the Past: Helen and the Body of Tragedy." In *Actualizing Absence,* ed. Mark Franko and Annette Richards. Hanover, forthcoming.

Beazley, J.D. "The New York 'Phlyax-Vase.' " *American Journal of Archaeology* 56 (1952): 193–95.

Benveniste, E. *Problems in General Linguistics.* Miami, 1971.

Bergren, Ann L.T. "Language and the Female in Early Greek Thought." *Arethusa* 16 (1983): 69–85.

Bernal, Martin. *Black Athena: The Afroasiatic Roots of Classical Civilization.* Vol. 1, *The Fabrication of Ancient Greece, 1785–1985.* New Brunswick, 1987.

Bieber, M. *The History of the Greek and Roman Theater.* Princeton, 1961.

Blamire, A. "Pausanias and Persia." *Greek, Roman, and Byzantine Studies* 11 (1970): 295–305.

Block, Elizabeth. "Clothing Makes the Man: A Pattern in the *Odyssey*." *Transactions of the American Philological Association* 115 (1985): 1–11.

Blundell, Mary Whitlock. "*Ēthos* and *Dianoia* Reconsidered." In *Essays on Aristotle's Poetics*, ed. Amelie Oksenberg Rorty, 155–76. Princeton, 1992.

Boardman, J. "Herakles, Peisistratos, and Sons." *Revue Archéologique*, n.s., 1–2 (1972): 57–72.

———. "Herakles, Peisistratos, and the Unconvinced." *Journal of Hellenic Studies* 109 (1989): 158–59.

Bonfante, Larissa. "Nudity as a Costume in Classical Art." *American Journal of Archaeology* 93 (1989): 543–70.

Boswell, J. *Christianity, Social Tolerance, and Homosexuality*. Chicago, 1980.

Boyer, M. Christine. *The City of Collective Memory: Its Historical Imagery and Architectural Entertainments*. Cambridge, Mass., 1994. Reprint 1996.

Brecht, Bertolt. *Brecht on Theatre: The Development of an Aesthetic*. Trans. John Willett. New York, 1964.

Broneer, Oscar. "The Tent of Xerxes and the Greek Theatre." *University of California Publications in Classical Archaeology* 1 (1944): 305–12.

Burkert, Walter. "Greek Tragedy and Sacrificial Ritual." *Greek, Roman, and Byzantine Studies* 7 (1966): 87–121.

———. *Structure and History in Greek Mythology and Ritual*. Berkeley, 1979.

———. *Homo Necans: The Anthropology of Ancient Greek Sacrificial Ritual and Myth*. Trans. Peter Bing. Berkeley 1983.

———. *Greek Religion*. Trans. John Raffan. Cambridge, Mass., 1985.

———. "Oriental and Greek Mythology: The Meeting of Parallels." In *Interpretations of Greek Mythology*, ed. J. Bremmer, 10–40. London, 1987.

Burnett, Anne Pippin. *Catastrophe Survived: Euripides' Plays of Mixed Reversal*. Oxford, 1971.

Butcher, S.H. *Aristotle's Theory of Poetry and Fine Art*. 1894. New York, 1951.

Butler, Judith. *Gender Trouble*. New York, 1990a.

———. "Performative Acts and Gender Constitution: An Essay in Phenomenology and Feminist Theory." In *Performing Feminisms*, ed. Sue-Ellen Case, 270–83. Baltimore and London, 1990b.

Calder III, William. "Gold for Bronze: *Iliad* 6.232–6." In *Studies Presented to Sterling Dow*, ed. K.J. Rigsby, 31–35. *Greek, Roman, and Byzantine Monographs*, vol. 10. Durham, 1984.

Cameron, Alan. *Bread and Circuses: The Roman Emperor and His People*. London, 1973.

Camp, John M. *The Athenian Agora: Excavations in the Heart of Classical Athens*. New York, 1986.

Carpenter, T.H. *Dionysian Imagery in Archaic Greek Art*. Oxford, 1986.

Case, Sue-Ellen. "Classic Drag: The Greek Creation of Female Parts." *Theatre Journal* 37 (1985): 317–27.

———. *Feminism and Theatre*. New York, 1988.

Chadwick, John. *The Mycenaean World*. Cambridge, 1976.

Clifford, James. *The Predicament of Culture: Twentieth-Century Ethnography, Literature, and Art.* Cambridge, Mass., 1988.

Clover, Carol. "Her Body, Himself: Gender in the Slasher Film." *Representations* 20 (1987): 187–228.

Cohen, David. *Law, Sexuality, and Society: The Enforcement of Morals in Classical Athens.* Cambridge, 1991.

Cole, Susan G. "Could Greek Women Read and Write?" In *Reflections of Women in Antiquity,* ed. Helene Foley, 219–45. New York, Paris, London, Montreux, and Tokyo, 1981.

Connor, W.R. "Tribes, Festivals, and Processions; Civic Ceremonial and Political Manipulation in Archaic Greece." *Journal of Hellenic Studies* 107 (1987): 40–50.

———. "City Dionysia and Athenian Democracy." In *Classica et Mediaevalia,* vol. 11, *Aspects of Athenian Democracy,* ed. W.R. Connor et al., 7–32. Copenhagen, 1990.

Daston, Lorraine. "Marvelous Facts and Miraculous Evidence in Early Modern Europe." In *Questions of Evidence: Proof, Practice, and Persuasion across the Disciplines,* ed. James Chandler, Arnold I. Davidson, and Harry Harootunian, 243–74. Chicago, 1994.

de Certeau, Michel. *The Writing of History.* Trans. Tom Conley. New York, 1988.

de Jong, Irene J.F. *Narrators and Focalizers: The Presentation of the Story in the Iliad.* Amsterdam, 1987.

de Lauretis, Teresa. "Desire in Narrative." In *Alice Doesn't: Feminism, Semiotics, Cinema,* 103–57. Bloomington, 1984.

———. "The female body and heterosexual presumption." *Semiotica* 67 (1987a): 129–79.

———. *Technologies of Gender: Essays on Theory, Film, and Fiction.* Bloomington, 1987b.

Delcourt, Marie. *Hermaphrodite: Mythes et rites de la bisexualité dans l'Antiquité classique.* Paris, 1958.

Denniston, J.D. *The Greek Particles.* Oxford, 1934.

Derrida, Jacques. *Of Grammatology.* Trans. Gayatri Chakravorty Spivak. Baltimore, 1976.

———. *Dissemination.* Trans. Barbara Johnson. Chicago, 1981.

de Ste. Croix, G.E.M. *The Class Struggle in the Ancient Greek World.* Ithaca, 1981.

Diels, H. and W. Kranz, eds. *Die Fragmente der Vorsokratiker,* 6th ed. 3 vols. Berlin 1951–52.

Doane, Mary Ann. *Femme Fatales: Feminism, Film Theory, Psychoanalysis.* New York, 1991.

Dodds, E.R. *The Greeks and the Irrational.* Berkeley: Sather Classical Lectures, vol. 25, 1951.

———. *Euripides Bacchae.* 2d ed. Oxford, 1966.

Doherty, Lillian. "The Internal and Implied Audiences of *Odyssey* 11." *Arethusa* 24 (1991): 145–76.

Dolan, Jill. *The Feminist Spectator as Critic*. Ann Arbor, 1988.

Dover, K.J. *Greek Homosexuality*. Cambridge, Mass., 1989.

———. *Frogs, Aristophanes*. Oxford, 1993.

duBois, Page. *Centaurs and Amazons: Women and the Prehistory of the Great Chain of Being*. Ann Arbor, 1982.

———. *Sowing the Body: Psychoanalysis and Ancient Representations of Women*. Women in Culture and Society. Chicago, 1988.

———. *Sappho Is Burning*. Chicago, 1996.

Easterling, P.E., and E.J. Kenney, ed. *The Cambridge History of Ancient Literature*. Vol. 1, part 2. Cambridge, 1989.

Edmonds, J.M. *The Fragments of Attic Comedy*. Vol. 3. Leiden, 1961.

———. *Elegy and Iambus*, vol. 1. *The Loeb Classical Library*. Cambridge, Mass. 1961.

Edwards, Mark W. "Homer and Oral Tradition: The Type-Scene." *Oral Tradition* 7, no. 2 (1992): 284–330.

Ehrenberg, Victor. "Polypragmosune: A Study in Greek Politics." *Journal of Hellenic Studies* 67 (1947): 46–67.

Elam, Keir. *The Semiotics of Theatre and Drama*. London and New York, 1980.

———. *Shakespeare's Universe of Discourse: Language-Games in the Comedies*. Cambridge, 1984.

Elderkin, George W. "The Stoa of the King." *Archaeological Papers* 4, no. 1 (1942): 11–12.

Eliade, M. *Patterns in Comparative Religion*. Trans. R. Sheed. New York, 1963.

Else, Gerald F. *Aristotle's Poetics: The Argument*. Cambridge, Mass., 1957a.

———. "The Origin of ΤΡΑΓΩΙΔΙΑ." *Hermes* 85 (1957b): 17–46.

———. *The Origin and Early Form of Greek Tragedy*. Cambridge, Mass., 1965.

Faraone, Christopher A. "Aphrodite's ΚΕΣΤΟΣ and Apples for Atalanta: Aphrodisiacs in Early Greek Myth and Ritual." *Phoenix* 44 (1990): 219–43.

———. "Sex and Power: Male-Targeting Aphrodisiacs in the Greek Magical Tradition." *Helios* 19 (1992): 92–103.

Farnell, L.R. *Cults of the Greek States*. Vol. 5. Oxford, 1909a.

———. "Dionysia: The Megala Dionysia and the Origin of Tragedy." *Journal of Hellenic Studies* 29 (1909b): xlvii.

Ferrari, Gloria Pinney. "Coming of Age in Ancient Greece." In *Gender, Race, and Identity*, ed. Craig Barrow, Katherine Frank, John Phillips, and Reed Sanderlin, 99–110. Chattanooga, 1993.

Ferris, Lesley. *Acting Women: Images of Women in Theatre*. New York, 1989.

Fineman, Joel. "The History of the Anecdote: Fiction and Fiction." In *The New Historicism*, ed. H. Aram Veeser, 49–76. New York, 1989.

Finley, John H. *Three Essays on Thucydides*. Cambridge, Mass., 1967.

Foley, Helene. " 'Reverse Similes' and Sex Roles in the *Odyssey*." *Arethusa* 11 (1978): 7–26.

———. "The 'Female Intruder' Reconsidered: Women in Aristophanes' *Lysistrata* and *Ecclesiazusae*." *Classical Philology* 77–78 (1982–83): 1–21.

———. *Ritual Irony: Poetry and Sacrifice in Euripides*. Ithaca, 1985.

———. "The Politics of Tragic Lamentation." In *Tragedy, Comedy, and the Polis: Papers from the Greek Drama Conference, Nottingham,* ed. A.H. Sommerstein, S. Halliwell, J. Henderson, and B. Zimmerman, 101–44. Bari, 1993.

Foley, John Miles. *The Theory of Oral Composition: History and Methodology.* Bloomington, 1988.

Fornara, Charles. *Herodotus: An Interpretive Essay.* Oxford, 1971.

Forsyth, N. "The Allurement Scene: A Typical Pattern in Greek Oral Epic." *California Studies in Classical Antiquity* 12 (1979): 107–20.

Foucault, Michel. *The Archaeology of Knowledge.* Trans. Alan Sheridan. London, 1972.

———. "What Is an Author." In *Textual Strategies: Perspectives in Post-Structuralist Criticism,* ed. Josue V. Harari, 141–60. Ithaca, 1979.

Fox Keller, Evelyn, and Christine R. Grontkowski. "The Mind's Eye." In *Discovering Reality: Feminist Perspectives on Epistemology, Metaphysics, Methodology, and Philosophy of Science,* ed. Sandra Harding and Merrill R. Hintikka, 207–24. Dordrecht, 1983.

Frame, Douglas. *The Myth of Return in Early Greek Epic.* New Haven, 1978.

Freeman, Kathleen. *The Life and Work of Solon.* New York, 1926.

Freud, Sigmund. "Medusa's Head." 1922. In *The Standard Edition of the Complete Psychological Works of Sigmund Freud,* trans. James Strachey, 18:273–74. London, 1940.

———. "The Horror of Incest." In *Totem and Taboo: Some Points of Agreement between the Mental Lives of Savages and Neurotics,* trans. James Strachey, 1–17. New York, 1952.

———. "Fetishism." 1927. In *The Standard Edition of the Complete Psychological Works of Sigmund Freud,* trans. James Strachey, 21:152–57. London, 1953–74.

———. *The Interpretation of Dreams.* 1900. Trans. James Strachey. New York, 1965.

Frontisi-Ducroux, Françoise, and François Lissarrague. "From Ambiguity to Ambivalence: A Dionysiac Excursion through the 'Anakreontic' Vases." In *Before Sexuality,* ed. David H. Halperin, John J. Winkler, and Froma I. Zeitlin, 211–55. Princeton, 1990.

Frost, Frank. "Toward a History of Pisistratid Athens." In *The Craft of the Ancient Historian,* ed. John W. Eadie and J. Ober, 57–78. Lanham, 1985.

Fuss, Diana. *Identification Papers.* New York, 1995.

Garber, Marjorie. *Vested Interests: Cross-Dressing and Cultural Anxiety.* New York, 1992.

Gaster, Theodor H. *Thespis: Ritual, Myth, and Drama in the Ancient Near East.* Garden City, N.Y., 1961.

Geddes, A.G. "Who's Who in Homeric Society?" *Classical Quarterly* 34 (1984): 17–36.

———. "Rags and Riches: The Costume of Athenian Men in the Fifth Century." *Classical Quarterly* 37 (1987): 307–31.

Geertz, Clifford. *Negara: The Theatre State in Nineteenth-Century Bali.* Princeton, 1980.

Girard, Rene. *Violence and the Sacred.* Trans. Patrick Gregory. Baltimore, 1977.

Golden, Leon. *Aristotle on Tragic and Comic Mimesis.* American Classical Studies, vol. 29. Atlanta, 1992.

Golder, Herbert. "Making a Scene: Gesture, Tableau, and the Tragic Chorus." *Arion,* 3d ser., 4, no. 1 (1996): 1–19.

Goldhill, Simon. "The Great Dionysia and Civic Ideology." In *Nothing to Do with Dionysos? Athenian Drama in Its Social Context,* ed. John J. Winkler and Froma I. Zeitlin, 97–129. Princeton, 1990.

———. *Foucault's Virginity: Ancient Erotic Fiction and the History of Sexuality.* Cambridge, 1995.

———. Review of *The Craft of Zeus: Myths of Weaving and Fabric,* by John Scheid and Jesper Svenbro. *Bryn Mawr Classical Review* 8, no. 3. (1996).

Goldman, Michael. *The Actor's Freedom: Toward a Theory of Drama.* New York, 1975.

Gomme, A.W. *A Historical Commentary on Thucydides.* Oxford, 1959.

Gould, John. "Dramatic Character and 'Human Intelligibility' in Greek Tragedy." *Proceedings of the Cambridge Philological Society* 204 (1978): 43–67.

———. "Law, Custom, and Myth: Aspects of the Social Position of Women in Classical Athens." *Journal of Hellenic Studies* 100 (1980): 38–59.

Goux, Jean-Joseph. "The Phallus: Masculine Identity and the 'Exchange of Women.' " *differences: A Journal of Feminist Cultural Studies* 4, no. 1 (1992): 40–75.

Greenblatt, Stephen. *Marvellous Possessions: The Wonder of the New World.* Chicago, 1991.

Greetham, D.C. *Textual Scholarship: An Introduction.* New York, 1992.

Griffin, Jasper. "Homeric Words and Speakers." *Journal of Hellenic Studies* 106 (1986): 36–57.

Griffith, Mark. "Brilliant Dynasts: Power and Politics in the *Oresteia.*" *Classical Antiquity* 14 (1995): 62–129.

Griffiths, J. Gwyn, ed. *Plutarch's De Iside et Osiride.* Cardiff, 1970.

Griswold, Charles. *Self-Knowledge in Plato's Phaedrus.* New Haven, 1986.

Hall, Edith. *Inventing the Barbarian: Greek Self-Definition through Tragedy.* Oxford, 1989.

Halliwell, Stephen. *Aristotle's Poetics.* Chapel Hill, 1986.

Halperin, David. "Plato and Erotic Reciprocity." *Classical Antiquity* 5 (1986): 60–80.

———. *One Hundred Years of Homosexuality.* New York, 1990.

———. "Plato and the Erotics of Narrativity." In *Innovations of Antiquity,* ed. Ralph Hexter and Daniel Selden, 95–131. New York, 1992.

Halverson, John. "Havelock on Greek Orality and Literacy." *Journal of the History of Ideas* 53 (1992): 148–63.

Hansen, M.H. *The Athenian Democracy in the Age of Demosthenes: Structure, Principles and Ideology.* Trans. J.A. Crook. Oxford, 1991.

Hanson, Victor. *The Western Way of War: Infantry Battle in Classical Greece.* New York, 1989.

————. "Hoplites into Democrats: The Changing Ideology of Athenian Infantry." In *Demokratia: A Conversation on Democracies, Ancient and Modern,* ed. Josiah Ober and Charles Hedrick, 289–312. Princeton, 1996.

Haraway, Donna. *Simians, Cyborgs, and Women: The Reinvention of Nature.* New York, 1991.

Harris, W.V. *Ancient Literacy.* Cambridge, Mass., 1989.

Hartog, François. *The Mirror of Herodotus: The Representation of the Other in the Writing of History.* Trans. Janet Lloyd. Berkeley, 1988.

Harvey. F.D. "Literacy in the Athenian Democracy." *Revue des études grecques* 79 (1966): 585–635.

Havelock, Eric A. *Preface to Plato.* Cambridge, Mass., 1982.

————. *The Literate Revolution in Greece and Its Cultural Consequences.* Princeton, 1982.

————. *The Muse Learns to Write: Reflections on Orality and Literacy from Antiquity to the Present.* New Haven, 1986.

Heiden, Bruce. "Tragedy and Comedy in the *Frogs* of Aristophanes." *Ramus* 20 (1991): 95–111.

Henderson, Jeffrey. *Aristophanes: Lysistrata.* Oxford, 1987.

————. *The Maculate Muse: Obscene Language in Attic Comedy.* 2d ed. New York, 1991.

Henrichs, A. "Greek Maenadism from Olympia to Messalina." *Harvard Studies in Classical Philology* 82 (1978): 121–60.

Herington, John. *Poetry into Drama: Early Tragedy and the Greek Poetic Tradition.* Berkeley, 1985.

Heubeck, A. *Archaeologia Homerica: Die Denkmäler und das frühgreichische Epos.* Vol. 3, no. 10. Göttingen, 1979.

Hollander, Anne. *Seeing through Clothes.* New York, 1978.

Hölscher, Tonio. "The City of Athens: Space, Symbol, Structure." In *City States in Classical Antiquity and Medieval Italy,* ed. Anthony Molho, Kurt Raaflaub, and Julia Emlen, 355–80. Ann Arbor, 1991.

Holtsmark, E. "Spiritual Rebirth of the Hero: *Odyssey* 5." *Classical Journal* 61 (1965–66): 206–10.

Hölzle, R. *Zum Aufbau der lyrischen Partien des Aischylos.* Marbach, 1934.

Hooker, J.T. "The Composition of the *Frogs.*" *Hermes* 108 (1980): 169–82.

Hornblower, Simon, and Antony Spawforth, eds. *The Oxford Classical Dictionary.* 3d ed. Oxford, 1996.

How, W.W., and J. Wells. *A Commentary on Herodotus.* 2 vols. Oxford, 1968.

Immerwahr, H.R. *Attic Script.* Oxford, 1990.

Jacoby, Felix. *Atthis: The Local Chronicles of Ancient Athens.* Oxford, 1949.

Janko, R. *The Iliad: A Commentary.* Vol. 4. Cambridge, 1992.

Jenkins, I.D. "The Ambiguity of Greek Textiles." *Arethusa* 18 (1985): 109–32.

Jones, John. *On Aristotle and Greek Tragedy.* London, 1962.

Jones, W.H.S., ed. *Pausanias, Description of Greece,* vol. 2. The Loeb Classical Library. Cambridge, Mass., 1977.

Jung, Hwa Yol. "The Body as Social Discourse: An Introduction to Carnal Hermeneutics." Paper presented at the annual meeting of the International Association for Philosophy and Literature, Montreal, May 1991.

Kennedy, George. "Helen's Web Unraveled." *Arethusa* 19 (1986): 5–14.

Keuls, Eva. *The Reign of the Phallus: Sexual Politics in Ancient Athens.* New York, 1985.

Kirk, G.S. "The Formal Duels in Books 3 and 7 of the *Iliad.*" In *Homer: Tradition and Invention,* ed. Bernard C. Fenik, 18–40. Leiden, 1978.

———, ed. *The Iliad: A Commentary.* Vol. 1. Cambridge, 1985.

———, ed. *The Iliad: A Commentary.* Vol. 2. Cambridge, 1990.

Knox, Bernard. "Literature." In *Athens Comes of Age: From Solon to Salamis,* ed. W.A.P. Childs, 43–52. Princeton, 1978.

Kolb, Frank. "Die Bau-, Religions-und Kulturpolitik der Peisistratiden." *Jahrbuch des Deutschen Archäologischen Instituts* 92 (1977): 99–138.

———. "Polis und Theater." In *Das griechische Drama,* ed. Gustaf A. Seeck, 504–45. Darmstadt, 1979.

———. *Agora und Theater: Volks-und Festversammlung.* Berlin, 1981.

Konstan, David. "Persians, Greeks, and Empire." *Arethusa* 20 (1987): 59–73.

———. "Aristophanes' *Lysistrata:* Women and the Body Politic." In *Tragedy, Comedy, and the Polis: Papers from the Greek Drama Conference, Nottingham,* ed. A.H. Sommerstein, S. Halliwell, J. Henderson, and B. Zimmerman, 431–44. Bari, 1993.

Kris, Ernst, and Otto Kurz. *Legend, Myth, and Magic in the Image of the Artist: A Historical Experiment.* New Haven, 1979.

Kurke, Leslie. "The Politics of ἁβροσύνη in Archaic Greece." *Classical Antiquity* 11 (1992): 91–120.

Lacey, W.K. *The Family in Classical Greece.* Ithaca, 1968.

Laplanche, J., and J.-B. Pontalis, eds. *The Language of Psycho-Analysis.* New York, 1973.

Laporte, M. Paul. "The Passing of the Gorgon." *Bucknell Review* 17 (1969): 55–71.

Leaf, Walter, ed. *The Iliad.* 2d ed. Amsterdam, 1960.

Lefkowitz, Mary R., and Maureen B. Fant. *Women's Life in Greece and Rome.* Baltimore, 1982.

Létoublon, Françoise. "Le Messager Fidèle." In *Homer, Beyond Oral Poetry: Recent Trends in Homeric Interpretation,* ed. J.M. Bremer, I.J.F. de Jong, and J. Kalff, 123–44. Amsterdam, 1987.

Levine, Laura. "Men in Women's Clothing: Anti-theatricality and Effeminization from 1579 to 1624." *Criticism* 27 (1986): 121–43.

Lévi-Strauss, Claude. "History and Anthropology." In *Structural Anthropology,* 1–27. New York, 1963a.

———. "The Structural Study of Myth." In *Structural Anthropology,* 206–31. New York, 1963b.

Lewis, I. *Ecstatic Religion.* Middlesex and Baltimore, 1971.

Linforth, I.M. *Solon the Athenian.* Berkeley, 1919.

Lissarrague, F. "Autour du guerrier." In *Le Cité des images*, ed. Claude Berard, 35–47. Paris, 1984.

———. "The Sexual Life of Satyrs." In *Before Sexuality*, ed. David M. Halperin, John J. Winkler and Froma I. Zeitlin, 53–81. Princeton, 1990.

Lloyd, G.E.R. *Science, Folklore, and Ideology: Studies in the Life Sciences in Ancient Greece.* Cambridge, 1983.

Long, Timothy. *Barbarians in Greek Comedy.* Carbondale, 1986.

Longo, Oddone. "Tecniche della communicazione e ideologie sociali nella Grecia antica." *Quaderni urbinati di cultura classica* 27 (1978): 63–92.

———. "The Theater of the *Polis*." In *Nothing to Do with Dionysos? Athenian Drama in Its Social Context*, ed. John J. Winkler and Froma I. Zeitlin, 12–19. Princeton, 1990.

Loraux, Nicole. *Les enfants d'Athena: Idées athéniennes sur la citoyenneté et la division des sexes.* Paris, 1981.

———. *The Invention of Athens: The Funeral Oration in the Classical City.* Trans. Alan Sheridan. Cambridge, Mass., 1986.

———. "Herakles: The Super Male and the Feminine." In *Before Sexuality*, ed. David M. Halperin, John J. Winkler, and Froma I. Zeitlin, 21–52. Princeton, 1990.

Lorraine, Tamsin E. *Gender, Identity, and the Production of Meaning.* Boulder, 1990.

Lucas, D.W. *Aristotle: Poetics.* Oxford, 1968. Reprint 1986.

MacCary, W. Thomas. *Childlike Achilles: Ontogeny and Phylogeny in the* Iliad. New York, 1982.

Maehler, H., ed. *Carmina cum Fragmentis.* 2 vols. Leipzig, 1989.

Manganaro, Marc. *Myth, Rhetoric, and the Voice of Authority: A Critique of Frazer, Eliot, Frye, and Campbell.* New Haven, 1992.

Martin, Richard. *The Language of Heroes: Speech and Performance in the* Iliad. Ithaca, 1989.

Mason, Peter. *The City of Men: Ideology, Sexual Politics, and the Social Formation.* Göttingen, 1984.

Matson, Patricia, Philip Rollinson, and Marion Sousa, eds. *Readings from Classical Rhetoric.* Carbondale, 1990.

McDonnell, Myles. "The Introduction of Athletic Nudity: Thucydides, Plato, and the Vases." *Journal of Hellenic Studies* 111 (1991): 182–93.

McGlew, James F. *Tyranny and Political Culture in Ancient Greece.* Ithaca and London, 1993.

Méautis, Georges. "Le Dionysalexandros de Cratinos." *Revue des Études Anciennes* 36 (1934): 462–66.

Meltzer, Françoise. "Unconscious." In *Critical Terms for Literary Study*, ed. Frank Lentricchia and Thomas McLaughlin, 147–62. Chicago, 1990.

Merkelbach, R. and M.L. West, eds. *Fragmenta Hesiodea.* Oxford, 1967.

Michelini, Ann. *Euripides and the Tragic Tradition.* Madison, 1987.

Modleski, Tania. *The Women Who Knew too Much, Hitchcock and Feminist Theory.* New York and London, 1988.

Morris, Sarah P. "Daidolos and Kadmos: Classicism and 'Orientalism.' " *Arethusa* (1989): 39–54.

Muecke, Frances. " 'I Know You—By Your Rags': Costume and Disguise in Fifth-Century Drama." *Antichthon* 16 (1982): 17–34.

Mueller, Martin. *The Iliad*. London, 1984.

Mullaney, Steven. "Strange Things, Gross Terms, Curious Customs: The Rehearsal of Cultures in the Late Renaissance." *Representations* 3 (1983): 40–67.

Mulvey, Laura. "Visual Pleasure and Narrative Cinema." In *Visual and other Pleasures*, 14–26. Bloomington, 1989.

Munson, Rosaria. "The Madness of Cambyses (Herodotus 3.16–38)." *Arethusa* 24 (1991): 43–63.

Murnaghan, Sheila. *Disguise and Recognition in the* Odyssey. Princeton, 1987.

———. "Maternity and Mortality in Homeric Poetry." *Classical Antiquity* 11, (1992): 242–64.

Nagler, M.N. *Spontaneity and Tradition: A Study in the Oral Art of Homer.*. Berkeley, 1974.

Nagy, G. *The Best of the Achaeans: Concepts of the Hero in Archaic Greek Poetry.* Baltimore, 1979.

———. *Pindar's Homer: The Lyric Possession of an Epic Past*. Baltimore, 1990.

Nehamas, Alexander. "Pity and Fear in the *Rhetoric* and the *Poetics*." In *Essays on Aristotle's Poetics*, ed. Amelie Oksenberg Rorty, 291–314. Princeton, 1992.

Newton, Esther. *Mother Camp: Female Impersonators in America*. Chicago, 1979.

Nilsson, Martin. "Der Ursprung der Tragödie." *Neue Jahrbücher für das klassische Altertum* 27 (1911): 609–42, 673–96.

———. *Cults, Myths, Oracles, and Politics in Ancient Greece*. New York, 1972.

———. *Geschichte der griechische Religion*. Vol. 1. Munich, 1967.

Nussbaum, Martha. *The Fragility of Goodness: Luck and Ethics in Greek Tragedy and Philosophy*. Cambridge, 1986.

———. Review of *Sex and Suits: The Evolution of Modern Dress*, by Anne Hollander. *New Republic*, January 2, 1995, 32.

Ober, Josiah. *Mass and Elite in Democratic Athens: Rhetoric, Ideology, and the Power of the People*. Princeton, 1989.

Olender, Maurice. "Aspects of Baubo: Ancient Texts and Contexts." In *Before Sexuality*, ed., David M. Halperin, John J. Winkler, and Froma I. Zeitlin, 83–114. Princeton, 1990.

Ong, Walter. *Orality and Literacy*. London, 1982.

Oranje, H. *Euripides' Bacchae: The Play and Its Audience*. Mnemosyne Supplement 78. Leiden, 1984.

Orgel, Stephen. "Nobody's Perfect, or, Why Did the English Stage Take Boys for Women." *South Atlantic Quarterly* no. 88, 1 (1989): 7–29.

Osborne, Robin. "Archaeology, the Salaminio, and the Politics of Sacred Space in Archaic Attica." In *Placing the Gods: Sanctuaries and Sacred Space in Ancient Greece*, ed. Susan E. Alcock and Robin Osborne, 143–60. Oxford, 1994.

Ostwald, M. "The Athenian Legislation against Tyranny and Subversion." *Transactions of the American Philological Association* 86 (1955): 103–28.

———. *From Popular Sovereignty to the Sovereignty of Law: Law, Society and Politics in Fifth-Century Athens.* Berkeley, 1986.

Owens, Craig. "The Discourse of Others: Feminists and Postmodernism." In *Anti-aesthetic,* ed. Hal Foster, 57–82. Port Townsend, 1983.

Padel, Ruth. *In and Out of the Mind: Greek Images of the Tragic Self.* Princeton, 1992.

———. *Whom Gods Destroy: Elements of Greek and Tragic Madness.* Princeton, 1995.

Parke, H.W. *Festivals of the Athenians.* Ithaca, 1977.

Parker, Andrew, and Eve Kosofsky Sedgwick, eds. *Performativity and Performance.* New York, 1995.

Parker, Patricia. *Literary Fat Ladies: Rhetoric, Gender, Property.* London and New York, 1987.

Patterson, Cynthia. *Pericles' Citizenship Law of 451–50 B.C.* Salem, 1981.

Peradotto, John. "Texts and Unrefracted Facts: Philology, Hermeneutics, and Semiotics." In *Classics: A Discipline in Crisis?* ed. Phyllis Culham and Lowell Edmunds, 179–98. Lanham, New York, and London, 1989.

Pickard-Cambridge, Arthur. *Dithyramb, Tragedy, and Comedy.* Ed T.B.L. Webster. 2d ed. Oxford, 1962.

———. *The Dramatic Festivals of Athens.* Ed. John Gould and D.M. Lewis. 2d ed. Oxford, 1968.

Pöhlmann, E. "Die ABC-Komödie des Kallias." *Rheinisches Museum fur Philologie* 114 (1971): 230–40.

Pomeroy, Sarah. *Xenophon Oeconomicus, A Social and Historical Commentary.* Oxford, 1994.

Postlethwaite, N. "Thersites in the *Iliad.*" *Greece and Rome,* n.s., 35 (1988): 123–35.

Potts, Alex. *Flesh and the Ideal: Winckelmann and the Origins of Art History.* New Haven, 1994.

Powell, Barry. *Composition by Theme in the* Odyssey. Meisenheim am Glan, 1977.

Pucci, Pietro. *Hesiod and the Language of Poetry.* Baltimore, 1977.

Radt, S., ed. *Tragicorum Graecorum Fragmenta,* vol. 4. Göttingen, 1977.

Rhodes, P.J. *Commentary on the Aristotelian Athenaion Politeia.* Oxford, 1981.

Ridgway, Brunilde Sismondo. *The Archaic Style in Greek Sculpture.* Princeton, 1977.

Riviere, Joan. "Womanliness as Masquerade." In *Psychoanalysis and Female Sexuality,* ed. Hendrick Ruitenbeek, 209–20. New Haven, 1966.

Roach, Joseph. *Cities of the Dead: Circum-Atlantic Performance.* New York, 1996.

Rose, H.J. "Divine Disguisings." *Harvard Theological Review* 49 (1956): 63–72.

Rose, P. "Thersites and the Plural Voices of Homer." *Arethusa* 21 (1988): 5–25.

Rousselle, Aline. "Observation féminine et idéologie masculine: Le corps de la femme d'apres les médecins grecs." *Annales ESC* 35 (1980): 1089–1115.

————. *Porneia: On Desire and the Body in Antiquity.* Oxford and New York, 1988.

Rubin, Gayle. "The Traffic in Women: Notes on the 'Political Economy' of Sex." In *Toward an Anthropology of Women,* ed. Rayna Reiter, 157–210. New York, 1975.

Said, Edward. *Orientalism.* New York, 1979.

Saïd, Suzanne. "Féminin, femme et femelle dans les grands traités biologiques d'Aristote." In *La femme dans les sociétés antiques: Actes des colloques de Strasbourg (mai 1980 et mars 1981),* ed. Edmond Lévy, 93–124. Strasbourg, 1983.

————. "Deux noms de l'image en grec ancien: Idole et icône." *Comptes rendus de l'Académie des Inscriptions et Belles Lettres* (1987a): 309–30.

————. "Travestis et travestissements dans les comédies d'Aristophane." *Cahiers du groupe interdisciplinaire du theatre antique* 3 (1987b): 217–48.

Saussy, Haun. "Writing in the *Odyssey*: Eurykleia, Parry, Jousse, and the Opening of a Letter from Homer." *Arethusa* 29 (1996): 299–338.

Schechner, Richard. *Between Theory and Anthropology.* Philadelphia, 1985.

————. *Performance Theory.* New York, 1988.

Scheid, John, and Jesper Svenbro. *The Craft of Zeus: Myths of Weaving and Fabric.* Cambridge, Mass., 1996.

Seaford, Richard. "Dionysiac Drama and the Dionysiac Mysteries." *Classical Quarterly* 31 (1981): 252–75.

————. "Pentheus' Vision: *Bacchae* 18–22." *Classical Quarterly* 37 (1987): 76–78.

————. *Reciprocity and Ritual: Homer and Tragedy in the Developing City State.* Oxford, 1994.

Sealey, Raphael. *A History of the Greek City States, ca. 700–338 B.C.* Berkeley, 1976.

Segal, Charles. "The Character and Cults of Dionysus and the Unity of the *Frogs.*" *Harvard Studies in Classical Philology* 65 (1961): 207–42.

————. "The Two Worlds of Euripides' *Helen.*" *Transactions of the American Philological Association* 102 (1971): 553–614.

————. "The Menace of Dionysus: Sex Roles and Reversals in Euripides' *Bacchae.*" *Arethusa* 11 (1978): 185–202.

————. *Dionysiac Poetics and Euripides' Bacchae.* Princeton, 1982.

————. "Greek Tragedy: Writing, Truth, and the Representation of the Self." In *Interpreting Greek Tragedy: Myth, Poetry, Text,* 75–109. Ithaca, 1986.

————. "Time, Oracles and Marriage in the *Trachiniae.*" *Lexis* 9–10 (1992): 63–92.

————. "Female Mourning and Dionysiac Lament in Euripides' *Bacchae.*" In *Orchestra, Drama, Mythos, Bühne,* ed. Anton Bierl and Peter von Möllendorff, 12–18. Leipzig, 1994a.

————. "Philomela's Web and the Pleasures of the Text: Reader and Violence in the *Metamorphoses* of Ovid." In *Modern Critical Theory and Classical Literature,* ed. Irene J.F. de Jong and J.P. Sullivan. Leiden, New York, and Koln, 1994b.

——. "Sophocles' *Oedipus Tyrannus:* Freud, Language, and the Unconscious." In *Freud and Forbidden Knowledge,* ed. Peter Rudnytsky and Ellen Handler Spitz. New York, 1994c.

——. "Catharsis, Audience, and Closure in Greek Tragedy." In *Tragedy and the Tragic: Greek Theatre and Beyond,* ed. M.S. Silk, 149–72. Oxford, 1996.

Seltman, Charles. *Greek Coins.* London, 1933.

Shapiro, H.A. *Art and Cult under the Tyrants in Athens.* Mainz am Rhein, 1989.

Shear, T. Leslie. "The Athenian Agora: Excavations of 1970." *Hesperia* 40 (1970): 241–79.

——. "Tyrants and Buildings in Archaic Athens." In *Athens Comes of Age: From Solon to Salamis,* 1–19. Princeton, 1978.

Silk, M.S., and J.P. Stern. *Nietzsche on Tragedy.* Cambridge, 1981.

Silverman, Kaja. *The Threshold of the Visible World.* New York, 1996.

Sinos, Rebecca H. "Divine Selection: Epiphany and Politics in Archaic Greece." In *Cultural Poetics in Archaic Greece: Cult, Performance, Politics,* ed. Leslie Kurke and Carol Dougherty, 73–91. Cambridge, 1993.

Sissa, Giulia. "Maidenhood without Maidenhead: The Female Body in Ancient Greece." In *Before Sexuality,* ed. David M. Halperin, John J. Winkler, and Froma I. Zeitlin, 339–64. Princeton, 1990.

Slater, Philip. *The Glory of Hera: Greek Mythology and the Greek Family.* Boston, 1968.

Sörbom, Göran. *Mimesis and Art: Studies in the Origin and Early Development of an Aesthetic Vocabulary.* Stockholm, 1966.

Spariosu, Mihai I. *God of Many Names: Play, Poetry, and Power in Hellenic Thought from Homer to Aristotle.* Durham, 1991.

Spelman, Elizabeth. "Woman as Body: Ancient and Contemporary Views." *Feminist Studies* 8, (1982): 109–31.

——. *Inessential Woman: Problems of Exclusion in Feminist Thought.* Boston, 1988.

Stanford, W.B., ed. *The Odyssey of Homer.* 2d ed. London, 1959. Reprint 1977.

——. *Aristophanes: The Frogs.* 2d ed., New York, 1958. Reprint 1968.

Stehle, Eva. *Performance and Gender in Ancient Greece: Nondramatic Poetry in Its Setting.* Princeton, 1997.

Stone, Laura. *Costume in Aristophanic Comedy.* New York, 1977.

Sutton, Robert F., Jr. "Pornography and Persuasion in Attic Pottery." In *Pornography and Representation in Greece and Rome,* ed. Amy Richlin, 3–35. New York and Oxford, 1992.

Svenbro, Jesper. "The 'Interior' Voice: On the Invention of Silent Reading." In *Nothing to Do with Dionysos? Athenian Drama in Its Social Context,* ed. John J. Winkler and Froma I. Zeitlin, 366–84. Princeton, 1990.

——. *Phrasikleia: An Anthropology of Reading in Ancient Greece.* Trans. Janet Lloyd. Ithaca, 1993.

Taaffe, Lauren K. "The Illusion of Gender Disguise in Aristophanes' *Ecclesiazusae.*" *Helios* 18 (1991): 91–112.

——. *Aristophanes and Women.* London and New York, 1993.

Thalmann, W.G. "Thersites: Comedy, Scapegoats, and Heroic Ideology in the *Iliad.*" *Transactions of the American Philological Association* 118 (1988): 1–28.

Thomas, Keith. Review of *Rethinking Social History: English Society, 1570–1920, and Its Interpretation,* ed. Adrian Wilson. *Times Literary Supplement,* October 14, 1994.

Thomas, Rosalind. *Literacy and Orality in Ancient Greece.* Cambridge, 1992.

Thompson, Homer A., and R.E. Wycherley. *The Athenian Agora.* Vol. 14. *The Agora of Athens.* Princeton, 1972.

Thomsen, R. *The Origin of Ostracism: A Synthesis.* Copenhagen, 1972.

Trendall, A.D., and T.B.L. Webster. *Illustrations of Greek Drama.* London, 1971.

Tsantsanaglou, K., and G.M. Parassoglou. "Two Gold Lamellae from Thessaly." *Hellenika* 38 (1987): 3–16.

Turner, E.G. *Athenian Books in the Fifth and Fourth Centuries B.C.* London, 1952.

Veeser, H.A., ed. *The New Historicism.* London, 1989.

Vernant, J.P. "The Historical Moment of Tragedy in Greece: Some of the Social and Psychological Conditions." In *Tragedy and Myth in Ancient Greece,* ed. J.-P. Vernant and Pierre Vidal-Naquet, trans. Janet Lloyd, 6–27. Sussex, 1981.

———. "Le Dionysos masqué des *Bacchantes* d'Euripide." *L'Homme* 25 (1985): 31–58.

———. "Psuche: Simulacrum of the Body or Image of the Divine." In *Mortals and Immortals: Collected Essays,* ed. Froma I. Zeitlin, 186–94. Princeton, 1991.

Vidal-Naquet, P. *The Black Hunter: Forms of Thought and Forms of Society in the Greek World.* Trans. Andrew Szegedy-Maszak. Baltimore, 1986.

West, M.L., ed. *Hesiod: Theogony.* Oxford, 1966.

———. *Iambi et Elegi Graeci.* Oxford, 1971–72.

———. "The Early Chronology of Attic Tragedy." *Classical Quarterly* 39 (1989): 251–54.

Westlake, H.D. "The *Lysistrata* and the war." *Phoenix* 34 (1980): 38–54.

White, Hayden. "Historical Text as Literary Artifact." In *Tropics of Discourse: Essays in Cultural Criticism,* 81–100. Baltimore, 1978.

———. "The Value of Narrativity in the Representation of Reality." *Critical Inquiry* 7 (1980): 5–27.

———. "The Real, the True, and the Figurative in the Human Sciences." *Profession* 92 (1992): 15–17.

Whitman, Cedric. *Homer and the Heroic Tradition.* Cambridge, Mass., 1958.

Wilshire, Bruce. *Role Playing and Identity: The Limits of Theatre as Metaphor.* Studies in Phenomenology and Existential Philosophy, ed. James M. Edie. Bloomington, 1982.

Wilson, Adrian, ed. *Rethinking Social History: English Society, 1570–1920, and Its Interpretation.* New York, 1993.

Winkler, John J. "The Ephebes Song: Tragoidia and Polis." *Representations* 11 (1985): 26–62.

———. "The Ephebes' Song: *Tragoidia* and *Polis.*" In *Nothing to Do with*

Dionysos? Athenian Drama in Its Social Context, ed. John J. Winkler and Froma Zeitlin, 20–62. Princeton, 1990a.

———. "Penelope's Cunning and Homer's." In *The Constraints of Desire: The Anthropology of Sex and Gender in Ancient Greece,* 129–61. New York and London, 1990b.

Wiseman, T.P. *Historiography and Imagination: Eight Essays on Roman Culture.* Exeter Studies in History, ed. Jonathan Barry and Tim Rees, no. 33. Exeter, 1994.

Wohl, Victoria. "Eusebeias heneka kai Philotimias: Hegemony and Democracy at the Panathenaia." *Classica et Mediaevalia* 47 (1996): 25–88.

Wolin, Sheldon. "Democracy in the Discourse of Postmodernism." *Social Research* 57, no. 1 (spring 1990): 5–30.

Woodbury, Leonard. "The Judgment of Dionysus: Books, Taste, and Teaching in the *Frogs.*" In *Greek Tragedy and Its Legacy: Essays Presented to D.J. Conacher,* ed. Martin Cropp, Elaine Fantham, and S.E. Scully, 241–58. Calgary, 1986.

Woodford, Susan. *Greece and Rome.* Vol. 1 of *Cambridge Introduction to the History of Art.* Cambridge, 1982.

Woodman, A.J. *Rhetoric in Classical Historiography: Four Studies.* London, 1988.

Wycherley, R.E. *The Athenian Agora.* Vol. 3, *Literary and Epigraphical Testimonia.* Princeton, 1957. Reprint, 1973.

Zeitlin, Froma I. "Cultic Models of the Female: Rites of Dionysus and Demeter." *Arethusa* 15 (1982a): 129–57.

———. *Under the Sign of the Shield: Semiotics and Aeschylus' Seven against Thebes.* Rome, 1982b.

———. "Playing the Other: Theatre, Theatricality, and the Feminine in Greek Drama." In *Nothing to Do with Dionysos? Athenian Drama in Its Social Context,* ed. John J. Winkler and Froma I. Zeitlin, 63–96. Princeton, 1990a.

———. "Thebes: Theater of Self and Society in Athenian Drama." In *Nothing to Do with Dionysos? Athenian Drama in Its Social Context,* ed. John J. Winkler and Froma I. Zeitlin, 130–67. Princeton, 1990b.

———. "The Artful Eye: Vision, Ecphrasis and Spectacle in Euripidean Theatre." In *Art and Text in Ancient Greek Culture,* ed. Simon Goldhill and Robin Osborne, 138–96. Cambridge, 1994.

Zweig, Bella. "The Mute Nude Female Characters in Aristophanes' Plays." In *Pornography and Representation in Greece and Rome,* ed. Amy Richlin, 73–90. New York and Oxford, 1992.

Index Locorum

Aeschines
Against Timarchus
 131: 106n. 19
Against Ctesiphon
 66–68: 141f.
On the Embassy
 167–68: 218n. 58
Aeschylus
Persians
 226–80: 44n. 7; 725: 44n. 7; 813:
 44n. 7; 1601–3: 44n. 7
Archilochus
 frag. 6 (Diehl): 104n. 15; frag. 93
 (Bergk): 130n. 68
Aristophanes
Acharnians
 515ff.: 198; 530–39: 150n. 25
Birds
 286: 235n. 99; 712: 135n. 82;
 1649–52: 198
Clouds
 988–89: 103n. 13
Ecclesiazousae
 24–25: 70n. 70; 93–97: 137; 668:
 135n. 82
Frogs
 46–47: 234; 66–67: 234; 108ff.:
 235; 357: 230n. 81; 432–34: 235;
 631: 234; 668–69: 239; 943: 240n.
 111; 952: 157n. 36; 866ff.: 91n.
 115; 966: 137; 1011: 237; 1013ff.:
 239; 1014–15: 237n. 101; 1016–
 17: 215, 238; 1021: 173n. 58;
 1021–27: 243; 1022: 238; 1029ff.:
 238; 1043: 238; 1048: 238; 1050–
 51: 238; 1053–56: 238; 1054: 238;

1058–62: 237; 1060ff.: 238; 1063–
 66: 115; 1070–71: 237; 1087–88:
 237; 1099: 240; 1114: 89, 240;
 1119ff.: 240; 1200ff.: 240; 1245ff.:
 93n. 120; 1330ff.: 240; 1409:
 240n. 111; 1419–23: 234; 1468:
 237; 1468ff.: 241; 1475: 241
Lysistrata
 42–53: 108; 46–52: 186n. 84; 115:
 109; 124: 108; 631: 178n. 69; 800–
 828: 138n. 87
Thesmophoriazousae
 146–52: 238n. 107; 636: 135n. 82;
 643: 138; 1012ff.: 234n. 92
Wasps
 1279: 42n. 2
Scholia
 On *Archarnians* 243: 206
Aristotle
Athenaion Politeia
 2.2: 148; 14.1: 157, 166, 167n. 53,
 184n. 81; 14.2: 168n. 54, 169;
 14.4: 176n. 65; 15.1: 181; 15.3–6:
 182; 16.10: 189n. 91; 17.2: 185;
 18.1–19.6: 189; 22.6: 189n. 91;
 26.4: 198n. 10, 199n. 12
Historia Animalium
 538b7–8: 102
Poetics
 1443b4–8: 32; 1447a12: 23;
 1448a5–6: 27; 1448b4–8: 211n.
 36; 1448b5–6: 23, 24; 1448b4–19:
 41, 173n. 60; 1448b10–14: 226;
 1448b34–35: 6n. 14; 1448b37–38:
 6; 1449a11: 208n. 29; 1449a15–
 19: 42n. 2; 1449b24–28: 42n. 1;

General Index